GREEN LOGISTICS

Improving the environmental sustainability of logistics

EDITED BY
ALAN MCKINNON, SHARON CULLINANE,
MICHAEL BROWNE, ANTHONY WHITEING

**The Chartered Institute of
Logistics and Transport (UK)**

KoganPage

LONDON PHILADELPHIA NEW DELHI

First published in Great Britain and the United States in 2010 by Kogan Page Limited

120 Pentonville Road	525 South 4th Street, #241	4737/23 Ansari Road
London N1 9JN	Philadelphia PA 19147	Daryaganj
United Kingdom	USA	New Delhi 110002
www.koganpage.com		India

© Alan McKinnon, Sharon Cullinane, Michael Browne and Anthony Whiteing, 2010

ISBN 978 0 7494 5678 8
E-ISBN 978 0 7494 5874 4

British Library Cataloguing-in-Publication Data

A CIP record for this book is available from the British Library.

Library of Congress Cataloging-in-Publication Data

Green logistics : improving the environmental sustainability of logistics / Alan McKinnon ... [et al.].
     p. cm.
   Includes bibliographical references.
   ISBN 978-0-7494-5678-8
  1. Business logistics--Environmental aspects. I. McKinnon, Alan C., 1953-
   HD38.5.G696 2010
   658.7--dc22

                              2009037392

Typeset by Saxon Graphics Ltd, Derby
Printed and bound in India by Replika Press Pvt Ltd

Contents

Contributor biographies   ix

**Part 1 ASSESSING THE ENVIRONMENTAL EFFECTS OF
         LOGISTICS**   1

1 Environmental sustainability: a new priority for logistics
   managers   3
   Alan McKinnon
   Introduction 3; A brief history of green logistics research 5;
   Green logistics: rhetoric and reality 17; A model for green
   logistics research 19; Outline of the book 22; Notes 25;
   References 25

2 Assessing the environmental impacts of freight transport   31
   Sharon Cullinane and Julia Edwards
   Introduction 31; Environmental impacts 32; Environmental
   standards 39; measuring the environmental impact of freight
   transport 42; Notes 45; References 45

3 Carbon auditing of companies, supply chains and products   49
   Maja Piecyk
   Introduction 49; Guidelines for carbon footprinting 50; The
   carbon footprinting process 51; Success factors in carbon
   footprinting 59; Case study: carbon auditing of road freight
   transport operations in the UK 60; Conclusions 65;
   References 66

4   Evaluating and internalizing the environmental costs of logistics 68
Maja Piecyk, Alan McKinnon and Julian Allen
Introduction 68; Arguments for and against the internalization
of environmental costs 69; Monetary valuation of
environmental costs 72; Internalization of the external costs
imposed by road freight vehicles in the UK 79; Conclusions
93; Notes 95; References 95

Part 2   STRATEGIC PERSPECTIVE   **99**

5   Restructuring of logistics systems and supply chains   101
Irina Harris, Vasco Sanchez Rodrigues, Mo Naim and
Christine Mumford
Introduction 101; Current state of knowledge of traditional
supply chains 102; Green supply chains 111; Gaps in our
understanding and priorities for research 116; Consequences
and conclusions 119; References 120

6   Transferring freight to 'greener' transport modes   124
Allan Woodburn and Anthony Whiteing
Background 124; Characteristics of the main freight transport
modes 126; Environmental impacts of the main freight
transport modes 129; Case study: container train load factors
130; The policy framework 131; Examples of measures aimed
at achieving modal shift for environmental benefit 133; Rail
and water industries 135; Conclusions 138; References 139

7   Development of greener vehicles, aircraft and ships   140
Alan McKinnon, Julian Allen and Allan Woodburn
Introduction 140; Road freight 141; Rail freight operations 150;
Air freight 153; Shipping 157; Conclusions 162; Notes 162;
References 163

8   Reducing the environmental impact of warehousing   167
Clive Marchant
Introduction 167; Scale of the environmental impact 168;
Increasing resource intensity 171; Framework for assessing
the environmental impact of warehouses 173; Ways of
reducing the environmental impact 173; Conclusion 189;
References 190

Part 3   OPERATIONAL PERSPECTIVE   **193**

9   Opportunities for improving vehicle utilization   195
     Alan McKinnon and Julia Edwards
     Introduction 195; Measuring vehicle utilization 196; Factors
     affecting the utilization of truck capacity 199; Conclusion 210;
     Note 210; References 210

10   Optimizing the routing of vehicles   215
     Richard Eglese and Dan Black
     Introduction 215; Vehicle routing problems 216; Types of
     problem 217; Environmental impact 221; Conclusions 224;
     References 225

11   Increasing fuel efficiency in the road freight sector   229
     Alan McKinnon
     Introduction 229; Fuel efficiency of new trucks 230; Vehicle
     design: aerodynamic profiling 231; Reducing the vehicle tare
     weight 232; Vehicle purchase decision 233; Vehicle
     maintenance 234; Increasing the fuel efficiency of trucking
     operations 235; Benchmarking the fuel efficiency of trucks 237;
     More fuel-efficient driving 238; Fleet management 239;
     Conclusions 240; References 240

12   Reverse logistics for the management of waste   242
     Tom Cherrett, Sarah Maynard, Fraser McLeod and Adrian Hickford
     Introduction 242; Waste management in the context of reverse
     logistics 243; The impact of waste treatment legislation 246;
     Reuse, refurbishment markets and take-back schemes 250;
     Managing waste as part of a sustainable reverse process 253;
     Conclusions 256; References 259

Part 4   Key issues   **263**

13   The food miles debate   265
     Tara Garnett
     Introduction 265; Transport and GHGs: is further worse? 266;
     Transport, the second order impacts and the implications for
     GHGs 272; Local versus global and the self-sufficiency
     question 274; Notes 277; References 277

14 Sustainability strategies for city logistics 282
Julian Allen and Michael Browne
Introduction 282; Urban freight research and policy making
283; Efficiency problems in urban freight transport 285; Urban
freight transport initiatives 288; urban consolidation centres
290; Joint working between the public and private sectors 294;
Environmental zones 296; Conclusions 301; References 302

15 Benefits and costs of switching to alternative fuels 306
Sharon Cullinane and Julia Edwards
Introduction 306; The main types of alternative fuels 307;
Current use of AFs in the freight industry 316; The future 318;
Notes 318; References 319

16 E-business, e-logistics and the environment 322
Julia Edwards, Yingli Wang, Andrew Potter and Sharon Cullinane
Introduction 322; Business-to-business (B2B) 323; Business-to-
consumer (B2C) 327; Restructuring of the supply chain 330;
the environmental impact of e-commerce 330; Case study:
online book supply chain 333; The future 335; References 335

Part 5 Public policy perspective **339**

17 The role of government in promoting green logistics 341
Alan McKinnon
Introduction 341; Objectives of public policy on sustainable
logistics 344; Policy measures 344; Reducing freight transport
intensity 347; Shifting freight to greener transport modes 349;
Improving vehicle utilization 351; Increasing energy efficiency
353; cutting emissions relative to energy use 355; Government-
sponsored advisory and accreditation programmes 356;
Conclusion 357; Note 358; References 358

Index *361*

Contributor biographies

Julian Allen is a Senior Research Fellow in the Transport Department at the University of Westminster, where he is involved in research and teaching activities relating to freight transport and logistics. His current research interests are urban freight transport, the impact of manufacturing and retailing techniques on logistics and transportation systems and the history of freight transport.

Daniel Black is a Research Associate at the Department of Management Science in Lancaster University Management School. His research interests include the environmental impact of vehicle routing and scheduling decisions, stochastic inventory control and optimization problems with particular reference to developing computer-based models.

Michael Browne directs freight transport and logistics research at the University of Westminster. Recent projects include: research on the energy use implications of global sourcing, potential benefits from improved city logistics strategies and forecasting future trends in logistics. He has worked on studies for Transport for London, the European Commission, the UK Department for Transport, the Research Councils and commercial organizations. He represents the University on many external committees and boards and chairs the Central London Freight Quality Partnership.

Tom Cherrett B.Sc., Ph.D, MCILT is a Senior Lecturer in the Transportation Research Group, University of Southampton. His main research areas include developing sustainable strategies for the collection and disposal of waste and the distribution of goods in urban areas, including distribution strategies for sustainable home delivery. He has considerable experience in the areas of incident detection and journey time estimation using urban traffic control infrastructure. He has management and logistics experience from working in the chilled distribution sector.

Sharon Cullinane gained her PhD in logistics 20 years ago from Plymouth University. Since then she has continued to lecture, research and publish in the field of transport policy and the environment around the world. Her most recent post was as Senior Lecturer at Heriot-Watt University in Edinburgh. Prior to that she was employed at the University of Hong Kong, Oxford University, the Egyptian National Institute of Transport, the Ecole Superieur de Rennes and Plymouth University. She is now an independent consultant. She is widely published internationally.

Julia Edwards is a Research Associate at the Logistics Research Centre in the School of Management and Languages at Heriot-Watt University, Edinburgh. She joined Heriot-Watt in 2006, as part of the multi-university 'Green Logistics' project. Prior to that she was a Senior Lecturer in Environmental Management at the University of Wales, Newport. Dr. Edwards has been researching and teaching in the areas of transport and environmental issues for the last 16 years. Currently, her research interests include carbon auditing of supply chains, e-commerce and the environment, and consumer travel and shopping behaviour.

Richard Eglese is a Professor of Operational Research at the Department of Management Science in Lancaster University Management School. His research interests concern mathematical and computational modelling for logistics and focus on optimization techniques, particularly heuristic methods, applied to problems of vehicle routing and scheduling. He has worked on a variety of applications including food distribution to supermarkets and winter gritting for road surfaces. In 2010–2011 he is President of the Operational Research Society.

Tara Garnett set up and runs the Food Climate Research Network based at the University of Surrey (www.fcrn.org.uk). Her work focuses on the contribution that the food system makes to greenhouse gas emissions and the scope for emissions reduction, looking at the technological, behavioural and policy options. She is also interested in the relationship between emissions reduction objectives and other social and ethical concerns, including human health, animal welfare, international development and biodiversity.

Irina Harris is a research student at Cardiff University. Her research project on 'Multi-Objective Optimization for Green Logistics' is jointly supervised by Cardiff School of Computer Science and Cardiff Business School. The objective is to investigate the feasibility of building a multi-objective optimization decision support tool for modelling the physical infrastructure of a logistics network where traditional and environmental objectives are considered simultaneously. The approach focuses on producing a set of viable alternatives for a decision-maker in contrast to calculating objectives as a constraint or prioritizing them.

Clive Marchant is a senior teaching fellow at Heriot-Watt University, Edinburgh, where he teaches freight transport systems as well as distribution centre design and management. He is an active member of the Chartered Institute of Logistics and Transport as well as member of the Warehouse Education Research Council in the USA. Prior to obtaining a Masters at Edinburgh and Heriot-Watt Universities he had a 25 year career in the third party logistics sector encompassing roles in operational management and the design of distribution networks and warehousing.

Sarah Maynard BSc, MSc, is a researcher at the Transportation Research Group (TRG), University of Southampton, UK. Since joining TRG in 2004 she has specialized in waste transport research and has been involved in a number of projects funded by the Engineering and Physical Sciences Research Council. Recent research has investigated the transport impacts associated with household waste recycling centres and the benefits of using reverse logistics processes to collect returns and waste generated by different retail supply chains in urban centres.

Alan McKinnon is Professor of Logistics and Director of the Logistics Research Centre at Heriot-Watt University, Edinburgh. A graduate of the universities of Aberdeen, British Columbia and London, he has been researching and teaching in freight transport/logistics for 30 years and has published extensively in journals and books. Alan has conducted studies for numerous public and private sector organizations, and has been an adviser to several UK government departments and parliamentary committees and various international agencies. He is also a member of the World Economic Forum's Global Agenda Council on the Future of Transportation.

Fraser McLeod (B.Sc. in mathematics, M.Phil. in passive sonar) is a Research Fellow with the Transportation Research Group, University of Southampton, with over 20 years experience of working on transport-related projects. In recent years his work has focused on Intelligent

Transport Systems (ITS), freight distribution and on the logistics of collecting household and trade waste. The common theme of the research is to suggest methods for improving transport efficiency and evaluating them through the use of simulation modelling, routeing and scheduling methods and mathematical analyses.

Christine Mumford obtained her PhD from Imperial College, London in 1995, and is a Senior Member of the IEEE. She is currently a Senior Lecturer at Cardiff University in the School of Computer Science. Her research interests include evolutionary computing and other metaheuristics, multi-objective optimization, and applications focused on combinatorial optimization, particularly vehicle routing, logistic network design, scheduling, timetabling and cutting and packing.

Mohamed Naim is a Professor in Logistics and Operations Management at Cardiff Business School. He is a Chartered Engineer and a Member of the Institution of Engineering and Technology and the Chartered Institute of Logistics and Transport. He is a Director of the Logistics Systems Dynamics Group and the EPSRC funded Cardiff University Innovative Manufacturing Research Centre. Mohamed is a former Editor-in-Chief of the International Journal of Logistics and is an Advisory Committee Member for the International Symposium on Logistics.

Maja Piecyk is a Research Associate in the Logistics Research Centre at Heriot-Watt University in Edinburgh. She has MSc degrees in economics and logistics. Her research interests focus on the environmental performance of supply chains and sustainability of freight transport operations. Much of her current work centres on the CO_2 auditing of businesses and the forecasting of long-term trends in the energy demands and environmental impacts of logistics.

Andrew Potter is a senior lecturer in transport and logistics at Cardiff University. His research has particularly focused on how freight transport can become more integrated within supply chains. While much of the focus has been on traditional supply chain performance measures, more recently consideration has also been given to environmental performance. He has published in a wide range of logistics and operations management journals. Andrew is also a member of the Chartered Institute of Logistics and Transport (UK).

Vasco Sanchez-Rodrigues has a first degree in Chemical Engineering from the Simon Bolivar University in Venezuela and an MBA from the University of Cardiff. Since 2005 he has been a researcher in the Cardiff

Business School, initially on the Fabric-to-Furniture project and over the past three years on the multi-university Green Logistics project. His main research interests are the trade-offs between supply chain management and green logistics under conditions of uncertainty. He is now in the process of completing a PhD on this topic.

Yingli Wang is a lecturer in logistics and operations management at Cardiff Business School. Before working at Cardiff University, she had a variety of managerial roles in Nestlé China, before completing an MBA in the UK. Her current research focuses on the application of technology in B2B logistics and transport management. In particular, her research has focused on electronic logistics marketplaces. This research formed the basis for her PhD thesis, which won the CILT(UK) James Cooper Memorial Cup in 2009.

Anthony Whiteing is a Senior Lecturer in the Institute for Transport Studies at the University of Leeds. His main areas of expertise are in freight transport economics, distribution, logistics and supply chain management. An academic with some 30 years experience, he has been involved in a wide range of UK and European research projects primarily in the field of freight transport, and is the Principal Investigator on the 'Green Logistics' research project.

Allan Woodburn is a Senior Lecturer in Freight and Logistics in the Transport Studies Department at the University of Westminster, London. He is involved in a wide range of teaching, research and consultancy activities in the field of freight transport, both within the UK and internationally. Allan completed his Doctorate examining the role for rail freight within the supply chain in 2000. Since then, his main research focus has been on rail freight policy, planning and operations, focusing specifically on efficiency and sustainability issues.

Part 1

ASSESSING THE ENVIRONMENTAL EFFECTS OF LOGISTICS

1

Environmental sustainability

A new priority for logistics managers

Alan McKinnon[1]

INTRODUCTION

Logistics is the term now widely used to describe the transport, storage and handling of products as they move from raw material source, through the production system to their final point of sale or consumption. Although its core activities have been fundamental to economic development and social well-being for millennia, it is only over the past 50 years that logistics has come to be regarded as a key determinant of business performance, a profession and a major field of academic study. During this period the dominant paradigm for those managing and studying logistics has been commercial. The prime, and in many cases sole, objective has been to organize logistics in a way that maximizes profitability. The calculation of profitability, however, has included only the economic costs that companies directly incur. The wider environmental and social costs, traditionally excluded from the balance sheet, have been largely ignored – until recently.

Over the past 10–15 years, against a background of increasing public and government concern for the environment, companies have come under mounting pressure to reduce the environmental impact of their logistics operations. This impact is diverse, in terms of the range of externalities and the distances over which their adverse effects are experienced. The distribution of goods impairs local air quality, generates noise and vibration, causes accidents and makes a significant contribution to global warming. The impact of logistics on climate change has attracted increasing attention in recent years, partly because tightening controls on pollution and road safety improvements have alleviated the other environmental problems, but also because new scientific research has revealed that global warming presents a much greater and more immediate threat than previously thought.

It is estimated that freight transport accounts for roughly 8 per cent of energy-related CO_2 emissions worldwide (Kahn Ribeiro and Kobayashi, 2007). The inclusion of warehousing and goods handling is likely to add around 2–3 per cent to this total. In the road transport sector, the amount of energy used to move freight is increasing at a faster rate than the energy consumed by cars and buses, and, in the European Union, may overtake it by the early 2020s (European Commission, 2003). If CO_2 emissions from shipping grow at their forecast rate while governments cut emissions from their national economies by an average of 50 per cent by the middle of the century in line with current targets, shipping alone could account for 15–30 per cent of total CO_2 emissions by 2050, even allowing for a 33–50 per cent improvement in its energy efficiency by then (Committee on Climate Change, 2008). It is hardly surprising, therefore, that governments and inter-governmental organizations are developing carbon abatement policies for the freight transport sector.

Making logistics 'sustainable' in the longer term will involve more than cutting carbon emissions. Despite recent improvements, the potential still exists to cut the other environmental costs of logistics by a significant margin. Furthermore, sustainability does not only have an environmental dimension. Sustainable development was originally portrayed as the reconciliation of environmental, economic and social objectives (Brundtland Commission, 1987). The expression 'triple-bottom line' is often used in the business world to convey this notion of a three-way trade-off. The concept also underpins government strategies on sustainable distribution, such as that of the UK government (DETR, 1999a). In practice, however, many of the measures that reduce the environmental impact of logistics, the so-called 'green-gold' measures, also save money, avoiding the need to trade off economic costs against environmental benefits. While the main focus of this book is on ways of reducing the environmental effects of logistics, frequent reference is also made to their economic and social implications.

The issues discussed in this book are topical, important and currently engaging the attention of company managers and policy makers in many countries around the world. They are examined from both corporate and public policy perspectives. The book aims to provide a broad overview of technical, managerial, economic and policy aspects of green logistics, and as a result to improve understanding of the various problems that have to be overcome in assessing and addressing the environmental consequences of logistical activities. It contains case studies and examples of the types of initiatives that can be taken at different levels, ranging from those within a single company to those that span an entire supply chain and possibly involve businesses in several countries. The book also explores the range of approaches and analytical tools available to academics and practitioners working in the field of green logistics.

Green logistics is a relatively young but rapidly evolving subject. This is a good time to take stock, reflect on the work that has been done to date and assess the challenges ahead. The remainder of this chapter lays a foundation for the book by reviewing the development of the subject over the past 50 years. It also presents an analytical framework for the study of green logistics and concludes with a brief outline of the other 16 chapters.

A BRIEF HISTORY OF GREEN LOGISTICS RESEARCH

It is difficult to decide when research on green logistics began. One possible starting point would be the publication of the first paper on an environmental theme in a mainstream logistics journal. This, however, would ignore a large body of earlier research on the environmental effects of freight transport undertaken before logistics gained recognition as a field of academic study. While concern was expressed about the damaging effects of freight transport in the 1950s, most of the substantive research on the subject dates from the mid-1960s. Murphy and Poist (1995: 16) assert that: 'prior to the 1960s, there was relatively little concern regarding environmental degradation. For the most part, the environment's ability to absorb wastes and to replace resources was perceived as being infinite.' This review is therefore confined to the last 40 years, but it 'casts its net wide' to capture a broad assortment of relevant literature in journals, books and reports. In their review of 10 logistics, supply management and transport journals over the period 1995–2004, Aronsson and Brodin (2006) found that only 45 papers out of 2,026 (2.2 per cent) addressed environmental issues. When the publication horizons are extended by time and type of output, however, one uncovers a large, well-established and vibrant field of research.

What we now call 'green logistics' represents the convergence of several strands of research that began at different times over the past 40 years. Figure 1.1 groups these strands under five headings: reducing freight transport externalities, city logistics, reverse logistics, corporate environmental strategies towards logistics and green supply chain management. This extends the three-fold classification of green logistics research adopted by Abukhader and Jonsson (2004), which comprises environmental assessment, reverse logistics and green supply chains. Figure 1.1 also proposes a tentative chronology for research activity on these topics and depicts three more general trends that have, since the 1960s, altered the context and priorities of the research. These are shown as wedges to reflect a broadening perspective:

1. Public-to-private: Much of the early research was driven by a public policy agenda as newly emergent environmental pressure groups began to lobby for government intervention to mitigate the damaging effects of freight movement and public agencies sought to improve their understanding of the problem and find means of addressing it. Through time, this public sector interest in the subject has been complemented by a growth in private sector involvement in green logistics research as businesses have begun to formulate environmental strategies both at a corporate level and more specifically for logistics.
2. Operational-to-strategic: A second general trend has been a broadening of the corporate commitment to green logistics, from the adoption of a few minor operational changes to the embedding of environmental principles in strategic planning.
3. Local-to-global: In the 1960s and 70s the main focus was on the local environmental impact of air pollution, noise, vibration, accidents and visual intrusion. No reference was made to the global atmospheric effects of logistical activity. Indeed in the 1970s some climate models predicted that the planet was entering a new ice age! The transcontinental spread of acid rain (from sulphur emissions) and depletion of the ozone layer (caused mainly by chlorofluorocarbons) during the 1980s demonstrated that logistics and other activities could have a more geographically extensive impact on the environment. With climate change now the dominant environmental issue of the age, the impact of logistics on global atmospheric conditions has become a major focus of research.

The context within which research on green logistics has been undertaken has also been evolving in other ways. Over the past 40 years, logistics has developed as an academic discipline, extending its original focus on the

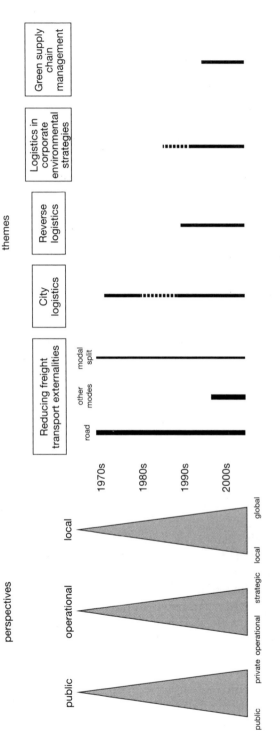

Figure 1.1 Evolving perspectives and themes in green logistics

outbound movement of finished products (physical distribution) to companies' entire transport, storage and handling systems (integrated logistics) and then to the interaction with businesses upstream and downstream (supply chain management). This has extended the scope of green logistics research in terms of the functions, processes and relationships investigated (McKinnon, 2003). Other major contextual trends include the growth of environmental awareness, the proliferation of environmental regulations, and the development of national and international standards for environmental reporting and management that many companies now adopt as part of their corporate social responsibility (CSR) programmes. Partly as a result of these trends, the volume of statistics available to green logistics researchers has greatly expanded and companies have become more willing to support studies in this field.

In reviewing the development of green logistics as a field of study, one detects international differences in research priorities. Although a survey by Murphy and Poist (2003) of samples of US and 'non-US' companies found strong similarities in the environmental perceptions and practices of logistics management, research efforts have tended to be skewed towards topics of national interest. In the UK, for example, much of the early research on green logistics was a response to a public dislike of heavy lorries. In Germany, research on reverse logistics was stimulated by the introduction of radical packaging-waste legislation in the early 1990s. Until recently, reverse logistics attracted much more attention from US researchers than other aspects of green logistics, with much of the corporate interest in the subject related to its impact on costs and profitability rather than on the environment.

Reducing freight transport externalities

Much of the early research on the environmental impact of logistics was motivated by the growth of lorry traffic at a time when lorries were much noisier and more polluting than today. Numerous studies were conducted in the 1970s to assess the nature and scale of these effects, many of them in the UK. Their focus was on the local environmental impact of lorries. Reports published by environmental pressure groups catalogued the environmental damage they were causing and demanded government action to contain the 'lorry menace'. Campaigners were particularly alarmed by official forecasts that freight traffic volumes would continue to grow steeply for the foreseeable future. In the UK, the government responded by setting up an inquiry to examine the effects of lorries on the environment and explore ways of minimizing them (Pettit, 1973). This led to the formation of the Lorries and the Environment Committee, an organization which between 1974 and 1979 published several reports on ways of rationalizing the movement of freight by road. The UK government, nevertheless, felt it necessary to commission a much wider investigation of 'lorries, people and the environment'. The Report of this Inquiry (Armitage, 1980) provided a useful review of lorry-related externalities, the causes of road freight growth and the options for mitigating its environmental effects. It was preoccupied, however, with local planning and regulatory issues, and antagonised environmental groups at the time by recommending an increase in the maximum gross lorry weight from 32 to 44 tonnes. At an international level, the OECD (1982) also published a report on the effects of heavy trucks on the environment and explored ways in which they might be reduced.

Advances in vehicle technology and tightening regulations on emission levels gradually reduced transport externalities per vehicle-km. It was recognized, however, that much of the environmental improvement being achieved at the individual vehicle level was being eroded by the underlying growth in road freight traffic (Adams, 1981; Whitelegg, 1995). Reducing the environmental burden imposed by freight transport would, therefore, entail much more than improved fuel efficiency and lower exhaust emissions. More radical measures to contain the growth of road freight traffic would be required. This might be difficult to achieve, however, without jeopardizing future economic growth. Bennathan, Fraser and Thompson (1992: 7) had established, for a sample of 17 developed countries, that 'the partial elasticity of ton-kilometres by road with respect to GDP [was] about unity (1.02).' This meant that road freight traffic was growing almost exactly in line with the economy.

Individual sectors of the economy, however, were experiencing rates of freight traffic growth well above the average and faster than the rate at which output was growing. Paxton (1994) showed how wider sourcing of food products was increasing the demand for freight transport or what she called 'food miles'. Around the same time, Böge (1994) conducted a much-publicized study in Germany of the amount of road transport generated by the production and distribution of a pot of strawberry yoghurt. By mapping the supply chains of all the ingredients and components contained in this product she was able to demonstrate that for every pot of yoghurt sold in a German supermarket, a truck had to travel nine metres. She went on to assess the environmental impact of all the related freight transport, using this case study to illustrate how the logistical requirements of even a fairly cheap basic product could be responsible for significant amounts of pollution and noise.

These and other studies highlighted the need for more research on the process of road freight traffic growth and the extent to which it could be influenced by public policy interventions. This need was addressed by a plethora of studies conducted in several countries during the 1990s. These studies examined, to varying degrees, three methods of decoupling economic growth from road freight traffic levels: reducing the transport intensity of the economy (generally defined as the ratio of road tonne-kms to GDP), altering the freight modal split (to displace freight on to alternative modes) and improving vehicle utilization (to reduce the ratio of vehicle-kms to tonne-kms). Table 1.1 lists some of the major freight-rationalization studies undertaken during the 1990s and shows which of the three decoupling options they considered.

Much of this research adopted a broader logistical perspective, acknowledging that the restructuring of companies' logistical systems was one of the main drivers of freight traffic growth. Research by McKinnon and Woodburn (1996), McKinnon (1998) and Cooper, Black and Peters (1998) identified a series of logistics and supply chain trends responsible for freight traffic growth. The nature of the relationship between these trends and freight traffic growth in different countries and sectors

Table 1.1 Freight transport rationalization studies conducted during the 1990s

Author / organization	study area	date	modal split	transport intensity	vehicle utilization
Hey et al. EURES / Greenpeace	Europe	1992	*	*	*
Peters Werkgroep 2000	Netherlands	1993	*		*
DIW / ifeu / IVA / HACON	Germany	1994	*		*
Royal Commission on Environmental Pollution	UK	1994	*	*	*
Plowden and Buchan Civic Trust	UK	1995	*	*	*
Bleijenberg CE	Europe	1996	*	*	*
Holman T&E	Europe	1996	*	*	*
Pastowski Wupperthal Institute	Germany	1997		*	
Schipper et al. International Energy Agency	OECD	1997	*	*	*

was subsequently investigated by two European Commission-funded projects called REDEFINE and SULOGTRA. In its 2001 transport White Paper, the European Commission stated that 'we have to consider the option of gradually breaking the link between economic growth and transport growth' (2001: 15). Ironically, over the previous decade the link had been broken, with freight tonne-kms growing at a faster rate than the EU economy as a whole. The policy aim, however, was to decouple these variables in the opposite direction. Evidence of this 'positive' form of decoupling had begun to emerge in some countries, such as the UK and Finland, stimulating research into the reasons for it occurring (Tapio, 2005; McKinnon, 2007). If the underlying growth in freight movement were to slacken, it would be easier for governments to make logistics more environmentally sustainable (DETR , 1999a). The main goal, however, should be to decouple economic growth from freight-related externalities rather than the growth in traffic volumes. This involves manipulating a series of key logistical parameters each of which is amenable to public policy initiatives. In the section on 'A model for green logistics research', we present an analytical framework built around these key parameters, which has its heritage in the earlier studies outlined above and can serve as a model for the greening of logistics.

In this section we have charted the development of research into ways of reducing freight-related externalities at national and international levels. It is in towns and cities, however, where high freight traffic and high population densities coincide, that these externalities are at their greatest. A separate strand of green logistics research has focused on the specific issues raised by the distribution of goods in urban areas.

City logistics

The first major studies of the distribution of freight in urban areas were conducted in the 1970s and early 1980s. Major cities such as London and Chicago commissioned, usually for the first time, surveys of freight movements, while academics began to research specific aspects of urban freight systems, often exploiting the new supply of urban freight data. This research was comprehensively reviewed by Ogden (1992), who identified the 'minimization of adverse effects' as one of the three main issues addressed by goods movement research. Many of the urban freight studies conducted at this time, especially in the United States, emphasized the other two issues of 'economic development' and 'transport efficiency'. Efficiency and environmental concerns converged in one of the most extensively researched urban freight topics at the time, namely the 'small order problem' (Jackson, 1985). The dispersal of freight in small consignments by poorly loaded vehicles to a multitude of locations was found to impose high economic and environmental costs. Numerous studies were then done to find ways of consolidating loads and, thereby, cut traffic levels, energy use, emissions and costs (eg Rushton, 1979). The most popular idea was to set up transhipment or consolidation centres in and around urban areas where inbound loads could be disaggregated and outbound loads aggregated. Feasibility studies at that time, particularly in the UK, suggested that the insertion of these centres into companies' supply chains would be disruptive, expensive and yield, at best, only modest environmental benefit (Sharp and Jennings, 1976).

The 1980s and early 1990s was a relatively fallow period for research on urban freight, partly because funding for large-scale urban goods transport studies dried up. Ogden (1992: 12) suggests that 'the decade of the 1980s may be described as a time of consolidation. While many of the aspirations of the early 1970s did not come to fruition, there has been at least in some quarters a clearer recognition of the role of freight, and ways of accommodating it.' Many of the environmental problems associated with the urban movement of freight in heavy lorries remained unsolved, however (Civic Trust et al, 1990). Partly for this reason, there was a major revival of interest in the subject during the 1990s and 2000s, supported by multinational research initiatives in Europe. As part of the European COST 321 programme, the effectiveness of a range of urban freight measures on 'ecology, traffic, economy and safety' was assessed across 28 cities in 11 European countries (European Commission, 1998). More recently the EU's Best Urban Freight Solutions (Bestufs) programme has fostered research and dissemination in this field. Japanese researchers have also become particularly active in the study of logistics (Taniguchi et al, 2001). Greater priority is now being given to environmental issues in urban freight research, despite the fact that, over the past 30 years, the tightening of pollution and noise limits on new vehicles has greatly reduced localized freight-related externalities while much freight-generating activity has migrated from inner urban areas to suburban and out-of-town locations. Other new strands in urban freight research in the last decade include the increase in the diversity and extent of service-related transport to commercial and residential locations, as well as the growing importance of home deliveries. The economic contribution of goods and service transport to major cities is also gaining wider recognition. This is beginning to result in a reconsideration of the priority given to urban freight transport in decisions concerning the allocation of road space and transport investment. There has also been a resurgence of interest in the scope for urban consolidation centres in specific sectors, including retailing and construction, based on new business models (Browne, Sweet et al, 2005).

Reverse logistics

Jonathan Weeks, a former chairman of the UK Institute of Logistics defined logistics as 'the movement of materials from the earth through production, distribution and consumption back to the earth'. This incorporates the return of waste product and packaging for reuse, recycling and disposal, an activity that is now regarded as a key part of green logistics. Research interest in this topic developed in the early 1990s when governments and businesses began to reform the management of waste, reducing the proportion of waste material being dumped in landfill sites or incinerated and increasing the proportion that was recycled and reused. This fundamentally transformed the logistics of waste management and stimulated research interest in the return flow of product back along the supply chain. In a White Paper prepared for the Council of Logistics Management, Stock (1992) set out an agenda for future academic research on this topic. He used available statistical data from the United States to highlight the scale of the problem, assessed the current state of knowledge and identified a series of research issues requiring further investigation. An early contribution by Jahre (1995) showed how the basic principles of logistics, such as those of postponement and speculation, could be applied to the return flow of waste from homes. In their state-of-the-art review some years later, however, Carter and Ellram (1998) lamented the lack of theory development and empirical research in this field. They identified a series of 'drivers and constraints' in reverse logistics and suggested that they become the foci of future 'theoretically-grounded' research (p 99). Over the past decade, there have been many more theoretical and analytical contributions to the reverse logistics literature (eg Jayaraman, Guide and Srivastava, 1999; Beamon, 1999; Dekker et al, 2004), reflecting a greater emphasis on the optimization of return flows of waste and other products. As the volume of waste being recycled and reused has grown, new waste management systems have evolved and government regulations have tightened, expanding opportunities for research in this field.

Corporate environmental strategies

Prior to the 1980s, companies' environmental initiatives were typically ad hoc and reactive, often implemented in response to government regulations or public protest. It thereafter became more common for businesses to formulate environmental strategies based on wide-ranging assessments of their impact on the environment. In a sample of 133 US firms surveyed by Murphy and Poist (1995: 16), 61 per cent had a 'formal or written environmental policy', almost three-quarters of which had been introduced since 1980. With such a strategy in place, the efforts of different departments to 'green' their operations could be more effectively coordinated and the business as a whole could become more proactive in environmental management. New international standards, such as ISO 14000, were introduced to accredit companies' environmental programmes and help customers ensure that suppliers had the required environmental credentials. As with quality management standards, however, this accreditation became more of a business 'qualifier' than a competitive differentiator. For a company wanting to extract more value from the adoption of green practices it was necessary to make the environment a key element in the business model.

It is against this background that companies have been developing environmental strategies for their logistics operations. Some companies claim to have had a specific environmental policy for logistics for many years; a survey by PE International (1993) in the UK, for example, found that 19 per cent of companies had such a policy. The survey by Murphy and Poist (1995) undertaken around the same time may have found that 60 per cent of logistics managers belonged to companies 'with formal or written environmental policies' (p 16), but these managers reported that they had only a 'minor role in both policy formulation and implementation'. This ran counter to the view of Wu and Dunn (1995: 20), that, 'because the nature of logistics management is cross-functional and integrative and since so many logistical activities impact on the environment, it makes sense for logistics managers to take the initiative in this area.' In their seminal paper they went on to illustrate the numerous ways in which a company could reduce the environmental impact of each stage in its value chain extending from the procurement of supplies to the after-sales service. This outlined the scope of what they termed 'environmentally responsible logistics' (ERL).

More recent surveys have revealed the widening diffusion of green logistics/supply chain strategies across the business world and suggested that transport and distribution activities have a prominent role in these strategies (Insight, 2008; Eyefortransport, 2007). The Insight survey of 600 supply chain professionals across Europe, the United States and Japan in 2008 found that an average of 35 per cent of their companies had a green supply chain strategy, with this proportion rising to 54 per cent for firms with an annual turnover in excess of $1 billion. Of the various activities covered by these strategies, logistics is one that the largest proportion of companies (81 per cent) have modified for environmental reasons (Insight, 2008).

These surveys have also provided empirical support for a claim frequently made in the academic literature (eg Wu and Dunn, 1995; Aronsson and Brodin, 2006) that, in many spheres of logistics management, economic and environmental objectives are closely aligned. Research by Rao and Holt (2005: 912) suggested that 'if they green their supply chains not only would firms achieve substantial cost savings, but they would also enhance sales, market share, and exploit new market opportunities to lead to greater profit margins.' It seems too that those firms that most effectively apply logistics best practice in terms of economic efficiency and customer service are also the best placed to green their logistics operations. In an international questionnaire survey of 306 logistics managers, Goldsby and Stank (2000: 199) found 'strong empirical evidence of a positive relationship between overall logistics competence and the implementation of ERL'.

This does not necessarily mean, however, that applying commercial best practice in logistics automatically minimizes its environmental impact. As companies do not have to bear the full cost of this impact (for reasons discussed in Chapter 4), the cost and service trade-offs that logistics managers make generally underestimate environmental effects. The resulting decisions may optimize logistics operations in economic terms to the detriment of the environment. Numerous studies have illustrated how practices such as the centralization of inventory (Matthews and Henrickson, 2003), just-in-time replenishment (Rao, Grenoble and Young, 1991; Whitelegg, 1995; Bleijenberg, 1996) and wider sourcing of supplies (Garnett, 2003) can carry a significant environmental penalty. It has frequently been argued that if companies factored all environmental costs into logistical trade-off analyses more sustainable systems would be created, characterized by more dispersed inventory, longer order lead times and more localized sourcing.

Other research, however, has challenged the conventional view that inventory centralization, JIT and globalization are inevitably bad for the environment. McKinnon and Woodburn (1994) and Kohn and Huge-Brodin (2008), for instance, contend that the centralization of distribution systems can reduce the environmental impact of logistics by, *inter alia*, consolidating freight flows. Garreau, Lieb and Millen (1991), Tracey et al (1995) and the Department of the Environment, Transport and the Regions (1999b) show how companies can implement JIT in ways that does not generate much additional freight traffic, while Smith et al (2005) and others assert that minimizing the distance goods travel from suppliers need not minimize their environmental footprint when measured on a life cycle basis.

Green supply chain management

Green supply chain management (GSCM) can be defined as the 'alignment and integration of environmental management within supply chain management' (Klassen and Johnson, 2004). It is based on the recognition that an individual firm's environmental impact extends well beyond its corporate boundaries. The origins of GSCM can be traced back to two functional areas in which companies' environmental responsibilities interfaced with external agencies: green purchasing/supply and reverse logistics.

Companies applying green principles to their internal operations naturally wish to ensure that their purchases of goods and services come from suppliers that also meet certain minimum environmental standards. At the very least, they want to minimize any environmental liability associated with purchased goods and services (Sarkis, 2000). Lamming and Hampson (1996: s61) envisaged 'the prospect of environmental soundness becoming a recognized feature of a supplier's overall performance'. A US survey by Gavaghan et al (1998) examined the extent to which companies were using four sets of environmental criteria in assessing suppliers, under the headings of regulatory compliance, environmental management systems, eco-efficiency and green design. The greening of purchasing activities has since become a fertile area of research considering issues such as the environmental criteria for supplier selection and environmental accreditation (eg Min and Galle, 2001). Walton, Handfield and Melnyk (1998), Bowen et al (2001) and others adopted a broader supply management perspective on the subject, examining ways in which vendors could work with their suppliers to improve their joint environmental performance. A key element in these collaborative initiatives is the physical movement of products between supply chain partners. In their definition of 'green supply' Vachon and Klassen (2006: 797), for example, include 'co-operation between organizations to minimize the logistical impact of material flows'.

Some authors have argued that research on GSCM has its origin in the reverse logistic studies undertaken in the 1990s. Van Hoek (1999), for example, saw the main locus of environmental research in logistics as being within the reverse channel for waste products, and advocated the extension of this research effort to environmental management of the whole chain from raw material source to after-sales service. The detailed review of literature on green supply chain management undertaken by Srivastava (2007) also exhibits a strong bias towards reverse logistics, devoting only a brief paragraph to the environmental effects of 'forward logistics' and giving 'logistics and distribution' a fairly subordinate role within his GSCM framework. This framework, like that of Sarkis

(2003), is based on a broad definition of GSCM that encompasses product design, all stages of manufacturing and distribution and all aspects of reverse logistics. Physically distributing products is seen as only one component in a much more broadly defined GSCM system. It is worth recalling, however, that in the recent survey by Insight (2008) four-fifths of the companies that were greening their supply chains had instigated measures related to logistics, a much higher proportion than were modifying other elements in the chain.

As the scope of GSCM has widened it has developed greater analytical depth. Srivastava (2007) found that a diverse range of mathematical and statistical techniques have been applied to the analysis of GSCM. Researchers have also adopted and adapted principles and techniques from the long established field of life cycle analysis (LCA) in assessing environmental impacts across the 'end-to-end' supply chain (eg Browne, Rizet et al, 2005; Faruk et al, 2001). Recent developments in the carbon auditing of supply chains have drawn heavily on LCA (Carbon Trust, 2007), and many new software tools (or 'carbon calculators') have been constructed to help companies and researchers to analyse carbon footprints at supply chain, company, process, facility and even product levels. Although GSCM is a relatively new field of study it has already achieved a fair degree of methodological maturity.

GREEN LOGISTICS: RHETORIC AND REALITY

A large body of survey evidence has accumulated to show that companies around the world are keen to promote their green credentials through the management of logistics. It is difficult to gauge, however, how far this reflects a true desire to help the environment as opposed to enhancing public relations. In concluding their assessment of the 'maturity' of the green supply chain, Insight (2008: 7) argue that 'when companies take action, they are typically taking the easy route of reputation and brand protection on green messaging.' This scepticism is echoed by Gilmore (2008) who argues that 'the corporate support for Green is as much for the potential to sell new products and technologies as it is about saving the planet'.

Recent surveys have enquired about the key drivers behind company initiatives to green their logistical systems and supply chains (Table 1.2). Although the survey methodologies, sample sizes and composition and questionnaire formats have varied, the same general messages have emerged, suggesting a strong emphasis on corporate image, competitive differentiation, cost saving and compliance with government regulation. Rather curiously, none of these surveys make explicit reference to the need to protect the environment. In business terms, after all, the most fundamental of all green objectives should be to maintain a physical environment that can support a high level of economic activity in the longer term.

On the other hand, it is very encouraging that companies responding to these surveys recognize that a healthy stream of conventional business benefits can flow from the greening of logistics (Table 1.3). This marks an important contrast with the situation in the early 1990s, at least in the UK. A UK study by PE International (1993) found companies essentially reacting to external pressures for environmental improvement, mainly from European and UK government regulations, with two-thirds of respondents expecting 'these pressures to increase operational costs'. A negative impression was given of businesses rather grudgingly trading off higher costs and lower profits for a better environment. While regulatory

Table 1.2 Key drivers for the greening of logistics and supply chains

EyeforTransport (2007)	Aberdeen Group (2008)	Insight (2008)
'Key Drivers for Instigating Green Transport/Logistics'	*'Top Five Pressures Driving the Green Supply Chain'*	*'Main Drivers for Green Logistics'*
Improving public relations (70%)	Desire to be thought leader in sustainability (51%)	Optimise logistics flow (18%)
Improving customer relations (70%)	Rising cost of energy/fuel (49%)	Improve corporate image (16%)
Part of their corporate responsibility agenda (60%)	Gaining competitive advantage/differentiation (48%)	Reduce logistics costs (15%)
Financial return on investment (60%)	Compliance with current/ expected regulation (31%)	Achieve regulatory compliance (15%)
Government compliance (60%)	Rising cost of transportation (24%)	Satisfy customer requirements (14%)
Decreasing fuel bills (60%)		Differentiation from competitors (11%)
Increasing supply chain efficiency (55%)		Develop alternative networks (10%)
Decreasing risk (50%)		
Improving investor relations (38%)		

compliance is still an important driver, it has slipped down the rankings and been superseded by a series of mainstream business motives. Green logistics is now regarded as good business practice and something that can have a positive impact on many financial and operational metrics.

A MODEL FOR GREEN LOGISTICS RESEARCH

A model has been devised to map the complex relationship between logistical activity and its related environmental effects and costs (Figure 1.2). These effects and costs mainly arise from freight transport operations and, for this reason, most of the boxes and links in the diagram are associated with the movement of goods. Reference is also made, however, to externalities from warehousing, materials handling and logistics IT activities. The model can be applied equally to the outbound movement of goods (forward logistics) and the return flow of products back along the supply chain (reverse logistics). In essence it decomposes

Table 1.3   Benefits of greening supply chains

Aberdeen Group (2008)	Insight (2008)
'Best-in-class Goals for Sustainability Initiatives'	*'Benefits of the Green Supply Chain'*
Reduce overall business costs (56%)	Improve brand image (70%)
Enhance CSR (54%)	Satisfy customer requirements (62%)
Improve profits (48%)	Differentiate from competitors (57%)
Reduce waste/improve disposal (43%)	Reduce logistics costs (52%)
Improve visibility of green supply drivers (41%)	Establish a competitive advantage (47%)
Increase use of recyclables/reusables (37%)	Optimise logistics flow (40%)
Improve fuel efficiency (35%)	Expand to new markets (38%)
Reduce emissions (33%)	Optimise manufacturing (35%)
Win new customers/develop new products (26%)	Reduce manufacturing costs (32%)
Reduce use of toxic materials (19%)	Other (2%)
Improve employee satisfaction (9%)	

the relationship between the material outputs of an economy and the monetary value of the logistics externalities into a series of key parameters and statistical aggregates. This relationship pivots on a set of nine key parameters:

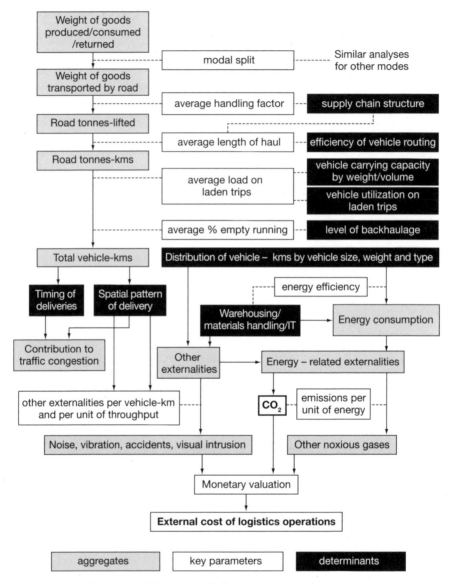

Figure 1.2 Analytical framework for green logistics

- Modal split indicates the proportion of freight carried by different transport modes. Following this split, subsequent parameters need to be calibrated for particular modes. As road is typically the main mode of freight transport within countries, the rest of Figure 1.2 has been defined with respect to this mode.[2]

- Average handling factor: this is the ratio of the weight of goods in an economy to freight tonnes-lifted, allowing for the fact that, as they pass through the supply chain, products are loaded on to vehicles several times. The handling factor serves as a crude measure of the average number of links in a supply chain.

- Average length of haul: this is the mean length of each link in the supply chain and essentially converts the tonnes-lifted statistic into tonne-kms.

- Average payload on laden trips and the average per cent empty running are the two key vehicle utilization parameters. Average payload is normally measured solely in terms of weight, though as the average density of freight is declining, for reasons discussed in Chapter 9, and an increasing proportion of loads is volume- rather than weight-constrained, it would be helpful to measure the physical dimensions of freight consignments. Very little data is available, however, to permit a volumetric analysis of vehicle loading.

- Energy efficiency: defined as the ratio of distance travelled to energy consumed. It is a function mainly of vehicle characteristics, driving behaviour and traffic conditions.

- Emissions per unit of energy: the quantity of CO_2 and noxious gases emitted per unit of energy consumed can vary with the type of energy/fuel, the nature of the engine converting this energy into logistical activity (such as movement, heating, refrigeration, IT) and exhaust filtration systems. For consistency, full well-to-wheel assessments should be made of the various pollutant emissions, wherever possible.

- Other externalities per vehicle-km and per unit of throughput: not all logistics-related externalities are a function of energy consumption. Allowance must also be made for other environmental effects such as noise irritation, vibration and accidents. This can be expressed either with respect to vehicle-kms in the case of transport, or with reference to the throughput of warehouses, terminals etc.

- Monetary valuation of externalities: the final stage in the framework converts physical measures of logistics-related externalities into monetary values. Money then becomes the common metric against which the environmental effects can be compared. This valuation also makes it possible to assess the extent to which environmental costs are recovered by the taxes imposed on logistical activity.

By altering these nine critical parameters, companies and governments can substantially reduce the environmental impact of logistics. Businesses devising green logistics strategies and government ministries developing sustainable logistics policies need to exploit this full range of parameters rather than rely on a few narrowly defined initiatives. As the 'determinant' boxes in Figure 1.2 illustrate, modifying the parameters requires different levels of logistical decision making. McKinnon and Woodburn (1996) differentiated for four levels:

- Strategic decisions relating to numbers, locations and capacity of factories, warehouses, shops and terminals.
- Commercial decisions on product sourcing, the subcontracting of production processes and distribution of finished products. These establish the pattern of trading links between a company and its suppliers, distributors and customers.
- Operational decisions on the scheduling of production and distribution that translate the trading links into discrete freight flows and determine the rate of inventory rotation in warehouses.
- Functional decisions relating to the management of logistical resources. Within the context defined by decisions at the previous three levels, logistics managers still have discretion over the choice, routing and loading of vehicles and operating practices within warehouses.

There has been a tendency for firms to confine green initiatives to the bottom end of this decision-making hierarchy where they usually yield economic as well as environment benefits. These functional-level initiatives typically focus on truck fuel efficiency, backloading, vehicle routing and energy conservation in warehouses. Although they are very welcome, much of their environmental benefit can be offset by the effects of higher-level strategic and commercial decisions, relating for example to inventory centralization or wider sourcing, which make logistics systems more transport-intensive and hence environmentally intrusive. The challenge is now for companies to instil green principles into the strategic planning of logistics and coordinate environmental management at all four levels of decision making. As Aronsson and Brodin (2006: 414) observe, there has been a 'lack of theories and models for connecting different logistics decisions on different hierarchical decision levels to each other and to their environmental impact'.

OUTLINE OF THE BOOK

The green logistics framework in Figure 1.2 provides a structure for this book. Each of the nine key parameters is addressed by at least one chapter.

Some chapters discuss more general issues that underpin efforts by companies and governments to make logistics more environmentally sustainable. The chapters have been grouped into four sections.

The remaining chapters in Section 1 assess the environmental effects of logistics, consider how they can be evaluated in monetary terms and ask to what extent these environmental costs are covered by taxation. In the first of these chapters, Cullinane and Edwards look at various ways in which freight transport adversely affects the environment over different geographical scales. They also consider the imposition of environmental standards on freight transport and show how environmental impacts can be measured at both macro- and micro-levels. This measurement theme continues into the next chapter, where Piecyk explains how carbon emissions from logistical activity can be audited at company, supply chain and individual product levels. Standard procedures are outlined and a case study used to show how a company can assess the carbon footprint of its road freight transport operation. The final chapter in this section by Piecyk, McKinnon and Allen deals with the monetary valuation of the environmental, infrastructural and congestion effects of freight transport and assesses the degree to which the taxes paid by lorries and vans in the UK internalize these external costs.

Section 2 takes a strategic perspective on green logistics. It begins with a chapter on the opportunities for making the structure of logistics systems and supply chains more environmentally sustainable. This chapter by Harris, Sanchez Rodrigues, Naim and Mumford reviews the current state of knowledge about supply chain structure and dynamics, highlights the need to include environmental metrics into supply chain analysis and shows how the design of logistics systems influences their environmental impact. Another major determinant of this impact is the choice of freight transport mode. In their chapter, Woodburn and Whiteing consider the environmental benefits of shifting freight from road to rail and water-borne transport and then review, with the help of case studies, what governments, freight operators and shippers can do to promote the use of these greener modes. In Chapter 7, McKinnon, Allen and Woodburn also adopt a cross-modal perspective in forecasting the future potential for 'greening' trucks, vans, freight trains, aircraft and ships. They focus on opportunities for technical improvements that would allow freight to be carried in larger quantities, more energy efficiently and with less pollution per tonne-km. The concluding chapter in this section by Marchant assesses the environmental impact of warehousing and examines the broad range of design, construction and operational measures that can be applied to minimize this impact and possibly even create, in the longer term, carbon neutral warehousing.

Section 3 takes more of an operational perspective on greening logistics. It starts with a chapter by McKinnon and Edwards on ways of improving vehicle utilization to achieve both environmental and economic savings. They consider the various ways of measuring vehicle-fill and the logistical trade-offs that companies must make in trying to raise vehicle load factors and cut empty running. Better loading should be accompanied by more efficient routeing and scheduling. This is the subject of the contribution by Eglese and Black, which begins by defining the vehicle routing and scheduling problem (VRSP) and then explores some of the problems that arise when trying to solve this problem in the real world, such as dealing with specified time windows, backhauling, mixed vehicle fleets and traffic congestion. Chapter 11, by McKinnon, explores the opportunities for improving fuel efficiency in the road freight sector. He argues that companies need to deploy a broad range of technical, behavioural and operational measures within properly coordinated fuel management programmes. The concluding chapter in this section, by Cherrett, Maynard, McLeod and Hickford, addresses a series of operational issues in the expanding field of reverse logistics. It examines the various options for recycling, refurbishing and reusing waste products, assesses the impact of waste regulations and considers how the return flow of waste can be made more environmentally sustainable.

In Section 4 authors discuss four key issues that have generated a good deal of discussion in the field of green logistics in recent years. The 'food miles' debate, which has extended well beyond academic circles into the public domain, is comprehensively reviewed by Garnett. She asks whether, in environmental terms, 'further is worse' and shows how the issue is much more complex than is generally suggested in the media. In recognition of the fact that much of the environmental impact of logistics is concentrated in urban areas, the chapter by Allen and Browne reviews a range of initiatives, such as the establishment of consolidation centres and creation of environmental zones, that can improve the sustainability of freight deliveries in towns and cities. Cullinane and Edwards weigh up the costs and benefits of freight operators switching from conventional fossil fuels to alternative energy forms such as biofuels, hydrogen, natural gas and battery power. Much of their chapter focuses on the sustainability of biofuels, an issue that is proving particularly contentious. The penultimate chapter, by Edwards, Wang, Potter and Cullinane, considers how the development of e-commerce, at both the business-to-business (B2B) and business-to-consumer (B2C) levels, is influencing the environmental footprint of logistics operations.

In Section 5, the final chapter provides a public policy perspective on green logistics. McKinnon reviews the objectives of sustainable logistics policies and the various measures that governments can use to influence the key parameters in the green logistics framework (Figure 1.2) and thereby decouple the environmental effects of logistics from the growth of the economy. As the free market on its own is unlikely to deliver the necessary level of environmental improvement, particularly in terms of climate change, governments will play a critical role in the future development of green logistics.

NOTES

1. Sharon Cullinane and Michael Browne also contributed to this chapter.
2. In the later sections average handling factor and length of haul are discussed before modal split as they are related to freight movement by all modes.

REFERENCES

Aberdeen Group (2008) *Building a Green Supply Chain*, Aberdeen Group, Boston

Abukhader, S and Jonsson, G (2004) Logistics and the environment: is it an established subject? *International Journal of Logistics: Research and Applications*, **7** (2), pp 137–49

Adams, JGU (1981) *Transport Planning: Vision and practice*, Routledge and Kegan Paul, London

Armitage, A (1980) *Report of the Inquiry into Lorries, People and the Environment*, HMSO, London

Aronsson, H and Brodin, MH (2006), The environmental impact of changing logistics structures, *The International Journal of Logistics Management*, **17** (3), pp 394–415

Beamon, B (1999) Designing the Green Supply Chain, *Logistics Information Management*, **12** (4), pp 332–42

Bennathan, E, Fraser, J and Thompson, LS (1992) What determines demand for freight transport, Working paper WPS 998, Infrastructure and Urban Development Department World Bank, Washington, DC

Bleijenberg, A (1996) *Freight Transport in Europe: In search of a sustainable course*, Centrum voor Energiebesparing en schone technologie (CE), Delft

Böge, S (1994) The well travelled yogurt pot: lessons for new freight transport policies and regional production, *World Transport Problems and Practice*, **1** (1), pp 7–11

Bowen, FE, Cousins, PD, Lamming, RC and Faruk, AC (2001) The role of supply management capabilities in green supply, *Production and Operations Management*, **10** (2), pp 174–89

Browne, M, Rizet, C, Anderson, S, Allen, J and Keita, B (2005) Life cycle assessment in the supply chain: a review and case study, *Transport Reviews*, **25** (6), pp 761–82

Browne, M, Sweet, M, Woodburn, A and Allen, J (2005) *Urban Freight Consolidation Centres*, report for the Department for Transport

Brundtland Commission (1987) *Our Common Future*, Oxford University Press, Oxford

Carbon Trust (2007) *Carbon Footprints in the Supply Chain*, Carbon Trust, London

Carter, CR and Ellram, LM (1998) Reverse logistics: a review of the literature and framework for future investigation, *Journal of Business Logistics*, **19**, pp 85–102

Civic Trust, County Surveyors Association, and Department of Transport (1990) *Lorries in the Community*, HMSO, London

Committee on Climate Change (2008) *Building a Low Carbon Economy*, Committee on Climate Change, London

Cooper, JC, Black, I and Peters, M (1998) Creating the sustainable supply chain: modelling key relationships, in *Transport Policy and the Environment*, ed D Banister, pp 176–203, E&FN Spon, London

Dekker, R, Fleischmann, M, Inderfurth, K and Van Wassenhove, LN (eds) (2004) *Reverse Logistics: Quantitative models for closed loop supply chains*, Springer, Berlin

Department of the Environment, Transport and the Regions (DETR) (1999a) *Sustainable Distribution: A strategy*, HMSO, London

DETR (1999b) *Efficient JIT Supply Chain Management: Nissan Motor Manufacturing (UK) Ltd*, Good Practice Case Study 374, Energy Efficiency Best Practice Programme, Harwell

DIW, ifeu, IVA/HACON (1994) *Reduction of Air Pollution and Noise from Long Distance Freight Transport by the Year 2010*, Research project no 104 04 962, Federal Environment Agency (Umweltbundesamt), Berlin

European Commission (1998) *COST 321: Urban goods transport – final report of the Action Directorate General Transport*, European Commission, Brussels

European Commission (2001) *Transport Policy for 2010: Time to Decide*, European Commission, Brussels

European Commission (2003) *European Energy and Transport Trends to 2003*, DG TREN, Brussels

Eyefortransport (2007) Green transportation and logistics, available at eyefortransport.com

Faruk, AC, Lamming, RC, Cousins, PD and Bowen, FE (2001) Analyzing, mapping and managing environmental impacts along supply chains, *Journal of Industrial Ecology*, **5** (2), pp 13–36

Garnett, T (2003) *Wise Moves: Exploring the relationship between food, transport and CO₂*, Transport 2000 Trust, London

Garreau, A, Lieb, R and Millen, R (1991) JIT and corporate transport: an international comparison, *International Journal of Physical Distribution & Logistics Management*, **21** (1), pp 46–49

Gavaghan, K, Klein, RC, Olson, JP and Pritchett, TE (1998) The greening of the supply chain, *Supply Chain Management Review*, **2** (2), pp 76–84

Gilmore, D (2008) How real is the green supply chain? *Supply Chain Digest*, 7 August

Goldsby, TJ and Stank, TP (2000) World class logistics performance and environmentally responsible practices, *Journal of Business Logistics*, **21** (2), pp 187–208

Hey, C, Hickmann, G, Geisendorf, S, Schleicher-Tappeser, R (1992) Dead end road, Eures/Greenpeace, Freiburg

Holman, C (1996) *The Greening of Freight Transport in Europe*, Report 96/12, European Federation of Transport and Environment, Brussels

Insight (2008) How mature is the green supply chain, *2008 Supply Chain Monitor*, Bearing Point Inc

Jackson GC (1985) A survey of freight consolidation practices, *Journal of Business Logistics*, **6** (1), pp 13–34

Jahre, M (1995) Household waste collection as a reverse channel, *International Journal of Physical Distribution & Logistics Management*, **25** (2), pp 39–55

Jayaraman, V, Guide, VDR and Srivastava, R (1999) A closed-loop model for remanufacturing, *Journal of the Operational Research Society*, 50, pp 497–508

Kahn Ribeiro, S and Kobayashi, S (2007) Transport and its infrastructure, in *Fourth Assessment Report: Climate change 2007 – mitigation of climate change*, Inter-governmental Panel on Climate Change, Geneva

Klassen, RD and Johnson, F (2004) The green supply chain, in *Understanding Supply Chains: Concepts, critiques and futures*, ed SJ New and R Westbrook, pp 229–51, Oxford University Press, Oxford

Kohn, C and Huge-Brodin, M (2008) Centralized distribution systems and the environment: how increased transport work can decrease the environmental impact of logistics, *International Journal of Logistics: Research and Applications*, **11** (3), pp 229–45

Lamming, R and Hampson, J (1996) The environment as a supply chain management issue, *British Journal of Management*, 7, pp s45–s62

Matthews, HS and Henrickson, CT (2003) The economic and environmental implications of centralized stock keeping, *Journal of Industrial Ecology*, **6** (2), pp 71–81

McKinnon, AC (1998) Logistical restructuring, road freight traffic growth and the environment, in *Transport Policy and the Environment*, ed D Banister, pp 97–110, Spon, London

McKinnon, AC (2003) Logistics and the environment, in *Handbook of Logistics and Supply Chain Management*, ed D Hensher and K Button, pp 665–85, Elsevier, Amsterdam

McKinnon, AC (2007) The decoupling of road freight transport and economic growth trends in the UK: an exploratory analysis, *Transport Reviews*, **27** (1), pp 37–64

McKinnon, AC and Woodburn, A (1994) The consolidation of retail deliveries: its effect on CO_2 emissions, *Transport Policy*, **1** (2), pp 125–36

McKinnon, AC and Woodburn, A (1996) Logistical restructuring and freight traffic growth: an empirical assessment, *Transportation*, **23** (2), pp 141–61

Min, H and Galle, WP (2001) Green purchasing practices of US firms, *International Journal of Operations & Production Management*, **21** (9), pp 1222–38

Murphy, PR and Poist, RF (1995) Role and relevance of logistics to corporate environmentalism: an empirical assessment, *International Journal of Physical Distribution & Logistics Management*, **25** (2), pp 5–19

Murphy, PR and Poist, RF (2003) Green perspectives and practices: a 'comparative logistics' study, *Supply Chain Management: An international journal*, **8** (2), pp 122–31

OECD (1982) *Impacts of Heavy Freight Vehicles*, OECD, Paris

Ogden, KW (1992) *Urban Goods Movement: A guide to policy and planning*, Ashgate, Aldershot

Pastowski, A (1997) *Decoupling Economic Development and Freight for Reducing its Negative Impacts*, Wupperthal paper no 78, Wupperthal Institute for Climate, Environment and Energy

Paxton, A (1994) *The Food Miles Report: The dangers of long distance transport of food*, Safe Alliance, London

PE International (1993) *Going Green: The logistics dilemma institute of logistics and distribution management*, PE International, Corby

Pettit, D (1973) *Lorries and the World We Live In*, HMSO, London

Plowden, S and Buchan, K (1995) *A New Framework for Freight Transport*, Civic Trust, London

Rao, K, Grenoble, W and Young, R (1991) Traffic congestion and JIT, *Journal of Business Logistics*, **12** (1), pp 105–21

Rao, P and Holt, D (2005) Do green supply chains lead to competitiveness and economic performance? *International Journal of Operations & Production Management*, **25** (2), pp 898–916

Royal Commission on Environmental Pollution (RCEP) (1994) *Transport and the Environment*, HMSO, London

Rushton, A (1979) *Improving Goods Delivery*, National Materials Handling Centre, Cranfield

Sarkis, J (2000) Supply chain management and environmentally conscious design and manufacturing, *International Journal of Environmentally Conscious Design and Manufacturing*, **4** (2), pp 43–52

Sarkis, J (2003) A strategic decision framework for green supply chain management, *Journal of Cleaner Production*, **11** (4), pp 397–409

Schipper, L, Scholl, L and Price, L (1997) Energy use and carbon emissions from freight in 10 industrialized countries: an analysis of trends from 1973 to 1992, *Transportation Research part D*, **2** (1), pp 57–76

Sharp, C and Jennings, A (1976) *Transport and the Environment*, Leicester University Press, Leicester

Smith, A, Watkiss, P, Tweddle, G, McKinnon, AC, Browne, M, Hunt, A, Treleven, C, Nash, C and Cross, A (2005) *The Validity of Food Miles as an Indicator of Sustainable Development*, Department of the Environment, Food and Rural Affairs, London

Srivastava, SK (2007) Green supply-chain management: a state-of-the-art literature review, *International Journal of Management Reviews*, **9** (1), pp 53–80

Stock, J (1992) *Reverse Logistics*, Council of Logistics Management, Oak Brook

Taniguchi, E, Thompson, RG, Yamada, T and van Diun, JHR (eds) (2001) *City Logistics: Network modelling and intelligent transport systems*, Pergamon, London

Tapio, P (2005) Towards a theory of decoupling: degrees of decoupling in the EU and the case of road traffic in Finland between 1970 and 2001, *Transport Policy*, **12**, pp 137–51

Tracey, M, Chong Leng Tan, Vonderembse, M and Bardi, E (1995) A re-examination of the effects of just-in-time on inbound logistics, *The International Journal of Logistics Management*, **6** (2), pp 25–38

Vachon, S and Klassen, RD (2006) Extending green practices across the supply chain, *International Journal of Operations & Production Management*, **26** (7), pp 795–821

Van Hoek, R (1999) From reversed logistics to green supply chains, *Supply Chain Management: An international journal*, **4** (3), pp 129–35

Walton, SV, Handfield, RB and Melnyk, SA (1998) The green supply chain: integrating suppliers into environmental management processes, *Journal of Supply Chain Management*, **34** (2), pp 2–11

Werkgroep 2000 (1993) *A New Course in Freight Transport*, Amersfoort, Netherlands

Whitelegg, J (1995) *Freight Transport, Logistics and Sustainable Development*, World Wide Fund for Nature, London

Wu, H-J and Dunn, SC (1995) Environmentally-responsible logistics systems, *International Journal of Physical Distribution & Logistics Management*, **25** (2), pp 20–38

2

Assessing the environmental impacts of freight transport

Sharon Cullinane and Julia Edwards

INTRODUCTION

Logistics is responsible for a variety of externalities, including air pollution, noise, accidents, vibration, land-take and visual intrusion. This chapter examines these various externalities and discusses how their impact can be assessed. As climate change is now considered to be the most serious environmental challenge facing mankind, the main focus will be on greenhouse gas (GHG) emissions from freight transport.

In measuring the environmental effects of logistics it is important to distinguish first-order and second-order impacts. The first-order environmental impacts are those directly associated with freight transport, warehousing and materials handling operations. Second-order impacts result indirectly from these logistics operations and take various forms. For instance, advances in logistics have facilitated the process of globalization so that goods are now sourced from previously little-developed parts of the world. Partly to accommodate the consequent growth in freight traffic in such areas, governments have expanded transport infrastructure and this has often encroached on sensitive environments. The increase in air freight and other traffic resulting from global sourcing is a first-order effect, whereas the increase in infrastructure, such as road building in sensitive areas, is a second-order effect. In this chapter we concentrate on the first-order impacts and make only brief reference to the wider, second-order effects. Since the majority of the first-order impacts emanate from the transport of goods, rather than their storage and handling, the attention will focus on this activity. Chapter 8 specifically examines the environmental impact of warehousing.

ENVIRONMENTAL IMPACTS

Atmospheric emissions

Emissions from freight transport largely depend on the type of fuel used. As discussed in Chapter 15, various alternative fuels now exist. However, the main fuel used by goods vehicles continues to be diesel, with relatively small amounts of freight moved in petrol-engined vans. Trucks and vans emit pollution mainly because the combustion process in their engines is incomplete. Diesel and petrol contain both hydrogen and carbon. If it were possible to achieve perfect combustion, 100 per cent of the hydrogen would be converted into water and all the carbon into CO_2. However, because combustion is not complete, tailpipe emissions of pollutants such as hydrocarbons, carbon monoxide and nitrogen oxides result (Holmen and Niemeier, 2003).

In most countries, relatively small amounts of freight are moved in electrically powered road vehicles or freight trains. In the case of these operations, the pollution arises at the point where the electricity is generated and the nature of that pollution depends on the primary energy source used. In countries such as France and Switzerland where only a small proportion of electricity is produced using fossil fuels, the carbon intensity of electrified rail freight services is very low (IRU, 2002).

Diesel and petrol have slightly different environmental impacts as their mix of pollutant emissions varies. Diesel engines emit more CO_2 per unit of energy, but because they are more energy efficient, the overall impact of diesel engines on CO_2 emissions is less than that of an equivalent-sized petrol engine (Schipper and Fulton, 2003). The standard fuel CO_2 conversion factors for various types of fuel are given in Table 2.1. Diesel engines emit much higher levels of particulate matter and nitrogen oxides than an equivalent petrol-powered engine (Holmen and Niemeier, 2003). It is difficult to measure emissions of particulates precisely, because of their ultra-fine nature. PM10 particles, for instance, have a radius of 10 microns or less (a micron is a hundredth of a millimetre). Measuring these particles when the vehicle is stationary is difficult enough; measuring them under different driving conditions and speeds introduces additional complexities. Calculating the impact of these tiny soot particles on human health presents further problems, although there is growing evidence of their effects on respiratory problems as well as on general morbidity (Pope et al, 2002).

The pollutants emitted by transport can be divided into local, regional and global effects (see Table 2.2). Local pollutants remain close to the source of the emission. At the kerbside of major roads, concentrations

Table 2.1 Standard road transport fuel conversion factors

Fuel type	Total units used	Units	×	Kg CO_2 per unit	Total
Petrol		litre		2.3154	
Diesel		litre		2.6304	
CNG		kg		2.7278	
LPG		litre		1.4975	

Source: DEFRA (2008).

Table 2.2 Geographical extent of pollutant effects

Effect	PM	HM	NH_3	SO_2	NOx	NMVOC	CO	CH_4	CO_2	N_2O
Global										
Greenhouse – indirect					X	X		X		
Greenhouse – direct							X	X	X	
Regional										
Acidification		X	X	X						
Photochemical					X	X		X		
Local										
Health and air quality	X	X	X	X	X	X		X		

PM – particulates, HM – heavy metals, NH_3 – Ammonia, SO_2 – sulphur dioxide, NOx – Oxides of nitrogen, NMVOC – non-metallic volatile organic compounds, CO – carbon monoxide, CH_4 – Methane, CO_2 – carbon dioxide, N_2O – Nitrous Oxide.

Source: Hickman (1999).

of the primary pollutants can be two to three times higher than the background urban level, while inside vehicles travelling along major roads, concentrations can be on average five times higher than the background levels (RCEP, 1994). Regional effects can occur far away from the source of the emission and affect wider geographical areas, sometimes spanning several adjoining countries. GHG emissions, on the other hand, affect the global atmosphere. The same pollutants, such as sulphur dioxide or nitrogen dioxide, can have an adverse effect on the environment over differing distance ranges.

We turn first to the global effects as they have become the main cause of environmental concern. This is partly because scientific discoveries over the past two decades have revealed the severity of the climate change problem, but also because tightening controls on the emissions of other noxious gases have eased pollution problems at local and regional levels.

Global effects of atmospheric pollution

According to the United Nations Inter-governmental Panel on Climate Change (UN IPCC, 2007), scientific evidence that human activity is the main cause of global warming is now 'unequivocal'. It explains that 'greenhouse gases are the gaseous constituents of the atmosphere, both natural and anthropogenic, that absorb and emit radiation at specific wavelengths within the spectrum of thermal infrared radiation emitted by the Earth's surface, the atmosphere itself, and by clouds' (2007: 82). The greenhouse effect arises because GHGs and some particles in the atmosphere allow more sunlight energy to filter through to the surface of the planet relative to the amount of radiant energy that they allow to escape back up to space. The UN IPCC (1996) lists 27 greenhouse gases. These are combined into six categories in the Kyoto Protocol agreed in December 1997 (United Nations, 1998), namely:

- Carbon dioxide (CO_2);
- Methane (MH_4);
- Nitrous oxides (NOx);
- Hydrofluorocarbons (HFC);
- Perfluorocarbons (PFC);
- Sulphur hexafluoride (SF_6).

Greenhouse gas emissions are defined as the total mass of a GHG released to the atmosphere over a specified period of time. Each gas has a different global warming potential (GWP). The GWP of a given GHG is calculated by multiplying the 'radiative forcing' impact of one mass-based unit (eg a tonne) of this gas relative to an equivalent unit of carbon dioxide over a given period.[1] GHG emissions tend to be reported in carbon dioxide equivalents (CO_2e), which are calculated by multiplying the mass of a given GHG by its GWP. CO_2e is a unit used for comparing the radiative forcing of a GHG to that of carbon dioxide. In the UK an official set of GWPs for reporting purposes is published by DEFRA based on international guidance produced by the IPCC (Table 2.3).

The GWP assesses the effects of various GHG emissions relative to those of an equivalent mass of CO_2 over a set time period, normally 100 years. Thus, methane has 21 times the global warming effect of CO_2 over 100 years and sulphur hexafluoride almost 24,000 times.

Carbon dioxide accounts for by far the largest proportion (approximately 85 per cent) of GHGs in the atmosphere, which is why there is so much attention focused on this particular gas. Although DEFRA now recommends expressing gases in terms of CO_2e, CO_2 emissions are sometimes converted into carbon emissions. One tonne of carbon is contained in 3.67 tonnes of CO_2. Other GHGs are frequently expressed in terms of carbon equivalent by multiplying their emissions by their GWP and then dividing by 3.67 (DEFRA, 2006).

At a global level, the movement of freight accounts for roughly a third of all the energy consumed by transport (UN IPCC, 2007). In the UK in 2004, transport accounted for 23 per cent of total energy-related CO_2 emissions, with freight transport responsible for around 8 per cent (McKinnon, 2007) or 33.7 million tonnes of CO_2. Road transport accounted for 92 per cent of this total, split in the ratio 86:14 between HGVs and vans. Rail and waterborne transport together represented

Table 2.3 The global warming potential (GWP) of the six Kyoto greenhouse gases

Greenhouse gas	Global Warming Potential (GWP) DEFRA	Global Warming Potential (GWP) IPCC
Carbon dioxide (CO_2)	1	1
Methane (CH_4)	21	25
Nitrous oxide (N_2O)	310	298
Hydrofluorocarbons (HFCs)	140–11,700	124–14,800
Perfluorocarbons (PFCs)	6,500–9,200	7,390–12,200
Sulphur hexafluoride (SF_6)	23,900	22,800

Source: DEFRA (2008).

just under 8 per cent of freight-related CO_2 emissions, with domestic air freight producing a negligible proportion.

Regional effects of atmospheric pollution

Airborne pollutants can diffuse widely from their original source, particularly when carried by the prevailing winds. The two main examples of air pollution extending over extensive areas are:

- Acid rain. This is caused by the emission of sulphur dioxide and nitrogen oxides into the atmosphere. It interferes with the growth of flora and fauna and with water-life. Mainly as a result of the adoption of low and ultra-low-sulphur diesel in the trucking sector and, to a lesser extent, by rail freight companies, land-based freight transport is now responsible for a very small proportion of acid rain. The high sulphur content of the bunker fuels used in shipping presents a much more serious environmental problem, particularly around ports, although the International Maritime Organization (IMO) has implemented new regulations under Annex 6 of its MARPOL convention to radically reduce SOx emissions (IMO, 2008).
- Photochemical smog. Photochemical smog is caused by the reaction of sunlight with nitrogen dioxide, especially during periods of still, settled weather (ie high pressure). It can extend over whole urban regions. Such smog can cause loss of lung efficiency and is thought to exacerbate asthma problems.

Local effects of atmospheric pollution

These effects are experienced in the immediate vicinity of the pollution source, where the concentration levels are high.

- Nitrogen oxides (NOx). Nitric oxide and nitrogen oxide result from combustion at high temperatures where nitrogen and oxygen combine. Short-term effects are rarely noticed but long-term exposure to fairly low levels can affect the functioning of the lungs. At higher levels, emphysema may occur (EPA, 2008).
- Hydrocarbons (HCs). Hydrocarbons result from the incomplete combustion of organic materials. Included within this category are volatile organic compounds (VOCs). Many hydrocarbons, such as benzene, are known to be carcinogenic, though the actual levels likely to cause damage are not known precisely (US Dept of Health and Human Services, 1999).

- Ozone (O_3). Ozone is formed when nitrogen oxides and VOCs react with sunlight. Exposure to high levels of ground level ozone can lead to respiratory problems and nausea. Children, asthmatics and the elderly may be more susceptible or vulnerable to the effects (Royal Society, 2008).
- Particulates. Particulates come in various sizes and from a variety of sources. In the case of vehicles, the majority take the form of soot emitted by diesel engines, particularly those that are badly tuned. There are concerns over the likely carcinogenic effects, particularly of the smaller PM10 particles (EPA, 2009). These particles are also linked to respiratory and cardiovascular problems and to asthma. It has been estimated that in the UK, PM10 pollution causes the premature deaths of 12,000–24,000 people annually and adds £9.1bn–£21bn to the national health budget (Rogers, 2007).
- Carbon monoxide (CO). Carbon monoxide results from the incomplete combustion of carbon-based fuels. It binds well with haemoglobin, which carries oxygen around the body. It binds 200 times more easily than oxygen and so reduces the circulation of oxygen. At low levels of exposure, perception and thought are impaired but at high levels it can cause death (HPA, 2009).
- Sulphur dioxide (SO_2). Fossil fuels, particularly diesel, contain sulphur. When they are burned in the engine, the remaining sulphur is converted into sulphur dioxide, an acidic gas which is then emitted through the exhaust pipe. Normally, it causes irritation to the eyes, nose and throat of those exposed to it. At low levels it may also temporarily make breathing difficult for people with predisposed respiratory illness, such as asthma (HPA, 2008).

Noise pollution

Road traffic is the main cause of environmental noise at the local level. The immediate adverse effects of noise disturbance include annoyance, communication difficulties, loss of sleep and impaired cognitive functioning resulting in loss of work productivity; longer-term, physiological and psychological health issues may also arise (den Boer and Schroten, 2007). Currently, around 30 per cent of the European Union's population is exposed to road traffic noise and 10 per cent to rail noise levels above 55 dB(A). Data on aircraft noise exposure is less reliable, though it is thought that around 10 per cent of the EU population may be highly disturbed by air transport noise (EEA, 2003).

In the UK 90 per cent of people hear road traffic noise while at home and 10 per cent of these regard this noise source as highly annoying (Watts et al, 2006).

Trucks generate road noise from three sources:

- propulsion noise (power train/engine sources), which dominates at low speeds (less than 50kmph);
- tyre/road-contact noise, which is the main cause of noise at speeds above 50kmph;
- aerodynamic noise, which increases as the vehicle accelerates.

European vehicle noise standards for individual vehicles were introduced in the early 1970s (Directive 70/157/EEC), when the permitted noise emissions for trucks were set at 80 dB(A). Noise standards have been tightened several times since then (Affenzeller and Rust, 2005). Significant reductions in noise levels have been achieved by technical advances in engine design, tyres and the aerodynamic profiling of vehicles. Nevertheless, overall noise levels have not improved, as the growth and spread of traffic in space and time has largely offset both technological improvements and other abatement measures (INFRAS, 2004)

The European Union in 2001 launched regulations that limited the levels of noise generated by vehicle tyres (Directive 2001/43/EC). Tyre noise was targeted specifically for two reasons. First, tyre rolling noise is generally the main source of noise from trucks at medium and high speeds (see Sandberg and Ejsmont, 2002); and second, as tyres are replaced more frequently than vehicles, implementing tyre noise standards was considered to be one of the fastest ways to achieve road noise reductions.

In addition to quietening the vehicle, it is possible to cut noise levels by altering the acoustic properties of the road surface. FEHRL (2006) outline a range of noise-abatement measures that can be applied in the design and construction of road infrastructure.

As in road transport, technological improvements in air transport (from engine improvements and airframe design) have substantially reduced the noise of individual aircraft, but these performance improvements have been eroded by the growth of air traffic (Janić, 2007).

Accidents

Accidents cause personal injury and death for those involved, and general inconvenience for other road users. Overall, accidents involving HGVs by distance travelled are fewer than for cars, although there is a higher likelihood of an HGV being involved in a fatal accident, as shown in Table 2.4. This is partly a reflection of HGVs greater momentum, and partly due to the relatively high proportion of time that they are driven on faster roads.

The accident rate in the EU varies enormously, as shown in Table 2.5. The country recording the highest fatality rate in accidents involving HGVs (Poland) has over six times more fatalities per million population than the country with the lowest rate (Italy). This difference is likely to be caused by a variety of factors, including driver behaviour, age of vehicles, vehicle maintenance, road standards and the nature and enforcement of safety regulations. The figures are also distorted by international variations in the statistical definition of a fatal traffic accident, which centres around the maximum length of time elapsing between the accident and the death. Table 2.5 also shows that in every country where comparable figures exist, the number of fatalities has dropped considerably over the period 1997–2006, in some cases more than halving.

In the EU14, 13 per cent of fatalities in accidents involving HGVs and 12 per cent involving LGVs (<3.5 tonnes gross weight) are in urban areas, much lower proportions than for cars and taxis (22 per cent). Although the number of LGVs has been increasing through time, the total annual number of fatalities in this category in the EU14 fell from 2,973 in 1997 to 2,511 in 2005 (ERSO, 2008).

ENVIRONMENTAL STANDARDS

Environmental standards can be divided into two types; those that are mandatory and those that more environmentally responsible companies meet voluntarily. The former type is mostly technical, while the latter type is often more management orientated.

Table 2.4   Vehicle involvement rates by accident severity in the UK, 2007 (rate per 100 million vehicle-kms)

Severity	HGVs	Cars
Killed	1.6	0.8
Killed or seriously injured	6.6	7.5
All	36	63

Source: Department for Transport (2008).

Table 2.5 Fatalities in accidents involving HGVs – EU (fatalities in HGVs plus all other fatalities)

Country	1997	2006	Rates per million population, 2006
Belgium	195	133	12.6
Czech Republic	n/a	215	20.9
Denmark	93	49	9.0
Estonia	n/a	37	27.5
Spain	888	664	15.1
France	1113	683	10.8
Ireland	85	n/a	12.7
Italy	476	n/a	5.7
Luxembourg	6	n/a	25.4
Hungary	n/a	239	23.7
Malta	n/a	1	n/a
Netherlands	177	n/a	9.7
Austria	150	120	14.5
Poland	n/a	n/a	37.4
Portugal	356	130	12.3
Finland	112	82	15.6
Sweden	97	83	9.1
Great Britain	554	443	7.3

Source: European Road Safety Observatory (2008).

Mandatory standards

EURO emission standards

Since the early 1990s, emissions from diesel-engined HGVs have been strictly controlled by EU legislation. New HGVs have been the subject of progressively tightening environmental standards, known as EURO emission standards. Emissions of nitrogen oxides and particulate matter have been targeted particularly and will be almost negligible after 2013

(Table 2.6). One vehicle manufacturer has produced an enhanced environmentally friendly vehicle (EEV) that, compared with Euro V standards, emits 50 per cent less soot, 87 per cent less CO and 88 per cent less HC. Many responsible logistics companies have been proactive, implementing the standards before the enforcement date.

Voluntary/management standards

Environmental management standards (EMS)

Environmental management was first developed as a response to new environmental regulations being imposed on companies. It soon evolved beyond its initial, narrow, technical approach as managers started to perceive environmental issues as realities that needed to be incorporated into business strategy (Walley and Whitehead, 1994). Environmental management has both short and long-term consequences, affecting the current performance and long-term sustainability of businesses. Carbon management is a relatively new part of this process, gaining in significance in light of the climate change threat. Carbon management should not, however, be implemented in isolation. It is important to create one comprehensive environmental strategy and understand the potential trade-offs between its constituent parts. The Institute of Environmental Management and Assessment (IEMA, 2008) defines an EMS as 'a structured framework for managing an organization's significant impact on the environment'. These impacts can include business waste, emissions, energy use, transport and consumption of materials and, increasingly, climate change factors.

Table 2.6 Emission standards for heavy-duty diesel engines (g/kWh)

Tier	Date of implementation	CO	HC	NOx	PM
Euro I	1992 (>85kw)	4.5	1.1	8.0	0.36
Euro II	1998	4.0	1.1	7.0	0.15
Euro III	2000	2.1	0.66	5.0	0.10
Euro IV	2005	1.5	0.46	3.5	0.02
Euro V	2008	1.5	0.46	2.0	0.02
Euro VI	2013	1.5	0.13	0.4	0.01

Source: www.nao.org.uk.

ISO 14000 and 14001
For companies that want certification of their environmental credentials there exists a series of international standards, namely the ISO 14000 series. These are a set of voluntary standards and guideline references for companies aiming to minimize their environmental impact. ISO 14001, which was published in 1996, is the only standard in the ISO 14000 series for which certification by an external authority is available, and concerns the specification of requirements for a company's environmental management system.

Eco-Management and Audit Scheme (EMAS)
This is a voluntary European-wide standard introduced by the European Union and applied to all European countries. It was formally introduced into the UK in April 1995. According to the Institute of Environmental Management and Assessment (IEMA, 2008), the aim of EMAS is 'to recognize and reward those organizations that go beyond minimum legal compliance and continuously improve their environmental performance'. Participating organizations must regularly produce a public environmental statement, checked by an independent environmental verifier that reports on their environmental performance.

BS7750
The UK has its own standard, designed to be compatible with EMAS and ISO 14001. BS7750 is designed to help companies to evaluate their performance and to define their policy, practices, objectives and targets in relation to the environment. It requires the support of senior management, and describes policies for the benefit of both staff and the general public.

MEASURING THE ENVIRONMENTAL IMPACT OF FREIGHT TRANSPORT

Macro-level assessment

Although the importance of measuring the environmental impact of pollution is universally recognized, in practice it is complex and there is no single, agreed method of so doing. Instead, there are several measurement methods, all yielding slightly different figures. The UK government makes a distinction between emissions from the 'end user' and emissions from 'source'. End-user figures include an estimate of emissions from upstream sources such as power stations and refineries, which are allocated to activities that use the electricity or fuel. This estimate equates to the 'well-to-wheel' definition. Source figures, on the other hand, allocate emission figures according to where the fuel is consumed and do not include the emissions from upstream sources. Tail-pipe emissions are an even narrower category of emissions measurement that measures the pollution that is emitted from the tail-pipe (or the exhaust pipe) of a vehicle. This is probably the crudest of all measures as it ignores all upstream pollution sources and all other output sources (such as those from the engine).

An important distinction can be made between top-down and bottom-up approaches to the estimation of energy use and emissions (McKinnon and Piecyk, 2009). The former approach measures total fuel consumption by transport and uses standard conversion factors to translate it into macro-level emission figures. In the UK, however, diesel fuel purchases are not differentiated by vehicle type at point of sale, making it very difficult to estimate the quantity of fuel consumed by freight vehicles (as opposed to buses and diesel cars). As far as road freight is concerned, the bottom-up approach is now deemed the more accurate. This involves surveying a large sample of HGV operators (as part of the Continuing Survey of Road Goods Transport) and enquiring about the distances their vehicles travel and quantities of fuel consumed. These fuel consumption estimates are grossed-up for the truck fleet as a whole and converted into emission values. No comparable surveys of fuel consumption are undertaken in the UK rail, air and shipping services, making it difficult to derive UK-specific emission estimates for these modes.

Within Europe, several organizations have compiled databases showing the environmental impact of the different freight transport modes (eg INFRAS, 2004; IFEU, 2008; TREMOVE, 2008). Table 2.7 summarizes one set of energy consumption and emissions estimates for the most atmospheric pollutants. It highlights the wide variations in the levels of emissions per tonne-km and potential benefits of shifting freight to more environmentally friendly transport modes, such as rail and water. The opportunities for modal shift are discussed in Chapter 6.

One must exercise caution, however, in interpreting comparative environmental data for freight transport modes (McKinnon, 2008), as the relative environmental performance of a particular mode can be affected by:

- differing assumptions about the utilization of vehicle capacity;
- use of tonne-kms as the denominator, misrepresenting modes specializing in the movement of lower-density cargos;
- extrapolation of emissions data from one country to another with different transport and energy systems;
- allocation of emissions between freight and passenger traffic sharing the same vehicles (such as aircraft and ferries);

Table 2.7 Average emission factors for freight transport modes within Europe

		EC (kj/tkm)	CO_2 (g/tkm)	NOx (mg/tkm)	SO_2 (mg/tkm)	NMHC (mg/tkm)	PMdir (mg/tkm)
Aircraft		9,876	656	3,253	864	389	46
Truck >34–40-t	Euro 1	1,086	72	683		75	21
	Euro 2	1,044	69	755		55	10
	Euro 3	1,082	72	553	90	54	12
	Euro 4	1,050	70	353		59	2
	Euro 5	996	66	205		58	2
Train	Diesel	530	35	549	44	62	17
	Electric	456	18	32	64	4	4.6
Water-way	Upstream	727	49	839	82	84	26
	Down-stream	438	29	506	49	51	16

EC = energy consumption, NMHC = non-methane hydrocarbons.

Source: IFEU (2008).

- neglect of emissions associated with the construction and maintenance of infrastructure;
- restriction of the analysis to emissions at source rather than 'well-to-wheel' data.

Micro-level assessment

The externalities associated with freight transport can be disaggregated in various ways:

- By geographical area: local authorities now closely monitor air quality and noise levels and, in some cases, can attribute these environmental impacts to particular categories of traffic. Transport for London, for example, estimated that prior to the introduction of the Low Emission Zone, road transport accounted for roughly half of all NOx and PM10 emissions in Central London, with most of them coming from the exhausts of HGVs (Fairholme, 2007).

- By company: an increasing number of businesses, as part of their corporate social responsibility (CSR) programmes, are monitoring the environmental impact of their freight transport operations. Major logistics companies such as UPS and DHL now publish annual environmental reports detailing the levels of pollutant emissions from their transport fleets.
- By customer: some companies can now estimate the environmental effects of distributing their products to particular customers. They can offer their client distribution by different modes and routes, each with a differing set of environmental impacts.
- By product: life cycle analysis (LCA) is a 'technique to assess the environmental effects and resource costs associated with a product, process, or service' (Environmental Protection Agency, 2006: 1). It generally does this on a 'cradle-to-grave' basis from raw material source through production, distribution and consumption to the point where the materials return to the earth. Freight transport is an integral part of this process and has its environmental impacts disaggregated to product level in the course of LCA.

In recent years, the assessment of environmental impacts at the company and product levels has been focused on GHG emissions. As climate change has risen up political and corporate agendas there has been a steep growth of interest in carbon footprinting. Unlike LCA, which inherently analyses a broad range of external effects, carbon footprinting is confined to GHG emissions (PAS 2050, 2008). The next chapter examines in detail how it is being applied both by individual companies and across supply chains.

NOTES

1. Radiative forcing is the difference between the amounts of incoming and outgoing radiation energy measured at the troposphere.

REFERENCES

Affenzeller, J and Rust, A (2005) Road traffic noise: a topic for today and the future, paper delivered at the VDA Technical Congress, Ingolstadt, Germany, March

den Boer, LC and Schroten, A (2007) *Traffic Noise Reduction in Europe: Health effects, social costs and technical and policy options to reduce road and rail traffic noise*, CE Delft, The Netherlands

Department for Environment, Food and Rural Affairs (DEFRA) (2006) *Environmental Key Performance Indicators*, DEFRA, London

DEFRA (2008) *Guidelines to DEFRA's GHG Conversion Factors*, DEFRA, London

Department for Transport (2008) *Road Casualties Great Britain 2007*, Department for Transport, London

Environmental Protection Agency (EPA) (2006) *Life Cycle Assessment: Principles and practice*, EPA/600/R-06/060, May

EPA (2008) *Integrated Science Assessment for Oxides of Nitrogen: Health criteria*, EPA/600/R-08/071, July

EPA (2009) [accessed 20 March 2009] Particulate matter [Online] www.epa.gov/air/particlepollution/

European Environment Agency (EEA) (2003) *Europe's Environment: The third assessment*, Environmental Assessment Report No10, EEA,

European Road Safety Observatory (ERSO) (2008) [accessed 13 October 2008] *Traffic Safety Basic Facts 2008* [Online] www.erso.eu

Fairholme, N (2007) London: low emission zone, Paper presented to ICLEI Europe conference, Seville, 21–24 March

FEHRL European National Highway Research Laboratories (2006) *Tyre/Road Noise Final Report*, S12408210

Health Protection Agency (HPA) (2008) [accessed 8 May 2009] Air quality: sulphur dioxide [Online] http://www.hpa.org.uk/web/HPAweb&HPAwebStandard/HPAweb_C/1195733804968,

HPA (2009) Carbon monoxide: health effects of chronic/repeated exposure (human) [Online] hpa.org.uk

Hickman, A (1999) *Deliverable for EU MEET Project*, Contract ST-96-SC204, Brussels

Holmen, BA and Niemeier, DA (2003) Air quality, in *Handbook of Transport and the Environment*, ed DA Hensher and KJ Button, Chapter 4, Elsevier, Oxford

Institute of Environmental Management and Assessment (IEMA) (2008) [accessed 22 October 2008] Introducing EMAS [Online] iemanet/ems/emas

IFEU (2008) *EcoTransIT: Ecological transport information tool, environmental methodology and data*, IFEU, Heidelberg

INFRAS (2004) *External Costs of Transport: Update study*, Final Report, INFRAS, Zurich/Karlsruhe

International Maritime Organization (IMO) (2008) *International Convention for the Prevention of Pollution from Ships, 1973, as Modified by the Protocol of 1978 Relating thereto (MARPOL)*, Annex VI, Prevention of Air Pollution from Ships, Amendments – revised, IMO, London

IRU (2002) *Comparative Analysis of Energy Consumption and CO$_2$ Emissions of Road Transport and Combined Transport Road/Rail*, International Road Transport Union, Geneva

Janić, M (2007) *The Sustainability of Air Transportation: A quantitative analysis and assessment*, Ashgate, Aldershot

McKinnon, A (2007) CO_2 *Emissions from Freight Transport in the UK*, CfIT, London

McKinnon, A (2008) Potential of economic incentives to reduce CO_2 emissions from goods transport, paper delivered at the 1st International Transport Forum on Transport and Energy: The Challenge of Climate Change, Leipzig, 28 May [accessed 3 November 1008] [Online] www.internationaltransportforumrg/Topics/Workshops/WS3McKinnonpdf

McKinnon, A and Piecyk, M (2009) *Measurement of CO_2 Emissions from Road Freight Transport: A review of UK experience*, LRC, Heriot-Watt University [accessed 18 June 1009] [Online] www.greenlogistics.org

PAS 2050 (2008) *Guide to PAS 2050: How to assess the carbon footprint of goods and services*, BSI British Standards, London

Pope, CA, Burnett, RT, Thun, MJ, Calle, EE, Krewsi, D, Ito, K and Thurston, GD (2002) Lung cancer, cardio-pulmonary mortality and long term exposure to fine particulate air pollution, *Journal of the American Medical Association*, **287**, pp 1132–41

Rogers, P (2007) *Rogers Review: National enforcement priorities for local authority regulatory services*, UK Cabinet Office, London

Royal Commission on Environmental Pollution (RCEP) (1994) *Eighteenth Report: Transport and the environment*, Cm 2674, HMSO, London

Royal Society (2008) *Ground-level Ozone in the 21st Century: Future trends, impacts and policy implications*, Science Policy Report 15/08, October, Royal Society, London

Sandberg, U and Ejsmont, JA (2002) *Tyre/Road Noise Reference Book*, Informex, Kisa, Sweden

Schipper, LJ and Fulton, L (2003) Carbon dioxide emissions from transportation: trends, driving forces and factors for change, in *Handbook of Transport and the Environment*, ed DA Hensher and KJ Button, Chapter 11, Elsevier, Oxford

TREMOVE (2008) EU project on transport activity and emissions [Online] www.tremove.org

United Nations (1998) *Kyoto Protocol to the United Nations Framework Convention on Climate Change*, United Nations, New York

United Nations Inter-governmental Panel on Climate Change (UN IPCC) (1996) *Guidelines for National Greenhouse Gas Inventories*, United Nations, New York

UN IPCC (2007) *Climate Change 2007: Fourth assessment report*, United Nations, New York

US Department of Health and Human Services (1999) *Toxicological Profile for Total Petroleum Hydrocarbons (TPH)*, Public Health Service Agency for Toxic Substances and Disease Registry, Atlanta

Walley, N and Whitehead, B (1994) It is not easy being green, *Harvard Business Review*, **72** (3), pp 54–64

Watts, GR, Nelson, PM, Abbot, PG, Stait, RE and Treleven, C (2006) *Tyre/ Road Noise: Assessment of the existing and proposed tyre noise limits*, TRL report PPR077, TRL, Crowthorne

3

Carbon auditing of companies, supply chains and products

Maja Piecyk

INTRODUCTION

In recent years, international organizations and national governments have been setting greenhouse gas (GHG) emission reduction targets for the next 10–40 years (eg EU by 20 per cent by 2020, UK Climate Change Act 80 per cent by 2050, both relative to 1990 emission levels). They have also been introducing measures to help meet these targets, including mandatory or voluntary GHG reporting programmes, emission trading schemes, carbon or energy taxes, regulations, or energy efficiency and emissions standards for buildings and equipment. Consequently, companies will need to understand and manage their GHG emissions so as to meet reporting and regulatory requirements, ensure long-term competitive advantage and be prepared for future government policies on climate change (WBCSD/WRI, 2004).

A common system of measurement needs to be found to enable a comparison of GHG emissions from different activities, individuals, organizations and products. This process has been termed 'carbon footprinting'. A carbon footprint can be defined as the total amount of carbon dioxide and other GHGs (expressed in CO_2 equivalents) emitted directly and indirectly from an entity (Carbon Trust, 2007). Figure 3.1 illustrates three types of carbon footprint: at a product (either a good or a service), a single company or a supply chain level. Carbon auditing of a supply chain or a product is more complicated than the auditing of a single organization because it includes other actors upstream and downstream. One of the main challenges lies in defining the boundaries of the system to be carbon footprinted.

Carbon footprinting is supported in the UK by various bodies, in both the private and public sectors, but the main one is the government-sponsored Carbon Trust. It has developed a methodology to 'build the carbon footprint of different products by analysing the carbon emissions generated by energy use across the supply chain' (Carbon Trust, 2006: 3). Once the carbon footprint of a particular product's supply chain has been measured, efforts can be made to minimize the footprint, thereby reducing the carbon emissions required to deliver a product to the end consumer.

GUIDELINES FOR CARBON FOOTPRINTING

Several guidelines have been published by different organizations to support companies in measuring, reporting and managing their carbon footprints. The most important include:

- PAS 2050: *Specification for the Assessment of the Life Cycle Greenhouse Gas Emissions of Goods and Services* (British Standards Institution, 2008a);
- The Greenhouse Gas Protocol: *A corporate accounting and reporting standard* (WBCSD/WRI, 2004);

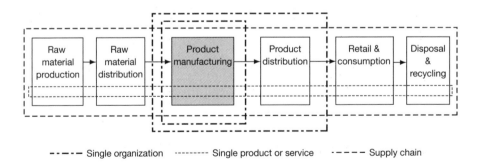

Figure 3.1 Different types of carbon footprint

Source: Based on Carbon Trust (2006).

- ISO 14064:1, *Greenhouse Gases – Part 1: Specification with guidance at the organization level for quantification and reporting of greenhouse gas emissions and removals* (ISO 14064:1, 2006);
- Carbon footprints in the supply chain: a guide, with examples of how the supply chains of newspapers and potato crisps were carbon audited (Carbon Trust, 2006).

The published guidelines differ in their details but the main assumptions and methodologies are similar. The same GHG auditing and reporting principles ought to be applied to all aspects of the calculation of a company's carbon footprint. The following principles are now widely adopted (WBCSD/WRI, 2004, ISO 14064-2, 2006, British Standards Institution, 2008a, 2008b):

- Relevance: a GHG emission report should appropriately reflect the environmental impact of the company, supply chain or service. It needs to contain all information that internal and external users need for their decision making.
- Completeness: all GHG emission sources within the chosen reporting boundary need to be included in the carbon footprint calculations. Any exclusions should be adequately justified and clearly specified in the GHG report.
- Consistency: calculation procedures should be applied in a manner that ensures that GHG emission data are comparable over time. If there are any changes in methodology, data or any other factors that may affect GHG emission estimates, these should be explicitly documented and justified.
- Accuracy: estimation of the GHG emissions should be compiled in such a way that it ensures maximum precision and minimizes the risk of both over and under-reporting. Uncertainties should be reduced as much as possible to give internal and external users confidence in the integrity and credibility of the reported information.
- Transparency: information on GHG emissions should be reported in a factual, neutral and coherent manner based on a clear audit trail. Any assumptions should be clearly disclosed and appropriate references to the reporting guidelines and data sources need to be included in the report.

THE CARBON FOOTPRINTING PROCESS

This process, as outlined by the Carbon Trust (2006), is summarized in Figure 3.2. Each of these steps will now be examined in detail.

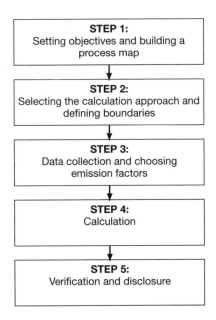

Figure 3.2 Steps to calculating the carbon footprint

STEP 1: Setting objectives and building a process map

Measuring and reporting GHG emissions is a first step in a carbon management process. For the reporting company, environmental objectives can be achieved in synergy with other strategic and financial goals. In a wider perspective, final customers can also benefit from improvements in the sustainability of businesses and industries, although these gains may be more difficult to measure directly.

Typically, the benefits of environmental auditing and management include (DEFRA, 2006):

- Compliance with legislation: this is the minimum requirement that companies must meet.
- Better use of resources and cost savings: measures to mitigate emissions often reduce costs as they focus on reducing waste, transport, energy consumption and the like, and promote more efficient use of resources.
- Competitive advantage: by demonstrating to the public that their activities are environmentally friendly, companies can promote a green image. As customers are becoming more environmentally aware, a company's green credentials can exert greater influence on customer behaviour.

- Improved attractiveness as a potential supplier: as organizations are increasingly requiring their suppliers and contractors to conform to their environmental standards, reporting on environmental performance can help to confer a preferred-supplier status.
- Increased attractiveness to the investment community: the sustainability of operations is becoming an important factor in investment decision making. Documenting how the environmental risks are reduced can also be required by insurers.
- Product and service innovation: measuring and managing environmental impacts drives innovation in product and service development, helping to secure new markets or safeguard existing ones.
- Employee recruitment: a good environmental reputation can be an important factor in an employee's choice of employer.

At this stage, the objectives of the carbon footprint exercise should be agreed, as they help to determine the methodology to be applied. For example, if the main objective is to obtain ISO 14000 series certification, the ISO guidelines must be followed. If a company intends to use the carbon footprint internally, it can decide which guidelines to apply but the methodology used should be explained in the final report.

A process map identifying all materials, activities and processes that contribute to the carbon footprint should be constructed. The complexity and scope of this map will depend on the type of carbon footprint required, in particular the level of disaggregation (eg at supply chain, company, business unit, facility or product level). The carbon footprinting of a product will typically be based on the life cycle assessment; in other words, it will include all product-related emissions from the raw material source, throughout the manufacturing and distribution stages, to impacts related to its use, disposal or recycling (Environmental Protection Agency, 2006). A sample process map has been constructed for yoghurt to illustrate the stages in the production and distribution system for which carbon data would have to be collected (Figure 3.3.)

The process map will be drawn at a relatively high level at the initial stage and can be refined during the carbon footprinting process. Having a graphical representation of the processes involved helps to identify the main sources of emissions and guides data collection process.

STEP 2: Selecting the calculation approach and defining boundaries

In the next stage, the scope for the carbon footprint calculations needs to be defined. In the case of a company or supply chain carbon footprint, the organizational boundaries will be particularly important. The company

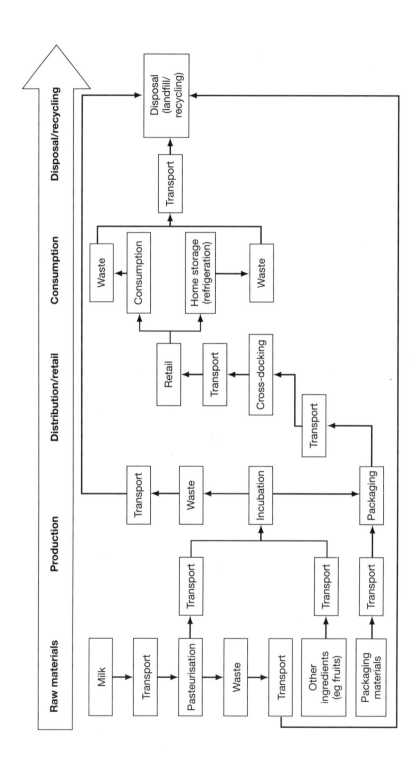

Figure 3.3 Process map for yoghurt

Source: Adapted from British Standards Institution (2008b).

may comprise one or more facilities and include wholly owned operations, joint ventures and/or subsidiaries. In setting the organizational boundaries a company effectively defines 'businesses and operations that constitute the company for the purpose of accounting and reporting GHG emissions' (WBCSD/WRI, 2004).

There are two approaches to consolidating GHG emissions within a boundary (ISO 14064-1, 2006):

- The control approach: the boundary is drawn to include all the activities over which the company has financial and/or operational control.
- The equity share approach: the organization assumes partial responsibility for GHG emissions from facilities in which it holds a share of the equity.

In order to avoid double counting of emissions, it is important to ensure that when a facility is controlled by several organizations, they all adopt the same consolidation approach. Further:

> where possible, organizations should follow the organizational boundaries already in place for their financial accounting, provided these are explicitly explained and followed consistently. When applying these concepts, the underlying assumption of 'substance over form' should be followed. That is, GHG emissions and removals should be quantified and reported in accordance with the organization's substance and economic reality and not merely its legal form. (ISO 14064-1, 2006)

This means that the boundaries of the carbon footprinting analysis should be set in a way that reflects business reality, fits with other requirements already in place (eg accounting reporting regulations) and be practical in terms of data collection.

After the organizational boundaries have been set, it is time to delimit the operational boundaries. This process involves identifying GHG emissions from the sources within the agreed organizational boundaries, grouping them into the categories listed below, and choosing the scope of reporting for indirect emissions.

The GHG emissions can be divided into three categories (WBCSD/WRI, 2004):

- Scope 1 emissions: these are direct GHG emissions from sources owned or controlled by the audited company, for instance emissions from combustion of fuel on site or in vehicles owned/controlled by the organization, from chemical reactions in production processes, and so on.
- Scope 2 emissions: these are indirect GHG emissions from the generation of electricity purchased from external suppliers.

- Scope 3 emissions: other indirect GHG emissions – emissions, other than indirect GHG emissions, that are a consequence of the audited company's activities but arise from sources owned or controlled by other organizations, for instance emissions from outsourced activities (such as logistics), waste disposal, product use, employee commuting, business travel in vehicles owned/controlled by other organizations and so on.

At a minimum, carbon footprinting should take account of Scope 1 and 2 emissions. The organization may also include Scope 3 emissions in the calculations. This is optional but considered to be good practice, particularly where the following circumstances apply (WBCSD/WRI, 2004):

- They are large relative to the Scope 1 and 2 emissions.
- They contribute to the organization's risk exposure.
- They are considered critical by key stakeholders (for instance customers, suppliers or investors).
- There are opportunities for emission reductions that can be exploited or influenced by the company.

All GHGs covered by Kyoto protocol should be included in the assessment. Other GHG emissions may also be included, like CFCs, halons or HCFCs. However, these are already regulated by the Montreal Protocol, which dealt with their contribution to ozone depletion rather than their contribution to global warming. ISO 14064, the Carbon Trust and the Greenhouse Gas Protocol guidance focus on reporting the Kyoto gases emissions, with the latter leaving the decision on data about other GHGs to the discretion of the reporting organization. According to the British PAS 2050, all GHGs including those covered by the Montreal Protocol have to be included.

STEP 3: Data collection and choosing emission factors

After establishing what needs to be included in the scope of carbon footprint calculations, the next step is to collect all the necessary data. A data collection plan should be prepared specifying what information is needed, the required format of the data and who holds or has access to the relevant records. Before requesting data from supply chain partners, it is considered good practice to introduce and explain the objectives of the project to them and, hopefully, get their buy-in and active support. When data is required from outside the organization, it is useful to have designated people in all companies involved, so that they can coordinate and manage the data collection process internally.

Primary data can be collected using either a top-down or a bottom-up approach. In a top-down approach, energy usage data is collected at an aggregate level, for example annual electricity consumption for the whole company. Where individual processes can be monitored separately and their specific energy requirements/GHG emissions can be measured, the carbon footprint can be built 'bottom-up' from these component measurements. Typically, some reconciliation between the two approaches will be needed. Because it is almost impossible to monitor all processes separately, the bottom-up estimates should be compared with the top-down results to ensure the accuracy of the carbon footprint calculation. In general, the top-down approach can provide reliable overall emission estimates, while the data collected using the bottom-up technique is more useful at later stages in the carbon management process when opportunities for efficiency improvements are being assessed.

As primary data is generally more reliable, it should be always considered first. Where it is not available, secondary data can be substituted. This usually comes in the form of generic emission factors for a given activity. In the course of life cycle analysis, inventories of data have been compiled on the emissions of different gases from a broad range of production, distribution, consumption and recycling/disposal activities. Industry-standard data on GHG emissions can be obtained from these inventories. Secondary data is often adequate for activities that make small contributions to total GHG emissions, and the time, effort and resources required to obtain primary data cannot be justified in such cases. The reasons why the organization decided to use secondary data instead of primary measurements should be explained in the final report. It is also important to consider the reliability and credibility of the source when obtaining the secondary data. Official government publications or recognized auditing standards should be the preferred sources of relevant energy-conversion and emissions factors.

Two other forms of secondary data are critical to the carbon footprinting calculation. These are the emission factors for different energy sources and global warming potential (GWP) of GHGs (Tables 2.1 and 2.3, Chapter 2). The official values for these should be applied to ensure comparability and consistency across different products, companies and supply chains.

STEP 4: Calculation

The actual carbon footprint calculation at a company or a supply chain level is relatively straightforward. All computations can be performed using a basic spreadsheet package, though more sophisticated software packages, such as CarbonView and Maersk's 'Carbon Check' are now available to facilitate the management and analysis of carbon data. The data are aggregated and the GHG emissions calculated by applying conversion factors for the different types of energy input or activity type. They should be then converted to carbon dioxide equivalent (CO_2e) by using the relevant GWP factor listed in Table 2.1. It is worth noting what DEFRA recommends, that 'for consistency, all changes in greenhouse gas emissions should be expressed as carbon dioxide equivalent, rather than carbon equivalent. However, referring to carbon is an acceptable shorthand for carbon dioxide equivalent, so long as this is made clear, and all figures are in CO_2e' (DEFRA, 2008a).

The calculations related to a product carbon footprint may require a slightly different approach. A process map will be very useful at this stage. It provides an overview of all the processes that a product undergoes at each stage in the end-to-end supply chain. If many different products are handled at a single site or moved on a single freight journey, a method must be found of allocating the emissions that are common to groups of products, for instance their share in warehouse electricity consumption or the fuel used by a truck. The calculation must also allow for any by-products of processes that are not accounted for separately. The emission values will be then summed to obtain a total carbon footprint of the product measured across its whole supply chain.

The issue of greenhouse gas sinks needs also to be considered. A GHG sink is defined as a 'physical unit or process that removes GHG from the atmosphere' (ISO 14064-1, 2006). Carbon storage may occur where carbon of biogenic origin forms part or all of an entire product, such as wooden furniture, or where atmospheric carbon is absorbed by a product over its life cycle. Emission reductions from storage of carbon in GHG sinks should be deducted from the total carbon footprint by applying appropriate removal factors. The detailed instructions on how to calculate the impact of carbon storage and what can be included in the assessment are provided in PAS 2050. Where a company in the supply chain engages in carbon offsetting (eg paying another company to cut CO_2 on its behalf), the quantities of CO_2 that are offset should not be deducted from the carbon footprint calculation. The general rule is that any changes to the footprint should be directly attributable to modifications to the product itself or the process involved in its production and distribution. Carbon reductions resulting from unrelated activities like the purchase of carbon credits or offsets do not qualify (British Standards Institution, 2008b).

STEP 5: Verification and disclosure

Before reporting any GHG information, companies should try to verify their carbon footprint estimates to confirm their accuracy and consistency. Verification minimizes the risk of human error and of decision makers forming the wrong judgements on the basis of misleading carbon footprint information. The level of verification will depend on the main objectives of the carbon footprinting exercise. If the emissions data is only to be used internally, self-verification will usually suffice. This involves asking somebody else within the organization to check the collected documentation and all the calculations independently, in order to detect any errors or missing data. The verifier should be able to confirm that the carbon footprint information fulfils the criteria of relevance, completeness, accuracy, transparency and consistency.

If companies want to disclose the carbon footprint information publicly, independent verification by a third party is encouraged. The highest level of validation would be offered by an accreditation body providing official certification. Non-accredited third-party organizations also offer external validation services.

The final GHG report should present relevant information on GHG emissions, assessment boundaries, the methodology applied and the period of assessment. The required level of detail and scope of the report will also depend on the audience at which it is targeted and the main objective of the carbon footprinting process. However, it should always be based on the best available data at the time of publication, while being open and honest about its limitations (WBCSD/WRI, 2004). Additionally, if the carbon footprint is calculated periodically, information on trends in GHG emission levels should be enclosed.

SUCCESS FACTORS IN CARBON FOOTPRINTING

Measuring a carbon footprint is a challenging and time-consuming task, particularly if it covers the activities of more than one organization in the supply chain. It should be perceived as an ongoing long-term project that is likely to bring benefits to all the parties involved. Critical success factors for carbon footprinting include:

- senior management support, devoting the necessary attention and resources;
- buy-in from all partners involved and a good level of cooperation across the supply chain;

- adoption of straightforward data collection procedures incorporating standardized questions and data input formats that are aligned with other applications already in use;
- a timetable for the project with firmly defined milestones for the different steps in the carbon footprinting exercise;
- employee involvement and understanding of the environmental impact of the carbon auditing and reduction programme.

CASE STUDY: CARBON AUDITING OF ROAD FREIGHT TRANSPORT OPERATIONS IN THE UK

Although freight transport typically constitutes a relatively small part of the total carbon footprint of a product or service, it is an activity whose carbon intensity can be significantly reduced at little or no net cost (McKinnon, 2007). CO_2 accounts for around 96 per cent of all GHG emissions from road transport (UK Air Quality Archive, 2008), thus the main focus should be on the CO_2 element.

The carbon footprinting of road freight operations would normally include Scope 1 and Scope 2 emissions, with Scope 3 emissions left to the reporting entity's discretion. All CO_2 emitted by freight vehicles owned and/or controlled by the company will be considered as Scope 1 emissions. Scope 2 emissions would only arise from battery-powered operation of vans and small rigid vehicles recharged with purchased electricity from the grid. The transport of goods in vans or lorries owned or controlled by another entity would be classed as Scope 3 emissions (WBCSD/WRI, 2005).

Two approaches can be used to calculate CO_2 emissions from road freight operations:

- fuel-based;
- activity-based.

Fuel-based approach

The amount of fuel used in a carbon accounting period is multiplied by the standard CO_2 conversion factor for each fuel type (Table 2.1). Data on fuel consumption can be obtained from the following sources:

- Fuel receipts, showing the quantity and type of fuel purchased.
- Direct measurements of fuel use, for example readings from fuel gauges or storage tanks.

- Financial records on fuel expenditures. Where no better data is available, reports on fuel expenditures can be converted to fuel consumption by using average fuel prices.

When using fuel receipts as the source of fuel consumption data, it is important to remember that not all fuel purchased may have been used in a calculation period. Any stocks remaining at the end of this period should be excluded from the carbon footprint estimate. Similarly, any fuel in the vehicle tank(s) at the beginning of the accounting period but purchased previously should be included in the calculations.

Activity-based approach

Emissions can be calculated by using activity-based conversion factors. In this case, data on activity level by vehicle type are needed. This should be available from a company's records, based, for example, on tachograph readings, despatch notes and other sources (WBCSD/WRI, 2005). The UK government produces a series of conversion tables to enable companies to convert their road freight activity levels into carbon footprints (Table 3.1).

Table 3.1 illustrates the fact that in terms of carbon dioxide emissions, for each category of vehicle (either rigid or articulated) the higher the gross vehicle weight (GVW) the higher the emissions per vehicle-km but the lower the emissions per tonne-km, suggesting that use of fewer heavier vehicles is better for the environment than more lighter vehicles. It is also interesting to note that on a tonne-km basis, rigid vehicles are actually more polluting than articulated ones. On a macro-level, it has been estimated that the heaviest articulated vehicles (with GVWs of over 33 tonnes) carry 72 per cent of all road tonne-kms (DfT, 2007) but are responsible for only around 47 per cent of all the external costs of road freight transport and for only 49 per cent of the total CO_2 emissions from HGVs. Conversely, rigid vehicles account for 48 per cent of the total external costs and 47 per cent of the CO_2 emissions while carrying only 24 per cent of all road tonne-kms (Piecyk and McKinnon, 2007). This is due to differences in the use patterns of these two categories of truck. Heavy articulated lorries move larger/heavier loads on long-haul, inter-urban trunk movements, where they achieve much higher energy efficiency than rigid vehicles, which typically distribute smaller, lighter loads on multiple-drop rounds within urban areas (DfT, 2008).

While vans (with a GVW of under 3.5 tonnes) run more kilometres per litre of fuel consumed than trucks, their much lower carrying capacity gives them a relatively high carbon intensity, expressed in terms of g CO_2 per tonne-km (Table 3.2). Using a diesel-powered light commercial

Table 3.1 CO_2 conversion factors for heavy goods vehicles (vehicle km basis, based on UK average load for each vehicle type and tonne-km basis)

Vehicle type (GVW tonnes)	Total vehicle-kms travelled		Conversion factor (kg CO_2 per vehicle-km)	Total kg CO_2	Total t-km travelled		Conversion factor (kg CO_2 per t-km)	Total kg CO_2
Rigid >3.5t–7.5t		×	0.563			×	0.591	
Rigid >7.5t–17t		×	0.747			×	0.336	
Rigid >17t		×	0.969			×	0.187	
All rigids (UK average)		×	0.895			×	0.276	
Articulated >3.5t–33t		×	0.817			×	0.163	
Articulated >33t		×	0.929			×	0.082	
All artics (UK average)		×	0.917			×	0.086	
All HGVs (UK average)		×	0.906			×	0.132	

Source: DEFRA (2008b).

vehicle releases approximately the same carbon dioxide emissions as an average rigid vehicle per tonne-km, and a small petrol-engined van produces considerably more. However, one needs to be careful when applying the tonne-kms conversion factor for vans. The values shown in Table 3.2 are based on an assumption that the average van carries a 50 per cent payload. This appears rather high, as results of the Department for Transport's survey of company owned vans for the period 2003 to 2005 shows that on 38 per cent of the distance travelled vans were less than one-quarter full (DfT, 2006). Also, when compared with the average lading factor of small rigid vehicles in the 3.5–7.5 tonne category (40 per cent) (DfT, 2008), the assumed 50 per cent load factor for vans seems to be too high.

The carbon footprint of road freight operations is strongly related to the capacity utilization of the vehicle. Table 3.3 shows its impact on carbon dioxide emissions for a typical articulated vehicle with a GVW over 33 tonnes. When a vehicle is empty, it still produces approximately two-thirds of the CO_2-related pollution of a fully laden vehicle, and the higher the vehicle capacity utilization, the lower the emissions per tonne of goods carried. Measures to improve vehicle utilization are examined in Chapter 11.

When deciding on the method of calculating carbon footprint, the fuel-based approach should be the preferred option as the fuel consumption records tend to be more reliable. However, if data are only available for an organization as a whole, this can require the calculation of a top-down estimate of the CO_2 emissions. In this case it may be difficult to disaggregate impacts by vehicle class. The activity-based (bottom-up) approach should then be used to allocate emissions to different vehicle classes in order to identify the most promising areas for improving energy efficiency and reducing CO_2 emissions. Disaggregated emissions data allow managers to target specific efficiency measures on particular categories of vehicles, types of operation or members of staff. Using both approaches simultaneously is not essential but it is a good way to validate calculations and ensure the reliability of the results.

In essence, the CO_2 emissions from road freight transport are a function of two factors: the nature of the vehicle and how it is used (Figure 3.4). In order to reduce CO_2 emissions from the road freight transport operation, managers can manipulate both sets of factors. As CO_2 emissions are directly proportional to the amount of fuel used, a reduction in fuel consumption will yield savings in CO_2 levels. Measures to improve the fuel efficiency of trucking are discussed in Chapters 7 and 11.

Table 3.2 Van/light commercial vehicle conversion factors based on a UK average vehicle

Vehicle type (GVW tonnes)	Total vehicle-km travelled	×	Conversion factor (kg CO$_2$ per vehicle-km)	Total kg CO$_2$	Total t-km travelled	×	Conversion factor (kg CO$_2$ per t-km)	Total Kg CO$_2$
Petrol up to 1.25t		×	0.224			×	0.449	
Diesel up to 3.5t		×	0.272			×	0.272	

Source: DEFRA (2008b).

Table 3.3 Conversion factors for one particular vehicle class at various capacity utilizations

	% weight laden	Total vehicle-kms travelled	×	Conversion factor (kg CO$_2$ per vehicle-km)	Total kg CO$_2$
Articulated vehicle >33t GVW	0		×	0.667	
	50		×	0.889	
	100		×	1.111	
	59 (UK average)		×	0.929	

Source: DEFRA (2008b).

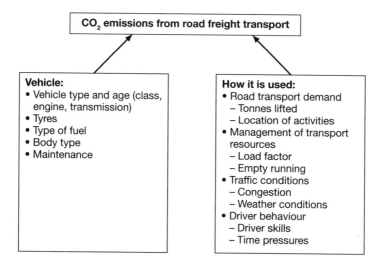

Figure 3.4   Factors affecting CO_2 emissions from road freight transport

CONCLUSIONS

Although still a relatively new concept, the carbon auditing of business activities has evolved rapidly in recent years. To date it has been conducted mainly at a company level, promoted both by government regulation and voluntary initiatives such as the Carbon Disclosure Project (www.cdproject.net). It is now developing in vertical and horizontal dimensions (Figure 3.5). Its vertical extension involves the disaggregation of CO_2 data by business unit, process, activity and even product, giving managers deeper understanding of the carbon-generating characteristics of their businesses. At the same time, carbon footprinting is being extended horizontally from individual companies across supply chains, making it possible to track the amounts of CO_2 released at different stages in the production and distribution of individual products. Several attempts have been made to use this data to label consumer products such as potato crisps and fruit juice. Given the complexity and high cost of product-level carbon auditing of supply chains, and uncertainty about consumer responses to carbon labelling, it is doubtful that this practice will become widespread, at least for the foreseeable future. The case study of carbon auditing in the road freight sector, however, illustrates how the disaggregation of CO_2 data to an activity, if not product, level can provide a quicker and more cost-effective means of finding opportunities for decarbonization within a logistics operation.

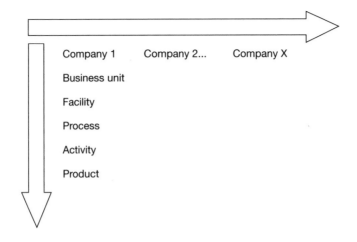

Company 1   Company 2...   Company X

Business unit

Facility

Process

Activity

Product

Figure 3.5 Horizontal and vertical dimensions of carbon footprint

REFERENCES

British Standards Institution (2008a) *PAS 2050: Specification for the Assessment of the Life Cycle Greenhouse Gas Emissions of Goods and Services*, BSI British Standards, London

British Standards Institution (2008b) *PAS 2050: Guide to PAS 2050 – How to assess the carbon footprint of goods and services*, BSI British Standards, London

Carbon Trust (2006) [accessed 11 February 2009] Carbon footprints in the supply chain: the next steps for business, November [online] www.carbontrust.co.uk

Carbon Trust (2007) *Carbon Footprinting: An introduction for organizations*, The Carbon Trust, London

Department for Environment, Food and Rural Affairs (DEFRA) (2006) *Environmental Key Performance Indicators*, DEFRA, London

DEFRA (2008a) *How to use Shadow Price of Carbon in Policy Appraisal*, DEFRA, London

DEFRA (2008b) *Guidelines to DEFRA's GHG Conversion Factors*, DEFRA, London

Department for Transport (DfT) (2006) *Road Freight Statistics* 2005, Department for Transport, London

DfT (2007) *Road Freight Statistics 2006*, Department for Transport, London

DfT (2008) *Road Freight Statistics 2007*, Department for Transport, London

Environmental Protection Agency (2006) *Life Cycle Assessment: Principles and practice*, EPA/600/R-06/060, May 2006

ISO 14064-1 (2006) *Greenhouse Gases - Part 1: Specification with guidance at the organization level for quantification and reporting of greenhouse gas emissions and removals*, International Organization for Standardization, Geneva

ISO 14064-2 (2006) *Greenhouse gases - Part 2: Specification with guidance at the project level for quantification, monitoring and reporting of greenhouse gas emission reductions or removal enhancements*, International Organization for Standardization, Geneva

McKinnon, A (2007) *CO_2 Emissions from Freight Transport in the UK*, Commission for Integrated Transport, London

Piecyk, M and McKinnon, A (2007) *Internalising the External Costs of Road Freight Transport in the UK*, Heriot-Watt University, Edinburgh

UK Air Quality Archive, (2008) [accessed 20 February 2009] Databases [online] http://www.airquality.co.uk/archive/reports/cat07/0804161424_GBR-2008-CRF.zip

World Business Council for Sustainable Development and World Resources Institute (WBCSD/WRI) (2004) *The Greenhouse Gas Protocol: A corporate accounting and reporting standard*, revised edition, World Business Council for Sustainable Development, Geneva and World Resources Institute, Washington, DC

WBCSD/WRI (2005) *Calculating CO_2 Emissions from Mobile Sources*, World Business Council for Sustainable Development, Geneva and World Resources Institute, Washington, DC

4

Evaluating and internalizing the environmental costs of logistics

Maja Piecyk, Alan McKinnon and Julian Allen

INTRODUCTION

All the environmental impacts of logistics impose costs. Some of these costs, arising for example from damage to business premises or injuries to employees, are borne by the company performing the logistics activities and appear in its balance sheet. Others have wider effects on the community and ecosystem that are not costed in the conventional sense and are excluded from a company's financial accounts. The term 'externality' is often used to describe these effects. A strong case can be made for estimating the costs of these externalities and 'internalizing' them within company budgets: in other words, applying the 'polluter-pays principle'.

The proposition that wider environmental (or 'social') costs be internalized in higher taxes was originally advanced by Pigou (1920) and has been refined by other studies, many of which are reviewed in ECMT (1998). Environmental pressure groups have campaigned for many years for full internalization of the external costs of transport, arguing that, in the absence of such internalization, markets will be distorted to the detriment of the environment. National governments and international organizations, most notably the European Commission, have accepted the need for such internalization. The 'fair and efficient pricing' policy promoted by the European Commission (2001 and 2006) aims to ensure that all external damage caused by personal and freight movement is fully internalized in the price of transport. It argues that pricing should be fair, meaning that 'polluters' are obliged to pay the marginal social cost of their activities, and efficient, giving them an economic incentive to reduce the negative effects of these activities (EEA, 2006). The Commission recently funded a major study of the issues to be resolved in applying the polluter-pays principle to transport (CE Delft, 2008) and is currently negotiating with the European Parliament and Council of Ministers on how it can be implemented. One of the most contentious parts of the proposal relates to the internalization of the environmental costs of road freight transport. It is proving difficult to secure international agreement on how this should be done and how the extra revenue generated should be spent.

In Europe and elsewhere, companies and trade bodies often oppose internalization, partly on matters of principle, but also because of the practical difficulties encountered in attaching monetary values to environmental and social effects and in devising an acceptable method of translating these values into charges on businesses and individuals.

In the next section, we review the arguments for and against internalizing the external costs of logistics. The third section explains how economists have placed monetary values on the range of environment effects discussed in Chapter 2, primarily the emission of air pollutants and greenhouse gases, traffic noise and accidents. The remainder of the chapter then summarizes the results of a study undertaken in the UK to determine the extent to which the taxes currently paid by trucks and vans cover the wider environmental, infrastructural and congestion costs they impose.

ARGUMENTS FOR AND AGAINST THE INTERNALIZATION OF ENVIRONMENTAL COSTS

The case for levying environmental taxes rests mainly on three arguments. First, on grounds of social justice, its seems only fair that a company should be made to pay for any damage that it inflicts on the environment. The environment, after all, should not be seen as a 'free good' that businesses and citizens can exploit and despoil with impunity. Second, internalizing environmental costs gives companies a financial incentive to reduce their level of pollution. It forces them, for example, to take account of environmental costs when appraising new investments. The third argument is that the imposition of environmental taxes raises additional revenue that can be used to fund a range of green initiatives, including:

- pollution-mitigation measures, such as noise barriers and double-glazing along busy roads;
- compensation for individuals and businesses adversely affected by the environmental effects;
- financial inducements to companies to 'green' their operations, reinforcing the effects of the environmental taxation.

There is no guarantee that governments will hypothecate 'green' taxes to finance environmental projects. But even where the revenue is absorbed into general taxation, some of it can still be spent on environment-related activities.

Numerous arguments have been advanced against internalizing the environmental costs of transport. Some object to this policy at a fundamental level while others question its practical application.

The economic logic underpinning the polluter-pays principle has been challenged by Coase (1960) and others, who reject the view of the environment being a 'victim' subject to harm inflicted by a polluter who must be charged accordingly. Their alternative view sees externalities as being caused by all the parties involved and the objective as finding the most economically efficient way of dealing with the problem. Coase advocated an alternative 'cheapest cost avoider' principle that determines which party can prevent or mitigate the adverse environmental effects at minimum cost. This can be the polluter, in which case 'the cheapest cost avoider analysis incorporates "polluter pays" as a possible outcome' (Schmidtchen et al, 2007). In other situations, however, it may be cheaper for the 'pollutee' to take the necessary action. For example, it might be cheaper to erect sound barriers along busy roads than to impose a charge on truck traffic to recover notional noise costs. It is argued that forcing the polluting company to pay for all the environmental damage caused does not necessarily maximize economic welfare. Some organizations representing the road freight sector, such as the IRU (2008), have used these arguments to challenge the current efforts of the EU to internalize the environmental cost of freight transport.

Maddison et al (1996), on the other hand, question the applicability of Coase's theory to transport. For them the key questions are who 'owns the relevant property right to the environmental amenity' and how the 'generator of the pollution' and the 'victim' can bargain. Given the huge number of organizations responsible for logistics-related externalities and the even larger number of 'victims', such negotiation would be impractical. The delayed effect of many of the externalities, such as climate change, also makes it impossible for those responsible for pollution today to enter into transactions with those who will suffer the consequences decades from now. Maddison et al also point out that 'some important environmental amenities, like air quality, [are] "public goods", meaning that the benefits of reduced pollution are not specific to the individuals who contribute to their upkeep.' So the 'cheapest avoider principle' also has significant shortcomings, particularly when applied in the transport arena.

Another complaint sometimes levelled at the polluter-pays principle is that there is no guarantee that internalizing environmental costs will raise the price of logistical activity sufficiently to induce the behavioural change necessary to get pollution down to an acceptable level. There is a greater likelihood of the desired environmental outcome being achieved if the extra tax revenue raised is invested in environmental initiatives. As mentioned earlier, however, it often goes into general taxation. The imposition of environmental taxes can also have an undesirable second-order effect by reducing the financial resources available to freight operators to upgrade their vehicle fleets and to introduce other green measures.

Further problems can emerge when the polluter-pays principle is not applied uniformly across a national economy. If it is being more rigorously applied in one sector than in others, this will cause market distortions and unfairness in the implementation of environmental policy. Market distortions can also occur geographically, where environmental costs are internalized to differing degrees and in different ways within neighbouring countries and regions. This is well illustrated by the European road haulage market where the proportion of environmental and congestion costs recovered by taxation varies enormously from country to country (see the section on 'Internalization of external HGV costs', below). As the variation in truck taxation is due mainly to differences in fuel duty, carriers can gain a competitive advantage by purchasing their fuel in countries where duty levels are low (indulging in a practice known as 'tank tourism') (ECMT, 2003). Foreign hauliers entering the UK market, for example, purchase almost all their fuel in neighbouring countries. It was estimated in 2008 that this gave them a 6–7 per cent price advantage in the UK market over domestic hauliers. This partly explains the steep increase in cabotage in the UK road freight market over the past decade.[1] Britain's 'fuel duty escalator' policy which, between 1994 and 1999, annually increased fuel taxes by 5–6 per cent in real terms, ostensibly for environmental reasons, largely precipitated the 'fuel crisis' of September 2000 when truckers and farmers blockaded oil refineries and blocked roads. This highlighted the difficulty of a single country trying to introduce a radical environmental tax policy unilaterally within an open, international market.

Some critics of internalization have also questioned the validity of the monetary valuations of externalities. They point to inconsistencies in the approaches and methods used, the large amount of subjective judgement that often has to be exercised and the general uncertainty about many of the values. Evidence of this uncertainty can be found when comparing the results of different studies of the environmental costs of transport (ECMT, 2003). Estimates of the total external costs of transport in the EU in the early 2000s, for example, vary by a factor of four, between €129 bn (UNITE, 2003) and €650 bn (INFRAS, 2004). Such variability undermines confidence in the economic basis of internalization policies. Despite these reservations, the detailed review of internalization methodologies carried out recently for the European Commission concluded that, 'the scientists have done their job. Although the estimation of external costs has to consider several uncertainties, there is consensus at a scientific level that external costs of transport can be measured by best practice approaches and that general figures (within reliable bandwidths) are ready for policy use' (CE Delft, 2008: 13).

The general message is that the internalization of environmental costs is not a panacea, is controversial and difficult to implement. Its effectiveness as a policy measure depends on the way in which it is applied and coordinated with other sustainability measures.

MONETARY VALUATION OF ENVIRONMENTAL COSTS

As discussed earlier, externalities are not normally taken into account in the decisions made by transport users. Internalization aims to correct this anomaly by increasing the price of transport services in proportion to all the relevant social and environmental costs imposed (Beuthe et al, 2002; Baublys and Isoraite, 2005). Placing an appropriate value on the external costs of freight transport is therefore fundamental to their internalization.

The external costs normally included in this calculation relate to the negative effects of air pollution, greenhouse gas emissions, noise, accidents and traffic congestion. Freight vehicles' contribution to the cost of providing, operating and maintaining transport infrastructure is not an externality as such, but has to be calculated to determine its share of the taxes paid by freight transport. It is out of the remaining taxes that the environmental and congestion costs can be recovered. For this reason, internalization calculations have to include freight vehicles' allocated share of infrastructure costs.

It is possible to attach monetary values to externalities in many different ways. A broad distinction can be drawn between methods that try to value the damage done to the environment, the so-called Damage

Function approach (Adamowicz, 2003), and those that estimate the cost of avoiding this damage.

Cost of environmental damage

Some of the physical damage can easily be measured and costed. For example, a vehicle accidentally crashing into a building will inflict structural damage. This externality would be valued by adding the cost of repairing the damage to other losses incurred while use of the building is constrained. Often, however, the damaging effects of logistical activity are much less direct and observable. The adverse health effects of atmospheric pollution, for example, are much more difficult to quantify and cost. Freight vehicles after all, may be only one of many sources of a particular pollutant, and that pollutant may be one of many factors contributing to ill-health. Placing a monetary value on health problems exacerbated by pollution, such as asthma, is also fraught with difficulty as it should take account of subjective valuations of the patient's reduced quality of life (and possibly death) as well as more tangible costs, such as the cost of providing medical treatment and loss of output while the patient is unable to work. Even if the degradation of a local environment affected by traffic pollution, noise and vibration does not cause significant health problems, local citizens can still perceive a loss of amenity and this too must be valued.

In making monetary valuations of environmental effects such as air pollution and noise, researchers generally employ the Impact Pathway Approach, originally devised for a major EU study called ExternE on the external costs of energy production (European Commission, 2003). This comprises a series of measurements, some assessing the physical impact of the emissions, others monetizing this impact (Figure 4.1). The approach starts by calculating the emissions from a logistics activity, charting their diffusion and, in the case of gases, their chemical conversion and concentration at different spatial scales. The next stage is an examination of the response of 'receptors' (eg people, animals, vegetation, physical objects) to these emissions, using so-called 'dose-response' models. These responses will normally be negative, representing losses of welfare and environmental quality. These losses are quantified and translated into monetary values. Two general methods are used to derive these monetary values (Mitchell and Carson, 1989):

- Stated preference surveys: in these surveys people are generally asked how much they would be willing to pay (WTP) to have the externality removed or to accept (WTA) in compensation. The most commonly used stated-preference technique is the Contingency Valuation

Method. This has three elements: 'a description of the scenario in which the respondent is to imagine himself placed; questions from which values are to be inferred… and questions relating to the respondent himself' (Maddison et al, 1996). The survey context is inevitably fairly artificial and the responses can be partly conditioned by the way the questions are asked.

- Revealed preference studies: it is sometimes possible to infer an environmental cost from actual changes in people's behaviour. For example, as people generally prefer not to live beside a busy road, there will be less demand for housing along the route and this will be reflected in lower property prices. The house price differential between an area seriously affected by traffic noise and pollution and another area comparatively free of these externalities can be used to monetize their negative effects (using so-called 'hedonic pricing methods'). This method too can be problematic, however, as environmental quality is only one of several factors likely to influence house prices in an area.

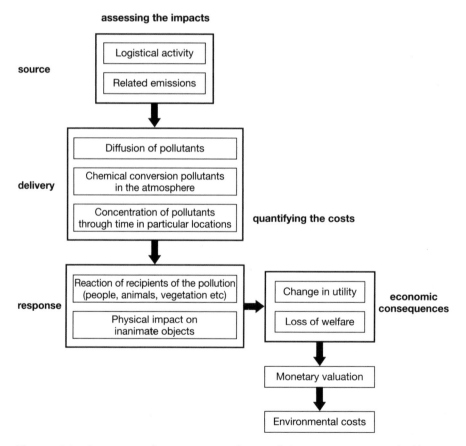

Figure 4.1 Impact pathway approach to valuing environmental effects

Source: Adapted from Bickel and Friedrich (2005).

One of the most contentious issues in the field of environmental economics is the monetary value to be placed on a human life lost as a result of an accident or pollution (Adams, 1981). Almost everyone would be likely to place an infinite value on their continued existence, but it is not possible to factor infinite values into the cost side of the internalization equation. Instead economists have derived ways of calculating the 'value of a statistical life', which is defined 'as the marginal willingness to pay to avoid the risk of a fatal accident aggregated over a large number of people' (Maddison et al, 1996). This value can be estimated by a mix of stated and revealed preference enquiries. A stated preference survey can ask how much people are prepared to pay to reduce the risk of a fatal accident by a given percentage, while revealed preferences can be observed in the wage premium paid to workers in more dangerous jobs, and in insurance premiums.

Cost of avoiding environmental damage

Rather than assessing the cost of the environmental damage once inflicted, one can try to calculate what it would cost to avert it. Often the objective is not to eliminate the environmental effect completely but to reduce it to what, in public policy terms, is considered to be an acceptable minimum. This approach, for example, has been used by the UK government in estimating a 'shadow price' for carbon that assumes the concentration of CO_2 in the atmosphere will be limited to 550 ppm by 2050 (DEFRA, 2007a). Account must be taken of the cost of the various measures that would have to be implemented to meet this target. A range of mitigation measures can also be applied at the local level to minimize the environmental impact of logistics, such as sound-proofing, locating distribution centres away from residential areas and switching to battery-powered vehicles. The additional cost of these measures can be used as a surrogate value for the environmental impact.

Summary of environmental costs

Different methods are used to attach monetary values to the various externalities. Table 4.1 summarizes the adverse effects of the range of externalities associated with logistical activity, identifies their key cost components, outlines the main methods used to value them and lists some of the major studies that have undertaken this valuation. Table 4.2 presents some of the monetary values that have been derived in the EU for key elements in the external cost calculation for transport (CE Delft, 2008).

Table 4.1 Nature, costs and valuations of logistics-related externalities

Externality	Adverse effects	Cost elements	Methods of valuation	Studies
Air pollution	Ill-health Discomfort Agricultural damage Other vegetative damage Physical damage to buildings	Medical treatment Value of statistical life/years lost Personal suffering Loss of agricultural output Loss of biodiversity Loss of amenity/landscape value Building value loss/repairs	Health care costs analysis Labour output analysis WTP/WTA assessments Agricultural surveys RP analysis or property prices Building repair costs	ExternE (EC, 2003) INFRAS (2004) UNITE (2003) COPERT (2009) TREMOVE (2009)
Climate change	Sea-level rise Extreme weather events Animal extinctions Water shortages Agricultural damage Other vegetative damage Human health problems Ecosystem destruction	Medical treatment Value of statistical life/years lost Personal suffering Loss of agricultural output Loss of biodiversity Loss of amenity/landscape value Flood protection Population relocation Physical adaptation etc	Use of climatic models to predict temperature rise Assessment of future damage to human activity/ecosystems Costing of the damage Calculation of marginal abatement costs	Stern (2006) INFRAS (2004) COPERT (2009) TREMOVE (2009)
Noise	Irritation Sleep disturbance Ill-health	Medical treatment Personal suffering Loss of amenity Building value loss/repairs Sound-proofing	WTP/WTA assessments RP analysis or property prices Estimate of sound proofing cost	INFRAS (2004) UNITE (2003) COPERT (2009) TREMOVE (2009)
Traffic accidents	Death and injury to humans and animals Damage to property	Medical treatment Value of statistical life/years lost Personal suffering Building value loss/repairs	Healthcare costs analysis Labour output analysis WTP/WTA assessments Costing of property damage	INFRAS (2004) UNITE (2003) COPERT (2009) TREMOVE (2009)

Table 4.2 Mid-range valuations of external costs

Health-related costs of air pollution:	Euros
Mean value of a statistical life	2,000,000
Mean value of life year lost	120,000
Case of chronic bronchitis	190,000
Hospital admission with respirator / cardiac problem	2,000
Loss of day's output through ill-health	83
Climate change (2010 central value)	
Per tonne of CO_2	25
Noise-related costs per person/annum (from road traffic – Germany):	
Noise level Lden dB(A) ≥70	175
Noise level Lden dB(A) ≥80	365
Traffic accident	
Fatality	1,815,000
Severe injury	235,100
Slight injury	18,600

In attaching monetary values to the future external effects of logistical activities performed today, economists must apply a discount rate to calculate their net present value. The choice of discount rate is discussed by Ricci and Friedrich (1999) and others, and has become a very contentious issue in the estimation of a social cost (or shadow price) for CO_2. Stern (2006), for example, has been criticized by Nordhaus (2006) and others for setting the discount rate too high in his analysis of the economics of climate change and thereby exaggerating its long-term social costs.

Cost of traffic congestion

Congestion is not, in the strict sense, an environmental externality, since its effect on transport cost is taken into account by carriers and reflected in their pricing (Beuthe et al, 2002). However, an extra vehicle entering the road system causes delays to the other vehicles on the network, imposing an additional cost upon them known as the marginal congestion cost (Sansom et al, 1998). Thus, road users should be required not only to absorb the direct cost of congestion which they experience themselves, but also the marginal cost they impose on other road users (Beuthe et al, 2002).

Traffic congestion also has an adverse effect on fuel consumption and the emissions of CO_2 and other noxious gases. Figure 4.2 shows the impact of vehicle speed on CO_2 emissions per vehicle kilometre. When the traffic speed drops below 20 km/h, fuel consumption and CO_2 emitted per vehicle-km rise steeply (SMMT, 2005). It has also been estimated that, for a 40-tonne articulated lorry, making 'two stops per kilometre leads to an increase of fuel consumption by roughly a factor of 3' (International Road Union, 1997). The related environmental effects of traffic congestion are generally recorded separately under the air pollution heading.

Use of marginal or average/aggregated costs for externalities

Externalities can be valued on a marginal or average cost basis. The former should involve a 'bottom-up' analysis of the additional external

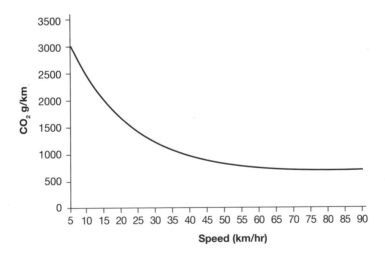

Figure 4.2 Vehicle speed and CO_2 emissions: articulated vehicle over 40 tonnes gvw

Source: Based on test-cycle data supplied by the Department for Transport.

costs imposed by an extra freight vehicle joining a traffic flow. External costs, on the other hand, can be averaged by vehicle, trip or freight consignment, by dividing a 'top-down' estimate of total environmental costs by the total number of units. In the case of those external costs whose relationship with traffic volumes is non-linear, such as congestion and noise, the marginal costs can be much higher than the average costs. The choice of costing method depends on the objectives of the exercise and 'nature of the policy question being addressed' (Ricci and Friedrich, 1999). The use of marginal costing is more appropriate in assessments of the cost-effectiveness of sustainability measures targeted on specific traffic flows. For example, the application procedure for Freight Facilities and Waterborne Freight Grants in the UK, which are designed to divert specific freight flows from road to rail or water, employ marginal costing to estimate the monetary value of the 'sensitive lorry miles' saved, namely 'the valuation of the environmental and other social benefits of removing one lorry mile of freight from road and transferring it to rail or water' (DfT, 2009). Where the objective is to compare, at a macro level, the total taxes paid by freight vehicles with the total infrastructural and external costs they impose, average or aggregated values are more applicable. This was the approach adopted in a recent internalization study of European road haulage for the European Federation of Transport and Environment (CE Delft, 2009) and in our research on the UK road freight sector. The results of this research are reported in the next section.

INTERNALIZATION OF THE EXTERNAL COSTS IMPOSED BY ROAD FREIGHT VEHICLES IN THE UK

The remainder of this chapter presents the results of an analysis of the extent to which the taxes paid by lorries (or heavy goods vehicles – HGVs), with gross weights of over 3.5 tonnes, and vans (or light goods vehicles – LGVs), with gross weights of up to and including 3.5 tonnes, in the UK cover their environmental, congestion and infrastructure costs. This analysis was based on vehicle activity levels and costs in 2006.

Taxes and charges borne by road freight operators

Fuel-related taxes represent over 90 per cent of the tax paid by operators of HGVs and vans in the UK. Vehicle ownership also incurs vehicle excise duty (VED). Apart from one motorway link and a few tolled bridges and tunnels, there are no direct infrastructure charges in the UK. Freight vehicles entering central London during the working week are subject to a congestion charge. The following calculation excludes both road tolls and congestion charges as they represent a tiny fraction of the total public revenue raised from the road freight sector.

The calculations were based on the average bulk and retail diesel fuel prices at 1 July 2006: 79.15 pence per litre (ppl) and 83.66 ppl, respectively. In the case of HGVs, an assumption was made that 80 per cent of the fuel used was purchased in bulk (FTA, 2006), yielding an average diesel fuel price of 80.05 ppl. Approximately 3 per cent of vans run on petrol rather than diesel. The average bulk and retail prices of petrol were, respectively, 81.65 ppl and 83.32 ppl in July 2006. Assuming that 80 per cent of fuel was purchased in bulk by drivers of company-owned LGVs and 50 per cent purchased in bulk by drivers of privately registered LGVs, an average duty rate of 47.10 ppl was estimated for all the fuel consumed by vans.

Although most HGV operators and many commercial operators of vans are VAT-registered and can recover this tax through VAT transactions, VAT passes along the supply chains and it is finally borne by one of the direct or indirect transport users. Hence, VAT has been included in the estimate of income generated by duties and taxes from road freight transport. Other internalization studies have excluded VAT on the grounds that, as operators normally claim it back, 'it is not counted by the user at the point of use... and is not really part of a user's marginal cost' (MRTU, 2008). As the current calculation is based on aggregate rather than marginal cost and revenue values, the inclusion of VAT is deemed appropriate.

In 2006, nearly £5.8 billion was collected in diesel fuel duty, VED and VAT paid by truck operators and £4.12 billion by van operators (Tables 4.3 and 4.4). In the case of HGVs, 95 per cent of the revenue was from fuel-related taxes and only 5 per cent from VED. For vans, the corresponding proportions were 90 per cent and 10 per cent.

External costs allocated to road freight vehicles

The estimates of congestion, noise and infrastructure costs were based on valuations used in a recently published report on the external costs of food distribution in the UK (DEFRA, 2007b) (Table 4.5). The infrastructure, noise, accidents and congestion cost values were originally expressed in 2005 prices and have been inflated to 2006 values on the basis of the change in GDP over the same period.

Emission factors for carbon dioxide (CO_2), hydrocarbons (VOCs), nitrogen oxide (NOx) and particulate matter (PM10) were derived

Table 4.3 Duties and taxes paid by HGV operators in 2006

2006 (£ million)	Rigid				Articulated		All vehicles
	Over 3.5 tonnes – not over 7.5 tonnes	Over 7.5 tonnes – not over 17 tonnes	Over 17 tonnes – not over 25 tonnes	Over 25 tonnes	Over 3.5 tonnes – not over 33 tonnes	Over 33 tonnes	
Fuel duty (47.1 ppl)	752	144	557	523	278	2,029	**4,283**
VAT (17.5%)	224	43	166	156	83	603	**1,274**
VED	25	11	29	55	14	136	**271**
Total	**1,001**	**198**	**752**	**734**	**374**	**2,769**	5,828

Table 4.4 Duties and taxes paid by LGV operators in Britain in 2006

2006 (£ million)	LGVs up to 1.8 tonnes gvw				LGVs 1.8–3.5 tonnes gvw				All LGVs
	Company-owned		Privately-owned		Company-owned		Privately-owned		
	Diesel	Petrol	Diesel	Petrol	Diesel	Petrol	Diesel	Petrol	
Fuel duty (47.1 ppl)	377	17	215	23	1,526	55	525	107	**2,846**
VAT (17.5%)	112	5	65	7	454	17	159	33	**852**
VED	47	1	55	4	153	4	144	17	**425**
Total	**537**	**24**	**335**	**34**	**2,132**	**76**	**828**	**157**	**4,123**

from the National Atmospheric Emissions Inventory (NAEI).[2] This contains values for different types of HGVs and LGVs. The cost of carbon emissions was calculated using the values quoted by DEFRA (2007b). The *Air Quality Damage Cost Guidance* report (DEFRA, 2006) was used to calculate the cost of PM10, NOx and SO_2 emissions. These cost values were given in 2005 prices and updated to the 2006 level in accordance with *The Green Book* (HM Treasury, 2003). The *Mode Shift Benefit Values* report (DfT, 2009) was the source of cost data on VOCs emissions (Table 4.6).

Table 4.5 Infrastructure, noise, congestion and accident costs in 2006

External costs (pence per km)	Motorway	Rural	Urban
Infrastructure			
LGV	0.01	0.09	0.09
Rigid over 3.5 tonnes – not over 7.5 tonnes	0.46	2.16	2.42
Rigid over 7.5 tonnes – not over 17 tonnes	1.00	4.66	5.21
Rigid over 17 tonnes – not over 25 tonnes	1.43	6.65	7.44
Rigid over 25 tonnes	2.49	11.57	12.93
Artic over 3.5 tonnes – not over 33 tonnes	2.72	8.33	9.35
Artic over 33 tonnes	4.87	14.89	16.73
Noise			
LGV	0.16	0.07	0.32
Rigid	0.42	0.21	1.23
Artic	0.80	0.35	2.35
Congestion			
LGV	2.84	2.22	19.59
Rigid	5.35	4.19	43.08
Artic	6.52	5.09	72.06
Accidents			
LGV	1.98	1.98	1.98
Rigid	6.77	6.77	6.77
Artic	5.45	5.45	5.45

We will consider the external costs and the extent to which they are internalized for HGVs and LGVs separately, and then combine the results to make an overall assessment of cost internalization for the UK road freight sector as a whole.

Table 4.6 Air pollution costs (2006 prices)

Emission costs (£ per tonne)	Low	Central	High
CO_2	22.28	24.76	29.22
NOx	698.03	896.88	1,017.83
PM (motorway, rural)	11,042.33	14,117.33	16,026.90
PM (urban)	74,459.07	91,262.76	108,066.44
VOCs	27.92	35.88	40.71
SO_2	1,238.20	1,533.40	1,740.45

Heavy goods vehicles

A spreadsheet was constructed based on freight and traffic data from the UK government's Continuing Survey of Road Goods Transport (CSRGT) (DfT, 2006) and National Road Traffic Survey (NRTS) (DfT, 2007a). It modelled the relationship between HGV activity in the UK and a series of freight transport-related externalities, including climate change, air pollution, noise and congestion.

The full external costs by HGV class are shown in Table 4.7. These include environmental, infrastructural and congestion costs. The total costs have been estimated at £8.6 billion, £8.7 billion and £8.9 billion using, respectively low, medium and high values for air pollution costs. The heaviest articulated vehicles (with gross weights of over 33 tonnes) carry 72 per cent of all road tonne-kms (DfT, 2007a) but are responsible for only around 45 per cent of all the external costs of road freight transport. Conversely, rigid vehicles account for 49 per cent of the total external costs while carrying only 24 per cent of total tonne-kilometres. These differing proportions show how larger/heavier trucks have lower external costs per tonne-km, assuming loading factors and empty running figures at current levels.

Overall, 42 per cent of the total external costs were attributable to congestion, 22 per cent to infrastructure, 20 per cent to traffic accidents, 14 per cent to air pollution and greenhouse gas emissions and only 2 per cent to noise (Figure 4.3). As some gases, such as methane and carbon monoxide, contribute both to global warming and to air pollution, it was possible to split the external costs associated with these emissions between climate change and reductions in air quality. An indication of the climate change component can be given by focusing on CO_2 emis-

Table 4.7 Total external costs of road freight transport

Total external cost of HGV activity in the UK (£ million)	Rigid				Articulated		All vehicles
	Over 3.5 tonnes – not over 7.5 tonnes	Over 7.5 tonnes – not over 17 tonnes	Over 17 tonnes – not over 25 tonnes	Over 25 tonnes	Over 3.5 tonnes – not over 33 tonnes	Over 33 tonnes	
Low estimate	1,922	307	1,138	860	`555	3,798	8,579
Medium estimate	1,945	312	1,154	872	568	3,893	8,744
High estimate	1,971	317	1,174	888	584	4,012	8,945

sions from lorry exhausts as these have no effect on air quality. On this basis, climate change costs would represent around 9 per cent of the total external costs of road freight transport in the UK.

Figure 4.4 shows the extent to which the taxes and duties paid by different classes of HGV covered their allocated external costs using medium estimates of air pollution costs.

The duties and taxes paid internalized on average 67 per cent of the total external costs (ie environmental, congestion and infrastructure costs) imposed by UK-registered HGVs in the UK in 2006. In the case of rigid vehicles between 51 per cent and 84 per cent of the costs were recovered by taxation, depending on the weight class of the vehicle. The taxes paid by articulated vehicles with gross weights in excess of 33 tonnes internalized roughly two-thirds of the externalities.

Congestion costs constitute approximately 42 per cent of the full external costs of lorry traffic in the UK. If these congestion costs are excluded, it appears that taxes exceeded the value of the remaining externalities for all of the HGV weight classes. In 2006, the average truck in the UK paid 16 per cent more in duties and taxes than its allocated infrastructural and environmental costs (excluding congestion costs).

In the light of recent re-assessments of the impact of climate change, these estimates of the degree of internalization may turn out to be too optimistic. Stern (2006) suggests that this element of external costs may have a significantly higher value than previously assumed. If so, the tax-to-cost ratio would be lower than calculated, reinforcing the case for sustainability measures to reduce the environmental damage done by HGVs. The *Stern Review* argues that the cost of CO_2 should

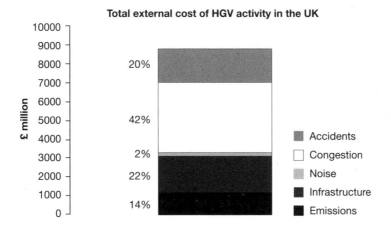

Figure 4.3 Total external costs of HGV activity in UK

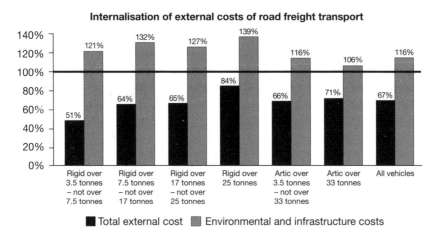

Figure 4.4 Internalization of external costs by HGV category

be around £72 per tonne in 2006 prices – roughly three times higher than the medium value of the shadow price of carbon factored into the above calculations. The adoption of this value would reduce the overall degree of external cost internalization for HGV operations in the UK to 57 per cent.

External costs imposed by foreign-registered HGVs

The estimates of external costs and their internalization reported in the previous section are based solely on the activities of UK-registered lorries. A significant proportion of road freight movement in the UK is handled by foreign-registered vehicles, and this share has risen sharply over the past decade. According to recent estimates compiled by the DfT, the number of foreign-registered HGVs travelling each year between Britain and mainland Europe grew from 461,000 in 1995 to over 1.5 million in 2006 (DfT, 2007b). This foreign HGV activity imposes an additional burden on the UK environment and transport infrastructure. This negative impact needs to be evaluated and included in the estimates of the external costs associated with road freight transport. As foreign trucks pay no VED in the UK and very little fuel duty, the degree to which their external costs are internalized is very much lower than that of UK-registered lorries.

NERA (2005) estimated the total environmental and track costs imposed by foreign-registered trucks in 2003 at £236.4 million (in 2004 prices). Burns (2005) calculated the annual track costs attributable to foreign goods vehicles to be £195 million, environmental costs £35 million and accident costs £33 million in 2005. His total of £263 million excluded congestion and noise costs. This section updates these earlier evaluations of the external costs imposed by foreign-registered goods vehicles travelling on British roads, including movements to and from the UK, cabotage journeys within the country and transit traffic.

The last official estimates of distances travelled by foreign-registered HGVs on UK roads were made in 2003 by the *Survey of Foreign Vehicle Activity in Great Britain* (FVA survey) (DfT, 2003). According to this survey, overseas-registered trucks travelled 924 million kilometres on Britain's roads in 2003. The average distance travelled per visit to the UK was 640 kilometres (DfT, 2003). If one scales up the 2003 estimate of foreign-HGV kilometres in proportion to the growth in the number of foreign trucks travelling between the UK and mainland Europe, the annual distance travelled by these vehicles would have been 1,058 million vehicle-kilometres in 2006. This assumes that the average distance travelled per visit to the UK remained constant between 2003 and 2006.

The methodology and cost estimates used in the foreign vehicle analysis were the same as those applied in the earlier analysis of UK-registered HGVs. For consistency, the vehicle categories used in the FVA survey were aligned with the weight classes used in this earlier analysis. Based on medium air pollution cost valuations, congestion constitutes 30 per cent of the external costs attributable to foreign-registered HGVs, followed by infrastructure wear (29 per cent), emissions (20 per cent), accidents (20 per cent) and noise (1 per cent) (Figure 4.5).

Eighty-three per cent of foreign lorries spend less than two days in the UK per visit and 93 per cent of visits last three or fewer days (DfT, 2003). Given the average distance travelled per visit (640 km), foreign-

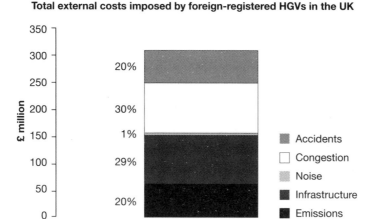

Figure 4.5 Total external costs imposed by foreign-registered trucks in the UK

registered lorries can undertake almost all their haulage work in the UK using fuel purchased outside the country. As the average price of diesel fuel in France, Belgium and the Netherlands was 28 per cent lower in 2006 than in the UK (McKinnon, 2007), foreign carriers had a strong financial incentive to fill their tanks before entering the UK. As a consequence, hardly any of the external costs imposed by foreign trucks in the UK are currently internalized. It is not known what proportion of the fuel consumed by foreign trucks in the UK is actually purchased here. As this is likely to be very low, however, it can be safely assumed that the level of internalization is minimal. If the estimated 1,058 million vehicle-kilometres run by foreign-registered lorries in 2006 had been run using diesel fuel purchased in the UK at an average level of fuel efficiency, an extra £177 million in duty would have been raised for the UK Exchequer. Full internalization of the external costs of foreign HGV activity in the UK would have raised around £300 million.

Combining UK and foreign-registered truck activity and assuming that none of the external costs imposed by overseas operators were internalized, the overall level of internalization of externalities associated with road freight transport in the UK in 2006 drops from 67 per cent to 64 per cent.

Internalization of external HGV costs across Europe

At a European level, according to the European Environmental Agency (EEA) (2006), distance-related charges (fuel taxes and infrastructure charges) levied on lorry transport fall well short of the minimum estimates of marginal external cost in all EU states (Figure 4.6). In 2002 the full external cost of HGV movements averaged €0.26 per vehicle-kilometre across the EU. More than 80 per cent of this external cost in Europe was related to accidents, climate change and air pollution.

According to the EEA estimates for 2002, taxes levied on HGVs in the UK internalized around 88 per cent of their external costs, a higher proportion than in any other EU country. At the other extreme, countries such as Poland, Greece and Luxembourg only internalized around 30 per cent of the external costs arising from truck traffic. These internalization estimates published by EEA cannot be directly compared with our valuations, however. Although the EEA does not explain the methodology used, it is clear that its internalization calculations involve comparing national taxes on HGVs with an EU-wide average figure for external costs per truck-km. Moreover, since 2002 there have been significant changes in the valuation of external costs and in tax levels.

The duty levied on diesel fuel in the UK remains the highest in Europe. In August 2007, it was 77 per cent higher than the European average (European Commission, 2008). It is likely that in 2007 UK-registered operators are still much closer to fully internalizing their external costs than most of their counterparts elsewhere in the EU. Since 2002, however, Germany and Austria have introduced road-tolling systems for trucks that have significantly increased their tax burden and helped to narrow

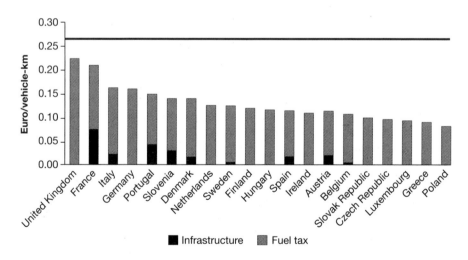

Figure 4.6 Distance-related charges and external costs of road freight transport (2002)

Source: EEA (2006).

the gap between external costs and taxes. Without knowing the corresponding external costs for each EU country it is not possible to compare international variations in the degree of internalization in 2006–07.

Light goods vehicles

Data on the van sector was obtained mainly from the government's Company Van Survey (DfT, 2004a), Survey of Privately Owned Vans (DfT, 2004b), the National Road Traffic Survey (NRTS) (DfT, 2007a), and Vehicle Licensing Statistics (DfT, 2008). The relationship between van activity and infrastructure, congestion and environmental costs was modelled in the same way as for HGVs.

The full infrastructural, congestion and environmental costs of van traffic are shown in Table 4.8, with the data disaggregated by vehicle ownership, weight class and fuel type. The total costs in 2006 have been estimated at £7.6 billion, £7.7 billion and £7.8 billion using, respectively, the low, medium and high emission cost values in Table 4.8.

Overall, 73–75 per cent of the total external costs were attributable to congestion, 17 per cent to traffic accidents, 6–8 per cent to air pollution and greenhouse gas emissions, 2 per cent to noise and only 1 per cent to infrastructure (Figure 4.7). Using a similar calculation to the HGV analysis, it is estimated that climate change costs represent around 4–5 per cent of the total external costs of van operations in Britain.

Unlike HGVs, vans perform other activities in addition to the delivery and collection of goods. They are also used to provide a wide range

Table 4.8 Total external costs of LGV operations in the UK (using road traffic count estimates of vehicle-kms)

2006 (£ million)	LGVs up to 1.8 tonnes gvw				LGVs 1.8 – 3.5 tonnes gvw				All LGVs
	Company owned		Privately owned		Company owned		Privately owned		
	Diesel	Petrol	Diesel	Petrol	Diesel	Petrol	Diesel	Petrol	
Low estimate	1,299	45	744	61	3,822	95	1,315	187	**7,569**
Medium estimate	1,309	45	753	61	3,896	96	1,341	189	**7,690**
High estimate	1,314	46	754	61	3,903	96	1,344	190	**7,708**

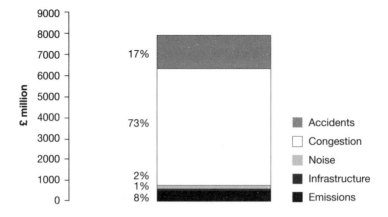

Figure 4.7 Total external costs of LGV activity in the UK (using medium emissions costs and road traffic count vehicle-km estimates)

of commercial services to establishments, and for commuting to and from work and personal trips (including, for example, shopping, leisure trips and visiting friends and relatives). Goods trips (ie those primarily involving the collection and delivery of goods) only account for, respectively, 34 per cent and 23 per cent of LGV vehicle kilometres for company and privately owned LGVs (30 per cent of all LGV vehicle kilometres). This conflicts with the widely held view that vans are used primarily for carrying goods. Table 4.9 shows estimates of external costs of the different types of LGV trip for company and privately owned LGVs, using medium air pollution cost values.

Table 4.9 Total external costs of LGV operations in the UK by trip type/purpose and vehicle ownership

2006 (£ million) Trip type/purpose	Company owned LGVs	Privately owned LGVs	All LGVs
Commercial: non-goods (ie service)	1,597	348	1,945
Commuting	1,735	1,057	2,792
Commercial: goods (ie delivery/collection)	1,805	537	2,342
Personal: goods and non-goods	209	402	611
Total	**5,346**	**2,344**	**7,690**

The degree of internalization was calculated for the different categories of van using medium cost figures for air pollution (Figure 4.8).

The duties and taxes paid by van operators cover on average 54 per cent of the total external costs (ie environmental, congestion and infrastructure costs) their vehicles impose. This varies from 41 per cent to 83 per cent depending on the category of van (with petrol-powered LGVs covering a greater proportion of their total external costs than diesel-powered vehicles). If congestion costs were excluded, the taxes substantially exceed the value of the remaining infrastructure and environmental costs for all categories of van. In 2006, the average van in the UK paid approximately twice its allocated infrastructural and environmental costs (excluding congestion costs) in duties and taxes.

Overview of internalization across the UK road freight sector

The estimated total external costs of LGV and HGV operations in the UK in 2006 were relatively similar (Table 4.10). The total costs of road freight operations by HGVs and LGVs in 2006 have been estimated at £16.1 billion, £16.4 billion and £16.7 billion using, respectively low, medium and high emission cost values. On the basis of medium emission cost values, HGVs accounted for 53 per cent of these external costs and LGVs for 47 per cent.

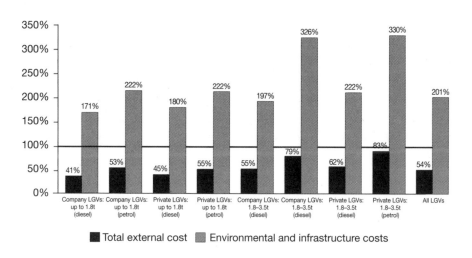

Figure 4.8 Internalization of external costs by LGVs in the UK

Table 4.10 Total external costs of LGV and HGV operations in the UK in 2006

2006 (£ million)	LGVs	HGVs	Total
Low estimate	7,569	8,579	**16,148**
Medium estimate	7,690	8,744	**16,434**
High estimate	7,708	8,945	**16,653**

Table 4.11 Importance of external cost categories for LGV and HGV operations in the UK in 2006

2006 (proportion of total external cost)	LGVs	HGVs
Emissions	8%	14%
Infrastructure	1%	22%
Noise	2%	2%
Congestion	73%	42%
Accidents	17%	20%
Total	100%	100%

Table 4.11 shows the proportion of total external costs accounted for by emissions, infrastructure, noise, congestion and traffic accidents for LGV and HGV operations, again based on the medium emissions cost values.

Congestion comprises a far greater proportion of total external costs for LGVs than for HGVs, reflecting the fact that their operations tend to be concentrated in and around urban areas, whereas HGVs run much of their annual mileage on less congested inter-urban trunk roads. Infrastructure costs, on the other hand, represent a much larger share of HGV costs because their heavier axle weights cause greater wear and tear on the road surface.

The duties and taxes paid by UK-registered LGV and HGV operators covered, on average, 54 per cent and 67 per cent respectively of the total external costs they imposed in 2006. All goods vehicles (ie LGVs and HGVs combined) covered 61 per cent of their total external costs in the UK. If congestion costs are excluded, LGV operators paid approximately twice as much in duties and taxes as their allocated infrastructural and environmental costs, while HGV operators paid about 16 per cent more than their infrastructural and environmental costs.

As discussed earlier, in contrast to HGVs, which are used almost entirely for the collection and delivery of goods, LGVs also perform a range of other non-goods carrying activities. In comparing the external costs of HGVs and LGVs as goods-carrying vehicles, one should really focus on the commercial goods trips performed by the latter. Using this narrower definition of goods-related van traffic, the total external costs of road freight activity in the UK in 2006 were calculated to be £11.1 billion (using medium cost estimates for air pollution). HGVs accounted for 79 per cent of these total goods-carrying vehicle external costs, and LGVs 21 per cent.

CONCLUSIONS

This chapter has examined the case for internalizing the environmental costs of logistics operations, in particular freight transport. While recognizing that there are strong theoretical and practical objections to applying the polluter-pays principle, it nevertheless argues that, on balance, internalization is likely to achieve a series of desirable public policy goals. Obtaining accurate and credible cost estimates for logistics-related externalities is difficult, however, particularly as the valuation process is both data-intensive and requires a good deal of subjective judgement. Different valuation methods need to be used for different externalities and a decision made as to whether it is more appropriate to use marginal or average costs in the internalization calculation.

A case study from the UK has been used to illustrate how it is possible to calculate, at a macro level, the extent to which taxes on road freight transport internalize its external costs. It was found that, in 2006, these taxes covered only 61 per cent of these costs. The tax shortfall was significantly greater for vans than for trucks. The figure for HGVs was also depressed by the failure to tax foreign-registered lorries for the environmental and infrastructural damage that they do while in the UK. Although, the monetary estimates of external costs vary widely at an international level (Walter et al, 2000), it seems likely that in 2006 the UK was much closer to fully internalizing the total external costs of its domestic road industry than most other EU countries.

There is a limit, however, in the extent to which any single country can unilaterally internalize the environmental costs of its freight transport. The resulting imposition of higher taxes on its transport operations can place its industry at a competitive disadvantage, particularly within an open market such as the EU. This is well illustrated in the case of the UK.

Ironically, Britain's high fuel duty policy has promoted increased pene-tration of its road haulage market by foreign operators who internalize very little of the external cost they impose on the country's environment and infrastructure. There is an apparent conflict between the European Commission's efforts to apply the polluter-pays principle to road freight transport and its rules on cross-border competition, which make it difficult for the UK government to 'level the fiscal playing field' between British and foreign hauliers and achieve 'internalization parity' between the two groups. Only the standardization of internalization policies across Europe will rectify this problem, though proposals currently being discussed in the EU would still give individual member states significant discretion over environmental taxation of the transport operations.

Even though duties and taxes on road freight traffic in the UK are very high by international standards, they would still need to be increased by 50 per cent for HGVs and 87 per cent for vans to fully internalize all the exter-nalities. It would clearly be very difficult and very unfair on road freight operators for the British government unilaterally to increase taxes by this margin. Moreover, UK-registered lorries currently pay significantly more tax than required to cover their environmental costs and share of road infrastructure costs. It is only when congestion costs are factored into the calculation that a tax shortfall results. If the government were to provide additional road space and/or use other traffic management measures to relieve traffic congestion, congestion costs would be reduced and the degree of internalization increased. This, however, would transfer costs from the congestion to infrastructure heading and not necessarily reduce the overall cost burden on freight operators.

The gradual upgrading of the new freight vehicles to higher EU emission standards and steady improvements in their fuel efficiency are reducing the total value of emission-related externalities. Increases in official esti-mates of the social cost of carbon and in the level of traffic congestion, however, will tend to counteract this downward pressure on external costs. It is difficult to predict what the net effect of these conflicting cost pressures will be on the future degree of internalization. The issue would be further complicated by the inclusion of road freight operations in the European Emissions Trading Scheme, as has been discussed by Raux and Alligier (2007).

Awareness of the full costs of freight transport services should help businesses to plan and manage their logistics in a way that achieves longer-term sustainability. Also, if the higher freight costs associated with greater internalization are passed down the supply chain, the purchasing behaviour of final consumers should also become more sensitive to the environmental impact of the distribution operations that keep them supplied with goods and services.

NOTES

1. Cabotage is domestic haulage work undertaken by foreign-registered carriers.
2. Available online at: http://www.naei.org.uk/datachunk.php?f_data-chunk_id=8.

REFERENCES

Adamowicz, W (2003) Valuation of environmental externalities, in *Handbook of Transport and the Environment*, ed D Hensher and K Button, Elsevier, Amsterdam

Adams, JGU (1981) *Transport Planning: Vision and practice*, Routledge and Kegan Paul, London

Baublys, A and Isoraite, M (2005) Improvement of external transport cost evaluation in the context of Lithuania's integration into the European Union, *Transport Reviews*, **25** (2), pp 245–59

Beuthe, M, Degrandsart, F, Geerts, J-F and Jourquin, B (2002) External costs of the Belgian interurban freight traffic: a network analysis of their internalisation, *Transportation Research Part D*, 7, pp 285–301

Bickel, P and Friedrich, R (2005) *ExternE: Externalities of Energy-Metholodology 2005 Update*, European Commission, Brussels

Burns, R (2005) *The Burns Freight Taxes Inquiry*, Freight Transport Association, Tunbridge Wells

CE Delft (2008) *Handbook on Estimation of External Costs in the Transport Sector*, Report for the European Commission, Delft

CE Delft (2009) *Are Trucks Taking their Toll? The environmental, safety and congestion impacts of lorries in the EU*, CE Delft, Delft

Coase, RH (1960) The problem of social cost, *Journal of Law and Economics*, **3** (1), pp 1–44

COPERT (2009) [accessed 15 May 2009] [Online] website: http://lat.eng.auth.gr/copert/

DEFRA (2006) *Air Quality Damage Cost Guidance*, DEFRA, London

DEFRA (2007a) *The Social Cost of Carbon and the Shadow Price of Carbon: What they are and how to use them in economic appraisal in the UK*, DEFRA, London

DEFRA (2007b) *Reducing the External costs of the Domestic Transportation of Food by the Food Industry*, Modelling Report, DEFRA, London

Department for Transport (DfT) (2003) *Survey of Foreign Vehicle Activity in Great Britain, 2003*, DfT, London

DfT (2004a) *Survey of Van Activity 2003*, DfT, London

DfT (2004b) *Survey of Privately Owned Vans: Results of survey, October 2002–September 2003*, SB (04) 21, DfT, London

DfT (2006) *Transport Statistics Great Britain: 2006 edition*, DfT, London

DfT (2007a) *Road Freight Statistics 2006*, DfT, London

DfT (2007b) *Road Goods Vehicles Travelling to Mainland Europe, 2007*, DfT, London

DfT (2008) Personal communication from the DfT Vehicle Licensing Statistics Team

DfT (2009) *Mode Shift Benefit Values: Draft technical report*, DfT, London

European Conference of Ministers of Transport (ECMT) (1998) *Efficient Transport in Europe: Policies for internalisation of external costs*, ECMT, Paris

ECMT (2003) *Efficiency Transport Taxes and Charges*, ECMT, Paris

European Commission (2001) *White Paper: European transport policy for 2010 – time to decide*, European Commission, Luxembourg

European Commission (2003) *External Costs: Research results on socio-environmental damages due to electricity and transport*, DG Research, Brussels

European Commission (2006) *Keep Europe Moving: Sustainable mobility for our continent*, European Commission, Luxembourg

European Commission (2008) [accessed 12 February 2009] Oil bulletin, Brussels [Online] http://ec.europa.eu/energy/observatory/oil/bulletin_en.htm

European Environmental Agency (EEA) (2006) *Transport and Environment: facing a dilemma; Term 2005: indicators tracking transport and environment in the European Union*, EEA, Copenhagen

Freight Transport Association (FTA) (2006) *Manager's Guide to Distribution Costs 2006*, FTA, Tunbridge Wells

HM Treasury (2003) *The Green Book, Appraisal and evaluation in central government*, TSO, London

INFRAS (2004) *External Costs of Transport: Update study*, INFRAS, Zurich/Karlsruhe

International Road Union (1997) *Driving towards Sustainable Development*, IRU, Geneva

IRU (2008) *IRU Position on the Internalisation of External Costs*, IRU, Geneva

Maddison, D, Pearce, D, Johansson, O, Calthrop, E, Litman, T and Verhoef, E (1996) *Blueprint 5: The true costs of road transport*, Earthscan, London

McKinnon, AC (2007) Increasing fuel prices and market distortion in a domestic road haulage market: the case of the United Kingdom, *European Transport*, **35**, pp 5–26

Mitchell, RC and Carson, RT (1989) *Using Surveys to Value Public Goods: The contingent valuation method*, Resources for the Future, Baltimore

MRTU (2008) *Heavy Lorries: Do they pay for the damage they cause?* MRTU, London

NERA (2005) *Costs Imposed by Foreign-Registered Trucks on Britain's Roads,* Report for the Freight Transport Association, London

Nordhaus, W (2006) *The Stern Review on the Economics of Climate Change,* NBER Working Paper No W12741, National Bureau of Economic Research, Yale

Pigou, AC (1920) *The Economics of Welfare,* Macmillan, London

Raux, C and Alligier, L (2007) A system of CO_2 tradable permits applied to freight transportation: is it feasible, could it work? Proceedings of the World Conference on Transport Research, University of California, Berkeley, 26–29 June 2007

Ricci, A and Friedrich, R (1999) *Calculating Transport Environmental Costs: Final report of the expert advisors to the High Level Group on Infrastructure Charging,* European Commission, Brussels

Sansom, T, Nash, C, Mackie, P, Shires, J and Watkiss, P (1998) *Surface Transport Costs and Charges: Great Britain,* Institute of Transport Studies, University of Leeds, Leeds

Schmidtchen, D, Koboldt, C, Monheim, J, Will, B and Haas, G (2007) *The Internalisation of External Costs in Transport: From the polluter pays to the cheapest cost avoider principle,* Centre for the Study of Law and Economics, Saarland University

SMMT (2005) *The UK Automotive Sector: Towards sustainability,* SMMT, London

Stern, N (2006) *Stern Review: The economics of climate change,* HM Treasury, London

TREMOVE (2009) [accessed 15 May 2009] Website [Online] http://www.tremove.org/

UNITE (2003) *Unification of Accounts and Marginal Costs for Transport Efficiency (UNITE): Final report,* Institute of Transport Studies, University of Leeds, Leeds

Walter, F, Neuenschwander, R, Sommer, H and Suter, S (2000) Monetary valuation of the external effects of transport: the state-of-the-art in Switzerland, *Swiss Political Science Review,* **6** (3), pp 134–45

Part 2

STRATEGIC PERSPECTIVE

5

Restructuring of logistics systems and supply chains

Irina Harris, Vasco Sanchez Rodrigues,
Mohamed Naim and Christine Mumford

INTRODUCTION

This chapter aims to review the current state of knowledge on the structural design of supply chain and logistics systems. Structural issues include physical flows, location of facilities and the use of information in decision-making protocols. In particular we will discuss the implications of dynamic behaviour and uncertainty of supply chain performance. We will determine the extent to which environmental criteria are being utilized in supply chain design vis-à-vis traditional cost and customer service metrics.

We will assess the current strengths and weaknesses of existing supply chain models and redesign methods, with the goal of highlighting future research challenges.

CURRENT STATE OF KNOWLEDGE OF TRADITIONAL SUPPLY CHAINS

Supply chain dynamics

Historically a supply chain has been defined as 'a system whose constituent parts include material suppliers, production facilities, distribution services and customers linked together by the feedforward flow of materials and the feedback flow of information' (Stevens, 1989). The main features of a traditional supply chain (Beamon, 1999) are illustrated in Figure 5.1, where the black arrows represent material flows and the dotted arrow represents information flow.

When designing a supply chain network, different levels of decisions need to be considered, from strategic through to operational. Strategic decisions typically have a planning period of many years and long-lasting effects. The identification of the number, locations and capacities of serving facilities, such as distribution centres (DCs) and warehouses, in a supply chain network, would normally be regarded as strategic planning. Tactical decisions involve a shorter planning horizon, and they are usually revised monthly or quarterly. Tactical activities include the selection of suppliers, assignment of products to DCs, and determining the distribution channel and the type of transportation mode. Finally, operational decisions, such as scheduling and routing activities, consider the day-to-day flow of products through the network, the amount of the inventory to be held by the facilities and so on. These decisions can be modified easily within a short period of time, for instance on a daily or weekly basis.

The complexity of a given supply chain is related to the number of echelons or cost centres present, where an echelon is identified as a place where inventory is kept (Tsiakis, Shah and Pantelides, 2001). There are

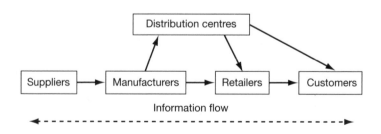

Figure 5.1 Traditional supply chain

Source: Based on Beamon (1999).

clear interfaces between each echelon, namely, suppliers/manufac-turers, manufacturers/distributors, distributors/retailers and retailers/customers. Material, cash and information flow across each interface. Typically, individual echelons embrace the following characteristics (Towill, 1991):

- perceived demand for products, which may be firm orders or simply forecasts;
- a production, or 'value-added', process;
- information on current performance (which may be high or low quality);
- 'disturbances', for example due to breakdowns, delays, absenteeism;
- decision points where information is brought together;
- transmission lags for both value-added and other activities;
- decision rules based on company procedures, for example, changing stock levels, placing new orders and production requirements.

Characteristics such as these can induce uncertainties within supply chains, which may not be due to any actual variations in market place demand. As far back as 1958 Forrester, in describing production–distribution systems, or what we now call supply chains, noted that demand in the marketplace can become delayed and distorted as it moves upstream in a supply chain, from customers through to raw material suppliers. At any one point in time, processes in various companies in the chain may be moving in different directions from each other and from the market, in response to order or production predictions.

Furthermore, traditional supply chains tend to 'amplify' marketplace variations. For example, the variations in orders placed on the factory may be much larger in magnitude than the fluctuations in the underlying marketplace demand. Critically, traditional supply chains can introduce 'periodicities' or 'rogue seasonality' (Thornhill and Naim, 2006), which can be misinterpreted as a consequence of seasonal variations in the marketplace, rather than a property of the supply chain itself. This 'law of industrial dynamics' phenomenon (Burbidge, 1984) has more recently been described as the 'bullwhip' effect (Lee, Padmanabhan and Whang, 1997a, 1997b) to include other forms of induced variations such as batching effects (Towill, 1997) and promotion activities (O'Donnell et al, 2006).

Bullwhip is an important measure as it is symptomatic of a poorly performing supply chain (Jones and Simons, 2000). It is a surrogate measure of production adaptation costs (Stalk and Hout, 1990) and implies the inclusion of 'just-in-case' stock holding to buffer against uncertainties. Evidence in many forms suggests that the bullwhip effect and Forrester's empirical conclusions are highly applicable to the vast majority of supply chains.

Forrester (1958) noted that attempts to reduce poor supply chain dynamic behaviour can exacerbate the problem. Counter-intuitive behaviour occurs because the causes of the behaviour are obscured from the decision makers in the chain. A recent example of this is given by Disney, Naim and Potter (2004). In a controlled experiment using the well-known MIT Beer Game, they implemented a number of scenarios including a traditional structure, electronic point of sales (EPOS) and vendor-managed inventory (VMI). The three supply chain scenarios researched are summarized in Figure 5.2. A traditional supply chain may be characterized by four 'serially linked' echelons in a supply chain. Each echelon only receives information on local stock levels and sales, and will determine its order on to its supplier using this knowledge, in conjunction with forecasts, work-in-process targets and inventory-holding requirements.

In the EPOS-enabled scenario, the end-consumer sales are transparent to all members of the supply chain. This is equivalent to the situation in grocery supply chains, where the data is available electronically directly from the retailer and can be used by all supply chain members to help in their stock-holding and ordering policies. However, each echelon still has to deliver, wherever possible, the goods ordered by its immediate customer. In the VMI scenario, the distributor in the two-echelon structure aims to take a holistic approach and simultaneously manage

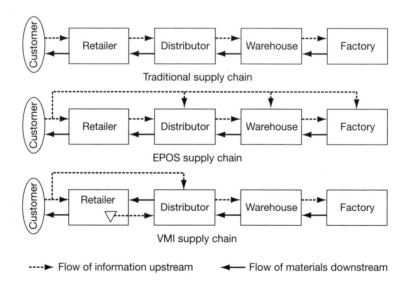

Figure 5.2 Three supply chain scenarios

Source: Based on Disney, Naim and Potter (2004).

both the retailer's and the distributor's stocks. The distributor is given information on the retailer's sales and stock levels. As a consequence, the retailer does not need to place orders on the distributor, because the distributor is at all times fully aware of the retailer's stock levels. Instead the distributor dispatches adequate amounts of material to ensure that there is enough stock at the retailer to satisfy customer service levels. The other echelons in this scenario, namely the warehouse and factory, retain the traditional ordering structure.

Disney, Naim and Potter (2004) made some interesting discoveries when investigating these three scenarios. The traditional supply chain behaved much as predicted, and extreme bullwhip was induced along the whole supply chain, resulting in increased inventory and backlog holding costs. In the EPOS scenario two modes were simulated: one in which no communication between players was allowed, and a second in which collaborative planning and replenishment was permitted. They discovered that EPOS, both with and without collaboration, incurred high negative inventory (backlog) costs. Nevertheless, EPOS with collaboration does well at reducing bullwhip in the supply chain.

The worst-performing scenario proved to be the VMI supply chain, which had both the highest inventory holding costs and the worst bullwhip chain. Although theory suggests that VMI should prove to be highly beneficial, due to its holistic approach to managing the supply chain (for example, see Hosoda et al, 2008), Disney, Naim and Potter (2004) found that the players had problems in implementing the concept even though they were provided with well-documented protocols.

An alternative to the above supply chain structures, which Disney, Naim and Potter (2004) also tested, was the elimination of one or more echelons in the supply chain; for example, goods may be shipped direct to a customer from the factory. Eliminating an echelon removes a decision point and reduces total lead times in one simple step. This approach was found to produce a better dynamic performance, in terms of bullwhip and inventory costs, than any other scenario (Wikner, Towill and Naim, 1991).

Taking the above principles into account, once a supply chain has been designed and implemented, it then has to be managed. Li et al (2005) have developed a list of sub-constructs for supply chain management practices to link them to performance. These constructs are:

- Strategic supplier partnership: long-term relationships between companies and their suppliers. This is designed to align the strategies of the companies with their suppliers.
- Customer relationship: practices aimed at defining how companies can manage customer complaints and develop long-term relationships with

them. Third-party logistics providers need to define who their main strategic customers are.

- Information sharing: the extent to which strategic information is shared with suppliers.
- Information quality: relates to how accurate, credible, current and adequate the information exchanged is.
- Internal lean practices: the extent to which there are practices of waste elimination and value creation within the supply chain.
- Postponement: represents the practice of delaying some activities within the supply chain. It has the goal of making the supply network more responsive.

Commensurate with the foregoing, Towill (1999) also developed a framework to enable the effective operations management of supply chains. He stated a number of preconditions that companies need to meet in order to simplify material flow. These preconditions, described as rules, require unbiased and noise-free information flows, compression and standardization of lead times in all work processes and choosing the smallest possible planning horizon.

Supply chain management and transport logistics

Supply chain management is a field that has traditionally been studied more from a marketing and manufacturing perspective, than from a transport point of view. Some recent papers indicate that the emphasis is changing, however. Stank and Goldsby (2000), for example, developed a decision-making framework that positions transport in an integrated supply chain. Meanwhile, Potter and Lalwani (2005) state that there has been little evidence of transport management techniques explicitly addressing supply chain issues, although there is evidence of demand variability, and subsequently, the bullwhip effect on transport operations. They go on to state that, although there is anecdotal evidence that bullwhip has a negative impact on transport performance, a negative relationship has not been proven. In addition, Potter and Lalwani developed a framework that integrates five main strategic themes, namely coordinated distribution network management, transport cost visibility, exploitation of ICT, collaborative relationships and information feedback.

Managing uncertainty in supply chains and transport

We have noted that serious problems such as bullwhip can arise as a result of uncertainty in supply chains. A considerable amount of research has been undertaken on uncertainty in supply chain management (Davis, 1993; Mason-Jones and Towill, 1999; Van der Vorst and Beulens, 2002; Geary et al, 2002; Peck et al, 2003), but in such work transport has typically been regarded as a marginal activity within supply chains (Stank and Goldsby, 2000) and has not been considered explicitly. To start to rectify these shortcomings, it is necessary to determine what forms of uncertainty affect transport operations. According to Van der Vorst and Beulens (2002), supply chain uncertainty refers to decision-making situations in which decision makers do not know what to decide. This indecision has many potential causes, including a shortage of one or more of the following: clear objectives, information processing capacity, or information about the supply chain or its environment. Such situations are hampered by an inability to accurately predict the impact of possible control actions on supply chain behaviour, or more simply, decision makers may lack effective control actions, per se. In response to such uncertainties at a strategic level, supply chain agility is proposed by Prater, Biehl and Smith (2001). This may be achieved through flexibility and speed in the three key activities of sourcing, manufacturing and delivery. Naim, Aryee and Potter (2007) specifically address the issue of transport flexibility as a response to supply chain uncertainties, stating that various types and degrees of transport flexibility are required for different supply chain needs. For example, different solutions may be needed for routine activities (simply moving goods from A to B) than would be appropriate when customized or tailored solutions are required, involving multi-modality, warehousing provision or inventory management. Types of transport flexibility include mix, routing, fleet and vehicle flexibility.

Davis (1993) was the first author to explicitly consider uncertainty as a strategic issue for supply chain performance when he stated 'there are three distinct sources of uncertainty that plague supply chains: suppliers, manufacturing, and customers. To understand fully the impact on customer service and to be able to improve performance, it is essential that each of these be measured and addressed.' This work produced a framework that was initiated in Hewlett-Packard in the early 1990s.

Building on the work of Davis (1993), Mason-Jones and Towill developed the Uncertainty Circle Model (Figure 5.3) as a way of defining the different sources of uncertainty that can affect supply chain performance. They confirmed that uncertainty is a strategic issue in supply chains, and suggested that it originates from four main sources: the supply side, the manufacturing process, the control systems and the demand side (Mason-Jones and Towill, 1999). Hence they extended Davis's work by adding a further source of uncertainty, the control systems. Moreover, they emphasized that uncertainty initiated in the supply side and/or in the manufacturing process can be mitigated by the application of lean-thinking principles. Uncertainty caused by control systems and/or on the demand side, on the other hand, requires an understanding of the dynamics of the whole system (Mason-Jones and Towill, 1999).

Another framework that takes uncertainty into account is the SCOR Model (Supply Chain Council, 2008). In a similar vein to Mason-Jones and Towill (1999), this model includes the supplier side as 'source', the manufacturing process as 'make' and the demand side as 'deliver'. It considers the logistics network concept by introducing the repetitive source–make–deliver sequences. Furthermore, the model extends the 'make' dimension by introducing the concept of 'value adding'. However, as with the Uncertainty Circle Model (Mason-Jones and Towill, 1999), it does not explicitly consider transport as a strategic supply chain process.

The Uncertainty Circle approach was further developed in research on the automotive industry by Geary et al (2002), where one of the main outcomes was an identification of the main issues associated with different types of uncertainty, examples of which are given in Figure 5.4. An attempt was also made to link the causes and effects of uncertainty or supply chain disruption. However, neither Van der Vorst and Beulens (2002) nor Geary et al (2002) considered transport as a strategic component of the supply chain or as a specific source of supply chain uncertainty. Instead they adopted a purely manufacturing perspective.

The recent body of work on supply risk and vulnerability has added an important new dimension of exogenous events to the Uncertainty Circle (Peck et al, 2003). Examples of such events might include terrorism, industrial action, disease epidemics or severe weather conditions. Transport operations may be seriously affected either directly through such events, or more indirectly through government regulations and controls aimed at preventing their occurrence or minimizing their impact. Furthermore, businesses may decide to change their strategies, including their supply

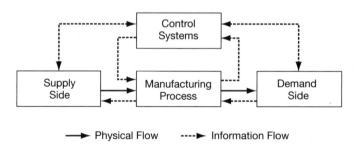

Figure 5.3 Uncertainty Circle Model

Source: Mason-Jones and Towill (1999).

Figure 5.4 Examples of bad practices from the four sources of supply chain uncertainty

Source: Geary, Childerhouse and Towill (2002).

chain policies, to minimize the future impact of government interventions such as taxation changes or new regulations that may be looming on the horizon but whose shape is not yet known for certain.

In the view of the present authors, work on the transport perspective of supply chain uncertainty is timely. Recently Prater (2005) developed an uncertainty framework that can be used to determine the causes of supply chain and transport uncertainty. This framework classifies uncertainty at both macro and micro-levels, as shown in Table 5.1. At the macro-level, uncertainty is typified in terms of general variation, foreseen uncertainty, unforeseen uncertainty and chaotic uncertainty. Getting down to the more micro-level, general variation consists of variable, multi-goal and constraint uncertainties. Foreseen uncertainty is caused by amplification of the demand from customers on inbound areas of the supply chain and parallel interactions between members of the supply network that are at the same horizontal level such as carriers and/or suppliers. Unforeseen uncertainty is the consequence of deterministic chaos that disrupts long-term planning, such as that resulting from road congestion. Finally, chaotic uncertainty is general non-deterministic chaos that cannot be predicted by a mathematical function, for example natural disasters or political problems that disrupt the supply chain flow and cannot be predicted with any accuracy.

Table 5.1 Micro-level types of uncertainty in supply chains

Macro-level	Micro-level
General variation	Variable, multi-goal and constraints
Foreseen uncertainty	Amplification, and parallel interactions
Unforeseen uncertainty	Deterministic chaos
Chaotic uncertainty	General non-deterministic chaos

Source: Prater (2005).

Sanchez Rodrigues et al (2008) have extended the Uncertainty Circle Model (Mason-Jones and Towill, 1999) from a manufacturing to a logistics triad perspective (Bask, 2001). The model is intended to provide a framework within which organizations, including logistics providers, can develop a supply chain strategy to mitigate the effects of uncertainty. By categorizing uncertainty into foreseen, unforeseen, chaotic and so on, organizations may determine where the greatest uncertainties lie, and hence develop a prioritized plan for supply chain re-engineering by initially targeting those uncertainties with the most significant implications for supply chain efficiency. The Logistics Triad Uncertainty Model is outlined in Figure 5.5.

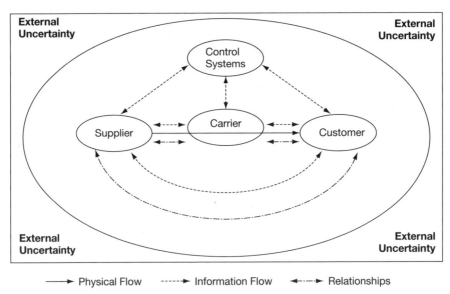

Figure 5.5 Logistics Triad Uncertainty Model

Source: Sanchez Rodriques et al (2008)

Performance measures for traditional supply chains

To ensure the efficient running of a supply chain, a range of performance measures have been developed over the years. Shepherd and Gunter (2006) presented a taxonomy and critical evaluation of performance measurements and various metrics for supply chains identified from 42 journal articles and books and from online resources published between 1990 and 2005. From their review, it is clear that different research studies classify the measures in very different ways. Nevertheless a taxonomy is presented according to the following classification:

- According to processes identified in the SCOR model: plan, source, make, deliver or return (customer satisfaction). This allows the identification of measures that are appropriate at the strategic, operational and tactical levels.
- Whether they measure cost, time, quality, flexibility or innovation. It is important to differentiate between cost and non-cost measures such as time and quality because if a supply chain relies only on cost measures, it can produce a misleading picture of supply chain performance (Chen and Paulraj, 2004).
- Whether they are qualitative or quantitative measures. Qualitative measures, such as customer satisfaction, reflect the happiness of the customers with the service and cannot be measured using a single numeric measure. Quantitative measures, such as cost, flexibility or customer responsiveness can be directly described numerically.

Shepherd and Gunter's review identified a total of 132 performance measures across different processes in the SCOR model. A very small proportion were related to the process of return or to customer satisfaction (5 per cent), compared with other processes such as plan (30 per cent), source (16 per cent), make (26 per cent) and deliver (20 per cent). Regarding the cost classification, the major proportion focused on cost (42 per cent) over non-cost measures such as quality (28 per cent), time (19 per cent), flexibility (10 per cent) and innovation (1 per cent). The quantitative measures (82 per cent) substantially exceeded the qualitative (18 per cent). One of the main problems with the all metrics discussed is that they do not capture the performance of the supply chain as a whole.

GREEN SUPPLY CHAINS

Beamon (1999a) recognized the essential objective of the green or extended supply chain as the evaluation of the total direct and eventual environmental effects of all processes and all products. A fully integrated supply chain (Figure 5.6) is described by Beamon as a supply chain having all the elements of the traditional configuration (Figure 5.1), but extended to incorporate product and packaging recycling as well as reuse and/or remanufacturing operations within a semi-closed loop. Consequently, it incorporates the elements of a reverse supply chain, reflecting the entire life cycle of the goods. Therefore, the main focus of a green supply chain is reducing energy consumption, emissions and waste, and increasing recycling and reuse.

To help deal with of the additional complexity of the extended supply chain, Beamon identified a new set of potential strategic and operational considerations:

● the number and location of facilities for product/packaging collection and re-use;
● the effects of traditional supply chain strategies (eg decentralized versus centralized facility location) on environmental performance;
● simultaneous operational and environmental supply chain optimization;
● incorporating environmental and operational goals into traditional analysis;

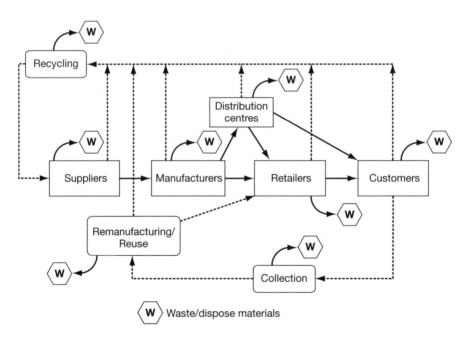

Figure 5.6 The extended supply chain

Source: Based on Beamon (1999).

- the level and location of buffer inventories in forward and reverse supply chains;
- the impact of the demand and recovery processes (which are not completely correlated) on the uncontrollable growth of unwanted parts or the non-availability of the critical parts and other decisions.

Green performance measures

A review of performance measurement systems and metrics under development for green supply chains is given by Hervani, Helms and Sarkis (2005). The selected list of metrics they identified range from atmospheric emissions to energy recovery. They include measures for on-site and off-site energy recovery, recycling and treatment, spill and leak prevention and pollution prevention. Additional general measures include total energy use, total electricity use, total fuel use, other energy use, total water use, habitat improvements and damages due to enterprise operations, cost associated with environmental compliance, and others. Hervani, Helms and Sarkis point out that organizations may choose their environmental performance measurements specifically to meet new government regulations on emissions, energy consumption or the disposal of hazardous waste.

From a logistics perspective, Aronsson and Huge-Brodin (2006), in their comprehensive literature review, identified the measurement of emissions as one of the most popular ways of assessing environmental impact. They noted, however, that even though the direct environmental impact can be assessed in terms of emissions, it is the root causes of these emissions that need to be addressed. Exactly what action to take needs to be determined by an appropriate analysis of the supply chain as a whole. Determining which sustainable measures to use and the difficulty of calculating them has been discussed by several researchers (Aronsson and Huge-Brodin, 2006; Hervani, Helms and Sarkis, 2005; Beamon, 1999).

Some researchers have noted that an improved environmental impact sometimes follows a supply chain redesign exercise based on traditional performance measures such as cost or customer service. In such cases improvements in environmental performance can be viewed as positive side effects of traditional methods, without having a fully integrated green supply chain. The factory gate pricing (FGP) concept, where the retailer is responsible for transportation of the product from the supplier, has been analysed for the UK grocery (Potter et al, 2003) and the Dutch retail industry (Le Blanc et al, 2006). Both studies show that cost reductions have brought significant environmental benefits, such as reduced congestion and transport kilometres/miles. Potter et al (2003) analysed the Tesco supply chain and suggested that by implementing FGP with consolidation centres for inbound deliveries, a reduction of 28 per cent in vehicle-miles required to transport products to DCs could be achieved, equating to over 400,000 miles per week.

Aronsson and Huge-Brodin (2006) describe three case studies, where companies had undergone changes in their distribution structures that had a positive effect not only on costs but also on the environment (reduced emissions). Among some of the typical changes made are new distribution structures with fewer nodes, larger warehouses, the introduction of new information systems, consolidation of flows, standardized vehicles and load carriers, and changes in transport mode.

Kohn and Huge-Brodin (2008) discuss two case studies that suggest improvements that can be made from an environmental perspective without impeding the cost-efficient provision of customer service when changing decentralized to centralized distribution systems. They point out that although centralization often results in an increase of total tonne-kilometres for transport work, at the same time it opens up other opportunities that can have a positive impact on the environment, such as shipment consolidation, change of transportation mode (eg from road transport to rail) and a reduction in emergency deliveries. Obviously, there are constraints and difficulties that can prevent companies from fully exploiting these opportunities. For example, a switch from road to rail would be difficult for many companies, as in the case of ITT Flygt discussed by Kohn and Huge-Brodin, due to limitations imposed by the rail infrastructure of the European Union, but for other companies, such as IKEA, modal change may be more realistic and beneficial.

As we can see from the above, the current approach is to assess the environmental impact following a redesign based on the optimization of traditional objectives, such as minimizing cost. The present authors believe there is a need to consider environmental measures explicitly during the optimization process at the same time as traditional objectives. Khoo et al (2001) use a simulation approach to select plant locations that balance low total market costs and low transport pollution, faster deliveries between plants, promotion of recycling of scrap metal and conservation of energy in a supply chain concerned with the distribution of aluminium metal. The simulation model was used to demonstrate the consequences of ignoring resource preservation and recycling activities as part of the network design. Other studies (Hugo and Pistikopoulos, 2005; Quariguasi Frota Neto et al, 2008) use multi-objective optimization techniques for evaluating the trade-offs between different objectives. Multi-objective optimization is discussed in more detail below.

As well as using individual sustainability measures, there is an increasing need to incorporate these measures into an assessment framework/methodology that will include environmental measures alongside economic and social metrics. Singh et al (2009) provide an overview of various sustainability indices that have been implemented. In their paper, they consider sustainability in its broadest sense, covering aspects other than the environment, such as product-based sustainability and quality of life. In total, 70 indices were grouped under 12 categories, including the following environmental indices: Eco-system-based indices (Eco-Index Methodology, Living Planet Index, Ecological Footprint); Composite Sustainability Performance Indices for Industry (Composite sustainable development index, ITT Flygt Sustainability Index, G Score method); Product-based Sustainability index (Life Cycle Index, Ford of Europe's Product Sustainability Index); Environmental Indices for Industries (Eco-Points, Eco-compass, Eco-indicator 99); Social and Quality of Life-Based indices (eg Index for sustainable society) and others.

An example of sustainable methodology use during supply chain design is described in Hugo and Pistikopoulos (2005). They present a generic mathematical programming model for assisting the strategic long-range planning and design of a bulk chemical network. Their multi-objective mixed integer programming problem is formulated to minimize the environmental impact resulting from the operations of the entire network whilst simultaneously maximizing the network's profitability. The method for impact assessment, the Eco-Indicator 99 method (Pré Consultants, 2000), is incorporated within the quantitative life cycle assessment model to formulate an appropriate environmental performance objective to guide strategic decision making. The Eco-Indicator 99 method attempts to model potential environmental impact on a European scale according to three categories: human health, ecosystem quality and resource depletion.

Another example involving the trading off of cost against environmental impact is described in Quariguasi Frota Neto et al (2008), where the reorganization of a European pulp and paper logistic network is described. The environmental impact was assessed using an environmental index proposed in Bloemhof-Ruwaard et al (1996). This index uses life cycle analysis and considers the diverse emissions produced in the supply chain: namely global warming, human toxicity, ecotoxicity, photochemical oxidation, acidification, nitrification and solid waste. The technique provides a single weighted measure for environmental impact for each phase of the supply chain.

To assess the environmental impact of supply chains, there is a pressing need for decision-making/support tools that incorporate green performance measurements. Hervani, Helms and Sarkis (2005) point out that, although environmental performance measures are being incorporated into existing tools at an increasing rate, current availability is far from adequate. They discuss the various tools that are available, including the analytical hierarchy process, balanced scorecard, activity-based costing, design for environmental analysis and life cycle analysis. Some of the tools could be directly applied to aspects of green supply chain management and performance, while others require adjustments and extensions. The authors point out that on the whole there is no perfect tool for traditional or green performance measurement systems, and that their usage is greatly dependent on acceptance by organizations. However, introducing new tools or tools with an 'unfamiliar feel' into a busy commercial environment can be challenging, if their adoption involves large capital investment, significant staff retraining or an unacceptable element of risk.

GAPS IN OUR UNDERSTANDING AND PRIORITIES FOR RESEARCH

There has been little research on the impact of supply chain practices on green logistics performance. In particular, the impact of fundamental supply chain management principles needs to be addressed. Where the body of knowledge on supply chains vis-à-vis transport exists, there has been a lack of explicit determination of the impact uncertainty, such as demand amplification, on transport performance, using either economic and/or environmental criteria. The impact of decision making, whether at strategic, planning or operational levels, needs due consideration with respect to balanced, or multi-objective, performance metrics that take environmental issues into account, in addition to economic costs and customer service levels.

Historically, most supply chain research considers the material producers, or 'suppliers', as the key players. However, recent research on the logistics triad sees the third-party logistics provider as a core constituent of the supply chain. Therefore, it is necessary to determine the impact of the relationship between all members of the triad and how various partnership arrangements may impact on green logistics performance. Again, historically, supply chain relationships have been considered from a vertical, forward material flow perspective. Other dimensions include reverse material flows and horizontal relationships, perhaps between carriers and their complementors and/or competitors. Complementary to the relationship issues, there is a need to address how best to use information in the supply chain so as to mitigate against a negative environmental impact. For example, to what extent is information sharing vital between third logistics providers and other members of the triad?

Logistics flexibility, as a response to uncertainty, is still little understood in terms of its economic impact let alone for its effect on green logistics. Therefore, the impact of transport providers' interactions and customer-transport providers' interactions should be established, since it could represent a very significant source of transport uncertainty, and as a consequence have a considerable impact on green logistics performance.

It is important to take a holistic view in establishing the impact of supply chain practices on the environmental performance of transport. Therefore, there should be a considerable degree of clarity about what aspects of uncertainty are relevant to green logistics. In order to determine this, future research should:

- determine and categorize all the sources of uncertainty that affect the supply chain and transport;
- consider the root causes and fundamental effects of each type of uncertainty;
- determine where each type of uncertainty originates from, whether in transport operations or other parts of the supply chain;
- determine the impact of the causes of uncertainty on green logistics performance;
- prioritize the causes of uncertainty and develop solutions, including flexibility strategies, to mitigate their implications;
- explore the full range of uncertainty, primarily related to the external environment, such as commodity availability, product prices, international trade regulations, taxes and duties.

Most measures lack the holistic perspective necessary for properly evaluating supply chain performance. There are relatively few examples where there is a systematic approach to the collation and utilization of supply chain measures. Shepherd and Gunter (2006) propose the following for future research:

- Measures of supply chain relationships in the supply chain as a whole need to be developed, rather than measures of intra-organizational performance. The lack of qualitative metrics and non-financial measures of innovation and customer satisfaction should also be addressed.
- The factors that influence the success or failure of attempts to implement measurement systems for supply chains need to be investigated.
- Measurement systems need to be treated as dynamic entities that must respond to environmental and strategic changes.

- The factors influencing the evolution of performance measurement systems for supply chains and ways to maintain these systems on an ongoing basis need to be investigated.
- Investigation is needed into whether it is cost-effective to implement measurement systems to evaluate supply chain performance, especially for small and medium enterprises.

With regard to environmental metrics and measures, Hervani, Helms and Sarkis (2005) identify the following issues for future research:

- The business and environmental outcomes of green supply chain management (GSCM) performance measurement systems and their impact within the organization and society at large need to be addressed. If as a result of such studies there is no immediate improvement, further research is needed to address when and if they will make the difference.
- There is a need for industry-specific research to address which performance measurement systems work best.
- There needs to be inter-organizational agreement on performance management and measurement.
- There is a need for tools to promote the development and improvement of green performance measures and supply chain management.
- Data and information issues relating to GSCM need to be addressed.
- The roles of new technologies including information technology in GSCM need to be better understood.

Singh et al (2009) point out that even though there is an international effort to measure sustainability, relatively few approaches consider environmental, economic and social aspects in an integrated way.

There is a lack of research into large-scale supply network problems, and such research would be conducive for multiple performance criteria assessment. Aronsson and Huge-Brodin (2006) have identified a general low level of interest in environmental issues in logistics. Their paper identified 'the lack of theories and models for connecting different logistics decisions on different hierarchical decision levels to each other and their environmental impact'. Hence, it is important to gain more insight into how companies can lower their costs and increase their competitiveness while at the same time reducing their environmental impact. In the cases where companies have undergone a strategic redesign of their supply chain or redesigned their distribution network, it appears that in many cases savings achieved in overall system costs also lead to environmental savings in terms of CO_2 emissions or energy savings.

CONSEQUENCES AND CONCLUSIONS

In this chapter we have reviewed the current knowledge of supply chain dynamics and identified a need to consider the environmental impact of business activities alongside the usual economic and customer service factors. We began with a survey of the current state of knowledge, discussing the strengths and limitations of some traditional supply chain models, particularly in relation to breakdowns and inefficiencies that result from poor supply chain dynamics. We identified uncertainty – and its mitigation – as a key issue in supply chain management. Most serious is the bullwhip effect, which tends to amplify marketplace variations and can result in alternating periods that produce vast surpluses and shortages of inventory, wasting resources and impacting on customer service levels. Clearly, supply chains that perform poorly from an economic and customer service perspective are also likely to perform badly when considered from an environmental viewpoint. Thus, addressing the weaknesses should produce simultaneous benefits for all stakeholders.

We noted that traditional supply chain management focuses primarily on market and manufacturing issues, and transport has typically been considered as a rather marginal activity. However we can identify several reasons why this emphasis needs to change, not least the increasing fuel costs. First of all, it is clear that the transport subsystem has a key role, and poor transport management will mean that goods are not delivered to where they are needed at the appropriate time, thus disrupting the operation of the whole supply chain. Second, transport activities have a high environmental impact, in terms of energy usage, carbon emissions, noise and pollution. Finally, the life cycle approach to supply chains adds considerable complexity, and requires much additional transportation to deal with returns, recycling and remanufacturing. We have identified a need for a more holistic approach to transport, and more horizontal and vertical collaboration between logistics operators.

Traditional and environmental performance measures were discussed in some detail in this chapter. Plainly, we rely on appropriate methods and measurements to give accurate information to decision makers. However there are very many aspects to sustainability, and there appears to be no general agreement on how to trade-off the different components such as energy and raw material usage, greenhouse gas emissions and the generation of scrap and waste. Furthermore, there are few tools to support the measurement of environmental KPIs.

It is clear to us that much more research is needed on how to quantify the impact of supply chain practices on green logistics performance, and the environmental impact of current supply chain management policies needs to be addressed as a matter of urgency. In particular, we need to look at how uncertainty in a supply chain impacts on transport performance, with respect to both economic and environmental criteria. Decision makers should consider environmental issues simultaneously with economic costs and customer service levels.

REFERENCES

Aronsson, H and Huge-Brodin, M (2006) The environmental impact of changing logistics structure, *The International Journal of Logistics Management*, **17** (3), pp 394–415

Bask, AH (2001) Relationships among TPL providers and members of supply chains: a strategic perspective, *Journal of Business & Industrial Marketing*, **16** (6), pp 470–86

Beamon, B (1999) Designing the green supply chain, *Logistics Information Management*, **12** (4), pp 332–42

Beamon, B (1999) Measuring supply chain performance, *International Journal of Operations & Production Management*, **19** (3), pp 275–92

Bloemhof-Ruwaard, JM, Van Wassenhove, LN, Gabel, HL and Weaver, PM (1996) An environmental life cycle optimization model for the European pulp and paper industry, *Omega*, **24** (6), pp 615–29

Burbidge, JL (1984) Automated production control with a simulation capability, Proceedings of the IFIP Conference, WG 5–7, Copenhagen, pp 1–14

Chen, IJ and Paulraj, A (2004) Understanding supply chain management: critical research and a theoretical framework, *International Journal of Production Research*, **42** (1), pp 131–63

Davis, T (1993) Effective supply chain management, *Sloan Management Review*, Summer, pp 35–45

Disney, SM, Naim, MM and Potter, A (2004) Assessing the impact of e-business on supply chain dynamics, *International Journal of Production Economics*, **89** (2), pp 109–18

Forrester, JW (1958) Industrial dynamics: a major breakthrough for decision makers, *Harvard Business Review*, **36** (4), pp 37–66

Geary, S, Childerhouse, P and Towill, D (2002) Uncertainty and the seamless supply chain, *Supply Chain Management Review*, **6** (4), pp 52–61

Hervani, AA, Helms, MM and Sarkis, J (2005) Performance measurement for green supply chain management, *Benchmarking: An International Journal*, **12** (4), pp 330–53

Hosoda, T, Naim, MM, Disney, SM and Potter, A (2008) Is there a benefit to sharing market sales information? Linking theory and practice, *Computers and Industrial Engineering*, **54**, pp 315–26

Hugo, A and Pistikopoulos, E (2005) Environmentally conscious long-range planning and design of supply chain networks, *Journal of Cleaner Production*, **13** (15), pp1428–48

Jones, DT and Simons, D (2000) Future directions for the supply side of ECR, in ECR in the Third Millennium, in *Academic Perspectives on the Future of Consumer Goods Industry*, ed D Corsten and DT Jones, pp 34–40, ECR, Brussels

Khoo, HH, Spedding, TA, Bainbridge, I and Taplin, DMR (2001) Creating a green supply chain, *Greener Management International*, 35, pp 71–88

Kohn, C and Huge-Brodin, MH (2008) Centralised distribution systems and the environment: how increased transport work can decrease the environmental impact of logistics, *International Journal of Logistics*, **11** (3), pp 229–245

Le Blanc, HM, Cruijssen, F, Fleuren, HA and de Koster, MBM (2006) Factory gate pricing: an analysis of the dutch retail distribution, *European Journal of Operational Research*, **174** (3), pp 1950–67

Lee, HL, Padmanabhan, P and Whang, S (1997a) Information distortion in a supply chain: the bullwhip effect, *Management Science*, **43**, pp 543–58

Lee, HL, Padmanabhan, V and Whang, S (1997b) The bullwhip effect in supply chains, *Sloan Management Review*, **38** (3), pp 93–102

Li, S, Ragu-Nathan, B, Ragu-Nathan, TS and Subba Rao, S (2005) Development and validation of a measurement instrument for studying supply chain management practices, *Journal of Operations Management*, **23** (6), pp 618–41

Mason-Jones, R and Towill, D (1999) Shrinking the supply chain uncertainty circle, *Institute of Operations Management, Control*, **24** (7), pp 17–22

Naim, M, Aryee, G and Potter, AT (2007) Transport provider's flexibility capability for mass customization, Proceedings of the 12th International Symposium on Logistics, 8–10 July, 2007, pp 483–89

O'Donnell, T, Maguire, L, McIvor, R and Humphreys, P (2006) Minimizing the bullwhip effect in a supply chain using genetic algorithms, *International Journal of Production Research*, **44** (8), pp 1523–43

Peck, H, Abley, J, Christopher, M, Haywood, M, Saw, R, Rutherford, C and Strathen, M (2003) *Creating Resilient Supply Chains: A practical guide*, Cranfield University, Cranfield

Potter, A and Lalwani, C, (2005) Supply chain dynamics and transport management: a review, In *Logistics Research Network 2005 Conference Proceedings*, ed J Dinwoodie, J Challacombe, E Madejski and D Song, pp 353–64, Chartered Institute of Logistics and Transport (UK), Corby

Potter, AT, Lalwani, CS, Disney, SM and Velho, H (2003) Modelling the impact of factory gate pricing on transport and logistics, Proceedings of the 8th International Symposium of Logistics, Seville, 6–8 July

Prater, E (2005) A framework for understanding the interaction of uncertainty and information systems on supply chains, *International Journal of Physical Distribution & Logistics Management*, **35** (7), pp 524–39

Prater, E, Biehl, M and Smith, MA (2001) International Supply chain agility: tradeoffs between flexibility and uncertainty, *International Journal of Operations & Production Management*, **21** (5–6), pp 823–39

Pré Consultants (2000) *The Eco-indicator 99. A damage oriented method for life cycle impact assessment: methodology report and manual for designers*, 2nd edn, Amersfoort, Netherlands

Quariguasi Frota Neto, J, Bloemhof-Ruwaard, JM, van Nunen, JAEE and van Heck, E (2008) Designing and evaluating sustainable logistics networks, *International Journal of Production Economics*, **111** (2), pp 195–208

Sanchez Rodrigues, V, Stantchev, D, Potter, AT, Naim, M and Whiteing, A (2008) Establishing a transport operation focused uncertainty model for the supply chain, *International Journal of Physical Distribution & Logistics Management*, **38** (5), pp 388–411

Shepherd, C and Gunter, H (2006) Measuring supply chain performance: current research and future directions, *International Journal of Productivity and Performance Management*, **55** (3–4), pp 242–58

Singh, RK, Murty, HR, Gupta, SK and Dikshit, AK (2009) An overview of sustainability assessment methodologies, *Ecological Indicators*, **9** (2), pp 189–212

Stalk, G Jr and Hout, TM (1990) *Competing Against Time: How time-based competition is reshaping global markets*, The Free Press, New York

Stank, T and Goldsby, T J (2000) A framework for transportation decision making in an integrated supply chain, *Supply Chain Management: An International Journal*, **5** (2), pp 71–78

Stevens, G (1989) Integrating the supply chain, *International Journal of Physical Distribution and Materials Management*, **19** (8), pp 3–8

Supply Chain Council (2008) *Supply-Chain Operations Reference-model*, Supply Chain Council, Washington, DC

Thornhill, NF and Naim, MM (2006) An exploratory study to identify rogue seasonality in a steel company's supply network using spectral principal component analysis, *European Journal of Operational Research*, **172** (1), pp 146–62

Towill, DR (1991) Supply chain dynamics, *International Journal of Computer Integrated Manufacturing*, **4** (4), pp 127–208

Towill, DR (1997) FORRIDGE: principles of good practice in material flow, *Production Planning and Control*, **8** (7), pp 622–32

Towill, DR (1999) Simplicity wins: twelve rules for designing effective supply chain control, *The Institute of Operations Management*, **25** (2), pp 9–13

Tsiakis, P, Shah, N and Pantelides, CC (2001) Design of multi-echelon supply chain networks under demand uncertainty, *Industrial and Engineering Chemistry Research*, **40** (16), pp 3585–604

Van der Vorst, J and Beulens, A (2002) Identifying sources of uncertainty to generate supply chain redesign strategies, Inter*national Journal of Physical Distribution & Logistics Management*, **32** (6), pp 409–31

Wikner, J, Towill, DR and Naim, MM (1991) Smoothing supply chain dynamics, *International Journal of Production Economics*, **22**, pp 231–48

6

Transferring freight to 'greener' transport modes

Allan Woodburn and Anthony Whiteing

For some journeys, road transport can be most efficient, but for others, combined options whether with rail, short-sea shipping or inland waterways, are better. Choosing the best option for any given journey will make transport operations more efficient, cost-effective, sustainable, and help our economies to become more competitive in a win-win environment.

(European Commission, 2006)

BACKGROUND

This chapter sets out the existing situation relating to the freight transport modal split in Britain and discusses ways in which freight can be transferred from road to alternative modes of transport that are perceived under most circumstances to have lower environmental impacts, particularly in relation to their contribution to climate change. The main focus of the chapter is on the greater use of rail and water – both inland waterway and coastal shipping – since these are the main alternatives to road for a broad range of commodity and flow types. In addition, short-sea shipping is considered in the context of freight flows between mainland Europe and Britain. Pipelines and air freight generally have been excluded due to the limited range of products they can reasonably carry.

The volume of freight transport has grown rapidly in the last three decades, with road gaining an increasing share of the total market. In 1976, the domestic freight market totalled just less than 150 billion tonne-kilometres, while by 2006 it had expanded to almost 250 billion tonne-kilometres. The rate of growth in freight transport movement has slowed considerably in the last decade, with an overall increase of just 8 per cent between 1996 and 2006 compared with increases of 20 per cent or more in each of the previous two decades. Of specific interest for this chapter, however, is the distribution of activity across the three transport modes under consideration. Road haulage has been dominant throughout the 30 year time period shown in Figure 6.1, its share rising from 65 per cent in 1976 to 69 per cent in 2006. It is evident that most of the growth in road haulage resulted from an increase in total freight activity, with the transfer of flows from other modes accounting for only a relatively small amount of road haulage growth.

The fortunes of the other two modes have been somewhat varied over the last 30 years, as can be seen from Table 6.1. Until the mid-1950s, rail had been the dominant mode of freight transport but its market share declined dramatically until the mid-1990s, by which time it retained just 7 per cent of the domestic market. In the last decade, this decline has been reversed and rail's share has edged upwards to 9 per cent in 2006. The proportion of freight moved by water rose considerably in the 1970s, largely due to the development of the North Sea oil and gas industry, but has since declined from its 1980s peak. Given the relatively limited extent

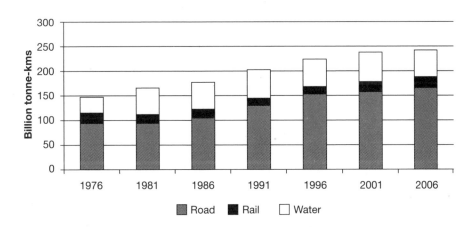

Figure 6.1 Domestic freight transport moved (Great Britain): by mode, 1976–2006

Source: Based on DfT (2007a).

of navigable inland waterways in the UK, domestic waterborne freight is dominated by seagoing flows.

While the share of domestic freight being moved by water has decreased, waterborne transport dominates when considering import and export flows. More than 95 per cent of trade by weight enters or leaves the UK by sea (DfT, 2007b), either short-sea to/from the rest of Europe or deep-sea to/from other continents, with most of the remainder travelling through the Channel Tunnel. Less than 0.5 per cent of the tonnage of international freight moves by air.

CHARACTERISTICS OF THE MAIN FREIGHT TRANSPORT MODES

The main freight transport modes all have different characteristics, which leads them to play different roles in the movement of goods. Rail and waterborne freight have natural advantages in the movement of bulk products, resulting mainly from their ability to carry large quantities in a single train or vessel. By contrast, the flexibility and convenience of road haulage lends itself to the movement of manufactured goods. Typically, then, rail and water come into their own for commodity movements in the early stages of the supply chain, where flow volumes tend to be larger and of relatively low value compared to their weight. Road caters for the majority of the flows that distribute products, where consignment values per tonne are typically higher and flows are of smaller volumes. Rail finds it hard to compete for shorter distance flows, except when very large volumes are on offer. Hence there are well-established, large variations in the average distance that goods move by

Table 6.1 Modal split (%) for freight transport moved (Great Britain), 1976–2006

	1976	1981	1986	1991	1996	2001	2006
Road	65	57	59	64	69	67	69
Rail	14	11	10	7	7	8	9
Water	20	32	31	29	25	25	22
Total*	100	100	100	100	100	100	100

* Totals may not add to 100 due to rounding.

Source: Based on DfT (2007a).

each mode, reflecting their different characteristics. The average road journey is 86 kilometres in length, while a rail movement averages 201 kilometres and for waterborne freight the figure is 410 kilometres (DfT, 2007b). Figure 6.2 demonstrates the dominance of waterborne freight in the movement of petroleum products, rail in the coal and coke market, and road in the carriage of other commodities. In recent times, the fastest growth has occurred in the movement of non-bulk commodities, favouring road haulage and strengthening its dominance of the UK freight market. Table 6.2 sets out an indicative mode suitability assessment for a range of commodity types.

The growth in the use of the freight container, and more recently the swapbody, has led to the development of intermodal transport, whereby more than one mode of transport is used for longer distance flows, with rail or water covering the majority of the distance and with road legs confined to the beginning and end of the journey. With intermodal transport, it is the unit in which the goods are conveyed that is handled at the point of modal transfer, rather than the goods themselves. This allows for greater standardization in terminal and transport equipment, reducing the cost and time of modal transfer. Domestic intermodal volumes by rail increased by more than 50 per cent in the five years to 2007–08, making this the fastest growing sector of the rail freight market (ORR, 2008a).

While the road haulage and waterborne modes have long been competitive markets, with considerable intra-modal competition for many commodities and flows, rail freight was part of the nationalized British Rail

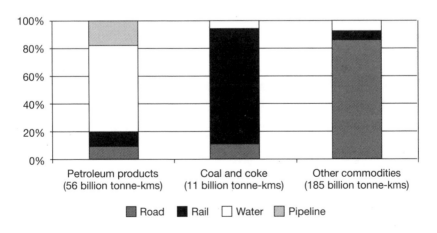

Figure 6.2 Domestic freight transport moved (Great Britain): mode share for selected commodities, 2006

Source: DfT (2007b).

Table 6.2 Mode suitability assessment for different commodity types

Commodity type/mode	Rail	Inland waterway	Short-sea shipping
Aggregates	Regular flows	Regular flows	Regular flows
Coal	Regular flows	Trial/irregular flows	Regular flows
Retail (non-food)	Regular flows	Trial/irregular flows	Regular flows
Retail (perishable food)	Trial/irregular flows	Not suited	Regular flows
Container	Regular flows	Trial/irregular flows	Regular flows
Automotive	Regular flows	Trial/irregular flows	Regular flows
Parcels	Regular flows	Not suited	Regular flows
Home delivery	Not suited	Not suited	Not suited
Waste	Regular flows	Regular flows	Regular flows
Oil and petroleum	Regular flows	Regular flows	Regular flows
Steel/scrap metal	Regular flows	Trial/irregular flows	Regular flows
Forest products	Regular flows	Trial/irregular flows	Regular flows

Key: ▣ Regular flows ▢ Trial/irregular flows ■ Not suited

Source: DfT (2008a).

monopoly provider until the mid-1990s. Since privatization, the rail freight market has become increasingly competitive and this is regularly cited as one of the major reasons for the revival of rail freight activity. As will be seen later, both European Union (EU) and UK government policies have favoured using competitive markets as a means of encouraging a more sustainable freight transport system, reflecting the inherent environmental advantages of certain non-road modes. While rail and water operations are almost exclusively in the private sector, government is involved in the provision of infrastructure for these modes. The British rail network is owned by Network Rail, nominally a private company but regulated by an independent regulatory authority and with no private shareholders, while many inland waterways are owned by British Waterways or the Environment Agency, both government agencies. By contrast, the majority of the biggest ports are now in the hands of private companies.

ENVIRONMENTAL IMPACTS OF THE MAIN FREIGHT TRANSPORT MODES

In addition to each of the modes having different operational character-istics, their environmental impacts also differ significantly. Various attempts have been made to assess the relative environmental impacts of freight modes, and a relatively consistent picture emerges from these different studies despite some differences in absolute values. Figure 6.3 presents the findings from a thorough assessment of the CO_2 emissions per tonne-km for a range of transport modes (McKinnon, 2007). In general, rail and waterborne modes of transport are less damaging to the envi-ronment than road haulage, with typical emissions from waterborne freight being four or five times less per tonne-km than for road, and in the case of rail it is seven times lower than road haulage. At either extreme, air (not shown in Figure 6.3) has significantly greater CO_2 emissions at around 1,600 grams per tonne-km, while pipeline has the lowest emis-sions rate. The role of these two modes in the freight transport system is particularly specialized. A shift to more pipeline traffic would be desirable for environmental reasons, but the practicalities of achieving this are limited. By contrast, it is clearly undesirable from a sustainability perspective to encourage greater use of air freight.

While most of the concern about the environmental impacts of freight transport relates to climate change, notably CO_2 emissions, the modes of transport also vary in terms of their other climate change and local air

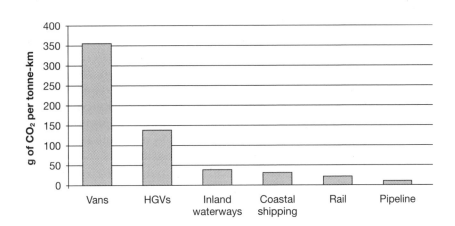

Figure 6.3 Estimated average CO_2 intensity values for freight transport modes

Source: McKinnon (2007).

pollution impacts. According to RSSB (2007), for example, rail freight is significantly better than road haulage in terms of the emissions of nitrogen oxides and particulates on a tonne-km basis, but is approximately three times worse than road for sulphur dioxide emissions. It is vital, therefore, to be clear on the environmental objectives to be achieved, in particular whether mitigating climate change impacts are the prime consideration or whether a trade-off between global and local emissions impacts is desirable. It should be borne in mind that these values are averages for each mode, which are helpful in identifying how each mode typically performs relative to the others but do not apply to every situation. The reality will be heavily influenced by the characteristics of the flow, not least the volume of goods to be moved, the efficiency and speed of the transport operation and the nature of the fuel consumed. For example, if a ship travels at 24 knots rather than 20 knots, it will typically use one third more fuel (DfT, 2008b), worsening its environmental performance.

CASE STUDY: CONTAINER TRAIN LOAD FACTORS

The two pictures in Figure 6.4 demonstrate dramatically different load factors for container train services, clearly showing that environmental performance per unit of freight moved may be significantly influenced by the level of operational efficiency. In the example on the left, with a far higher train load factor, the amount of fuel used (and the associated pollutant emissions) will be slightly higher than in the poorly loaded example shown on the right, but the emissions per container or per tonne carried will be far lower in the example of the better loaded train. In fact, it may well be the case that in the case of the poorly loaded train, the environmental impact of using road haulage would be lower than it is for rail, given that only a small number of HGVs would be required to move the small number of containers being carried. By contrast, the example on the left is highly likely to be less polluting per unit carried than road since a large number of HGVs would be needed to move all the containers on the train.

A recent study of container train utilization, carried out as part of the EPSRC Green Logistics project (Woodburn, 2008), found considerable variability in load factors by port served, direction of travel (ie import or export), rail freight operator and specific corridor. Overall, a 72 per cent load factor was identified, with 75 per cent loading for imports and 69 per cent in the export direction. Load factors varied from a high of 80 per cent at Felixstowe to just 55 per cent at Tilbury, while for the four rail freight

Figure 6.4   Examples of different load factors for container train services

Source: Author's collection.

operators there was variability from 90 per cent down to only 54 per cent. For specific services in the sample of almost 600 trains, load factors ranging from 100 per cent full to completely empty were found. The average train carried 44 20-foot equivalent units (TEUs), which avoids the use of more than 20 HGVs for each rail service operated. If all of these trains were fully loaded, though, at least 30 HGV journeys per train would be avoided.

THE POLICY FRAMEWORK

European Union

The momentum behind the promotion of policies designed to achieve a shift from road to 'greener' transport modes has grown since the late 1990s, at both the national and EU levels. In 1992, the European Commission published its first White Paper on Transport. This focused mainly on the liberalization of transport markets as part of the development of the Single European Market, but led to a strengthening of road's position in the freight market, at the expense of rail and inland waterways which both lost market share. The 2001 White Paper recognized this imbalance in the growth of the different transport modes and the consequent impacts on the environment, congestion and accidents. This second White Paper was published at a time when a consensus was forming within the scientific community as to the strong likelihood that human activities, of which transport is key, were responsible for the changing global climate. Reducing the dependence on oil-based fuel sources also favours a switch of traffic from road to rail, where the latter may have the opportunity to use electric traction, which raises the opportunity to use renewable or other non-fossil fuel power sources. At present, the waterborne freight sector is almost entirely dependent upon oil-based sources, so does not offer the same benefit over road, but of course is typically far more fuel efficient.

The EU is developing an Integrated Maritime Policy, which will have particular significance for the UK given its reliance on shipping for international trade and the importance of coastal traffic. The policy aims to balance the often-conflicting challenges of globalization and economic competitiveness, climate change, marine environment damage, maritime safety and energy security and sustainability. One specific objective is the reduction of CO_2 emissions from shipping. Other EU policies and regulations influence both freight transport mode choice and the environmental impacts of the different modes. For example, increasingly stringent emissions regulations relating to the sulphur content of diesel fuel have been implemented for road vehicles, and are now being widened to cover most non-road diesel engines, such as those used in railway locomotives.

UK government

In the UK, different levels of government have responsibilities that influence freight transport activity. The situation has become more complex in the last decade, with the introduction of devolved administrations in Scotland, Wales and Northern Ireland. It is not possible to thoroughly discuss the involvement of each of the different tiers of administration, so an overview of UK policy development relating to freight transport is provided. The key policy documents published in the last decade are:

- *A New Deal For Transport: Better for Everyone* – White Paper (1998);
- *Sustainable Distribution: A strategy* (1999);
- *Waterways for Tomorrow* (2000);
- *Modern Ports: A UK policy* (2000);
- *The Future of Rail* – White Paper (2004);
- *Future of Transport: A network for 2030* – White Paper (2004);
- *The Eddington Transport Study* (2006);
- *Delivering a Sustainable Railway* – White Paper (2007);
- *Towards a Sustainable Transport System: Supporting economic growth in a low carbon world* (2007).

The evolution of freight transport policy aims to balance two of the main strategic objectives of the UK government, these being the generation of economic growth and enhanced productivity and a reduction in the environmental impacts (particularly relating to climate change) of transport activity. Switching freight to modes with lower carbon intensity levels is a key element of the strategy, which in itself will form an important part of the broader programme to reduce the UK's carbon emissions. A range of practical measures to encourage modal shift from road to rail and water is identified in the next section.

EXAMPLES OF MEASURES AIMED AT ACHIEVING MODAL SHIFT FOR ENVIRONMENTAL BENEFIT

This section presents a selection of measures introduced by the European Union, UK government and the rail and water industries themselves to encourage the greater use of rail and waterborne modes. Finally, arguments are expounded that can be adopted to encourage freight users to consider switching from road. The aim is to show that a wide range of measures exists, rather than to provide a comprehensive review.

European Union

The EU has developed a Freight Action Plan (European Commission, 2007), in an attempt to coordinate policy initiatives relating to the performance of the freight sector. On modal shift, a number of initiatives are outlined, including the development of 'green' transport corridors for freight (including the establishment of a freight-oriented rail network), the removal of barriers that hinder the use of rail and water-based solutions, the promotion of best practice and the development of performance indicators measuring sustainability. Through its 'Greening Transport' initiative, the EU aims to allow national governments to introduce user-charging schemes to internalize the external costs associated with freight movement, particularly relating to the road haulage sector. Traditionally, road tolls have been allowed only to recoup infrastructure costs, although differential tariffs based on vehicles' environmental characteristics have been allowed since 2006. Proposals are being developed to allow a more comprehensive charging regime that will better reflect the environmental impacts of freight traffic. Implementation is expected by 2011, leading to more efficient road haulage operations (eg by encouraging more fuel-efficient and less polluting vehicles), as well as a shift of traffic to rail and water in situations where they become more cost-effective than road.

In conjunction with its programme to enhance transport interoperability and connectivity, the EU is using its Trans-European Network programme to try to influence the modal split in favour of more sustainable transport. Many of the 30 priority projects are focused on removing obstacles to using rail and water, together with promoting intermodal operations that use the most appropriate mode for each stage of a freight flow. The EU anticipates that completion of the TEN-T priority network will slow down the rate of increase of CO_2 emissions from freight transport operations through a combination of modal shift and more efficient operations. One specific priority project is known as 'Motorways of the Sea'. This concept is attempting to develop maritime-based supply chains in Europe that will be more sustainable, and should also be more commercially efficient, than traditional road-only transport. A sea-based network is expected to be developed by 2010, primarily covering routes in the Baltic, western European and Mediterranean regions. For example, major improvements are planned to the Rhine/Meuse–Main–Danube inland waterway system, and there are also proposed links between the Seine and the Scheldt to facilitate waterborne freight movements.

UK government

Strategic measures that aim to reduce the dominance of road haulage include land-use planning policies, investment in transport infrastructure provision and capability, and infrastructure charging policies. The Planning Bill seeks to establish an Infrastructure Planning Commission (IPC), which will evaluate nationally significant infrastructure projects in an attempt to address current concerns relating to the land-use planning process for the handling of strategic projects. Under the existing system, rail and water schemes that may offer broader environmental benefits have been rejected due to local concerns. For transport infrastructure, funding from the Transport Innovation Fund (TIF): Productivity has been awarded to upgrade key links in the rail network to allow the more efficient movement of high-cube containers by rail between major ports and their hinterland. Infrastructure charging policies are influenced by EU legislation but implemented by national governments, and mode choice can be influenced by decisions on road user charging and the level of rail track access charges, for example.

In addition, there are many practical initiatives supporting the transfer of freight to 'greener' modes. Two examples are identified here: freight mode shift grant support and the Freight Best Practice programme. From its Sustainable Distribution Fund, the Department for Transport provides three different types of grant: Freight Facilities Grants (FFG), the Rail

Environmental Benefit Procurement Scheme (REPS) and Waterborne Freight Grants (WFG). These grants work on the premise of gaining environmental and social benefits that arise from the use of rail or water transport rather than road. The Freight Best Practice programme has traditionally been focused on road freight transport but there is now increasing emphasis on providing guidance on multimodal transport solutions that offer environmental and commercial benefits. One such product of this expansion in the scope of the Best Practice scheme is a recent guide to *Choosing and Developing a Multi-modal Solution* (DfT, 2008a).

RAIL AND WATER INDUSTRIES

As has been seen, the rail and water industries typically have lower environmental impacts than road. It is important, therefore, not to make modal transfer from road more difficult through the introduction of policy measures, targets and regulations that make rail and water use more onerous. Equally, though, further improvements in environmental performance are desirable.

The privatized British rail freight operators have invested in more than 450 new Class 66 freight locomotives, replacing the vast majority of the older locomotive fleets inherited at the time of privatization. These new locomotives are more fuel efficient and less environmentally damaging than their predecessors. Indeed, the more recent batches of Class 66s to be delivered have significantly lower emissions of certain pollutants than those delivered earlier. According to Freightliner (2006), emissions of carbon monoxide are 95 per cent lower, hydrocarbons are reduced by 89 per cent and nitrous oxides are 38 per cent lower. Other measures that can be adopted to further reduce environmental impacts include shutting down locomotives between duties, which is more feasible with modern engines that readily restart, encouraging drivers to be more fuel efficient, and providing paths through the rail network that allow steady progress for freight trains rather than lots of acceleration, deceleration and idling in passing loops or yards. Steps are being taken to introduce sulphur-free diesel to replace the traditional gasoil used for rail freight operations. The Office of Rail Regulation has instructed Network Rail, the infrastructure manager, to accommodate a 30 per cent growth in freight services and a 25 per cent reduction in freight train delays caused by the infrastructure manager by 2014 (ORR, 2008b). Freight operating companies estimate that they can reduce their CO_2 emissions by between 15 and 21 per cent through the implementation of a series of planned initiatives, including auxiliary power units, the relocation of fuel points, in-cab driver advice systems and the adoption of best practice for drivers and ground staff (DfT, 2008b). Biofuels are also under trial. In the longer term, greater use of electric traction may provide further environmental benefits, particularly if renewable sources are used for electricity generation, though a significant shift in this direction would require investment in additional railway electrification. Such measures can assist with modal shift by improving the performance and reducing the cost of rail, and by projecting a more sustainable image for the industry in order to attract new custom. Organizations such as the Rail Freight Group and Freight on Rail also exist to lobby in favour of rail freight use and help to develop cost-effective and sustainable rail-based solutions.

The waterborne freight sector is more fragmented than the rail industry, but the Sea and Water organization was established in 2003 as a one-stop-shop to promote waterborne freight as a commercially viable and sustainable mode of transport. It argues for the development of a strategic waterway network, together with measures to encourage greater use of coastal and short-sea shipping. Initiatives intended to promote modal shift include raising awareness of the possibilities of using water-based transport within supply chains, educating potential users about the specific benefits to them of adopting water-based solutions, consolidating information provision about coastal shipping and inland waterway services, and promoting short-sea services to link the UK with the rest of Europe.

Freight users

There are a number of arguments that can be used to encourage freight users to consider the use of 'greener' transport modes:

- It may be possible for companies to generate cost savings at the same time as reducing environmental impacts, particularly at times of high oil prices since these affect overall road haulage costs proportionally more than those for the rail and water modes.
- Performance may be enhanced, leading to greater reliability and lower variability of freight operations. For example, the need for a rail network path gives greater certainty of journey time (and arrival time at the destination) than the 'turn-up-and-go' arrangements for accessing the road network, which is prone to unpredictable congestion effects.
- Companies may benefit from marketing their use of 'greener' modes, for example as part of their corporate social responsibility (CSR) strategy. This may give them a competitive advantage and lead to additional sales revenue.

- Organizations are becoming increasingly concerned about business continuity and supply chain resilience, particularly in relation to their ability to deal with risks that arise from external sources and over which they may have little control or ability to respond in the short term. In the context of freight activities there may be risks associated with using road exclusively, such as major fluctuations in fuel prices or an interruption to the availability of fuel. As such, forward-looking companies are attempting to 'future-proof' their supply chains by ensuring that they have a choice of modes available to them.

In general, companies may find that they are able to make improvements to the performance of their supply chain operations if they consider the role for 'greener' modes when making strategic changes to their logistical activities. Forcing the use of different modes into an otherwise unchanged supply chain is unlikely to be successful.

Good practice in achieving modal shift to rail and water

The multimodal guide referred to earlier in the chapter contains 35 case studies exemplifying the possibilities for using rail and water-based freight solutions (DfT, 2008a). These case studies feature logistics service providers, retailers, those involved in the movement of bulk products and container operators. Some of the key features of these case studies are highlighted below, using quantified benefits where possible.

Freight grants have been a fundamental ingredient in the success of a number of the flows that have shifted from road to 'greener' modes. In the retail sector, Asda uses shipping services to deliver products directly to its Import Deconsolidation Centre at Teesport in north-east England. The company uses rail for general merchandise and clothing products moving between the Midlands and central Scotland and also within Scotland. These initiatives are key to support Asda's target of reducing carbon emissions by 40 per cent by the end of 2010. Similarly, Tesco uses rail between the Midlands and central Scotland, saving more than 7 million road-kilometres per annum and leading to around 6,000 fewer tonnes of CO_2 being emitted each year. It has also begun to use the inland waterway system to move containerized wine that is imported through Liverpool and bottled in Manchester. The 60-kilometre barge transfer along the Manchester Ship Canal removes 50 lorry journeys each week. A similar barge operation moves grain between the terminal in the Port of Liverpool and flour mills in Manchester, saving more than 125 lorry movements per week.

Modal transfer has also occurred in the bulk sectors that traditionally make great use of rail and water, highlighting the fact that there is often scope for still greater use of 'greener' modes even where they already have significant market share. For example, significantly greater volumes of coal can now be handled at the port of Immingham as a result of investment in new equipment that can load 1,500 tonnes of coal into a train in 23 minutes. Investment in new equipment is fundamental to the success of many of these initiatives, and again grant funding is often available. Days Aggregates received grant funding to assist with the purchase of mobile handling equipment to unload aggregates at terminals in the London area. More strategically, as part of the expansion of the Haven ports, covering Felixstowe and Bathside Bay, Hutchison Ports has committed to investing in the rail network to enable more container trains to operate and to carry high-cube containers more efficiently. In this case, private finance is being used alongside government funding for the rail network, with the aim of increasing rail freight volumes from Felixstowe by 3 per cent each year.

Shipping lines have become increasingly involved in contracting train space on container services, in some cases even committing to regular full trainloads. Kuehne & Nagel uses a mix of dedicated trains, contracted space on multi-customer trains and spot hire of capacity, and is on record as stating that its container flows by rail are now more punctual than by road. Similarly, the development of rail services sponsored by logistics service providers has been one of the most successful developments in the past decade in attracting consumer products to rail. Logistics companies such as The Malcolm Group, Eddie Stobart Ltd and John G Russell (Transport) Ltd have become established players in the rail freight market, acting as consolidators to make up viable trainloads from their customer base and bridging the gap between the rail operators and freight customers. The Tesco rail freight example referred to earlier is an interesting example of supply chain cooperation, since Tesco provides 100 per cent of the northbound volume and 90 per cent of the southbound volume, with freight for other Eddie Stobart customers helping to fill the remaining southbound capacity. In the shipping sector, a number of container shipping lines such as Feederlink BV, OOCL and K-Line have developed short-sea and coastal services that move containers to ports that are closer to their ultimate destination, rather than relying on land-based onward movement from the major ports.

CONCLUSIONS

This chapter has outlined the reasons behind the desire for an increase in the share of freight being moved by rail and water, given that these modes are typically 'greener' than road haulage. The policy framework has developed over the last decade to reflect the growing concern about the environmental impacts of freight transport activity, primarily relating to climate change but also with respect to local air quality issues. There are some signs of success in encouraging the use of alternatives to road, particularly with the resurgent rail freight sector but also with new waterborne flows. There is potential for considerably greater transfer of freight from road, but progress is likely to be limited until many of the new EU and UK policy initiatives under discussion are implemented. It seems unlikely that CO_2 emissions targets will be met without more concerted action to achieve modal shift, given the ongoing reliance on fossil fuels in the road haulage sector.

REFERENCES

Department for Transport (DfT) (2007a) *Transport Statistics Great Britain 2007*, DfT, London

DfT (2007b) *Transport Trends 2007 Edition*, DfT, London

DfT (2008a) *Choosing and Developing a Multi-modal Solution*, DfT, London

DfT (2008b) *Carbon Pathways Analysis: Informing development of a carbon reduction strategy for the transport sector*, DfT, London

European Commission (2006) *European Freight Transport: Modern logistics solutions for competitiveness and sustainability*, Directorate-General for Energy and Transport, European Commission, Brussels

European Commission (2007) *Freight Transport Logistics Action Plan*, COM(2007) 607 final, European Commission, Brussels

Freightliner (2006) *Freightliner Limited/Freightliner Heavy Haul Limited Response to ORR Consultation Document on Sustainable Development*, Freightliner, London

McKinnon, AC (2007) *CO_2 Emissions from Freight Transport in the UK*, Report prepared for the Climate Change Working Group of the Commission for Integrated Transport, Edinburgh

Office of Rail Regulation (ORR) (2008a) *National Rail Trends 2007–08 Yearbook*, ORR, London

ORR (2008b) *Periodic Review 2008: Determination of Network Rail's outputs and funding for 2009–14*, ORR, London

Rail Safety and Standards Board (RSSB) (2007) *The Case for Rail 2007: The first sustainable development review of the mainline railways of Great Britain*, RSSB, London

Woodburn, AG (2008), An investigation of container train service provision and load factors in Great Britain, unpublished paper presented at the 40th Annual UTSG Conference, Southampton, 3–5 January 2008, Department of Transport Studies, University of Westminster, London

7

Development of greener vehicles, aircraft and ships

Alan McKinnon, Julian Allen and Allan Woodburn

INTRODUCTION

Many of the technical improvements that have been made to freight vehicles and vessels over the past few decades have reduced their environmental impact. Some of these improvements have been required to meet tightening environmental legislation, particularly on air pollution and noise. Others have been motivated mainly by commercial pressures to improve energy efficiency and vehicle loading, though they have indirectly yielded environmental benefits. The potential for future advances in vehicle technology to reduce environmental impacts further partly depends on the timescale. The Intergovernmental Panel on Climate Change notes that, as far as greenhouse gas (GHG) emissions from transport are concerned, 'the most promising strategy for the near term is incremental improvements in current vehicle techniques' (Kahn Ribeiro et al, 2007: 335). In the longer term, however, it is likely that freight vehicles will be more radically redesigned, primarily to cut their fuel consumption and CO_2 emissions.

In this chapter, we examine the extent to which new technology will contribute to the greening of companies' freight transport operations. It adopts a cross-modal perspective, considering the opportunities for technologically improving the environmental performance of trucks, vans, freight trains, ships and planes. While there is a strong commitment to decarbonize freight transport across all modes, individual modes can have particular environmental priorities. The shipping industry, for example, is under strong pressure to reduce sulphur emissions, while the use of ultra-low-sulphur fuels is now the norm in the trucking systems of developed countries. Research and development efforts can therefore have a different focus in particular sectors of the freight market.

Generally speaking, advances in vehicle technology can reduce the environmental impact of freight transport in three ways:

- increasing vehicle carrying capacity;
- improving energy efficiency;
- reducing externalities.

These advances are not always mutually reinforcing in environmental terms. For example, redesigning engines to reduce NOx emissions usually impairs fuel efficiency and increases emissions of CO_2. The potential for exploiting these advances also varies between modes. Regulations governing the size and weight of road vehicles tightly limit the scope for enlarging trucks, while in the air and maritime sectors capacity limits are set mainly by infrastructure, with the maxima well above the present levels. The duration of the vehicle/vessel replacement cycle also varies widely, from a few years in the case of vans to tens of years in the case of ships and locomotives. The economics and practicality of retrofitting new technology is similarly variable. As a result, technical innovations are adopted more rapidly in some freight modes than in others. Over a 20–30 year time horizon, however, the development and diffusion of clean vehicle technology is likely to reduce substantially the externalities from all the main modes of freight transport.

ROAD FREIGHT

Trucks

Carrying capacity

As discussed in Chapters 9 and 17, governments impose limits on the maximum gross weight and dimensions of vehicles. When these limits are relaxed, vehicles can be redesigned to maximize the resulting gain in carrying capacity. There has been much discussion in Europe and North America in recent years about the costs and benefits of allowing trucks to get longer and heavier, possibly raising the limits to those prevailing in Sweden and Finland and some US states. There are many variants of longer and heavier vehicles (LHVs) currently in operation in these countries and states. Liberalization of vehicle size and weight limits elsewhere would simply open other road haulage markets to existing types of LHV, probably with some customization of the equipment to regulatory, infrastructural and business requirements in particular areas.

In the UK, where there is no legal limit on vehicle height and clearances at most bridges and tunnels can accommodate trailers up to five metres high, there has been a proliferation of double-deck trailer designs. The past 20 years have seen extensive development of double-deck trailer technology, with many different variants produced for particular logistics applications. Arguably the main advance over the next few years will not be to the vehicles themselves, but rather to the external lifting equipment at reception bays. The installation of such equipment removes the need for expensive hydraulic lifts for mobile decks on the vehicles, which can carry a payload penalty of several tonnes. The refinement and diffusion of these external lifts could allow companies to achieve better utilization of double-deck trailers with consequent benefits for the environment.

The weight-carrying capacity of a truck can also be increased by reducing its tare (or empty) weight. The use of less dense materials in truck chassis can significantly cut the tare weight. According to the European Aluminium Association (2006), switching from steel to aluminium could cut around 3,000 kg from the weight of an articulated lorry. This would permit an 11.5 per cent increase in the payload of a vehicle registered at a gross weight of 40 tonnes. Research in the United States, however, suggests that the fuel savings from reducing tare weight are relatively modest, at roughly 0.5 per cent per 1,000 lbs (0.45 tonnes) (Southwest Research Institute, 2008; Greszler, 2009). Reference is also made in Chapter 11 to the 'light-weighting' of vehicles.

One of the major challenges for designers will be to maintain or even increase vehicle carrying capacity while improving the aerodynamic profiling of the truck. There is a trade-off between the degree of streamlining and the cubic capacity of the vehicle. Increasing the latter can reduce fuel efficiency, expressed on a vehicle-km per litre basis, but the more important energy metric of load-kms per litre is increased. Some truck manufacturers now argue that to maintain carrying capacity within a new generation of very low-drag vehicles it will be necessary to extend the legal length limit. The issue of aerodynamic profiling is discussed below.

Energy efficiency

The US Department for Energy expects that about two-thirds of future fuel efficiency gains in trucks will come from improvements to engine and exhaust systems. The largest gains are likely to come from:

- Use of turbocharging (involving the recycling of heat from exhaust gases) to make possible the downsizing of engines: allowing trucks to achieve the same power rating with lower fuel consumption.
- Application of hybrid technology to rigid lorries engaged in local delivery/collection operations. Research by Volvo suggests that combining diesel and battery power could ultimately improve fuel economy by 50 per cent. The limited range and stop–start nature of these operations make them particularly suited to the use of hybrids. Most of the main European truck manufacturers are currently developing hybrid rigids. Because of the limited range and relatively heavy weight of the battery and the greater fuel efficiency of diesel engines operating at constant speeds over long distances, hybrid technology is likely to have very limited application in long haul operations.
- Improving the energy efficiency of auxiliary equipment on the vehicle, such as pumps, fans, air compressor, heating, air conditioning and power steering. The installation of separate power systems for this equipment can also save fuel, as it decouples their operation from that of the main vehicle engine. Separate batteries can be used for this purpose. The US Department for Energy has indicated that fuel efficiency gains of 50 per cent can be achieved by overhauling these auxiliary systems.
- Technology can also be used to correct poor driving practice. For example, anti-idling devices automatically switch off the engine when the vehicle is not moving. Automatic gearboxes can be adjusted to ensure that gear changes minimize fuel consumption.

Chapter 11 discusses the fuel savings that can be achieved by applying currently available technology to aerodynamic profiling. For the foreseeable future, most of the savings from improved streamlining of vehicles are likely to come from wider diffusion of existing technology. In the longer term, however, vehicle manufacturers will adopt radically new truck designs that will yield step-change improvements in energy efficiency. One feature of these designs will be their integration of the tractor and trailer to permit optimal profiling of the complete vehicle and largely eliminate the turbulence created in the gap behind the tractor unit. It is predicted that it will be possible to reduce the coefficient of drag (CD) on articulated trucks from the current average of around 0.57 to the 0.30 achieved by some types of car. This has been achieved by a new 'concept vehicle' developed by MAN called the 'Dolphin' (*Commercial Motor*, 8 January 2009).

The so-called 'next generation' tyres should also be able to raise fuel efficiency by 3.5–8 per cent by reducing 'rolling resistance'. Improvements of this magnitude will only be achieved on motorway running, however.

Automatic pressure-monitoring and inflation of tyres will also yield significant fuel savings and improve tyre wear.

US research has assessed the overall prospects for improving the fuel efficiency of new heavy trucks with gross weights in excess of 25 tonnes (National Academies of Science, 2007). This suggests that a 36 per cent increase is possible (Figure 7.1). Consultation with major European truck manufacturers suggests that there is less potential to improve the energy efficiency of new trucks sold in Europe.

In Japan, truck manufacturers are now required to meet tightening fuel economy standards for new vehicles. The Japanese government's Energy Conservation Law made provision for the adoption of a 'top runner' fuel efficiency standard for trucks. The 'top runner' concept aims to make the best-in-class performance the average by a target date. For trucks this will entail improving the average fuel efficiency from 6.30 kms/litre in 2002 to 7.09 kms/litre in 2015 (Ministry of Economy, Trade and Industry, 2008). Different target improvements have been specified for different vehicle weight classes. Tax incentives are being used to promote this move to higher efficiency standards. The purchase tax is being reduced by 1–2 per cent for new vehicles meeting the target fuel efficiency standards. Both the US government and the European Commission are considering the adoption of fuel economy standards for trucks, though the diversity of vehicles types and the combination of different types of auxiliary equipment on a single vehicle will make this difficult. Individual truck manufacturers have much less control over the fuel performance of the final lorry than their counterparts in the car sector.

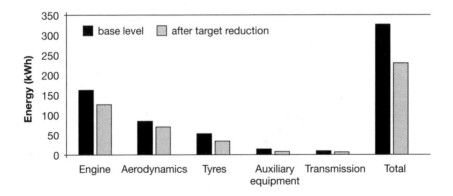

Figure 7.1   Target reductions in the energy consumption of heavy trucks in the United States

Source: National Academies of Science (2007).

Reducing externalities

A distinction can be made between externalities that are fuel-related (mainly air pollution and greenhouse gas emissions) and those with little or no relationship to energy use (accidents, noise, vibration etc). Improving fuel efficiency reduces the former but not the latter. These fuel-related externalities can also be reduced independently of fuel consumption in three ways:

- Altering the nature of the fuel/energy source: switching from conventional diesel to alternative fuels, such as compressed natural gas or biodiesel mixes, can significantly reduce emissions of particular gases per litre of fuel consumed, though allowance must be made for the lower calorific content of some fuels. The use of alternative fuels is discussed in Chapter 15. Existing trucks can be run on low per-cent mixes of biodiesel with conventional diesel, though high mixes or full substitution of biodiesel generally requires engine modification. The 'electrification' of trucks through the use of batteries either, as the sole or a supplementary power source, not only cuts diesel fuel consumption; it can also reduce externalities per unit of energy consumed. The planned 'decarbonization' of the electricity supply will indirectly reduce the carbon footprint of road freight operations. Reliance on battery power will also virtually eliminate local air pollution by road freight vehicles.
- Engine redesign: tightening emission standards have forced vehicle manufacturers to radically redesign truck engines over the past 20 years. Future 'cleaning' of diesel engines is likely to be marginal by comparison with what has so far been achieved, particularly if increased priority is given to minimizing fuel consumption and CO_2 emissions. As discussed in Chapter 11, alternative approaches to emission reduction have been adopted by vehicle manufacturers in recent years: exhaust gas recirculation (EGR) and selective catalytic reduction (SCR). Views differ on which of these systems will offer the more cost-effective means of meeting future emission standards. Proponents of EGR argue that, in the SCR system, downward pressure on NOx levels requires the addition of greater quantities of the AdBlue chemical at higher economic and environmental cost. To comply with the Euro 6 emission standard by 2013, however, it may be necessary to combine the EGR and SCR technologies, particularly if tighter CO_2 emission targets are to be met.
- Exhaust system: particulate traps are currently used in diesel exhausts to remove PM10s. The amount of particulate matter emitted by the engine depends on the temperature and completeness of the combustion process. In the EGR system, combustion temperatures

are lower, more particulate matter is emitted and, as a consequence, particulate filters must be installed to reduce PM10 emissions to the regulated levels. Such filters are not required by SCR systems. The future development of truck exhausts will partly depend therefore on the evolution of EGR and SCR systems, independently or in combination.

Other non-fuel-related improvements to the environmental performance of trucks are likely to be incremental. For example, the combination of quieter engines, air brake silencers, internal load restraint systems, low rolling resistance tyres, quieter refrigeration units and cab sound-proofing offers the potential for further noise reduction.

Vans

Carrying capacity

Unlike trucks, the maximum permissible weight of vans does not change over time as a result of governments relaxing restrictions on vehicle weights. Instead the weight limit for vans (also referred to as light goods vehicles, or light commercial vehicles) is fixed, as it defines whether the vehicle is a van or truck, and thereby the regulations that the vehicle and its owner and driver are subject to. In many countries the maximum permissible gross weight for vans is 3.5 tonnes (it is important to note that some vehicles are manufactured with van bodies with a gross weight of over 3.5 tonnes but these vehicles are treated as trucks in terms of driving and operational regulations).

Vehicle manufacturers produce a wide range of styles, weights and sizes of vans. These can be categorized by gross weight as small (car-derived/micro), medium and heavy vans. Table 7.1 provides a summary of the typical attributes of these three categories of van.

Vans have a far wider range of uses than trucks. In fact, only around one van trip in five actually carries freight. Survey work in Britain suggested that in the period 2002–03 commuting accounted for 39 per cent of all van journeys, servicing for 23 per cent, goods collection and delivery for 22 per cent, and personal journeys for 16 per cent (Allen and Browne, 2008).

This wide range of journey purposes means that van operators have extremely varying requirements in terms of load space, payload, vehicle length, vehicle height and vehicle body requirements, and put the load area of the vehicle to differing uses. For example, in the case of service activities often only tools, equipment and parts are transported (which may not be particularly heavy) and vans may be equipped with sophisticated racking systems for these purposes. In some operations drivers

Table 7.1 Summary of the typical size, weight and fuel efficiency attributes of vans

	Small vans	Medium vans	Heavy vans
Typical gross weight (tonnes)	Up to 1.8	1.8–2.6	2.6–3.5
Typical payload (tonnes)	0.4–0.8	0.8–1.2	1.2–2.0
Typical load space (m³)	1–3	4–8	7–17
Typical fuel consumption (mpg) (Litres per 100 km)	40–55 (7.1–5.1)	30–40 (9.4–7.1)	20–35 (14.1–8.1)
Example models	Vauxhall Corsa Citroen Berlingo Renault Kangoo	Ford Transit VW Transporter Renault Trafic	Ford Transit Mercedes Sprinter Iveco Daily

Source: Author's own estimates.

will require space to work inside the vehicle (for example, an electrician having to carry out preparatory work inside the vehicle, or a delivery driver sorting goods in a parcel delivery operation). As a result, the average lading factor (in terms of weight and volume) for the van population is likely to be lower than for trucks. In Britain, the Company Van Survey that was conducted between 2003–2005 showed that, overall, vans were more than half full (by volume) for only 34 per cent of total vehicle kilometres travelled (DfT, 2008a).

Even though vans have a maximum gross weight of 3.5 tonnes, the average gross weight and payload of vans can increase if operators purchase a greater proportion of heavier vans over time. This has been happening in the van sector. Analysis of the vans sold in Britain between 1990 and 2007 suggests that the average gross weight and payload of vans has increased by 10–20 per cent over this period.[1]

Regulations have not prevented manufacturers from increasing the length of vans. A growing proportion of the medium and heavy vans are being produced with long wheel bases (the wheel base is the distance between the front and rear wheels). The longer the wheel base, the bigger the load space in the vehicle. Vans with long wheel bases are often between ½–1½ metres longer than their medium wheel base equivalents. Assuming that the width and height of these vehicles are the same, the long wheel base varieties have approximately an additional 20 per cent load space for every extra ½ metre of length compared with shorter vans, with little or no difference in gross weight.[2]

As with trucks, van manufacturers try to use lighter materials (for the chassis, body and internal racking systems) where possible to reduce the tare weight of the vehicle and hence maximize payload.

Energy efficiency

Up until the 1990s the majority of vans in Europe were powered by petrol. However, diesel engines became increasingly popular among van operators as manufacturers overcame the problems of vehicle speed and noise associated with early diesel vans. In addition, diesel engines have greater fuel efficiency, are hardwearing and, due to technological advances such as fuel injection and turbo-charging, can now produce much greater power and torque (Momenta, 2006). It is estimated that diesel vehicles have a fuel economy advantage of approximately 20 to 40 per cent over petrol vehicles (EIA, 2009). In Britain, for example, 69 per cent of all vans were diesel-powered in 1998, but by 2007 this had risen to 92 per cent (DfT, 2008b). By contrast, in America diesel-powered vans have accounted for, on average, only about 4 per cent of new van sales each year for the past 20 years (EIA, 2009). The greater penetration of diesel vans in Europe is likely to be due to factors such as higher average fuel prices, more favourable tax policies for diesel, and less stringent emissions standards (which permit higher levels of NOx and PM in Europe than in America) (EIA, 2009).

As concern grows about fossil fuel consumption and emissions, leading to new regulations and tax regimes, it is likely that greater use will be made of new technologies that help to improve the fuel efficiency of vans such as hybrid vehicles, devices to reduce engine idling, and speed limiters (all of which are described in relation to trucks in the section on 'Energy efficiency'). Hybrid vehicles and anti-idling technologies have particular relevance to vans due to the high proportion of operations carried out in urban areas, involving stop–start traffic conditions and, in some cases, multi-drop delivery rounds.

It is also likely that further significant improvements in the fuel efficiency of diesel engines are possible through advanced turbo-charged engines with direct injection technologies. A senior director of a major van manufacturer was recently quoted as saying that they expected 'that small, highly efficient diesels capable of 100 miles per gallon will become commonplace' (Anon, 2008a).

A sizeable number of vans make use of auxiliary equipment including refrigeration, air conditioning, heating, pumps, fans and power steering.

As with trucks, the use of power sources other than the vehicle engine to fuel this equipment has the potential to reduce total fossil fuel consumption.

Aerodynamic profiling is generally less important for vans than trucks owing to their smaller sizes and because a greater proportion of van activity takes place in urban areas at lower average speeds. It has, nevertheless, been improving, as demonstrated by the streamlining of the Ford Transit van (Storey and Boyes, 2003).

Externalities

Euro emission standards apply to vans as well as trucks and are gradually tightening. Although CO_2 emissions are not part of these 'Euro' standards, this is about to change. The European Commission is planning to impose limits on the amount of CO_2 emitted by new vans, restricting it to 175 g/km CO_2 by 2012 and 160 g/km CO_2 by 2015 (European Commission, 2008). In the UK, vehicle manufacturers have been required to test the fuel consumption and CO_2 emissions of their vans since the start of 2008, but do not initially have to publish this data (Anon, 2008b). However, since June 2009 the CO_2 emissions and fuel consumption data for new van models on the UK market has been made available via an online database compiled by the Vehicle Certification Agency, Society of Motor Manufacturers and Traders, and Department for Transport (DfT, 2009). Producing this data is complicated by the number of van variants manufactured, the range of body types and the effect of vehicle lading, but once it is available this data should help operators to better include fuel efficiency and CO_2 considerations in their vehicle purchasing decisions. A recent report suggests that typical CO_2 emissions from vans have fallen from approximately 320 g/km in 1980 to 220 g/km in 2008 (based on data supplied by Ford) (VDA, 2008).

On a 'well-to-wheel' basis, diesel vans emit 15 per cent less greenhouse gas than petrol vans (EIA, 2009). A further 20–25 per cent greenhouse gas reduction can be achieved by switching to petrol or diesel-powered hybrid electric vehicles. It is important to note that diesel engines emit less CO and HC but relatively more NOx and PM than petrol engines.

A wide range of alternatively fuelled vans is available (including liquefied petroleum gas, compressed natural gas, biofuels, electric and hybrid vehicles). As well as the emissions benefits of these alternative fuels, electric vehicles also cut noise levels. However, the use of these alternative fuel vans is discouraged by their higher purchase price, higher operating costs, limited range and lack of refuelling infrastructure. Consequently, the market penetration of these vans has remained low;

for example, fewer than 1 per cent of vans in Britain are currently alternatively fuelled (DfT, 2008b).

Proximity sensors and additional mirrors are being offered by manufacturers to enhance van safety and reduce collisions, especially in urban
environments. Other equipment such as rear-view cameras are also being
developed to aid driver awareness. The Electronic Stability Program
(ESP), a computerized technology that detects and prevents skids, is
also available from some van manufacturers. At the same time, tyre grip
is also being enhanced, especially for wet weather conditions, thereby
reducing accident risk (Banner, 2008).

These improvements to the design of new vans make them safer and
more environmentally sustainable, but some of these benefits are eroded
by poor maintenance and inefficient operation. Official data in Britain,
for example, show that a significant proportion of vans are not well
maintained by operators (proportionately more vans failed their annual
vehicle test than any other vehicle type in 2007/08) and are regularly
overloaded (proportionately more often than trucks) (VOSA, 2008). These
can be important factors in vehicle accident involvement.

RAIL FREIGHT OPERATIONS

Carrying capacity

The key variables influencing train carrying capacity are weight and
length. For heavy flows, such as coal and steel, weight tends to be the
constraining factor, while for lighter weight flows, such as intermodal,
train length is more likely to constrain the carrying capacity. The EU is
developing policies to improve rail infrastructure capability, in terms of
train length, axle loads, loading gauge (ie maximum vehicle dimensions)
and maximum speed, to allow greater carrying capacity (European
Commission, 2007).

Across Europe, traditional two-axle wagons have gradually been
replaced by bogie wagons, which tend to offer a higher payload for a
given train length, as well as being less damaging to the rail infrastructure.
These new bogie wagons are far larger than those that they have replaced.
The bogie wagons now widely used for coal flows in Britain also offer a
slightly greater payload-to-tare-weight ratio per wagon and have led to
greater train payloads overall. On a selective basis, additional wagons
have been added to increase train payloads where route conditions allow.
Freightliner, Britain's biggest intermodal rail freight operator, placed
an order in 2007 from General Electric for a fleet of new locomotives
(Freightliner, 2007), which at 3,700 hp will be more powerful than the

existing 3,300 hp Class 66 design. This will make it possible to operate longer, heavier trains in situations where locomotive power currently constrains the maximum train weight. In North America, double stacking of containers is an efficient means of carrying a greater volume for a given train length, but this is not a realistic option in Europe due to the more restricted loading gauge. Instead, measures to increase train lengths are being examined, often requiring changes to signalling systems, passing loops and terminals. In the Freight Route Utilisation Strategy for the British rail network, measures to allow 775 or 900-metre-long trains are identified (Network Rail, 2007). In many cases, though, trains are currently loaded to neither their maximum weight nor length due to flow characteristics or operational inefficiencies, so potential often exists to make improvements within the existing weight and length limits.

Energy efficiency

The rail industry has gradually been improving its knowledge of energy use, both of electricity and diesel fuel, but has generally lagged behind the road haulage sector in achieving significant improvements. It is likely that there will be a greater focus on the energy efficiency for rail freight in the future, partly in response to increasing energy costs but also to preserve, and if possible reinforce, rail's environmental advantage over road in the movement of goods. According to *The Case for Rail* (RSSB, 2007), a range of initiatives to improve energy efficiency have been adopted by the British rail freight industry. For example, diesel engine shutdown when stationary for 15 minutes or more has reduced fuel consumption by 3–5 per cent. Fuel conservation may also result from better network operations management (eg optimization of train paths to reduce stop–start and acceleration–deceleration procedures) or reduced operating speeds, though this may result in longer journey times. Fuel consumption is affected by aerodynamic drag, particularly at speeds of around 60 mph (100 kph) or more. For intermodal trains in particular, drag can be reduced considerably by optimizing train loading to reduce the number and size of gaps between containers (Stehly, 2009).

For diesel operation, further improvements to engine design are achievable. For example, it is claimed that the previously mentioned General Electric locomotives under construction for Freightliner will have a 10 per cent fuel economy benefit. Regenerative braking is increasingly being adopted for electric traction, where electricity can be fed back either into the power supply system for use by other trains or returned to the National Grid to be used elsewhere. In addition, human factors are recognized as being important, with increasing attention being devoted to driver training and monitoring. It is likely that increased use will be made of computer simulators to train staff to drive locomotives more energy efficiently and safely (Ward et al, 2004)

Reducing externalities

In sharp contrast to several other European countries, the overwhelming majority of rail freight in Britain (around 90 per cent) is hauled by diesel locomotive. Per tonne-kilometre, diesel-powered rail engines typically generate far fewer externalities than road goods vehicles (RSSB, 2007). The exception, where road currently outperforms rail, is in sulphur dioxide. Rail is also considerably safer than road. As discussed in Chapter 6, freight transport externalities can therefore be reduced by effecting modal shift from road to rail. That said, as with energy efficiency, the road haulage sector has tended to implement measures to reduce externalities per tonne-kilometre at a faster rate than rail (largely in response to tightening regulatory controls on exhaust emissions). Considerable potential still exists to raise environment standards in the rail freight industry. Potential measures to reduce rail freight externalities include:

- Maximizing the use of electric traction: this makes zero carbon emission freight possible if electricity production is from non-fossil fuel sources. Currently, though, roughly three-quarters of electricity production in Britain is from fossil fuels (DBERR, 2007). Electric traction also has the benefit of removing air pollution at the point of use, and any pollutants arising from electricity generation may more easily be tackled at source.
- Continuing to invest in low-emission diesel locomotives where electric traction is not viable: almost the entire British diesel rail freight fleet has been replaced since privatization in the mid-1990s, leading to considerable reductions in externalities. The EU has introduced Non-Road Mobile Machinery (NRMM) legislation covering many gaseous and particulate pollutants, and the more recent batches of Class 66 locomotives are compliant.
- Low sulphur fuel: EU legislation under the Fuel Quality Directive is tackling rail's sulphur dioxide emissions, with standards for the sulphur content of fuel having been implemented in 2008. Future legislation, taking effect in 2012, is likely to result in dramatic reductions in sulphur emissions from rail, though at the expense of fuel efficiency and CO_2 emissions. The taxation system does not always favour the use of less polluting fuels by rail freight operators, so operators could be further incentivized to switch to cleaner fuels through taxation changes.

- Noise and vibration problems can be ameliorated through quieter engine technology, track lubrication, new braking systems and other improvements.

Across Europe, market liberalization has increased the number of organizations involved in infrastructure and service provision. The resulting fragmentation of responsibilities and actions makes it more challenging to implement large-scale initiatives to reduce externalities, creating a need for industry leadership. It is hoped that the Sustainable Rail Programme (RSSB, 2007) being developed for the British rail network will succeed in adopting a holistic approach, at least at the national level. For example, this may lead in time to more use of electric traction, countering the recent emphasis by individual freight operators on diesel engines due to their ability to be used network-wide.

AIR FREIGHT

Air cargo trends

The movement of freight by air is more damaging to the environment, on a tonne-km basis, than by any of the surface freight modes (see Chapter 2). One might, therefore, expect that if companies were serious about greening their logistics systems, future demand for air cargo services would be likely to drop. On the contrary, until recently the growth of air cargo tonne-kms was predicted to accelerate over the next 20 years, increasing from an average annual growth of 4.6 per cent between 1996 and 2006 to 5.8 per cent per annum between 2007 and 2026 (Boeing, 2008; Airbus, 2008). The sharp drop in global airfreight volumes during the current recession (down 22.6 per cent between December 2007 and December 2008 (Millward, 2009)) is causing a short-term deviation from this forecast trend. It was estimated that to accommodate the tripling of air freight traffic over the next 20 years, the global fleet of air freighters would have to expand by 150 per cent (Airbus, 2008). Assuming that the rate of airfreight growth returns to its pre-recession level, there will be a pressing need to cut externalities per tonne-km for air freight to mitigate the effects of this huge future increase in freight volumes. For aviation as a whole, it is argued that supply-side developments to cut emissions per tonne- or passenger-km will be more than offset by the predicted growth in traffic volumes (MacIntosh and Wallace, 2009).

Past environmental trends in aviation provide some grounds for optimism. Over the past 40 years the average fuel efficiency of commercial aircraft has risen by 70 per cent, while aircraft coming into service today are around 75 per cent quieter than their predecessors of 20 years ago (ICAO, 2007). Most of the environmental gains have come from improved engine technology, in particular the use of high bypass ratio turbofans and low emission annular combustion systems. The Advisory Council for Aeronautics Research in Europe asserts, however, that 'although there is scope for further improvement by evolving existing technologies, further substantial improvement will require the introduction of breakthrough technologies and concepts into everyday service' (ACARE, 2008: 61). The development, implementation and diffusion of these new technologies is likely to be relatively slow as aviation is essentially 'a long life cycle industry' (ICAO, 2007). It can take 10 years to design a new aircraft, which will then be manufactured for around 20–30 years, with each aircraft having a typical lifespan of 25–40 years. The investment cycle can be as long as 55 years (Committee on Climate Change, 2008). The uptake of new, more environmentally friendly technology is even slower in those sectors of the air freight market that use former passenger aircraft converted into freighters at a later stage in their life. It is estimated that by 2026, approximately two-thirds of the global fleet of 4,200 dedicated air-cargo aircraft will be converted from passenger aircraft. It is also predicted that 27 per cent of the airfreighter fleet of 2006 will still be in service in 2026 (Airbus, 2008).

Just over 40 per cent of air cargo tonne-kms are moved in the belly-holds of passenger aircraft (Airbus, 2008). This means that, to a substantial extent, environmental improvements in aviation are shared between passengers and freight and progress at a similar rate. It also has implications for the allocation of responsibility for externalities between people and goods travelling on the same aircraft, an issue that has yet to be satisfactorily resolved.

Increases in capacity

As with other transport modes, load consolidation in aviation reduces energy consumption and externalities per tonne-km. As passenger aircraft have increased in size, their belly-hold capacity has also grown, particularly on long haul routes, increasing the average air cargo payload. The development of new freighter versions of these aircraft and the conversion of these larger aircraft to cargo operations also expands carrying capacity. An Airbus 380 freighter, for example, will carry a maximum payload of 150 tonnes by comparison with a maximum of 124 tonnes on a 747–400 (Hanson and Guiliano, 2004). The belly-hold capacity of new passenger aircraft is also expanding. The Boeing 787 Dreamliner, for instance, will have 47 per cent more revenue-earning cargo space than previous aircraft of its type. Across the airfreighter fleet as a whole it is anticipated that the average payload weight will increase by a fifth, from 52.9 to 64.1 tonnes between 2006 and 2026 (Airbus, 2008). Future air cargo payloads will not only be a function of the carrying capacity of the aircraft, however. As this mode provides a rapid and reliable service for time-sensitive products, future capacity utilization will partly depend on the prevalence and rigidity of JIT scheduling. The fastest-growing sector of the air freight market has been that held by the integrated express carriers that cater mainly for time-critical consignments and often have to sacrifice load efficiency for service quality.

Improvements in fuel efficiency

The three main sources of fuel efficiency gains in aviation are the airframe, the engine and the air traffic management system (ATM):

- Airframe: this determines the weight and aerodynamic efficiency (or streamlining) of the aircraft. Aircraft with a given carrying capacity can be made lighter by increased use of special alloys and composites. The A320, which entered commercial service in 1988, comprised roughly 12 per cent composites, while the A380 introduced in 2008 had just over twice this percentage. Half of the primary structure of the new Boeing 787 Dreamliner will be made of composite materials. The switch to 'fly-by-wire', involving the replacement of hydraulic controls by wiring, has also reduced aircraft weight. Advances in aerodynamic profiling are also improving fuel efficiency, as well exemplified by the Dreamliner, which overall will be 20 per cent more fuel efficient than current aircraft of its type and capacity. Retrofitting 'winglets' to the ends of aircraft wings can also improve fuel efficiency by an average of 4–6 per cent (*Flight International*, 27 June 2008). Research for the Committee on Climate Change (2008: 316) suggests that 'evolutionary changes in airframe technology could conceivably deliver 20–30 per cent improvement in the efficiency of new aircraft' in 2025 as compared to 2006.
- Engine technology: ACARE (2008) estimated that the application of a series of engine-related technologies could cut the specific fuel consumption (SFC) of new aircraft by around 10 per cent between 2000 and 2010, with further 5–10 per cent savings over the following decade. This is broadly in line with estimates quoted by the Committee on Climate Change (2008: 316), which indicate that 'evolutionary changes in engine technology could deliver another 15–20 per cent improvement' in fuel efficiency between 2006 and 2025.

- Air traffic management: this includes the airborne routing of the aircraft as well as its taxiing on the ground. For example, following an IATA (2004) initiative, improvements have been made to 350 air routes worldwide, saving a total of 6 million tonnes of CO_2 in 2006 (ICAO, 2007). Routings through congested European airspace still carry a significant environmental, as well as economic, penalty, however. In 2007, such congestion added an average of approximately 50 km to the length of each flight (EUROCONTROL, 2008). This improved very slightly in 2008. An influential report by the IPCC (Penner et al, 1999) on the links between aviation and climate change indicated that an overhaul of the air traffic control (ATC) system could cut CO_2 emissions from aviation by up to 18 per cent. Thomas (2008: 68), however, argues that as much of the world 'languishes under a mountain of bureaucracy' this forecast for fuel savings 'in a perfect ATC world is a distant goal'. ACARE (2008: 64) estimates that 'between 13 per cent and 15 per cent of fuel is consumed through excessive holding either on-ground or in-flight and through indirect routing and non-optimal flight profiles'. It has set a target of 5–10 per cent fuel savings from 'radical changes to the air traffic management system'. These changes will be at least as dependent on international collaboration as on technological upgrading of ATM systems. By far the most important initiative in Europe to improve air traffic management is 'SESAR'. This is the European ATM modernization programme, which runs through to 2020. It seeks to combine technological, economic and regulatory measures and will use the Single European Sky legislation to synchronize the plans and actions of the different stakeholders and dedicate the necessary resources for improvements, in both airborne and ground systems. Planning is still at a relatively high level, with, as yet, very few specific references to freight.

Reduction in externalities

The main environmental impacts of aviation are greenhouse gas (GHG) emissions (mainly CO_2 and water vapour), nitrogen oxides (NOx) and noise. Per passenger and tonne-km, these externalities have been declining. Reference was made earlier to improvements in fuel efficiency and these correlate closely with GHG intensity. Over the past 15 years, NOx emissions from aircraft have come down by 50 per cent, while the number of people exposed to aircraft noise has declined by 35 per cent (Anon, 2009). Efforts are being made to maintain, and if possible accelerate, this rate of improvement.

ACARE (2008) has set four environmental targets for aviation by 2020. It wants the industry to reduce:

- fuel consumption and CO_2 emissions (per passenger/tonne carried) by 50 per cent;
- perceived external noise by 50 per cent;
- NOx emissions by 80 per cent;
- environmental impact of manufacture, maintenance and disposal of aircraft and parts.

ACARE (2008) has estimated the potential contribution of the airframe, engine and ATM to the targeted reduction in CO_2 at, respectively, 20–25 per cent, 15–20 per cent and 5–10 per cent (other estimates have been produced by other bodies).

Several of these environmental goals are in conflict, however. For example, NOx emissions can be reduced by lowering thrust levels at take-off, but this can make it more difficult to comply with local noise regulations (Somerville, 2003). The high engine temperatures required to minimize fuel consumption and hence CO_2, CO and hydrocarbon emissions promote the formation of NOx. One technical challenge, in aviation as in other modes, is therefore to minimize the fuel penalty associated with NOx reductions.

The electrification, using renewal or nuclear power, which offers large potential for the decarbonization of land-based freight modes, will not be a feasible option for aviation. The main requirement of an aviation power source is a very high ratio of energy to weight (ie energy density). There is no prospect, however, of the energy density of batteries coming anywhere close to that of kerosene in the foreseeable future (Committee on Climate Change, 2008).

Net emissions, measured on a life cycle basis, can be reduced by switching from kerosene to alternative fuels. To date, several airlines have made trial flights with one or more engines powered by biofuel/kerosene blends. While this has been shown to be feasible, 'no game-changing alternative to burning kerosene is foreseen in the short to medium-term' (Airbus, 2008: 18). This is supported by Somerville (2003: 227) who argues that 'kerosene is likely to remain the fuel for aviation for at least the next few decades.' As discussed in Chapter 15, doubts have also been raised about the potential carbon savings and wider environmental effects of a switch to biofuels.

SHIPPING

Shipping has traditionally been regarded as 'the most environmentally sound mode of transport' (Bode et al, 2002). Its relative environmental advantage stems from its low energy consumption per unit of freight movement: a 3,700 TEU[3] container ship, for example, uses only 0.026 kilowatts to move one ton one kilometre as opposed to 0.067 kWs for diesel-powered rail freight, 0.18 kW for a heavy truck and 2 kW for air freight moved in a Boeing 747–400 (Network for Transport and the Environment quoted by CSIS, 2009). However, emissions of pollutants, such as SOx, NOx and particulate matter (PM), per unit of energy consumed are much higher than for these other modes and have been declining at a much slower rate.

Sulphur is the environmental 'Achilles heel' of the shipping industry. Ships burn extremely dirty 'bunker fuel' rich in sulphur, which is left as a residual fraction in the refining process when cleaner 'distillate' fuels, mainly petrol and diesel used in surface transport, have been extracted. On average this bunker fuel contains around 27,000 parts per million (ppm) of sulphur, by comparison with 10–15 ppm in the fuels consumed by road vehicles in Europe and the United States (ICCT, 2007). This leads Kassel (2008) to describe ocean-going ships as the 'last bastion of dirty diesel engines'.

Ocean-going vessels are also responsible for around 17 per cent of total global emissions of NOx, and much higher percentages in the vicinity of ports and coastal channels (ICCT, 2007). It is sometimes argued that emissions from ships have attracted little public attention because they are much less visible than those from land-based transport. Roughly three-quarters of their output of noxious gases, however, are emitted within 400 km of land (ICCT quoted by Kassel, 2008) and can thus adversely affect coastal populations and ecosystems. The effects can be severe. Corbett et al (2007), for example, have estimated that around the world there are approximately 60,000 'premature mortalities' each year primarily as a result of the inhalation of ship-related PM emissions.

In recent years, several developments have turned the environmental 'spotlight' on shipping. Much more research has been done on the subject to improve our understanding of the nature and scale of the problem. Globalization has accelerated the expansion of international container shipping and annual growth rates of 7–8 per cent are expected at least until 2015 despite the recent economic slow-down (Heymann, 2008). Although international shipping was excluded from the Kyoto system of GHG accounting, its 2.5 per cent share of global emissions[4] is roughly equivalent to that of aviation and likely to be covered by future national and international GHG reduction targets. Impressive reductions in emissions per tonne-km by other transport modes have also eroded shipping's relative environmental advantage. Indeed the European Commission has predicted that total emissions of SOx and NOx from international shipping will exceed those of land-based sources of these gases by around 2015–2020. The International Maritime Organization (IMO) has responded to environmental pressures by establishing future limits for SOx and NOx emissions from ships both globally and for particular maritime zones. Individual shipping lines are also setting targets for cutting emissions, in many cases maintaining recent improvements in environmental performance. Between 2004 and 2007, for example, OOCL managed to cut average emissions per TEU-km of SOx, NOx and CO_2 by, respectively, 12 per cent, 12 per cent and 15 per cent (OOCL, 2009). Recent reductions in emissions have been due mainly to the commissioning of new, cleaner and more fuel-efficient vessels and the adoption of more fuel-efficient operating practices, such as reducing speeds.[5] What are the prospects for achieving more substantial greening of maritime operations in the longer term? These will be briefly assessed for deep-sea container shipping.

Carrying capacity

There has been a huge expansion in container ship capacity over the past 50 years, from the 58 TEUs handled by the *Ideal X* in 1956 to the 13,000 TEUs carried by the *Emma Maersk* in 2008. This increase in ship size has been driven by economies of scale, a component of which is the reduction in average fuel consumption per TEU and per tonne-km. Tozer (2004) also notes that in the future 'the scale economies associated with the largest ships may make it economically viable to install additional and more sophisticated equipment to improve environmental performance.' For example, as larger ships tend to be more stable they require less ballast water and hence consume less fuel transporting this additional weight.

The future trend in the maximum size of container ships has been a subject of much debate in recent years. Designs have been prepared for vessels capable of carrying 18,000 TEUs. The main constraint on vessel size is likely to be port and channel capacity rather than the exhaustion of technical scale economies. Relatively few ports would have the draught, dock and handling capacity to accommodate 'ultra-large' container ships, limiting their routing options and revenue potential. The average size of container ships is, nevertheless, likely to continue to rise and, if matched by a growth in traffic volumes on the major deep-sea routes, will maintain the downward trend in energy consumption per tonne-km.

Energy efficiency

The energy- and CO_2-efficiency of container ships have also been increasing independently of the growth in carrying capacity. It has been claimed that 'a container ship now typically emits about a quarter of the CO_2 it did in the 1970s as well as carrying up to 10 times as many containers' (CSIS, 2009). The major Japanese shipping line NYK (2009) has estimated that as a result of technical innovation a further 50 per cent improvement in energy efficiency might be achieved, half of which would accrue from redesign of the hull, 6 per cent from new propulsion systems and 5 per cent from waste heat recovery. NYK has also released an 'exploratory design' for a 'Super Eco Ship' which it believes could be launched by 2030 and offer a 69 per cent reduction in CO_2 per container handled. This vessel's environmental credentials would be enhanced by further light-weighting and streamlining of the hull and use of alternative power sources such as LNG-based fuel cells, solar cells and wind power. The use of sails as a supplementary power source has recently been successfully trialled. The company marketing this technology, SkySails (2009), claims that, 'Depending on the prevailing wind conditions, a ship's average annual fuel costs can be reduced by 10 to 35 per cent' by using this system.

Externalities

SOx emissions are reduced by removing sulphur from the fuel burned in ships. The IMO now limits the sulphur content in bunker fuel to 4.5 per cent and this maximum will drop to 1.5 per cent by 2020. In several maritime zones (or SO_2 Emission Control Areas – SECAs), such as the Baltic Sea, North Sea/English Channel and West Coast of the United States, the tighter limits are being introduced more rapidly. The International Council on Clean Transportation (2007: 9) is recommending that 'a uniform global fuel sulphur standard of 0.5 per cent be introduced in the medium term', which 'relative to the 2.7 per cent average sulphur content of current marine fuel... will reduce SO_2 emissions by approximately 80 per cent and PM emissions by approximately 20 per cent.' Imposing a 'global cap on sulphur content of marine fuels of 0.5 per cent by 2020' would present a formidable challenge to the oil industry and require massive investment in new refining capacity (Kanter, 2008). The American Petroleum Institute has estimated that an investment of $126 bn would be required, inflating the cost of a barrel of marine fuel by an average of $13–14. Bringing sulphur emissions from shipping down to the levels now prevalent in overland freight transport will, therefore, be very expensive.

The 'desulphurization' of marine fuel would also indirectly help to cut NOx levels. It would permit the installation of selective catalytic reduction (SCR) in marine engines to remove more NOx from exhaust emissions. Overall, the ICCT believes that new ship engines should be able 'to achieve NOx limits that are 40 per cent lower than the current standard in the near term'. Further deployment of 'additional emission control technologies' would allow NOx levels to fall by 95 per cent in the medium term. As in the case of the other freight transport modes examined in this chapter, this NOx reduction is likely to entail some loss of fuel efficiency and hence an increase in CO_2 emissions per tonne-km, forcing designers and operators of ships and regulatory authorities to balance environmental priorities. In the case of shipping, the trade-off between pollutants is complicated by the regional effect that sulphur aerosols can have in reducing 'radiative forcing' and hence countering global warming (Eyring et al, 2007).

Another technical development can help to reduce the externalities of shipping at the points where they are concentrated: that is, in the vicinity of ports. This can be done by stopping the ship's diesel-powered auxiliary engine from running while in port (so-called 'hotelling') and plugging the vessel into the local electricity grid using a system called 'cold-ironing'. By offering suitably equipped vessels this alternative power source, ports such as Gothenburg, Zeebrugge and Long Beach in California are managing to reduce local concentrations of SOx, NOx and PMs. Widespread application of this practice, however, will require the adoption of international standards of shore-side electricity supply to ensure compatibility of voltage and frequency between ship and port 'plug-in'.

Summary

Mainly because of intense market pressures and a lax regulatory regime, the rate of environmental improvement in the shipping sector has been slow. The rather complacent view that shipping is inherently 'green' has now been challenged, forcing regulators, shipping lines, ship designers, port operators and oil companies to place much greater emphasis on environmental performance. The rate of environmental improvement will be partly constrained by the relatively long lifespan and replacement cycle of the vessels.[6] The International Council on Clean Transportation (2007: 10) acknowledge that 'a low fleet turnover rate means that the largely uncontrolled vessels that make up the majority of the international shipping fleet today will continue to pollute for several decades before they are retired.' The potential exists to retrofit ships with devices that improve fuel efficiency and cut emissions, but Marintek et al (2000) expect the diffusion of environmental technology in the shipping industry to be primarily through new build rather than retrofitting. In response to the surge in demand for global shipping services since 2000, a large amount of new capacity has entered service in recent years that meets higher standards of fuel efficiency and emissions. Tightening emission controls, tougher environmental specifications from clients and, possibly, the future inclusion of shipping in emission trading schemes, will incentivize the adoption of cleaner technologies and practices across the shipping industry.

CONCLUSIONS

The redesign of vehicles and application of new technology offers the potential to reduce the environmental impact of all transport modes by a significant margin. In environmental terms, the rate of technological improvement has been faster in road freight transport than across the rail and waterborne sectors. This is partly because regulatory pressures to cut emissions have been stronger in this sector, but also because it has a higher energy intensity than rail and shipping and is thus more sensitive to rising oil prices. The 'electrification' of rigid trucks and vans over the next 20 years and their powering by low-carbon electricity will offer a quantum reduction in their environmental impact. The electrification of rail freight services should help them maintain their environmental advantage. While maritime and air freight services will remain heavily dependent on fossil fuels, major opportunities exist to cut their environmental costs per tonne-km.

To meet the environmental targets that have been set by governments and international organizations, efforts to design and commercialize greener vehicles are likely to intensify. Designers' environmental priorities are also likely to change. The overriding emphasis on minimizing noxious gases is likely to give way to a more holistic view of the 'green vehicle' that achieves a better balance of clean air, climate change, noise and safety objectives.

While vehicle design and technology have a key role to play in the greening of logistics, at least as much environmental benefit will accrue from more effective use of vehicles and a rationalization of the underlying demand for freight transport.

NOTES

1. This estimate is based on the author's own analysis of annual van licensing data provided by the SMMT.
2. This estimate is based on the author's own analysis of the effect of van length on load space.

3. Twenty-foot equivalent unit.
4. Recent reports suggest that it may be as high as 4.5 per cent (Vidal, 2008).
5. Reducing the speed of a 4,250 TEU container ship from 24.5 to 20 knots cuts fuel consumption by roughly 50 per cent (Seaspan quoted by Heymann, 2008).
6. In 2005 the average container ship was 11 years old and the average general cargo ship around twice that age (Deutsche Bank Research, 2006).

REFERENCES

Advisory Council for Aeronautics Research in Europe (ACARE) (2008) *Strategic Research Agenda 1: Volume 2 – Environment*, ACARE, Brussels

Airbus (2008) *Flying by Nature: Global market forecast 2007–2026*, Airbus, Paris

Allen, J and Browne, M (2008) *Using Official Data Sources to Analyse the Light Goods Vehicle Fleet and Operations in Britain*, report produced as part of the Green Logistics Project: Work Module 9 (Urban Freight Transport) [Online] http://www.greenlogistics.org/PageView.aspx?id=147&tid=147

Anon (2008a) Electric vans a partial solution, *What Van?* 1 May, [Online] http://www2.whatvan.co.uk/news_s.asp?id=5294

Anon (2008b) Van CO_2 and fuel consumption figures set for 2009 release, *What Van?* 30 June, [Online] http://www2.whatvan.co.uk/news_s.asp?id=5352

Anon (2009) [accessed 7 May 2009] Aviation in general [Online] http://www.enviro.aero/aviationenvironmentfactsfigures.aspx

Banner, S (2008) Marketplace – Tyres, *What Van?* 3 June [Online] http://www2.whatvan.co.uk/features.asp?id=5327

Bode, S, Isensee, J, Karsten, K and Michaelowa, A (2002) Climate policy: analysis of ecological, technical and economic implications for international maritime transport, *International Journal of Maritime Economics*, **4** (2), pp 164–84

Boeing (2008) *World Air Cargo Forecast 2008–9*, Boeing, Seattle

Committee on Climate Change (2008) *Building a Low Carbon Economy Part III*, Committee on Climate Change, London

Container Shipping Information Service (CSIS) (2009) Environment, [Online] http://www.shipsandboxes.com/eng/keytopics/environment/

Corbett, JJ, Winebrake, JJ, Green, EH, Kasibhatia, P, Eyring, V and Lauer, A (2007) Mortality from ship emissions: a global assessment, *Environmental Science and Technology*, **41** (24), pp 8512–18

Department for Business Enterprise and Regulatory Reform (DBERR) (2007) *Digest of United Kingdom Energy Statistics, 2007*, DBERR, London

Department for Transport (DfT) (2008a) *Road freight statistics 2006*, Transport Statistics Bulletin SB (06) 23, revised edition, Department for Transport, London

DfT (2008b) *Vehicle licensing statistics 2007*, Transport Statistics Bulletin SB (08) 15, Department for Transport, London

DfT (2009) *White Van Man goes Green*, press release, 8 June 2009

Deutsche Bank Research (2006) *Container Shipping*, Deutsche Bank Research, Frankfurt

Energy Information Administration (EIA) (2009) *Light-duty Diesel Vehicles: Market issues and potential energy and emissions impacts*, Office of Integrated Analysis and Forecasting, US Department of Energy, Washington

EUROCONTROL (2008) *Performance Review Report 2007: An assessment of air traffic management in Europe during the calendar year 2007*, EUROCONTROL, Brussels

European Aluminium Association (2006) *Moving Up to Aluminium: Light, strong and profitable*, European Aluminium Association, Brussels

European Commission (2007) *Towards a Rail Network Giving Priority to Rail Freight*, COM(2007) 608, European Commission, Brussels

European Commission (2008) Proposal to reduce CO_2 emissions from light duty vehicles, European Commission [Online] http://ec.europa.eu/environment/air/transport/co2/pdf/issue_paper.pdf

Eyring, V, Corbett, JJ, Lee, DS and Winebrake, JJ (2007) *Brief summary of the impact of ship emissions on atmospheric composition, climate and human health*, document submitted to the Health and Environment Sub-group of the International Maritime Organization

Freightliner (2007) *Freightliner Group Ltd has placed an order for 30 brand new locomotives*, Press release, 19 November, Freightliner, London

Greszler, A (2009) Heavy duty vehicle fleet technologies for reducing carbon dioxide: an industry perspective, in *Reducing Climate Impacts in the Transportation Sector*, ed D Sperling and JS Cannon, pp 101–16, Springer, New York

Hanson, S and Guiliano, G (2004) *The Geography of Urban Transport*, 3rd edition, Guilford Press, London

Heymann, E (2008) *Prospects for the Container Shipping Industry*, Deutsche Bank Research, Frankfurt

IATA (2004) *Environmental Review 2004*, IATA, Geneva

ICAO (2007) *ICAO Environmental Report 2007*, ICAO, Montreal

International Council on Clean Transportation (ICCT) (2007) *Air Pollution and Greenhouse Gas Emissions from Ocean-going Ships: Impacts, mitigation options and opportunities for managing group*, ICCT, Washington, DC

Kahn Ribeiro, S, Kobayashi, S, Beuthe, M, Gasca, J, Greene, D, Lee, DS, Muromachi, Y, Newton, PJ, Plotkin, S, Sperling, D, Wit, R and Zhou, PJ (2007) Transport and its infrastructure, in *Climate Change 2007: Mitigation*, ed B Metz, OR Davidson, PR Bosch, R Dave and LA Meyer, Contribution of Working Group III to the Fourth Assessment Report of the Intergovernmental Panel on Climate Change, Cambridge University Press, Cambridge

Kanter, J (2008) Making ships green, in port and at sea, *New York Times*, 26 April

Kassel, R (2008) Ocean-going ships are the last bastion of the dirty diesels [Online] http://switchboard.nrdc.org/blogs/rkassel/oceangoing_ships_are_the_last.html

MacIntosh, A and Wallace, L (2009) International aviation emissions to 2025: can emissions be stabilized without restricting demand, *Energy Policy*, **37**, pp 254–73

Marintek, Econ, Carnegie-Mellon and DNV (2000) *Study of Greenhouse Gas Emissions from Ships*, Final Report to the International Maritime Organization, Trondheim

Millward, D (2009) Air Cargo Traffic Plummets as Global Recession Worsens, *Daily Telegraph*, 29 January 2009

Ministry of Economy, Trade and Industry (2008) *Top Runner Program: Developing the world's best energy-efficient appliances*, Ministry of Economy, Trade and Industry, Tokyo

Momenta (2006) *LCV Scoping Study – Phase 1: Review of published literature*, Report to Department for Transport Logistics Policy Division, AEA Technology, Harwell

National Academies of Science (2007) *Report of the 21st Century Vehicle Partnership*, National Academies of Science, Washington, DC

Network Rail (2007) *Freight Route Utilisation Strategy*, Network Rail, London

NYK (2009) Presentation at the Scotch Whisky Association Seminar, Paisley, 6 March

OOCL (2009) Presentation at the Scotch Whisky Association Seminar, Paisley, 6 March

Penner, JE, Lister, DH, Griggs, DJ, Dokken, DJ and McFarland, M (1999) *Aviation and the Global Atmosphere*, Cambridge University Press, Cambridge

Rail Safety and Standards Board (RSSB) (2007) *The Case for Rail 2007*, RSSB, London

SkySails (2009) [accessed 27 April 2009] SkySails for cargo ships [Online] http://www.skysails.info/english/products/skysails-for-cargo-ships/

Somerville, H (2003) Transport energy and emissions: aviation, in *Handbook of Transport and the Environment*, ed DA Hensher and JK Button, pp 263–78, Elsevier, Amsterdam

Southwest Research Institute (2008) Heavy duty vehicle fuel consumption and GHG emissions improvement: preliminary simulation results, presentation to National Academy of Sciences hearing on Fuel Economy Standards, Washington, DC, 4–5 December

Stehly, M (2009) Technologies to address rising fuel impacts, Transportation Research Board (TRB) Conference, Washington, DC, 12 January

Storey, R and Boyes, G (2003) Van, in *Companion to British Road Haulage History*, ed J Armstrong, J Aldridge, G Boyes, G Mustoe and R Storey, pp 418–19, Science Museum, London

Thomas, G (2008) Making Air Traffic Management more Efficient is One of the Few Remaining Low-Hanging Fruits in the Effort to Save Fuel and Reduce Carbon Emissions, Air Transport World [Online] http://www.atwonline.com/channels/eco/article.html?articleID=2448

Tozer, D (2004) *Ultra-large Container Ships: The green ships of the future*, Lloyd's List, London

Vehicle and Operator Services Agency (VOSA) (2008) *Effectiveness Report 2007/08*, VOSA, Bristol

Verband der Automobilindustrie (VDA) (2008) The commercial vehicle: environmentally friendly and efficient, VDA [Online] http://www.vda.de/en/downloads/492/?PHPSESSID=a4rsqgkktu1m4bcimsal7n0q60

Vidal, J (2008) Shipping Boom Fuels Rising Tide of Global CO_2 Emissions, *Guardian*, 13 February

Ward, D, Tyler, P, Wilson, P and Eichinger, M (2004) *Developments in Rail Simulators and Computer Based Training to Increase Training Efficiency and Effectiveness*, Simulation Industry Association of Australia, Lindfield

8

Reducing the environmental impact of warehousing

Clive Marchant

INTRODUCTION

When considering issues of energy intensity, carbon footprints or sustainability within the supply chain, most attention has been given to understanding and mitigating the impact of transportation. By comparison little attention appears to have been given to evaluating the consequences of warehousing within the supply chain. However, like many other areas of business, the opportunity to place a 'green wash' on an activity by prefacing that activity with the accolade of 'green', 'eco' or 'carbon neutral' has not been missed and is indeed an increasing feature of headlines in supply chain practitioner publications. But what can we understand from the use of such terms? What actions can and should the warehouse sector be adopting today or anticipate undertaking to meet those environmental aspirations? This chapter will address these questions by reviewing the changing nature of warehouse activity, and the factors affecting and mitigating energy use and consequential emission, and so through this wider assessment place terms such as the 'green' or 'carbon neutral' or 'eco' warehouse into a wider reference framework.

It is not the purpose of this chapter to review or question the techniques of environmental assessment. Consequently the merits of the use of approaches such as life cycle analysis or sustainability strategies that encompass the reduction, reuse and, recycling of resources and renewable forms of energy are not debated (Tsoulfas and Pappis, 2005; Padgett et al, 2008). This chapter will therefore apply those approaches to the warehouse sector and at a level of the action an individual firm or warehouse manager could reasonably take. However, the discussion will go beyond considering just the micro-level actions of a firm and will consider wider macro-level impacts of emissions, land use, environment and ecology. Technical aspects of building design, the assessment of the thermal qualities of different materials or descriptions of building energy mass balances will also be left to others (Treloar et al, 2001).

The first section sets out the changing scale and energy use of warehousing relative to other commercial property activity, primarily in the UK. For the reader not familiar with an understanding of the role performed by today's warehouse, a short review of recent trends is included. From this a three-stage warehouse sustainability model that addresses the business, economic, environmental and social aspects will be put forward.

Once a baseline of impact and scope has been established, the next section will identify those actions that businesses can and are taking to reduce the energy intensity within their current operations. This is a 'business-as-usual approach' focusing on reducing demand and becoming energy efficient. From that position the next section moves on to consider to what extent warehouse operators can incorporate low emission and new forms of sustainable energy generation and resource management into their activities. The final section considers a deeper and wider range of measures and actions where companies are seeking to achieve minimal impact over the widest breadth of economic, resource, environmental and ecological features.

SCALE OF THE ENVIRONMENTAL IMPACT

The term warehousing in today's supply chain is a portmanteau one that includes a wide range of functions and activities from cross-dock, consolidation centre, regional distribution centre and composite warehouse to national distribution centre. Whilst the number of large and often anonymous grey buildings that cluster around our motorway intersections, primary ports and the outskirts of most large towns are easily visible, the activities within remain hidden. A warehouse may imply a point where goods are stored for a long period of time, and whilst this remains an important function the warehouse is more associated today with terms of flow, movement, the rapid fulfillment of customer orders, and the provision of customizing and value-adding services (Baker and Canessa,

2009; Frazelle, 2002). The term warehouse whenever it is used in this chapter refers to this wider intensive role, which is more often associated with the term distribution centre.

First it is necessary to quickly establish the scale of the sector in terms of area occupied and overall use of energy. By considering these trends in association with the main operational and business changes the drivers to achieving energy and resource efficiency will become clearer.

In assessing the overall impact of warehousing, consideration has to be given to the relative scale and trends in the extent of the land occupied, the direct energy used, the emissions produced (primarily carbon dioxide, CO_2), water consumed and embedded energy contained in building materials. The area under occupation is usually reported in terms of the internal floor area of the buildings in square metres and not the total land area of a location. The measure for energy used, regardless of the source (oil, gas, fossil generated electricity) or method of generation used, is kWh, which is again related to area and is expressed as kWh/m^2. Emissions for direct and embedded energy are measured as CO_2/m^2.

The range of official statistics that capture the range of information identified above is very limited. This is a consequence of sector and sub-sector definitions being constructed around broad industrial classifications rather than building activity, and of a high level of data aggregation (UK GBC, 2007). Warehousing for most statistical purposes is subsumed within larger industrial classifications or absorbed within broad commercial headings such as office, shops and factories. However, some major features can be identified:

- Globally it is estimated that buildings emit 15 per cent of all greenhouse gases, with commercial property accounting for 35 per cent of emissions compared with 65 per cent for residential property. In terms of emissions from the energy consumed, however, commercial property is more dependent on electricity than residential property, with 65 per cent of its emissions coming from that source (World Resources Institute, 2006).
- The warehouse sector in the UK by the end of 2004 totalled just under 152 million m^2, which constituted 25.5 per cent of all UK commercial properties (Figure 8.1). Between 1970 and 1994, as retail space increased by 54 per cent and office space grew by 100 per cent, warehouse space increased by 114 per cent (Scrase, 2000).
- The direct energy consumed by all UK commercial property has been estimated at 50 per cent, with the sector accounting for 40 per cent of all raw materials used (Saunders, 2008).
- Studies from the UK and United States suggest that the growth in electricity consumption and energy for all commercial property is closely coupled to the rate of increase in total floor space (Green Buildings.com, 2008).

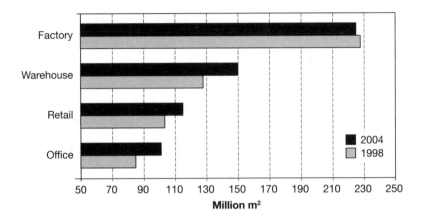

Figure 8.1 Changes in UK floor space by usage, 1998 to 2004 (million m²)

Source: Adapted from Department of Communities and Local Government (2007).

• Property developer Gazeley through its life cycle analysis suggests that between 65 and 90 per cent of energy is consumed in a warehouse during ongoing operational activity through power for heat, ventilation and air conditioning (HVAC), lighting and equipment (Gazeley, 2008).

The picture that emerges is that warehouse activity has a significant level of impact through the scale of its activities and in the consumption of resources (energy and land) and that whilst its total CO_2 level is lower than for offices and retail (Table 8.1), its impact is substantial and increasing. The next section will identify those changes in warehouse activity that have led to this increased resource intensity.

Table 8.1 Energy consumption and CO_2 emissions in the UK commercial office, retail and warehouse building stock

	Commercial offices	**Retail**	**Warehouses**
Fossil fuels (petajoules PJ)	54	55	22
Electricity (petajoules PJ)	56	82	50
CO_2 (kilotonne kT)	9,669	15,237	8,515

Source: Cited by Scrase (2000) and Pout et al (1998).

INCREASING RESOURCE INTENSITY

The warehouse or distribution centre is often one of the largest fixed and long-lived assets within any organization's supply chain. Investment decisions in warehouses are therefore of strategic importance, with the focus of decision making being on cost reduction and return on investment as well as improved customer service and operational performance. However, it should be remembered that logistics as a percentage of cost of sales in the fast-moving consumer goods sector averages around 6–8 per cent. Within overall logistical costs, warehouse activity contributes approximately 24 per cent of total logistics costs compared with 40 per cent for transportation (ELA, 2004). As a consequence, whilst warehousing has significant impact within a firm it is not surprising that more opportunity and management focus has been directed towards reducing transportation spend and emissions.

Significant growth in the total area occupied by warehousing has already been identified, but what has been of greater significance has been the increase in size, scale of throughput and duration of activity. This has occurred as company inventories have been centralized and the geographical market areas served expanded (McKinnon, 1998). Whilst the number of warehouses required have reduced, those warehouses that remain have increased in floor area. In 1996 the average newly built distribution centre was approximately 19,000 m^2 and this had increased to 34,000 m^2 by 2008 (KingSturge, 2008). In addition the height, and so the cubic capacity, of the buildings has increased as greater use was being made of high bay (AS/AR) systems or narrow aisle racking systems (Baker and Perotti, 2008) in order to accommodate ever larger product ranges. Minimizing the visual impact on the wider environment of these buildings, which can now often reach over 20 metres in height, has become a further issue as a consequence. At the local level a new generation of transshipment or cross-dock centres has emerged that place a premium on buildings of much lower heights but with large floor area, with banks of doors on opposite sides of a building to facilitate the rapid transshipment of orders. Both warehouse types are often being located in proximity to centres of population rather than points of supply. Consequently warehouses now cluster along the major arterial routes in what were often former green fields rather than brown-field land located within urban areas (Hesse, 2004).

Increasing the size of warehouses has also meant that capital invested in these buildings has increased. This has meant that the intensity with which these assets are operated has increased substantially in order to achieve faster investment paybacks and to reduce unit fixed costs. This intensification is also reinforced by retailer moves towards longer trading periods across the week and by industry adopting continuous replenishment and JIT production methods. Many warehouses now expect to work two shifts six days per week (Baker and Perotti, 2008). A typical grocery regional distribution centre (RDC) will today operate 24 × 7, 364 days per year. Sweating the asset in this way reduces unit fixed costs and defers the need for further capital investment but increases the operational consumption of energy for power, light and heat.

Concentration into fewer and larger warehouses has additionally meant that the numbers of inbound supplier vehicles and outbound customer deliveries serving these warehouses through a 24-hour period has increased. The road congestion effects around distribution parks are further compounded by an increasing proportion of those commercial vehicles being made up of articulated maximum-weight or capacity trucks. At the same time the number of staff employed within these warehouses has also increased. Again, a grocery RDC can now employ over 1,000 employees per eight-hour shift. This places pressure on increasing the size of onsite service areas, employee car parking and local road infrastructure. Whilst good connectivity to the trunk road network is a priority for new warehouse developments, connectivity to public transport service networks for staff is often very poor.

To cope with increased product ranges, reduced order lead times, greater customisation, and heath and safety regulation, greater use is being made of powered mechanical equipment in the form of forklift trucks, conveyors and automated order picking or sortation systems (Baker, 2006). This is in addition to other value-adding activities such as labelling or product assembly operations, which have been transferred from manufacturing as companies have adopted postponement strategies. To cope with this the warehouse has had to rapidly extend the use of IT support systems deployed at operator level, using wireless communications to support bar code readers, voice and light picking, and more recently RFID technologies. Against the accrued benefits of a 'paperless warehouse' has to set the overall increase in power needs to support additional IT infrastructure.

The final feature to be considered is the emergence of a multiplicity of market intermediaries and a separation between those who occupy, design, finance and manage buildings (Scrase, 2000; Hesse, 2004; Reed and Wilkinson, 2005). In this business environment it can be difficult to establish a consensus of how to balance long-term capital investment decisions against short-term operational savings in energy or resource consumption for a third party. 'Market capitalization and returns on investments are now becoming preferred in land-use decisions, whereas public institutions – obligated by environmental, transport or community needs – are losing influence' (Hesse, 2004: 167).

FRAMEWORK FOR ASSESSING THE ENVIRONMENTAL IMPACT OF WAREHOUSES

The previous review of major trends in warehouse activity has shown how diverse are the areas affected by warehousing and suggests that any mitigating actions require a systems-wide approach. On the one side there are the micro-level firm-based direct inputs associated with meeting operational needs that consume resources: these include energy, water and land and building materials. But there are also wider external macro-level outputs that go beyond the boundary of a single firm and affect the environment and society. These externalities are associated with the impact of land use, atmospheric emissions, waste management, traffic and congestion, public transport, visual intrusion and ecology. The systems approach clearly draws upon the life cycle analysis now widely used throughout supply chain analysis (Carbon Trust, 2006b; Tsoulfas and Pappis, 2005; Padgett et al, 2008).

The main elements of this framework are shown in Figure 8.2. The suggested framework is separated into a micro-level perspective, which emphasizes the individual firm and economic features, and a macro-level perspective where broader externalities related to the environment and society are considered. The scope of these two perspectives can be further classified by type of resource and related activities. Finally three developmental stages can be envisaged from a baseline of being energy efficient before seeking to adopt low-emission technologies and then achieving full sustainability.

For a firm, the immediate and business-as-usual objective is the efficient and economic use of energy inputs, typically fossil based, that provide power for equipment (forklift trucks, conveyors etc); and regulation of temperature (cooling or heating), light (internal and external) and water for personal hygiene and processes. This is a baseline that all warehouses should achieve as a minimum. The next section will map out the range of actions that can be taken for a warehouse to become energy efficient.

WAYS OF REDUCING THE ENVIRONMENTAL IMPACT

Stage 1: Improve energy efficiency

There is little published information on the actual cost structure of warehouse operations, and even less on direct spend on energy costs or energy consumption rates. The range of building types, and the range of use and

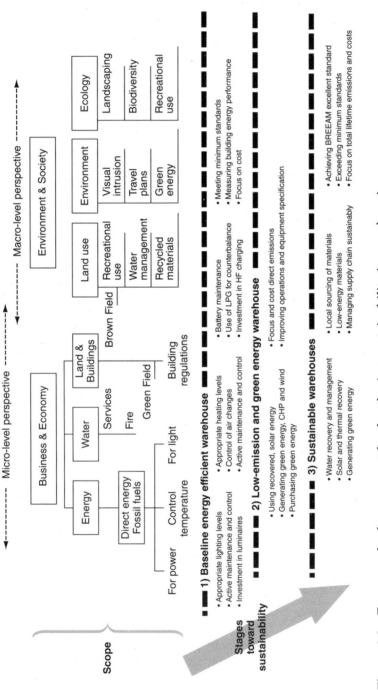

Figure 8.2 Framework of assessment for developing sustainability in warehousing

operating conditions make producing benchmarks or standards particularly challenging. This is further compounded by inconsistency in the building energy models (UK GBC, 2007), variation in boundary definitions for activities (Johnson, 2008; Padgett et al, 2008) and little or no central collation of energy data (Perez-Lombard, Ortiz and Pout, 2007). The Royal Institute of Chartered Surveyors (RICS) estimated that direct energy costs in warehouses account for 1 per cent of operational expenses, whilst property costs contribute around 10 per cent and labour up to 85 per cent (RICS Green Value Report, 2005, cited in KingSturge, 2007). Other sources suggests that energy costs of between 5 to 10 per cent may be more representative of general-ambient warehouses, while temperature-controlled warehouses operating at –26°C may well have costs closer to 15 to 20 per cent. Regardless of actual level, surveys undertaken by the UK government's Energy Efficiency Best Practice Programme suggest that 50 per cent of all direct energy used for heat, light and powered equipment could be saved by simple housekeeping measures (Carbon Trust, 2002a). Each of these major areas of energy use will be reviewed in the following sections.

Warehouse temperature

Fuel oil or gas is the primary source of energy for heating a warehouse, and electricity is used for cooling. The extent of the energy consumed is primarily determined by:

- The temperature required to maintain the stored products in a satisfactory condition. This may require intervention to maintain a maximum or minimum temperature level, as well as to control relative humidity.
- The background temperature of the internal space required for operatives to perform their work in comfort (known as the dry resultant temperature) in relation to extent of their physical exertion and location of the task being undertaken.

Further structural factors influencing the energy required will be the overall thermal mass of the building: the nature of the materials used in the construction of the building as well as levels of insulation; the orientation of the building relative to local prevailing wind and sun, and the heating or cooling degree days; the overall volume of the building; and thermal gain from internal processes and equipment such as forklift trucks or lights. Due to their greater overall thermal mass, larger buildings tend to require less energy per m², with heat loss through walls being relatively small. Reducing the internal target temperature has the largest effect on energy consumed, with a 1°C reduction typically producing a saving of 10 per cent. Setting local temperatures by zone in a way that is appropriate to the activity being carried out is therefore important. In areas where there is a high level of physical activity, such as loading bays, 13°C should be adequate, whilst for order picking or inspection 19°C would be required. In bulk storage areas for dry ambient products 10°C may be satisfactory (Carbon Trust, 2002a).

Once the building achieves its required temperature, the maintenance of that level is affected by the ventilation. This is expressed as the number of air changes per hour. All buildings require ventilation to maintain a satisfactory working and storage environment. High air-exchange rates are associated with high energy cost, as buildings or zones within a building have to recover heat loss or reduce gain in the case of temperature-controlled warehouses (Carbon Trust, 2002b, 2006a). Air changes are directly affected by the level of draughts, often the consequence of poor construction or maintenance but often more significantly affected by the number and type of doors and the time that the doors are left open. Stratification through convection as a result of warm air rising and cold air sinking is an additional feature in all buildings, and again is most prevalent in buildings with high air-exchange rates and not only taller buildings.

Significant savings can be achieved by (Carbon Trust 2002a);

- opening doors only in periods of vehicle activity;
- incorporating barriers such as close-fitting door locks, plastic strip barriers or fast-acting doors in areas frequented by forklift trucks;
- segregating intake or dispatch areas from other areas of activity;
- using zoned or time-controlled thermostats.

The source of heating used in the warehouse depends upon the size of areas to be controlled and the extent that local zone conditions have to be maintained. For large areas, or where there are high air-exchange rates across a building and where an overall minimum temperature is required, then ducted warm air systems are most efficient. These systems are usually powered by fuel oil or gas, although new biomass and combined heat and power systems are future options. For smaller areas local heating is usually provided by either suspended warm air heaters or radiant heaters, powered preferably by gas or fuel oil. Suspended heaters that are unflued have a high thermal efficiency of 100 per cent but are only suitable for large-volume buildings due to the build-up of by-products of combustion. Flued heaters should still achieve thermal efficiencies of 90 per cent and are best suited to large buildings with low air-change rates. Radiant heaters that emit infrared radiation from hot surfaces have a lower net thermal value of 50 per cent, but they are effective at providing localized heat in areas of high air-exchange rates, typically close to doors where operators require higher levels of comfort or are mainly engaged in low-activity or sedentary activities (Carbon Trust, 2002b).

Warehouse lighting

Managing lighting efficiently in terms of its functional performance, cost, energy use and resultant emissions is the most straightforward area within the warehouse to manage. A combination of simple housekeeping measures, use of known and available technologies, simple control methods, clear performance standards and methods of calculating comparative installed circuit demand in terms of Watts per m² all assist. Annual energy consumption is itself easily measured by multiplying the installed load by the floor area and hours of operation. A single 400W high-pressure sodium light bulb operated continuously for a year has been calculated to produce the equivalent of 1.69 tonnes of CO_2 according to Powerboss Eluma (Wyatt, 2007), so taking lighting seriously has considerable environmental and energy consequences as it is dependent upon electricity.

The term used to measure the amount of light in an area is lux and the required luminescence and colour-rending level is set by the nature of the task being undertaken. The extent that natural light needs to be complemented by additional light sources (known as luminaires) is affected by the extent and orientation of roof lights, the duration of daylight hours, height of buildings and aisle widths. Guidance lux values and installed circuit loads are reproduced in Table 8.2 from the Carbon Trust's *Good Practice Guide 319* (Carbon Trust, 2002a). Providing too much light is as disadvantageous as too little as it can cause glare and operator discomfort.

Table 8.2 Recommended light levels in open and racked warehouse areas

General warehouse lighting conditions		Target installed Circuit W/m²	
		300 Lux	500 Lux
General lighting in 'open' area		5–6	8–10
Constrained by aisle and height			
Aisle width (metres)	Mounting height (metres)	150 Lux	300 Lux
1.2	4.5	8	14
2.4	6.5	8	16
3.0	8.0	9	17

Source: Carbon Trust (2002a).

Simple cleaning of both roof lights and luminaires should be a regular feature of any energy efficiency strategy, as light levels can be reduced by 50 per cent in two years through the accumulation of dust and so increase operating costs by 15 per cent (ie energy consumed) (Carbon Trust, 2007). Regardless of type of lamps fitted, a replacement strategy based on average usage and not on failure is recommended. With buildings increasing in height, difficulties in accessibility can be more easily managed within a prescribed programme of replacement using access towers, which can also be linked to full cleaning of all luminaires.

The choice of lamp type and the control gear to switch lights on and off needs to take into account the activity to be undertaken, the likely frequency of switching, the lamps' run-up and restrike rate (time to reach optimum light from start or restart) and the average life of the lamp in relation to the ease of access for replacement. Removing old mercury discharge lamps with high-pressure sodium lamps (SON) should produce a 15 per cent saving in energy costs; replacing old style 38m (T12) tubular triphosphor-coated fluorescent lamps with 26m (T8) tubes will bring an 8 per cent saving, and if a high-frequency control gear is used, 20 per cent savings in energy consumed can be expected. Fitting high-performance lamps without adequate maintenance or placing them in luminaires without efficient optics or prismatic glass to direct the light falling into an area will considerably reduce these savings, as lamp power ratings or numbers or both would need to be increased (Carbon Trust, 2002a, 2007). Table 8.3 indicates the appropriate types of lighting for different activity areas around the warehouse.

Table 8.3 Appropriate lamps by activity area

Site location	Space use	Recommended lamp type
Internal	Offices	Triphosphor tubular fluorescent, compact fluorescent, low voltage tungsten halogen
	Factories	Triphosphor tubular fluorescent, high pressure sodium, metal halide, inductive
		Emergency directional LED
External	Car parks	High pressure sodium, metal halide, compact fluorescent
	Floodlighting	Metal halide and high pressure sodium

Source: Adapted from Carbon Trust (2007).

Mechanical handling equipment

To achieve the rapid and intensive movement of goods, all warehouses will use a range of mechanical handling systems for the movement and lifting of goods. A simple manual warehouse will use counterbalance forklift trucks to unload and vehicles to move and lift pallets of products into block stacks. Further types of forklift trucks such as reach trucks are required to achieve higher storage densities through the use of pallet racking. Higher labour efficiencies for case or item picking require the use of ride-on trucks, low-level order pickers or simple conveyors. Higher throughputs, wider product ranges and more intensive operations add further specialist electro-mechanical systems in the form of high-bay stacker cranes, sorting and collation conveyors, layer pickers, A-frames to robotics (Baker, 2006). To consider such a range of equipment is not possible and so only the largest single category, forklift trucks, will be reviewed.

Whilst the category of forklift trucks covers a very wide variety of types of truck, the choice of type of power unit and consequential fuel type is a simple one. The choice lies between those trucks that use an internal-combustion engine as their primary power source or those that use lead-acid electric-storage batteries. For combustion engine units, the power alternatives are diesel fuel or gas (LPG). The power unit provides propulsion to the truck whilst secondary motors power hydraulic pumps for lifting.

The starting point for the choice of equipment lies not in considering the energy source to be used but rather in wider equipment characteristics related to: the type of access to products (aisle width and lift height); whether the work is done in an open or closed environment (operating outside a building, on uneven surfaces or where fumes can affect personnel or goods); weight distribution (for stability of trucks, all require a heavy counterweight). Counterbalance trucks, whilst offering more energy options, are limited in the areas of the warehouse they can operate in due to their lower lift heights and wider turning radius. They are used predominantly in receiving and dispatch bays, where surfaces are uneven or open to the elements. Where counterbalance trucks are used externally LPG or diesel are alternatives, whilst for internal use the choice is between LPG and electric-storage batteries. For flexibility of function across the entire warehouse, electric-storage battery trucks predominate and are incorporated into a wider variety of reach trucks, narrow-aisle trucks and order-picking trucks.

Within this apparently narrow choice of alternatives there is a range of options that companies can take to reduce the levels of direct energy consumed, emissions produced and wider environmental impacts associated with manufacture and disposal, especially of batteries and these will be reviewed next.

As with all comparative analysis of energy consumed and emission balances, the issue is not with energy efficiency conversion factors or CO_2 emission rates but the definition of system boundaries. The difficulties in providing a straightforward answer to this are highlighted by Johnson in his review of carbon footprints for electric and LPG forklifts (Johnson, 2008). Studies have failed to agree on relative energy efficiencies as there is no standard industry test cycle and no consistency in the system boundaries, with CO_2 per kWh output boundaries that range from 'well-to-pump', 'well-to-wheel', 'outlet-to-battery', 'battery-to-wheel' or 'wheel-to-exhaust' all producing different relative positions for each fuel type. So whilst LPG has the highest energy efficiency at 89.3 per cent and lowest CO_2 emissions, one study showed it used six times more energy per operating cycle than electricity, but on a well-to-battery basis electric-storage batteries were less efficient. Overall Johnson concludes that 'fuel carbon footprints of electric and LPG forklifts are, in principle, about equal, while in actual practice, LPG's footprint is smaller than that of electricity' (Johnson, 2008: 1572). In a business-as-usual scenario where the choice is between LPG, diesel fuel or electric battery, this tends to reinforce a cost-of-ownership approach based around capital purchase and disposal values, fuel cost, fuel consumed and maintenance rather than a wider evaluation of total emissions.

Looking to the future there are new counterbalance design options starting to come into the market built around alternative engine technologies used also in the automotive industry. Internal-combustion power units using bio-diesel or hybrid fuel combinations and hydrogen fuel cell technologies are all coming on to the market. For hydrogen fuel cells these are still in the developmental stage, and although there are concept trucks from most of the main manufacturers the number of operational units remains very small (MacLeod, 2008).

The efficiency of lead-acid electric battery technology and consequential routes to achieving reduced energy inputs and so emissions are bounded by loss of power through the mains electricity transmission grid, the efficiency of the transfer process as batteries are charged from the mains supply, the internal efficiency of a battery to absorb and retain its charge over its life, and finally the manufacture and disposal of the lead battery itself (Trebilock, 2008).Whilst new battery types based around lithium ion are slowly emerging, especially for low-level pedestrian riders, in a business-as-usual setting the focus for current businesses is on achieving greater performance through enhancing current battery performance (MacLeod, 2008).

Improvements in lead-acid batteries from plate to tubular cell construction and from water-filled flooded units to low-maintenance sealed units have improved energy performance, although individual energy efficiency in the charging phase (grid to battery) remains at around 70–80 per cent. In a typical 10-hour charge cycle, 80 per cent of the charge is achieved in the first five hours, with the remaining time being required to complete the full charge cycle (Trebilock, 2008). Interrupting or exceeding this charge cycle reduces the power retained and overall life of the battery. Overcharging through this period can create additional heat, thus distorting the internal cell structure, which in turn reduces cell efficiency and life as well as causing the additional venting of potentially combustible gases. Batteries are usually charged to perform over a single shift of 8–10 hours, so for extended operating periods multiple batteries will be required. Typically, in multi-shift operations, a battery to truck ratio of 2:1 will be maintained. Managing this recharge cycle is important to minimize the energy required and achieve the maximum battery life, which is restricted to a fixed number of recharge cycles over the battery's life. For larger fleets, especially where continuous shifts are worked, the management of the total battery fleet using a combination of high-frequency fast charging, advanced battery management monitoring and individual battery monitoring over weekly recharge cycles reduces the ratio of batteries to vehicles required to 1.6 to 1, extends the operating life and minimizes waste heat and gases. In the short term, capital costs for high-frequency charges are higher but over a five-year period power consumption should be 11 per cent lower and whole-life cost savings of 10 per cent are projected (*SHD*, 2009).

The traditional approach to maintaining maximum operational efficiency over a working period has been to fit over-capacity sized batteries despite the disadvantage of additional energy costs, which are often not separately monitored. The introduction of 3-phase AC high-frequency fast-charging systems and opportunity-charge batteries has enabled batteries to be more appropriately specified. Opportunity charging can take the form of rapid charging from the mains during coffee breaks and short operational breaks, or direct charging by onboard regenerative motors, linked to returning energy produced during braking or the lowering of the mast and forks via the hydraulic system direct to the battery (Davies, 2009). Trials reported by Toyota Material Handling and Jungheinrich (Davies, 2009) suggest that using recovered energy reduces power consumption from the battery by between 15 and 25 per cent. These approaches are very effective at getting a battery back up to the 80 per cent capacity level when used with a correctly specified battery. However (even along with other truck improvement to lift controls, transmission and gearbox design, hydraulic systems and on-board performance diagnostics that have reduced the overall cost of ownership) 'fundamental improvements in truck design are currently limited by battery technology' (Davies, 2009: 16).

So far the actions considered for reducing the level of demand for energy have been centred on adopting technologies with lower energy inputs and better operational controls by relating equipment performance specification to activity and need. This is an essential first step, but to engage more actively with the need to reduce emissions a move to local and renewable sources of energy is the next phase towards achieving a sustainable warehouse.

Stage 2: Harness green energy

Green energy can be defined in terms of the generating of power from a range of low-carbon renewable sources close to or at the point of use. The primary aim of adopting green energy is to achieve a shift from carbon-intensive energy sources principally based on coal or oil, either directly or indirectly via the production of grid-based electricity. The main forms of renewable green energy sources include:

- biomass (wood chip or other waste), wind, solar thermal, solar photo-voltaics;
- recovered process waste energy, such as heat from refrigeration plants or air compressors;
- recovered kinetic energy;
- air, ground or water thermal-exchange units.

In addition, low-carbon alternatives such as natural gas and bio-diesel could be included although there are substantial additional sustainability issues associated with these fuels, which have been discussed elsewhere.

The suitability and potential applicability of the four sources of power on the energy mix for an individual warehouse depends upon a wide range of operational, cost, environmental and market factors. Principal amongst these are:

- the operational pattern of energy demand versus the generating characteristics of the alternative green energy supply;
- the cost and scalability of each green energy technology;
- the relative generating efficiency and life cycle emissions levels of alternative technologies;
- the rate of technology maturity and innovation;
- regulatory and market conditions affecting price, demand and supply conditions.

Demand for energy within the warehouse in the form of either electricity or heat is not constant. It is dictated by hourly and weekly throughput patterns as well as longer seasonal weather changes over the year. Further local variation in generating periods due to local weather conditions, the proximity and orientation of buildings or levels of associated activity adds further complexity. This creates issues of managing total energy demand against short-term fixed generating capacity, the availability and cost of sourcing variable additional short-term external energy supplies, and the disposal or sale of surplus green energy or a means of storing that surplus energy. Consequently, local generation of green energy is likely to provide only a partial solution. Studies looking at these demands and generating patterns suggest that 44 per cent of onsite renewable energy will be exported (sold) whilst only 38 per cent of demand can be satisfied by green energy (UK GBC, 2007).

Like most transformational processes the economics of power generation are subject to economies of scale and a balance between capital costs, fuel input costs versus lifetime operating costs and not just the greenhouse emissions and energy conversion rates. A review of each technology goes beyond the scope of this analysis but some studies suggest a 10-fold cost per kg-CO_2 benefit of using offsite renewable versus onsite generating (see Figure 8.3), highlighting the need for companies to proceed with caution in this area. On the other hand, recovered process energy systems or solar thermal systems for pre-heating water appear to lend themselves effectively to local site applications on an energy conversion, cost and operational basis. Similarly ground source heat pumps need only '100 kWh to turn 200 kWh of environmental or waste heat into 300 kWh useful heat' (Gazeley, 2004: 137).

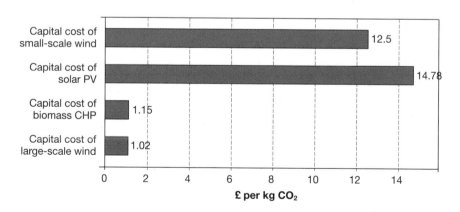

Figure 8.3 Comparison in estimated cost of on and offsite renewables

Source: Adapted from UK Green Building Council (2007: 48).

Technologies such as solar photovoltaics are still a maturing technology where current payback periods are still calculated in periods of 15–20 years, which is far longer than the current rate of technology improvement. The use of combination technologies such as self-cleaning transparent film technologies in conjunction with solar photovoltaic laminates such as ETFE roof-light panels may prove more cost and energy efficient, even in the medium term. These are reported as having 50 to 200 times less embodied energy, with a trial 33,900 m^2 distribution centre installation generating 80 MWh of power and saving 32 tonnes of CO_2 (Gazeley, 2008). By comparison, small wind generators with an estimated five-year payback may offer better short-term alternatives although these may convert only 30 per cent of the wind energy into electricity. By comparison, whilst a 600 kW wind turbine would have a capital cost of £400,000 and generate 1.5 gigawatts, a solar photovoltaic array would require an investment of £10 million and a roof space of 20,000 m^2 (UK GBC, 2007). In contrast, combined power and heat (CHP) systems using biomass are capable of achieving viability in the scale of generating low life cycle emissions at acceptable costs. However, studies do suggest that CHP systems require extended operating periods of 14 hours per day as well as proximity to other domestic and commercial users to achieve overall viability (UK GBC, 2007).

The final factor affecting the growth of green energy comes from regulation of developments and the regulatory regime within the wider energy market. In the UK many local authorities are adopting the 'Merton rule', which follows the London Borough of Merton's requirement in its planning regulations that all developments are required to generate 10 per cent of their generated energy needs from renewables. The true value of this policy needs to be set in the context of the factors high-lighted earlier, as well as broader UK renewable energy policy. The UK encourages new small capacity generators not via preferential 'feed' tariffs for micro-generators, as in the rest of Europe, but Renewable Obligation Certificates (ROCs) to the major power generators. Here the commercial generators and energy retailers are required by the regulator to make up an increasing percentage of their energy capacity from renewables sourced from either large or small generators that qualify for Renewable Obligation status. In cost terms, sourcing electrical energy from the retail market rather than local micro-generation may therefore in the medium term offer a more cost-effective and low-risk route than engaging with onsite micro-power generation.

This cautious approach, even when linked to reducing energy intensity, has been shown by several studies to be insufficient to achieve an overall reduction in energy intensity of warehouse operations. To go to the next stage of sustainability and approach zero emissions, companies need to incorporate many of the previously-mentioned features within their buildings and operations and then go beyond current building standards (UK Green Building Council, 2007; Reed and Wilkinson, 2005; Papadopoulos, Stylianou and Oxizidis, 2006). The next section highlights the advantages to be gained by designing sustainability, energy management and green energy generation into the next generation of buildings.

Stage 3: Design sustainability into buildings

Building regulations in the UK have principally been aimed at establishing minimum standards for the thermal characteristics of buildings' operator comfort in terms of light, heat and ventilation. The introduction of Non-Domestic Energy Performance Certificates in April 2008 in the UK for commercial buildings over 10,000 m² as part of the EU Energy Performance Buildings Directive aims to encourage progress towards higher energy efficiencies. Whilst undoubtedly these standards have both sought and have achieved higher energy efficiencies, as can be seen in Table 8.4, they have not necessarily challenged the commercial property sector to become either carbon neutral or fully sustainable. That challenge has been left to the market to achieve through the adoption of voluntary building certification systems and best practice programmes.

There are a number of voluntary sustainable building award schemes that encourage developers and users to go beyond current building and energy standards as well as incorporating a wider socioeconomic life cycle perspective. The main building benchmarking schemes are (Saunders, 2008):

Table 8.4 Energy consumption benchmarks for setting good practice design targets in storage and distribution property

	Building-related energy (kWh/m² per year)					
Building standard	Heating & hot water (fossil)	Fans, pumps controls (electricity)	Lighting (electricity)	Other (electricity)	Total electricity	Total
Typical	185	8	25	10	43	228
Improved	135	7	12	10	29	164
New	80	5	5	10	20	100

Source: Carbon Trust (2000).

- BREEAM (Building Research Establishment Environmental Assessment Method), established in the UK in 1990, encompasses all forms of public and commercial properties. It sets the standard for best practice in sustainable design and has an award banded from pass to excellent. Some 1,358 non-domestic buildings have been assessed, including new and refurbished ones (http://www.bream.org).
- LEED (Leadership in Energy and Environment Design) was established by the US Green Building Council in the United States in 1998. The voluntary audit, for domestic and commercial (new and refurbished) developments, grades buildings from certified to platinum. Some 1,283 commercial buildings have been audited (http://www.usgbc.org/).
- GREENSTAR is a voluntary environmental rating system based in Australia. Established in 2003, it has a six-star rating system, with some 50 non-domestic buildings audited to date (http://www.gbca.org.au/).
- CASBEE (Comprehensive Assessment System for Building Environmental Efficiency), inaugurated in 2004 by Japan Sustainable Building Consortium. Currently only 23 non-domestic buildings have been audited, with five grade bands from C to S (hhtp;//www.gbca.org.au/).

These schemes all seek to capture elements that encompass the resources used in terms of direct energy, water and land, but also the indirect energy embedded in the construction materials, the amount of recycled materials and the construction process itself. Wider social, ecological and environmental aspects are also included with reference to the quality of the working environment, transportation planning and management of the surrounding ecology. Within this broad approach there are considerable differences between each organizational standard in respect to assessment weighting, the method of assessment, input standards of performance, the means of accreditation and the final output measures (see Table 8.5). This undoubtedly creates substantial issues when undertaking any form of comparison between buildings across the world (Holmes and Hudson, 2002) in that each is highly adapted to local conditions, which means that, 'none of these systems, including BREEAM, travel well' (Saunders, 2008), but they have provided a catalyst for change in the market. A number of international commercial property groups such as Gazeley, Prologis, CB Richard Ellis and KingSturge have committed themselves to achieving the highest category of building certification for both their new and refurbished commercial properties. Prologis in 2007 had 0.53 million sq m in the United States and 0.34 million sq m in the UK meeting these higher standards. It should be recognized that whilst this is a small percentage of Prologis worldwide property holding of 44.9 million sq m, it does represent a significant percentage of its current build programme (Prologis, 2007). Adopting these higher standards offers developers benefits of shorter vacancy periods from construction to occupancy, and higher rental yields by providing long-term lower energy and operator costs for tenants and compliance with wider corporate social responsibility objectives (RICS Green Value Report, 2005, cited in KingSturge, 2007). But despite these advantages the perception of 67 per cent of smaller UK developers in 2005 remained that they would not go beyond the current minimum regulatory requirements due to concerns over their long-term rentals not offsetting higher capital costs (ibid). This mismatch between industry stakeholders remains a major structural barrier to achieving substantial environmental improvement (Hesse, 2004; Altes, 2008).

In the past five years, through initiatives such as Gazeley 'eco templates' (Gazeley, 2004) or Prologis 'low-carbon' warehouse, a number of exemplar developments that meet the BREEAM 'excellent' standard have been built in the UK and Europe both speculatively and on a client-commissioned basis. These buildings, by taking a holistic approach, have shown that the dilemmas of capital costs, emission levels, energy cost and environmental improvement can be commercially reconciled.

In 2007, Gazeley developed for the John Lewis Partnership, at Magna Park near Milton Keynes a 60,000 m^2 automated national distribution centre. To meet the CSR requirements of John Lewis the building incorporated 'rain water harvesting and recycling, energy efficient lighting, solar panels, low water appliances, photovoltaic panels, solar thermal

Table 8.5 per cent weighting factors attached to factors in building accreditation schemes

	BREEAM	LEED	GREEN STAR	CASBEE
Management	15	8	10	It is not
Energy & transport	25	25	20	possible to calculate the value of each issue
Health & well-being	15	13	10	category, as
Water	5	5	12	the value is dependent
Materials	10	19	10	on the final score
Land use & ecology	15	5	8	
Pollution	15	11	5	
Sustainable sites	–	16	–	

Source: Saunders (2008).

energy and local provenance vegetation'. These features added £1 million to a capital cost of £72m but achieved operational savings of £240,000 per annum (Ryan, 2007), with annual savings of 39 per cent in CO_2 emissions (1,826 tonnes), 40 per cent in energy usage (2,990 MWh) and 61 per cent in water usage (740,000 litres). Build time remained unaffected, with an overall construction and commissioning period of just 34 weeks.

A more ambitious scheme incorporates a brownfield development by property group Gazeley that includes extensive landscape recovery of the 74-hectare site at Chatterley Park, Staffordshire. This is claimed to be the first 'carbon positive' warehouse and was completed in February 2009. The 34,000 m^2 building (see Figure 8.4) achieves air tightness rates 25 per cent above current standards to minimize heat loss. Air circulation and ambient heat levels are enhanced by the use of under-floor heating ducts built into the floor slab, with south-facing walls incorporating solar-absorbing wall panels. Power for light and heat is provided by a biomass CHP power plant that can provide power to a further 650 nearby private homes. Energy needs are further reduced by using 15 per cent roof lights, rather than the standard 10 per cent, with the use of solar cell ETFE roof-light panels to generate energy and reduce night light pollution. Kinetic plates incorporated into the gatehouse area recover and convert energy from vehicles arriving and departing from the site. An innovative roof design recovers and manages rainwater for use within the warehouse as well as the overall site. Additional site access, landscaping and extensive planting have been incorporated to meet both site commercial and recreational use.

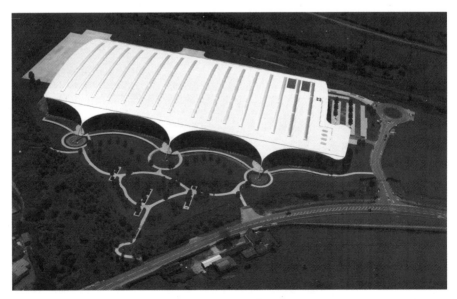

Figure 8.4 Chatterley Park Distribution Centre

Source: Photos supplied by Gazeley, 2009.

Whilst Gazeley describe this as a 'low-carbon' warehouse and it achieves the highest excellent rating, there is no objective measure in the BREEAM rating to measure total lifetime carbon levels that include operational use. Indeed research undertaken by the Green Building Council suggest that due to the size of these buildings, their continuous activity levels over extended periods and consequential direct energy needs make a zero-carbon warehouse virtually impossible even with onsite renewable generation. Further, it also highlights that 'the actual energy use of buildings appears higher than those modelled' (UK Green Building Council, 2007). This complements the observation that 'as with the heating benchmarks differences of + −15 per cent between site specific benchmarks and PI (performance index) should not be regarded as significant' (Carbon Trust, 2002b).

CONCLUSION

So where does this leave our understanding of the environmental impact of warehousing and the means of mitigating those effects? Certainly the change in scale and intensity of activity levels within warehouses has been and continues to be a challenge to achieving sustainability. This challenge extends beyond the operational needs of managing energy and resources such as fuel, and in particular electricity, water and land. Sustainability needs also to encompass wider economic, societal, ecological and environmental aspects. However, there appear to be many easy gains that firms can and should be taking by controlling and reviewing lighting and heating, and managing ventilation rates and heat loss, as well the use of LPG for counter balance or high-frequency charges for electric battery trucks. This simple business-as-usual strategy can reduce direct energy use and emissions by 50 per cent but by itself will not offset the overall growth in the energy intensity of warehouses. This energy efficient state should therefore be seen as the baseline from which further points of improvement should be measured rather than justifying any additional accolade.

To move beyond energy efficiency a firm needs to engage with more active steps through switching to green energy sources that are both more local and more sustainable. In many buildings small-scale improvements can be achieved through recovered heat and solar heating. For larger warehouses CHP may appear viable, although in the medium term the use of photovoltaic or small wind units for micro-power generation still remains questionable, as does the use of fuel cells and lithium ion batteries for forklift trucks. Purchasing green energy from major power generators seems both commercially and environmentally a better option, but one not fully understood by planning authorities. In this second stage towards sustainability only warehouses that both actively manage all forms of energy use and procure and generate viable green energy should be regarded as achieving low-emission status.

Addressing more significant and deeper changes that encompass the entire site requires more input from regulators. As with other commercial activities, most companies see compliance to regulation as the principal motivation for change despite the example of positive and short-term paybacks now emerging from leading developers and operators. International building standards such as BREEAM or LEED have been a motivator, but a lack of consistency in approach and measurement make these methods of accreditation in their current form difficult to use as objective measures towards the goal of sustainability. These systems have helped to close the historic separation in the market between the roles of developers, property managers and operators that have made investment decisions more difficult. There is some evidence that greater awareness is now entering the market, especially for new builds, in an effort to reduce operational costs and emissions rather than just concentrating on short-term rental yields and capital investment. However, the scale of the warehouse property footprint and the relatively long replacement cycle means that there will be a long time lag in achieving the goal of sustainability within the warehouse sector. Developments such as Chatterley Park show that with a holistic approach the term 'sustainable warehouse' does have a reality, although the lack of wider agreement on process boundaries or of incorporating building construction with use means that terms such as 'low carbon' are ambiguous and of greater use for publicity than as a means of classification.

REFERENCES

Altes, T (2008) Higher occupancy, higher lease rates for green buildings, *Environmental Building News*, **17** (5), p 5

Baker, P (2006) Designing distribution centres for agile supply chains, *International Journal of Logistics: Research and Applications*, **9** (1), pp 207–21

Baker, P and Canessa, M (2009), Warehouse design: a structured approach, *European Journal of Operations Management*, **193** (2), pp 425–36

Baker, P and Perotti, S (2008) *UK Warehouse Benchmarking Report 2008*, Cranfield School of Management, Cranfield University, Cranfield

Carbon Trust (2000) *The Designer's Guide to Energy-Efficient Buildings for Industry*, GPG 303, HMSO, London

Carbon Trust (2002a) *Good Practice Guide 319: Managing energy in warehouses*, HMSO, London

Carbon Trust (2002b) *Energy Consumption Guide 81: Benchmarking tool for industrial buildings – heating and internal lighting*, HMSO, London

Carbon Trust (2006a) *Refrigeration: Introducing energy saving opportunities for business*, CTV002, HMSO, London

Carbon Trust (2006b) *Carbon Footprints in the Supply Chain: The next steps for business*, CTC616, London

Carbon Trust (2007) *Lighting: Bright ideas for more efficient illumination*, CTV021, HMSO, London

Davies, J (2009) Innovative reach, *Logistics Manager*, February, pp 15–18

Department of Communities and Local Government (2007) [accessed 24 May 2009] Tables on commercial and industrial floor space and Rateable Value Statistics 2007 [Online] http://www.communities. gov.uk/planningandbuilding/planningbuilding/planningstatistics/ livetables/tablescommercialindustrialfloors/

European Logistics Association (ELA) (2004) *Differentiation for Performance Excellence in Logistics 2004*, Deutscher Verkehrs-Verlag GmbH, Hamburg

Frazelle, E (2002) *World-class Warehousing and Material Handling*, McGraw-Hill, New York

Gazeley (2004) Eco template a framework for increasingly environmental and socially responsible logistics development Gazely UK Limited, London

Gazeley (2008) Sustainability report 2008 [Online] http://www.gazeley. com/en-GB/Home_Corporate_Responsibility_Download.aspx

Green Buildings.com (2008) Green buildings impact report 2008 [Online] http://stateofgreenbusiness.com/greenbusinessreport/thank-you?sid=22443

Hesse, M (2004) Land for logistics: locational dynamics real estate markets and political regulation of regional distribution complexes, *Tijdschrift voor Economische en Sociale Geografie*, **95** (2), pp 162–73

Holmes, J and Hudson, G (2002) The application of BREEAM in corporate real estate: a case study in the design of a city centre office development, *Journal of Corporate Real Estate*, **5** (1), pp 66–78

Johnson, E (2008) Disagreement over carbon footprints: a comparison of electric and LPG forklifts, *Energy Policy*, **36**, pp 1569–73

KingSturge (2007) European property sustainability matters – reduce, reuse, recycle [Online] http://www.kingsturge.co.uk/research/

KingSturge (2008) *Logistics Property Today*, Spring 2008 edition

MacLeod, P (2008) House of Hanover, *SHD*, July, pp 38–46

McKinnon, AC (1998) Logistical restructuring, freight traffic growth and the environment, in *Transport Policy and the Environment*, ed D Banister, pp 97–109, Spon, London

Padgett, J, Steinemann, AC, Clarke, JH and Vandenbergh, MP (2008) A comparison of carbon calculators, *Environmental Impact Assessment Review*, **28**, pp 106–15

Papadopoulos, A, Stylianou, A and Oxizidis, S (2006) Impact of energy pricing on buildings' energy design, *Management of Environmental Quality: An International Journal*, **17** (6) pp 753–61

Perez-Lombard, L, Ortiz, J and Pout, C (2007) A review on buildings energy consumption information, *Energy and Buildings*, **40**, 394–98

Prologis (2007) Sustainability Report [Online] http://ir.prologis.com/ investors/SustainReport2007/index.html

Pout, CH, Moss, SA, Davidson, PJ, Steadman, JP, Bruhns, HR, Mortimer, ND and Rix, JHR (1998) *Non-domestic Energy Fact File*, Building Research Establishment, London

Reed, R and Wilkinson, S (2005) The increasing importance of sustainability for building ownership, *Journal of Corporate Real Estate*, **7** (4) pp 339–50

Ryan , J (2007) Green giants, *Retail Week*, 1 November [Online] www. retail-week.com/property/green_giants.html

Saunders, T (2008) [accessed 26 August 2009] A discussion document comparing international environmental assessment methods for buildings, BREEAM [Online] http://www.breeam.org/page. jsp?id=101

Scrase, I (2000) *White-collar CO_2 Energy Consumption in the Service Sector*, The Association for the Conservation of Energy, London

SHD Magazine (2009) Powerfully green, February, pp 30–31

Trebilock, B (2008) Battery basic, *Modern Material Handling*, November, pp 38–41

Treloar, G, Fay, R, Ilozor, B and Love, P (2001) Building materials selection: greenhouse strategies for built facilities, *Facilities*, **19** (3/4), pp 139–149

Tsoulfas, G and Pappis, C (2005) Environmental principles applicable to supply chains design and operation, *Journal of Cleaner Production*, **14**, pp 1593–1602

UK Green Building Council (UK GBC) (2007) *Report on Carbon Reductions in New Non-domestic Buildings*, Queen's Printer, London

World Resources Institute (2006) Hot Climate, Cool Commerce: A service sector guide to greenhouse gas management, World Resources Institute, Washington, DC [Online] http://pdf.wri.org/hotclimatecoolcommerce. pdf

Wyatt, K (2007) Taking light steps to cut carbon emissions, *UKWA*, August [Online] www.ukwa.org.uk

Part 3

OPERATIONAL
PERSPECTIVE

9

Opportunities for improving vehicle utilization

Alan McKinnon and Julia Edwards

INTRODUCTION

In most developed countries, road transport is the dominant mode of freight movement. The efficiency of the road freight sector is therefore a major determinant of the overall environmental impact of logistics. If all trucks and vans were fully laden on all trips, this environmental burden could be greatly reduced. The extent of the resulting environmental benefit is difficult to quantify at a national or international level as little official data is collected on the use of vehicle capacity, particularly in terms of floor area and cube. Some of the available statistics, however, indicate the degree of capacity under-utilization. For example:

- Approximately 25 per cent of truck kilometres in EU countries is run empty, while in Ireland it averages around 37 per cent (Eurostat, 2007).
- In the UK food supply chain, only about 52 per cent of the available space on laden trips is actually occupied by a load (Freight Best Practice Programme, 2006).
- 44-tonne trucks in the UK, which can carry a maximum payload of 29 tonnes, transport on average only 17.6 tonnes when laden and 12.7 tonnes if allowance is made for empty running (Knight et al, 2008).

Raising vehicle load factors is one of the most attractive sustainable distribution measures to companies because it yields substantial economic as well as environmental benefits. Increasing transport costs and the prospect of oil prices rising steeply in the future are giving companies a strong incentive to improve their vehicle loading. Gosier et al (2008: 2) argue that 'strategies such as just-in-time, lean manufacturing and even low-cost country-sourcing must be re-valuated in light of fuel prices. In every respect, we have entered a new era where different supply chain strategies are needed to engender high performance.' Improved vehicle loading and reduced empty running also cut traffic levels and ease congestion on the road network. Governments have recognized these economic, environmental and infrastructural advantages. In the UK, improving vehicle loading and minimizing empty running were key objectives of the government's original Sustainable Distribution Strategy (DETR, 1999) and recently reiterated in its 'logistical perspective' in the pursuit of a 'sustainable transport system' (DfT, 2008a). There have also been several industry-led initiatives to promote 'transport optimisation' across particular sectors, such as groceries (IGD 2003).

In this chapter we begin by examining the different measures that can be used to assess road vehicle utilization. We then review a series of constraints on truck utilization and outline various ways in which they can be relaxed.

MEASURING VEHICLE UTILIZATION

Different indices can be used to calculate the utilization of vehicle fleets, each giving a slightly different impression of transport efficiency. At a macro-level, most of the parameters measure freight in terms of weight rather than volume, reflecting a lack of government data on the cubic-volume of freight transported.

Tonne-kilometres per vehicle per annum

This indicator is essentially a measure of productivity, and as such, generally presents the trucking industry in a favourable light. Over the last half century in the UK there has been a five-fold increase in the number of tonne-kms carried annually by the average truck (Figure 9.1), owing mainly to increases in maximum truck weight and the use of vehicles for more hours in the day (McKinnon, 2007). Since the late 1990s this metric has levelled off for the UK truck fleet, despite two increases in the maximum truck weight since 1999 (DfT, 2008b). It is a rather poor

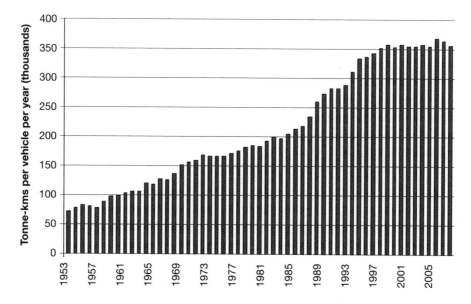

Figure 9.1   Improvement in truck productivity in the UK: tonne-kms per truck per annum

Data source: Department for Transport.

measure of the sustainability of the road freight sector as it gives no indication of the proportion of vehicle capacity actually utilized or the potential to raise load factors.

Weight-based lading factor

This measure is exclusively weight based and is generally expressed as the ratio of 'the actual goods moved to the maximum tonne-kilometres achievable if the vehicles, whenever loaded, were loaded to their maximum carrying capacity' (DfT, 2008b). It gives a less favourable impression of capacity utilization in the road freight industry. In the UK, for example, average load factors have declined from 63 per cent in 1990 to 57 per cent in 2007 (DfT, 2008b). Much of this reduction has, however, occurred since 1999 when maximum lorry weight was increased initially from 38 to 41 tonnes (on six axles) and then to 44 tonnes in 2001. These increases in maximum carrying capacity occur overnight, but it can then take several years for industry to adapt its ordering patterns to exploit this additional capacity. In the meantime, the average percentage load factor can drop. The recent decline in this lading factor can also be partly attributed to a decline in the average density of road freight, due to a switch from heavier materials such as metal and wood, to lighter plastics, and an increase in the amount of packaging. This increases the proportion of loads that 'cube-out' before they 'weigh-out' and is reflected in a decline in the weight-based measures of vehicle lading. For lower density products, space-related measures of lading are more appropriate.

Space-utilization/vehicle fill

Vehicle fill can be measured in three dimensions by the percentage of space occupied by a load or in two dimensions by the proportion of the floor (or deck) area covered. In the case of unitized loads (of, for example, pallets, roll cages or stillages), the actual number of units carried can be divided by the maximum number to calculate the percentage fill. This should be accompanied by an assessment of the internal loading of the units and the average height of the pallet-loads (Samuelsson and Tilanus, 1997). There is no systematic collection of volumetric data for road freight flows, so assessing vehicle fill at an industry level is very problematic. The Transport KPI surveys commissioned by the UK government over the past decade have become a useful source of this data (McKinnon, 2007).

Empty running

Empty running is generally expressed as the proportion of vehicle-kms run empty. It is an inevitable consequence of the uni-directional movement of freight consignments and difficulty of balancing freight flows in opposite directions. Usually the final leg of a multi-drop journey, or the initial leg in a multiple collection round, is also run empty. Within the EU, the empty-running of trucks varies considerably by country and averages around 27 per cent (Eurostat, 2007). The level of empty running tends to be inversely proportional to the length of haul, because the longer the journey the greater the economic incentive to find a backload.

Empty journeys are not only wasteful economically, but also carry an environmental penalty. Encouragingly, over the last 30 years the proportion of empty running by trucks in the UK has steadily declined, yielding significant economic and environmental benefits. McKinnon and Ge (2004) estimated that 'other things being equal, if the percentage of empty running had remained at its 1973 level, road haulage costs in 2003 would have been £1.3 bn higher and an extra 1.1 million of tonnes of CO_2 would have been emitted into the atmosphere by trucks.'

FACTORS AFFECTING THE UTILIZATION OF TRUCK CAPACITY

Companies do not wilfully under-load their vehicles. Nor is poor loading very often a result of careless management. There are many good reasons for trucks travelling around empty or only partly full. Figure 9.2 identifies the main constraints on vehicle loading and classifies them into five categories (McKinnon, 2007):

- market-related constraints associated with the spatial pattern of trade and fluctuations on the volume of freight flow;
- regulatory constraints governing the size and weight of vehicles, the timing of deliveries and health and safety aspects of vehicle loading/unloading;
- inter-functional constraints imposed on transport management by other departments within the business;
- infrastructural constraints related to the physical capacity of transport networks and storage capacity at both ends of a freight movement;
- equipment-related constraints resulting from the incompatibility of vehicles, handling equipment and loads.

We will now examine some of the more important constraints in greater detail and consider what, if anything, companies can do to ease them.

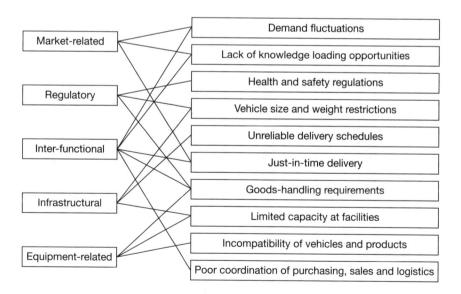

Figure 9.2 Five-fold classification of the constraints on vehicle utilization

This review reveals that in under-loading their vehicles companies are sometimes making perfectly rational trade-offs between transport efficiency and other corporate goals, such as minimizing inventory, optimizing the use of warehouse space or maximizing staff productivity at the loading bay. As a result total logistics costs may be minimized. When environmental costs are factored into the calculation, however, the trade-offs usually have to be rebalanced to give greater priority to vehicle utilization.

Demand fluctuations

Sales volumes can vary widely over daily, weekly, monthly and seasonal cycles. Figure 9.3, for example, illustrates the average daily flow of groceries in the UK food supply chain. Vehicle capacity is often planned to accommodate peak demand, inevitably leaving the fleet with surplus capacity at other times. Companies subject to pronounced, and quite predictable, seasonal fluctuations can hire additional vehicles or outsource more of their transport at peak periods. It is more difficult to adopt this strategy where there are wide and unpredictable variations in transport demand from day to day.

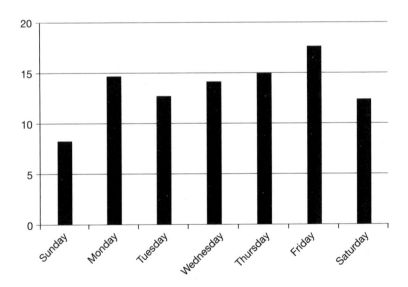

Figure 9.3 Daily demand fluctuation in the food sector: per cent by volume

Source: Department for Transport (2007).

If transport managers and carriers can be given more advanced warning of future demand they can plan the use of vehicle capacity much more effectively. One of the key objectives of Collaborative Transportation Management (CTM) is to involve managers responsible for the transport operation at an earlier stage in the logistics process (Browning and White, 2000). By creating an 'extended planning horizon' some carriers have been able to increase the utilization of their regional truck fleets in the United States by between 10 and 42 per cent, mainly as a result of improved backloading (Esper and Williams, 2003).

The Nominated Day Delivery System (NDDS) helps firms achieve much higher levels of transport efficiency by getting customers to adhere to an ordering and delivery timetable. They are informed that a vehicle will be visiting their area on a 'nominated' day, and that to receive a delivery on that day they must submit their order a certain period in advance. By concentrating deliveries in particular zones on particular days of the week, suppliers can achieve higher levels of load consolidation, drop density and vehicle utilization. This practice is, however, resisted by some sales managers on the grounds that it impairs the standard of customer service and can weaken the company's competitive position.

Some demand fluctuations are artificially induced by standard business practices. Promotional activity, for example, destabilizes the flow of goods, making it more difficult to manage transport capacity at a uniformly high level. The normal practice of paying bills at the end of the calendar month and giving sales staff monthly targets also causes freight volumes to peak at the start of the month. Vehicle capacity provided to meet this peak is often under-used later in the month. Relaxing the monthly payment cycle and moving to a system of 'rolling credit', in which customers are still given the same length of time to pay but from the date of the order rather than the start of a calendar month, can significantly improve vehicle utilization. It has been suggested, for example, that this could significantly cut supply chain costs and environmental impacts in the European chemical industry (McKinnon, 2004).

Lack of knowledge of loading opportunities

If transport operators had perfect knowledge of all the loads available for delivery in all locations at all times they would be able to attain much higher levels of vehicle loading on both outbound and return journeys. Many load matching opportunities are missed because of a lack of communication between potential carriers and shippers.

Traditionally it has been the role of intermediaries in the freight market, such as freight forwarders and brokers, to act as clearing houses for information about available loads and vehicles. They relied on market knowledge, personal networking and the telephone to arrange deals between shippers and carriers. With the advent of the internet, a new generation of freight exchanges has emerged, providing web-enabled tendering, online auctions and bulletin boards for road haulage services (Sarkis, Meade and Talluri, 2000; Lewis, 2001). This has greatly improved the opportunities for matching loads with vehicle capacity, particularly on backhauls. One online freight exchange has estimated that companies using its procurement services have been able to cut companies' transport costs by 8 per cent by increasing 'carrier's asset utilization while protecting their margins' (Mansell, 2006: 27). The impact of e-commerce on the freight and logistics sector is discussed more fully in Chapter 16.

Geographical imbalances in traffic flow

Unlike passengers, who normally make return journeys, almost all freight moves in one direction. The quantities of freight moved between pairs of countries and regions are seldom balanced. Even if there is parity in the level of trade in monetary terms, the physical amounts of freight moved in opposite directions can be quite different. It was estimated that in 2003 130,000 lorries travelled empty between Scotland and England, reflecting a ratio of 1:1.31 in the tonnage of freight moved by road between the two countries.

The main way in which carriers deal with such traffic imbalances is by adopting a practice called 'triangulation'. Instead of running vehicles on A-to-B-to-A bilateral routes, they send them on more complex inter-regional trips (eg A-to-B-to-C-to-A), which can allow them to exploit traffic imbalances in opposite directions along the route and thus raise the average load factor across the journey as a whole.

Just-in-time (JIT) delivery

The goal of JIT is to achieve a continuous flow of materials through the supply chain in an effort to keep inventory to a minimum. The synchronization of transport with the production process and time-criticality of JIT deliveries often results in supplies being delivered at short notice and in small quantities. Under these circumstances, efficient utilization of transport capacity can be sacrificed for lower inventory and more flexible production. Low-inventory policies and JIT delivery are now the norm across many industrial sectors. It is hardly surprising, therefore, that JIT receives much of the blame for the under-utilization of trucks and consequent growth in freight traffic. As discussed in Chapter 1, it is generally portrayed as being bad for the environment.

The adverse effects of JIT on transport efficiency can be eased by rationalizing the inbound logistics system. For example, some car manufacturers, like Nissan (DETR, 1998a), have employed logistics service providers to collect components from suppliers and consolidate them at a hub prior to JIT delivery directly to the production line. The clustering of suppliers' plants, vendor hubs and warehouses around car and computer assembly plants has also minimized JIT delivery distances. In the retail sector, the equivalent 'quick response' pressures, have resulted in the insertion of an additional 'primary consolidation' tier between the factory and the distribution centre where different manufacturers' products are aggregated into viably sized loads.

Lack of inter-functional coordination

Poor truck utilization can be a consequence of the departmental 'silo' structure in many businesses, which inhibits communication and coordination between functions. Lack of liaison between purchasing and logistics staff often results in potential opportunities for backloading being missed, while sales staff can make commitments to customers that entail the delivery of goods in poorly loaded vehicles. This problem can be alleviated by the application of good business practice, involving the replacement of silos with more effective cross-functional management of core processes, one of which is the fulfilment of customer orders (Christopher, 2005).

Priority given to the outbound deliveries

Companies naturally give priority to distribution of their products to customers and are reluctant to backload a vehicle when they fear that it may not return in time for reloading with the next outbound consignment. This fear has been identified as one of the main constraints on backloading, particularly where delivery schedules are unreliable (McKinnon and Ge, 2006). The main way of addressing this concern is to improve the reliability and 'visibility' of road freight operations so as to give managers greater confidence in distribution schedules. This is discussed in the next section.

Lack of cooperation across the supply chain

There is a limit to how much any individual company can do on its own to improve the utilization of vehicles carrying its products. The decisions of companies upstream and downstream in the supply chain can limit the opportunity to improve load factors and cut truck-kms. If supply chain partners are prepared to collaborate, much higher levels of utilization can be achieved. A distinction can be made between horizontal collaboration, where companies at the same level of the supply chain work together, and vertical collaboration, which involves collective action by trading partners at different levels in a supply chain. In both cases, logistics service providers can play a key role.

Horizontal collaboration

Newing (2008) has estimated that where two competing firms merge their logistics operations and vehicle deliveries they can cut their combined transport costs by 15–20 per cent. Such cross-company/ industry collaboration can take various forms. In the petroleum sector, for example, swap agreements between oil companies allow refineries to supply all the filling stations in a local area regardless of brand, maximizing drop density and minimizing empty backhaul distances. In the fast-moving consumer goods (FMCG) sector there are examples of firms merging their logistics operations at a shared distribution facility and combining vehicle loads. This is well exemplified by the consolidation of Unilever and Kimberly-Clark products for the Dutch retail market at a distribution centre operated for them by Kuehne and Nagel in Raamsdonksveer (Cruijssen, 2007). As a result of this collaboration the companies have been able to cut their logistics costs by 12–15 per cent while responding to retailers' demands for faster and more frequent delivery. In the UK, Nestlé and United Biscuits, which are competitors in the biscuit and confectionery markets, have worked together to cut empty running of trucks between Yorkshire and the Midlands (Clements, 2008). This is part of a wider food industry initiative involving '37 of the UK's leading food and consumer goods companies' that has 'removed the equivalent of 53 million journey miles from UK roads' (IGD, 2008a).

Vertical collaboration

There are also several different types of vertical collaboration. One of the most common is the collection of inbound supplies by a returning delivery vehicle. This is now common practice in the retail grocery sector where lorries returning from supermarkets make a triangular trip to pick up orders from suppliers and transport them to the distribution centre. This form of 'supplier collection' substantially reduces empty mileage (DfT, 2005a). A variant of this scheme, known as 'onward delivery', involves suppliers' vehicles delivering to the retailer's shops on their way back from the distribution centre to the factory. Through these forms of vertical collaboration with upstream suppliers, the UK supermarket chain Tesco was able to save around 3 million journeys per annum (DETR, 1998b).

Where trading partners in the vertical channel adopt a vendor-managed inventory (VMI) strategy, the supplier assumes control of the replenishment process and can then phase the movement of products in a way that optimizes the use of vehicle capacity. Disney, Potter and Gardner (2003) used simulation modelling to demonstrate the potential transport benefits of VMI over a 'traditional supply chain'. Although VMI can result in more inventory being held at the customer's premises, they would typically only be charged for supplies as they are actually used (or 'called off').

Higher transport efficiency can be achieved in local distribution to homes and commercial premises through the use of 'unattended delivery' (see Chapter 16). When customers install a reception box, the carrier can exercise much greater control over the delivery schedule, improving the efficiency of vehicle loading and routing while virtually eliminating the risk of failed delivery. Research in Helsinki has suggested that the use of reception boxes can cut transport costs, delivery distances and related externalities by as much as 40 per cent (Punakivi, Yrjölä, and Holmström, 2001).

Vertical collaboration in the field of reverse logistics can maximize the return flow of waste, damaged and unwanted products on backhauls. This offers considerable potential for reducing empty running and would contribute to the 20–40 per cent savings in transport costs that could be achieved if retailers were to rationalize the reverse flow for returned products from shops (Cranfield University, Sheffield Hallam University and CILT, 2004). Reverse logistics is the main focus of Chapter 11.

Unreliability in logistics schedules

To plan backhauls and the more complex routes that are often required to maximize vehicle loading, managers must have confidence in the scheduling. Fortunately, much traffic congestion is regular and predictable, allowing companies to accommodate related delays by building some slack into their supply chain operations (McKinnon et al, 2008). More problematic are the unforeseen, random traffic incidents, such as major accidents and road works, that can significantly increase transit time variability. It has been estimated that in the UK around 24 per cent of freight deliveries are delayed, and approximately 34 per cent of these delays are attributable mainly to traffic congestion (McKinnon, 2009). Deviations from schedule are also due to a range of other factors, including backdoor congestion at distribution centres, vehicle breakdowns and staff absenteeism.

Advances in IT and telematics now permit the tracking of trucks, providing advance warning of delays and allowing fleet managers to replan routes in real-time while the vehicle is on the road to minimize the impact of congestion. The rescheduling of deliveries into the evening and night can also reduce transit time variability. For delays originating in factories, warehouses and shops, some re-engineering of internal processes is often required and, in the case of backdoor congestion, the provision of additional capacity. Increasing the ratio of tractors to trailers in an articulated vehicle fleet (ie the 'articulation ratio') can decouple the transport operation from the loading/unloading activity, reducing the risk of inbound delays constraining the outbound load factor.

Design of packaging and handling equipment

The nature of the packaging influences the efficiency with which space is used in buildings and vehicles across the supply chain. Its shape, dimensions and stackability can result in poor use of vehicle capacity. In their choice of handling equipment companies often trade off lower vehicle cube utilization for faster and easier loading and off-loading of consignments.

Handling equipment can be modified to permit convenient handling as well as efficient use of transport and storage capacity. A French food manufacturer, for example, was able to improve vehicle fill by 35–41 per cent by packing orders into modules of varying heights (University of St Gallen, 2000). The total amount of packaging on products can also be reduced, often without increasing damage levels across the supply chain. The UK supermarket chain Asda, for example, is aiming to reduce the packaging on its own-label product range by 25 per cent (IGD, 2008b). Packaging can also be redesigned to improve its 'space-efficiency'. Efforts have been made, for example, to replace round cans with square ones to cut space requirements by 20 per cent in vehicles, warehouses and shops (Sonneveld, 2000).

Incompatibility of vehicles and products

Some vehicles are limited to carrying only certain commodities, restricting the types of load they can collect on a backhaul. It is not possible, for example, to carry palletized loads on a tanker, or refrigerated goods in a trailer without temperature control. This constrains the matching of loads with available vehicle capacity on particular routes.

It has been possible to redesign vehicles to accommodate a wider mix of products, often on the same journey. The compartmentalization of trucks has enabled grocery retailers and their contractors to combine the movement of products at different temperatures on a single journey. This form of 'composite distribution', for example, enabled the UK retailer Safeway to reduce the average number of vehicle trips required to deliver 1000 cases from five in 1985 to one in 1995 (Freight Transport Association, 1995).

Vehicle size and weight restrictions

As discussed above, many loads 'weigh-out' before all the vehicle space is filled or 'cube-out' before the vehicle reaches its maximum gross weight. Legal restrictions on vehicle weights and dimensions, therefore, result in either weight or volume-carrying capacity being under-utilized (McKinnon, 2005). As weight limits have been raised by a greater margin than size limits in recent decades, over a period when the average density of freight has been declining, a higher proportion of loads are now volume constrained than weight constrained. This is clearly illustrated in the UK, where just over twice as many of the loads carried by trucks with gross weights of over 38 tonnes are volume constrained as weight constrained (Figure 9.4).

Increasing the maximum size of trucks can therefore allow companies to consolidate loads, achieving greater vehicle fill and cutting truck-kms. It is possible to gain extra cubic capacity vertically or horizontally. In some countries, most notably the UK where bridge and tunnel clearances over the road network are relatively high (mainly to accommodate double-deck buses), it is possible to increase vehicle height and insert

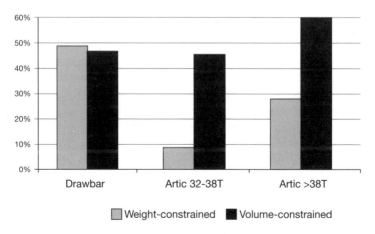

Figure 9.4 Percentage of lorry-kms travelled with weight and volume-constrained loads

a double-deck to permit the carriage of two layers of pallets.[1] Britain actually has no legal limit on vehicle height though, because of infrastructural constraints, five metres is generally considered the maximum. Companies carrying low-density products have the most to gain from the use of double-decks, and for this reason they are now extensively used by major retailers and parcel carriers in the UK (McKinnon and Campbell, 1997). One large UK retailer has demonstrated the benefits of double-decking by comparing operating parameters for deliveries using a double-deck vehicle and two single-deck vehicles with similar capacity. Unit delivery costs, vehicle-kms and CO_2 emissions were all around 48 per cent lower (DfT, 2005b).

Across much of the European mainland a four-metre height limit applies, tightly restricting, but not eliminating, opportunities for double-decking. In other European countries, such as Sweden, Finland and the Netherlands, companies have gained extra cube 'horizontally' by lengthening the vehicle. Often this increase in length and axle numbers has been accompanied by a relaxation of the maximum weight limit. Currently, within the EU, Council Directive 96/53/EC permits a maximum vehicle length of 18.75 m for a draw bar-trailer combination and 16.5 m for semi-trailer articulated vehicles. Trailers and semi-trailers that comply with these regulations can be combined to greater overall lengths of up to 25.25 m in the so-called European modular system. All EU member states have the right to operate these longer vehicles for domestic use (ie as long as they do not cross international borders or distort international competition in the transport sector). Until recently no EU country had introduced longer and heavier vehicles (LHVs) as a result of the 96/53/EC directive, though the use of LHVs in Sweden and Finland pre-dated their entry to the EU (McKinnon, 2008). In 2007, following a successful on-the-road trial, the Dutch government decided to permit 25.25-metre-long trucks up to a maximum gross weight of 50 tonnes (since raised to 60 tonnes). Studies of the environmental and economic impact of LHVs have also been conducted in Germany (UBA, 2007), Belgium (Debauche and Decock, 2007), Sweden (Vierth et al, 2008) and the UK (Knight et al, 2008). Partly in the light of this evidence, the governments of both countries have refused to legalize 25.25-metre vehicles, though Britain is considering increasing the maximum length of articulated vehicles with a single trailer from 16.5 to 18.75 metres. A recent EU-funded study concluded that LHVs could be widely introduced in Europe 'without harming European society as a whole', though it recognized the need for several 'counter-measures' to minimize the negative impact on alternative modes, allay safety concerns and prepare the road infrastructure (Transport and Mobility Leuven et al, 2008). Rail freight organizations (eg UIC et al, 2007) and environmental groups (eg European Federation of Transport and the

Environment, 2007) are vehemently opposed to the legalization of what they call 'mega-trucks'.

Health and safety regulations

These regulations constrain the height to which loads can be stacked on a vehicle to minimize the risk of operatives being injured. The double-decking of vehicles can help to relax this constraint without compromising safety, though only where vehicle height clearances permit.

Working time restrictions

Legal restrictions on drivers' hours and working time, which are also a form of health and safety regulation, can constrain the amount of freight that can be collected and/or delivered in a single shift. In particular, they can reduce the amount of time available for backhauling and hence increase the proportion of empty running. It was feared that the application of the Working Time Directive to European road freight operations in 2006 would frustrate efforts to improve vehicle loading. In reality, European governments have tended to adopt quite a liberal interpretation of 'periods of availability' in WTD regulations, giving vehicle operators greater flexibility than they had initially expected. Based on the UK experience, the WTD appears not to have had the adverse effect on vehicle utilization than some commentators were predicting.

Capacity constraints at company premises

The size of an order is often constrained by the amount of storage capacity available at the delivery point. In some sectors, this storage capacity has been shrinking, partly in line with the downward pressure on inventory but also to intensify the use of floor space. Retailers, for example, have been compressing back-storeroom areas in their shops to maximize the floor area available for product display and merchandizing. Where deliveries are to warehouses, the dimensions of slots in the racking systems can dictate the maximum pallet height. Under these circumstances, the size and shape of unitized loads may optimize space utilization in the warehouse but not in the delivery vehicle (AT Kearney, 1997).

In some sectors, such as chemicals and agriculture, lack of investment has prevented the ability of tanks and silos to increase in line with vehicle carrying capacity. Expanding their capacity would improve vehicle utilization and often yield a healthy return on investment. Where companies have deliberately scaled down their storage space at the expense of transport efficiency, it may be necessary to reappraise the cost trade-offs in the light of rising transport costs and environmental concerns.

CONCLUSION

It has been suggested that if all trucks had glass sides, people would be surprised by the amount of air they carried. This chapter has tried to show that the under-utilization of vehicle capacity has many causes and can sometimes be justified on solid commercial grounds. Companies cannot afford to be complacent, however, in the way that they manage this capacity. In response to a combination of economic and environmental pressures they are now giving greater priority to vehicle fill and trying much harder to overcome the traditional constraints on load size and weight. This requires an internal realignment of business objectives within companies as well as greater external collaboration along and between supply chains. Advances in vehicle, materials handling and information technology can assist efforts to improve loading, as can investment in more storage space at critical points in the supply chain. As discussed more fully in Chapter 17, government also has a role to play by optimizing vehicle size and weight limits for sustainable distribution, adopting charging mechanisms that incentivize efficient loading, and running best-practice programmes for road freight operators.

A sample of 100 logistics specialists recently surveyed in the UK predicted that by 2020 the proportion of truck kilometres run empty would drop by 19 per cent and the average payload weight on laden trips increase by 12 per cent (Piecyk and McKinnon, 2009). This confirms that the potential exists to achieve substantial improvements in vehicle loading and reap the resulting economic and environmental rewards.

NOTE

1. The floor of the vehicle can also be lowered by using smaller wheels.

REFERENCES

AT Kearney (1997) *The Efficient Unit Loads Report*, ECR Europe, Brussels
Browning, B and White, A (2000) *Collaborative Transportation Management: A Proposal*, Logility Inc, Atlanta
Christopher, M (2005) *Logistics and Supply Chain Management: Creating value-adding networks*, Financial Times/Prentice Hall, London

Clements, A (2008) Green collaboration, *Retail Week*, 26 September

Cranfield University, Sheffield Hallam University and CILT (2004) *The Efficiency of Reverse Logistics*, DfT [Online] http://www.ciltuk.org.uk/pages/revlog

Cruijssen, FCAM (2007) *Horizontal Co-operation in Transport and Logistics*, PhD thesis, University of Tilburg

Debauche, W and Decock, D (2007) *Working Group on Longer and Heavier Vehicles: A multidisciplinary approach to the issue*, Belgian Road Research Centre, Brussels

Department of the Environment, Transport and the Regions (DETR) (1998a) *Efficient JIT Supply Chain Management: Nissan Motor Manufacturing (UK) Ltd*, Good Practice Case Study 374, DETR, London

DETR (1998b) *Energy Savings from Integrated Logistics Management: Tesco plc*, Good Practice Case Study 364, Energy Efficiency Best Practice Programme, Harwell

DETR (1999) *Sustainable Development: A strategy*, DETR, London

Department for Transport (DfT) (2004) *The Future of Transport*, White Paper CM6234, DfT, London

DfT (2005a) *Make Back-hauling Work for You*, Freight Best Practice Guide, DfT, London

DfT (2005b) *Focus on Double Decks: Freight best practice programme*, HMSO, London

DfT (2007) *Key Performance Indicators for Food and Drink Supply Chains, Freight best practice programme*, HMSO, London

DfT (2008a) *Delivery a Sustainable Transport System: The logistics perspective*, DfT, London

DfT (2008b) *Road Freight Statistics 2007*, DfT, London

Disney, S, Potter, A and Gardner, B (2003) The impact of VMI on transport operations, *Transportation Research Part E: Logistics and transportation*, **39**, pp 363–80

Esper, TL and Williams, LR (2003) The value of collaborative transportation management (CTM): its relationship to CPFR and information technology, *Transportation Journal*, Summer, **42** (4), pp 55–65

European Federation of Transport and the Environment (2007) *Longer and Heavier Vehicles (LHVs) and the Environment*, Position Paper, European Federation of Transport and the Environment, Brussels

Eurostat (2007) Average loads, distances and empty running in road freight transport – 2005, *Statistics in Focus*, Transport 117/2007, Eurostat, Luxembourg

Freight Best Practice Programme (2006) *Key Performance Indicators for the Food Supply Chain*, DfT, London

Freight Transport Association (1995) *JIT: Time sensitive distribution*, Freight Matters 1/95, FTA, Tunbridge Wells

Gosier, R, Simchi-Levi, D, Wright, J and Bertz, BA (2008) *Past the Tipping Point: Record oil prices require new supply chain strategies to enable future high performance*, Accenture, [accessed 4 April 2009] [Online] http://www.accenture.com/NR/rdonlyres/3AFCE27E-F969-4053-8A0C-3608D2FFCC9C/0/PasttheTippingPointFinal.pdf

IGD (2003) *Transport Optimization: Sharing best practice in distribution management*, IGD, Watford

IGD (2008a) *On the Road to Greener Distribution*, IGD, Letchmore Heath [Online] http://www. igd.com/index.asp?id=1&fid=1&sid=5&tid=47&cid=564

IGD (2008b) *Sustainable Distribution in 2008*, IGD, Watford

Knight, I, Newton, W, McKinnon, A, Palmer, A, Barlow, T, McCrae, I, Dodd, M, Couper, G, Davies, H, Daly, A, McMahon, B, Cook, E, Ramdas, V and Taylor, N (2008) *Longer and/or Longer and Heavier Goods Vehicles (LHVs) – A study of the likely effects if permitted in the UK: final report*, TRL Published Project Report 285, TRL, Berkshire

Lewis, I (2001) Logistics and electronic commerce: an interorganisational systems perspective, *Transportation Journal*, **40**, (4), pp. 5–13

Mansell, G (2006) Transport tendering comes of age, *Transport and Logistics Focus*, **8** (4) , pp 26–28

McKinnon, AC (2004) *Supply Chain Excellence in the European Chemical Industry*, European Petrochemical Association/Cefic, Brussels

McKinnon, AC (2005) The economic and environmental benefits of increasing maximum truck weight: the British experience, *Transportation Research Part D*, **10**, pp 77–95

McKinnon, AC (2007) CO_2 *emissions from the freight transport sector*, paper prepared for the Climate Change Working Group of the Commission for Integrated Transport, London

McKinnon, AC (2008) Should the maximum length and weight of trucks be increased? A review of European research, in the Proceedings of the 13th International Symposium on Logistics, 6–8 July, Bangkok

McKinnon, AC (2009) Benchmarking road freight transport: review of a government-sponsored programme, *Benchmarking: An International Journal*, **16** (5) (in print)

McKinnon AC and Campbell, J (1997) *Opportunities for Consolidating Volume-constrained Loads in Double-deck and High-cube Vehicles*, Christian Salvesen Logistics Research Paper No 1, Heriot-Watt University, Edinburgh

McKinnon, AC and Ge, Y (2004) Use of a synchronized vehicle audit to determine opportunities for improving transport efficiency in a supply chain, *International Journal of Logistics: Research and Applications*, **7** (3), pp 219–38

McKinnon, AC and Ge, Y (2006) The potential for reducing empty running by trucks: a retrospective analysis, *International Journal of Physical Distribution & Logistics Management*, **36** (5) pp 391–410

McKinnon, AC, Palmer, A, Edwards, JB and Piecyk, M (2008) *Reliability of Road Transport from the Perspective of Logistics Managers and Freight Operators*, Report prepared for the Joint Transport Research Centre of the OECD and the International Transport Forum, Logistics Research Centre, Heriot-Watt University, Edinburgh

Newing, R (2008) Finding better ways to deliver the goods, *Financial Times*, 8 October

Piecyk, M and McKinnon, AC (2009) *Environmental Impact of Road Freight Transport in 2020: Full report of a Delphi survey*, Heriot-Watt University, Edinburgh

Punakivi, M, Yrjölä, H and Holmström, J (2001) Solving the last mile issue: reception box or delivery box? *International Journal of Physical Distribution & Logistics Management*, **31** (6), pp 427–39

Samuelsson, A and Tilanus, B (1997) A framework efficiency model for goods transportation, with an application to regional less-than-truckload distribution, *Transport Logistics*, **1** (2), pp 139–51

Sarkis, J, Meade, LM and Talluri, S (2000) E-logistics and the natural environment, *Supply Chain Management: An International Journal*, **9** (4), pp 303–21

Sonneveld, K (2000) What drives (food) packaging innovation? *Packaging Technology and Science*, **13**, pp 29–35

Transport and Mobility Leuven, TNO, LCPC and RWTH Aachen University (2008) *Effects of Adapting the Rules on Weights and Dimensions of Heavy Commercial Vehicles as Established within Directive 96/53/EC*, Report for the European Commission, Brussels

UIC, CER, EIM, UNIFE and ERFA (2007) *Mega-trucks versus Rail Freight*, UIC, Paris

Umwelt Bundes Amt (UBA) (2007) *Longer and Heavier on German Roads: Do megatrucks contribute towards sustainable transport?*, UBA, Dessau

University of St Gallen (2000) *The Transport Optimization Report*, ECR Europe, Brussels

Vierth, I, Berell, H, McDaniel, J, Haraldsson, M, Hammarströom, U, Lindberg, G, Carlsson, A, Yahya, MH, Ögren, M and Björketun, U (2008) *The Effects of Long and Heavy Trucks on the Transport System*, VTI, Stockholm

10

Optimizing the routing of vehicles

Richard Eglese and Dan Black

INTRODUCTION

A large proportion of freight distribution is carried out by road vehicles. Assigning customers to the vehicles, followed by routing and scheduling them, involves a set of decisions that can have a significant impact on the costs and levels of service provided. The problem of organizing and routing a fleet in such a way is called the vehicle routing and scheduling problem (VRSP). Where the set of customers and their demands change little, experience can lead to good sets of routes that meet constraints concerning the vehicles, such as their capacities and service requirements (for example time windows for deliveries at customers), and that are close to minimizing the economic costs of the operation. However, when the customer base and demands are changing, it is often advantageous to make use of a computer to solve the problem. A variety of VRSP software packages are available that will provide routes and schedules. It has been suggested that 'the use of computerized procedures for the distribution process planning produces substantial savings (generally from 5 per cent to 20 per cent) in the global transportation costs' (Toth and Vigo, 2001).

Reduction in costs comes partly from a reduction in unnecessary distance travelled by making use of better routes, which in itself can lead to a reduction in fuel consumption and hence a reduction in greenhouse gas emissions. However there are additional factors to be taken into account when aiming to reduce the environmental impact of a fleet of vehicles. Not only must each journey be driven in an efficient manner using the most appropriate route, but work items should be ordered in such a way that difficult journeys (for example, into a congested city centre) are scheduled for a time of day where their impact will be minimized.

Reducing commercial vehicle emissions is a key concern on the green logistics agenda. Commercial vehicles account for 22 per cent of CO_2 emissions in the UK. Many companies are looking at this area to help reduce their carbon footprint and improve their green credentials. Walmart is aiming to make its vehicle fleet 25 per cent more efficient within three years and 50 per cent in 10 years (Walmart, 2008). In the UK, supermarket chains Tesco and J Sainsbury intend to reduce transport emissions for a case of goods by 50 per cent in five years and 5 per cent in three years respectively (Tesco, 2008; J Sainsbury, 2008).

The aims of this chapter are to define the VRSP in its basic form, introduce some of the sub-problems that arise when considering real world features of VRSPs and discuss some of the issues relating to reducing emissions when solving VRSPs.

VEHICLE ROUTING PROBLEMS

The basic capacitated vehicle routing problem (CVRP) consists of a set of customer deliveries to be made by a vehicle fleet based at a central depot. The travelling distances between each pair of customers as well as to and from the depot are known, each delivery item is of a known amount and each vehicle has a fixed capacity. The aim of the problem is to minimize the total distance driven by the vehicles while satisfying all of the customer orders. Further problem objectives can also be considered, such as minimizing the fleet size or balancing the set of vehicle routes to make them as equal in length as possible.

The problem was first introduced by Danzig and Ramser (1959) and it has received considerable attention since. An overview of the work into the VRSP can be found in books by Golden and Assad (1988), Toth and Vigo (2001) and, more recently, Golden, Reghavan and Wasil (2008). The VRSP is classified as an NP-hard problem, which implies that as the problem size increases, the computation time required to find the optimum solution for any known method increases exponentially. Optimum solutions can be found for problems of limited size; however, in order to find an optimum solution an impractical amount of computation effort can be required to discount all non-optimal routes. In practice heuristic methods are usually applied. Heuristics are not guaranteed to find the optimum solution; however, a well-designed heuristic will find good quality solutions in a reasonable computation time.

There are many commercial software packages available to provide solutions to real-world VRSPs. Such packages offer significant advantages over any manual method through the use of heuristics. Software vendors are keen to publicize the significant sums of money that such an approach can save. However, most are only concerned with maximizing the economic savings, which are usually achieved through minimizing the total travel cost measured from the distance travelled or time taken and minimizing the fleet size. Such improvements will, inevitably, reduce the emissions produced by vehicles; however, none currently aim to minimize the environmental impact directly. *OR/MS Today* regularly publishes surveys of available packages. In the most recent survey only one software vendor highlighted environmental impact as a future feature/concern for its software package (*OR/MS Today*, 2008).

TYPES OF PROBLEM

The basic CVRP has been introduced in the previous section; however, routing problems are rarely so straightforward in practice. For example, additional constraints that can have a major impact on the operation include legal requirements on driving and working times, and the fact that certain customers require delivery by particular vehicles (for loading and unloading reasons). This section introduces some more of the problem features that can occur in practice, and some of the research into the resulting models.

Time windows

A very common constraint concerns when a delivery can be made. The time window for a delivery is defined by a start and an end time. Depending on the problem considered, the time window may be treated as either a hard or soft constraint. A hard constraint requires that a vehicle must wait until the time window begins before making a delivery or must not arrive until the time window begins. Once the time window ends the delivery cannot be made. A soft constraint allows the delivery to be made outside of the time window at a penalty cost. This cost can either be a fixed cost or can be proportional to the earliness or lateness of the delivery. Algorithms to find the exact solution to the problem with hard time windows have been developed by Kolen, Kan and Trienekens (1987) and Kallehauge, Larsen and Madsen (2006). Heuristic methods have been used by Bräysy (2002) and more recently by Lau, Sim and Teo (2003) and Fu, Eglese and Li (2008) who consider both hard and soft time windows.

Backhauls

Problems that allow backhauls include customers who require an item be collected and delivered to the depot. This is in addition to the customers expecting deliveries (also referred to as linehauls). It is common that any deliveries are made before backhauls are considered. Approaches giving exact solutions to problems of limited size have been developed, for example by Toth and Vigo (1997) or Mingozzi, Giorgi and Baldacci (1999). Heuristic methods have also been applied to the problem, see Duhamel, Potvin and Rousseau (1997), Brandão (2006) and Tavakkoli-Moghaddam, Saremi and Ziaee (2006).

Pick-up and delivery

In this case each item is picked up from one location and delivered to another (neither of which is the depot). Obviously, each pair (pick-up and delivery) must be assigned to the same vehicle and the pick-up must occur before the delivery. Again, there is a limit on the capacity of the vehicle at any one time. Berbeglia et al (2007) review a wide variety of such problems, including the dial-a-ride problem (DARP), which concerns itself with the transportation requests of bus passengers (usually the elderly or disabled). The DARP can include restrictions on the time between pick-up and delivery, which are more relevant to passenger transport. Cordeau and Laporte (2003) have devised a heuristic approach to the DARP and Wassan, Nagy and Ahmadi (2008) have tackled the more general pick-up and delivery problem.

A problem that is related to both the VRP with backhauls and the VRP with pick-up and delivery is the problem with simultaneous pick-up and delivery. In this case, items are delivered to a customer from the depot and, as the delivery is made, other items are returned to the depot. Originally introduced by Min (1989) to model the movement of library stock, a heuristic approach has recently been developed by Montané and Galvão (2006).

Non-homogeneous vehicles

The vehicle fleet is often made up of different types of vehicles with different characteristics, which may be critical when determining vehicle routes. The vehicles used may have different capacities, and this may affect how they are used. In addition, some items may only be delivered by certain vehicles either due to restrictions at the customer location (the site-dependent VRP) or the nature of the item (eg heavy or hazardous items). Nag, Golden and Assad (1988) were among the first to consider such restrictions and implement a heuristic that solves the problem by way of a three-stage process, assigning vehicles to deliveries before attempting to create vehicle routes. A more recent heuristic approach has been presented by Chao, Golden and Wasil (1999).

Open VRSP

The 'open VRSP' introduces the idea that routes need not start or end at a depot. This may better reflect the cost structure when distribution is assigned to a third-party logistics provider and the vehicle does not need to return to the depot after the last delivery, but is allowed to go elsewhere to undertake other jobs. Brandão (2004) considers this problem and discusses the subtle differences that occur when not routing to and from a central location. An exact approach to the open VRSP can be found in Letchford, Lysgaard and Eglese (2007).

Dynamic VRSP

The 'dynamic VRSP' allows the rescheduling of customer requests once some new information is known. This is different from the standard approach where all information is known and fixed schedules are generated at the start of the day. This new information can be in the form of new customer requests or information regarding possible travel delays. Scheduling new customer requests is the most common dynamic feature and has been tackled by, among others, Gendreau et al (1999) and more recently Ichoua, Gendreau and Potvin (2006). Papastavrou (1996) investigates the problem where there is no initial set of customers at the start of the day and all demands occur dynamically. The heuristics developed take into account traffic density, which would in practice allow the consideration of travel delay information. Taniguchi and Shimamoto (2004) consider dynamic routing to avoid congestion and apply their heuristic to a real-world problem with successful results.

Although there have been technical advances in being able to modify routes according to real-time demands and traffic conditions, there are limits to the benefits that can be achieved in practice. For example, if the logistics operation is concerned with distributing specific orders from a central depot to a set of customers, then the decision about which customers can be serviced on which route must be taken initially when the vehicles are loaded and cannot be subsequently changed, even if traffic conditions change in such a way that a different allocation of orders would have produced better routes.

Stochastic VRSP

In stochastic VRSPs, uncertainties in the demands or travel times are explicitly modelled. A stochastic demand model may be appropriate when the vehicles deliver a resource and the amount required by each customer is not known until the customer is visited. Using an estimate of the demand for each customer, an initial set of routes can be defined. However, should a customer require more of the resource than the vehicle contains, the vehicle will need to return to the depot to get more stock before it can satisfy the customer demand. Each time a delivery is made, a decision must be taken on whether to deviate from the planned route to either visit an alternative customer or return to the depot. Approaches to this problem are given in Yang, Mathur and Ballou (2000) and Secomandi (2001).

Travel times may also be treated as uncertain and modelled according to a probability distribution. Fu (2002) considers stochastic travel times for the dial-a-ride problem. A minimum service rate is defined on the maximum time between pick-up and drop-off for each passenger. A heuristic is used to produce a schedule that, on average, will satisfy this service rate. A different approach is taken by Ando and Taniguchi (2006), where a penalty cost is used to try to eliminate probable delays.

Arc routing problems

The problems discussed so far require serving customers located at specific locations on a road network. Arc routing problems arise when a set of roads have to be visited to provide a service or treatment. Practical examples of services are postal delivery or refuse collection. Examples of treatments are snow ploughing or winter gritting, when salt or some other substance is spread on the roads to prevent ice forming. Similar constraints may need to be considered as for the VSRP, such as the capacity of the vehicles used and any time constraints on the operation. Practical details need to be clear in the modelling, such as whether a vehicle can deliver the service or treatment to a road by travelling down it once in either direction (as is sometimes the case for refuse collection in suburban streets) or whether the vehicle needs to travel down the road twice, once in each direction (as is usually the case where a road has been divided into a dual carriageway). Algorithms and software have been developed for arc routing and take advantage of the different structure of the problem to the VRSP counterpart. Overviews can be found in Wøhlk (2008) and Dror (2000).

Transportation of hazardous materials

Research into the routing of hazardous materials tends to concern evaluating the environmental impact of different routes between two locations rather than scheduling routes between several locations. A main area of interest is the risk associated with a route. Erkut and Verter (1998) define risk as a combination of, for each section of the route, the probability of an accident and the population size affected. The different real-world routes generated by several measures of risk from this basic definition are examined. Karkazis and Boffey (1995) consider further issues on accident impact such as the weather. An overview of such risk evaluations is given by List et al (1991). Kara and Verter (2004) propose a system whereby a regulator restricts access to sections of the road network on the basis of risk assessments and the haulier subsequently optimizes routing decisions over the remaining network.

ENVIRONMENTAL IMPACT

The environmental impact of a fleet will be affected by factors other than the routes and schedules used, such as the size of the vehicles and the type of fuel used. Practical measures, such as the way the vehicles are driven, can have an impact on emissions. In the UK the SAFED programme provides driver training to encourage safe and fuel-efficient driving through a wide range of factors. Issues include aerodynamics and loading, braking technique, the use of gears, cruise control and the determination of optimal speeds. Companies can provide efficiency awards to drivers who achieve targets such as using less fuel. These methods emphasize the importance of the fleet's efficiency to the drivers who will be required to implement the results of any more complex analysis. Such measures have been shown to reduce fuel consumption by between 1.9 and 13.5 per cent (DfT, 2006) in one study and by 4.35 per cent in a before-and-after study of Greek bus drivers (Zarkadoula, Zoidis and Tritopoulou, 2007).

Emissions auditing

Emissions auditing is the process of calculating the amount of greenhouse gas or other pollutants released into the atmosphere by a given activity. When estimating vehicle emissions, a variety of factors can be taken into account, including load weight and distribution, vehicle age, engine size, vehicle design, driving style, road gradient and speed. Speed is the major factor with reference to vehicle routing, and a route generated while opti-mizing distance may emit more CO_2 or other polluting gases due to slower speeds than a longer alternative route.

A simple method of estimating emissions from a vehicle is to take the distance of the planned journey and assume an average driving speed or fuel consumption per mile/km. Such an approach is included in the model of Dessouky, Rahimi and Weidner (2003). However, this assumption implies a linear relationship between such an estimate and the total distance travelled that makes minimizing emissions in such a way equivalent to minimizing distance. A more detailed approach would break each journey down by road type (eg highways, major roads, minor roads, residential streets) and assume an average speed/fuel-consumption for each type. Such an approach is already used in many software packages to estimate driving times. However, speed, particu-larly within city centres, has been shown to vary substantially during the course of the day (Eglese, Maden and Slater, 2006; van Woensel, Creten and Vandaele, 2001). Figure 10.1 shows how the average speed for a particular section of a primary road varies. Any estimate of emissions that fails to take this variation into account will be limited in its accuracy. Furthermore, failure to consider congestion reduces the robustness of computer-generated schedules when implemented in the real world. Palmer (2007) has shown that routes took 10 per cent longer in practice than the estimates provided by computer software. Any environmental gains from the use of vehicle routing and scheduling software may be lost due to schedules being infeasible in practice or even ignored by the drivers through lack of faith in their predicted timings.

Congestion

It has already been mentioned that the average speed on a road will vary at different times of day. The main cause of this variability is congestion. Congestion prevents a vehicle from driving at an optimum speed and subsequently has a negative impact on total vehicle emissions. McKinnon (2007) identifies exposure to congestion as one of the key freight variables that the UK government needs to manage in order to reduce CO_2 emis-

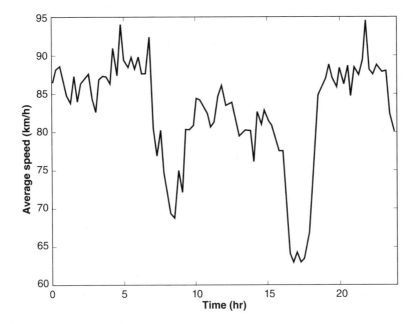

Figure 10.1   The average speed on a primary road in the UK

Source: Commercial data supplied by ITIS Holdings, 2009.

sions. Figure 10.2 shows the relationship between vehicle speed and fuel consumption (which varies directly in proportion to CO_2 emissions). As speed decreases below the optimal level, considerably more fuel is used. To make matters worse, congestion forces driving in a stop–start manner, which results in increased fuel consumption and emissions as the vehicle accelerates and brakes instead of travelling at a steady speed. This means that estimates of fuel consumption based on vehicle test cycle data may not accurately represent the fuel used in typical driving conditions, as discussed in McKinnon and Piecyk (2008).

Modern technology, particularly with the advent of GPS devices, allows the monitoring of vehicles. Data from vehicles are stored and then transmitted to a central location and analyzed. Typically, speed and location (accurate to a particular section of road) are recorded; however, modern devices also include information on fuel flow. It is hoped that in the future information on fuel consumption collected in this way will aid emissions auditing. However, in the meantime, data on vehicle speeds have been compiled so that the average speed for a section of road at each time of the day is known. This provides a way of measuring the congestion that occurs on a daily basis.

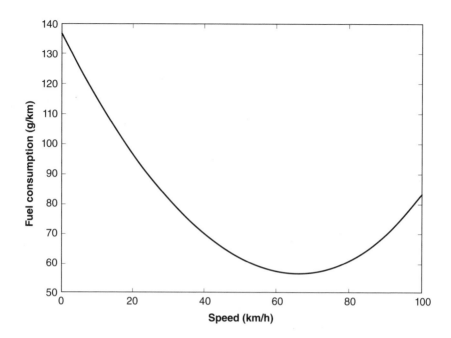

Figure 10.2 The relationship between speed and fuel consumption for a light duty diesel vehicle

Source: Estimates produced using the method of the *EMEP/CORINAIR Emission Inventory Guidebook*; European Environment Agency (2007).

This data has been used by Eglese, Maden and Slater (2006) and Maden (2006) to find solutions to VRSPs that minimize the total driving time. The aim of this approach is to produce more reliable vehicle schedules, but a potential environmental benefit is the construction of routes that tend to avoid congestion and the emissions produced in slow-moving traffic. Such an approach will also provide more robust schedules that will reduce overtime and improve customer satisfaction through more punctual deliveries and collections.

CONCLUSIONS

Modern computer software systems are able to produce efficient sets of vehicle routes for road freight deliveries that produce economic savings and environmental benefits compared with manual planning systems, particularly when the customers and demands vary from day to day.

Modern developments in tracking technology are opening up new opportunities to improve vehicle routing and scheduling further by taking account of expected congestion, and to modify routing plans dynamically by taking into account current traffic conditions. Baumgaertner, Léonardi and Krusch (2008) describe a qualitative survey of trucking companies and software providers that is used to assess the importance of computerized vehicle routing systems and other technologies to reduce fuel consumption and CO_2 emissions.

Vehicle routing and scheduling is only one of many factors that will influence the economic and environmental performance of a distribution system, but good routing and scheduling have the potential to contribute to reductions in greenhouse gas emissions and other pollutants.

REFERENCES

Ando, N and Taniguchi, E (2006) Travel time reliability in vehicle routing and scheduling with time windows, *Networks and Spatial Economics*, **6** (3–4), pp 293–311

Baumgaertner, M, Léonardi, J and Krusch, O (2008) Improving computerized routing and scheduling and vehicle telematics: a qualitative survey, *Transportation Research Part D*, **13**, pp 377–82

Berbeglia, G, Cordeau, J-F, Gribkovskaia, I and Laporte, G (2007) Static pickup and delivery problems: a classification scheme and survey, *TOP*, **15** (1), pp 1–31

Brandão, J (2004) A tabu search algorithm for the open vehicle routing problem, *European Journal of Operational Research*, **157** (3), pp 552–64

Brandão, J (2006) A new tabu search algorithm for the vehicle routing problem with backhauls, *European Journal of Operational Research*, **173** (2), pp 540–55

Bräysy, O (2002) Fast local searches for the vehicle routing problem with time windows, *INFOR*, **40** (4), pp 319–30

Chao, I-M, Golden, BL and Wasil, E (1999) A computational study of a new heuristic for the site-dependent vehicle routing problem, *INFOR*, **37** (3), pp 319–36

Cordeau, J-F and Laporte, G (2003) A tabu search heuristic for the static multi-vehicle dial-a-ride problem, *Transportation Research Part B*, **37** (6), pp 579–94

Danzig, GB and Ramser, JM (1959) The truck dispatching problem, *Management Science*, **6**, pp 81–91

Department for Transport (DfT) (2006) [accessed 15 September 2008] Companies and drivers benefit from SAFED for HGVs, *Freight Best*

Practice [Online] http://www.freightbestpractice.org.uk/download. aspx?pid=119&action=save

Dessouky, M, Rahimi, M and Weidner, M (2003) Jointly optimizing cost, service, and environmental performance in demand-responsive transit scheduling, *Transportation Research Part D*, **8** (6), pp 433–65

Dror, M (2000) *Arc Routing: Theory, solutions and applications*, Kluwer Academic Publishers, Norwell, Mass

Duhamel, C, Potvin, J-Y and Rousseau, J-M (1997) A tabu search heuristic for the vehicle routing problem with backhauls and time windows, *Transportation Science*, **31**, pp 45–59

Eglese, RW, Maden, W and Slater, A (2006) A road timetable to aid vehicle routing and scheduling, *Computers and Operations Research*, **33** (12), pp 3508–19

Erkut, E and Verter, V (1998) Modeling of transport risk for hazardous materials, *Operations Research*, **46** (5), pp 625–42

European Environment Agency (2007) *EMEP/CORINAIR Emission Inventory Guidebook: Group 7 road transport*, Technical report No 16/2007

Fu, L (2002) Scheduling dial-a-ride paratransit under time-varying stochastic congestion, *Transportation Research Part B*, **36** (6), pp 485–506

Fu, Z, Eglese, R and Li, LYO (2008) A unified tabu search algorithm for vehicle routing problems with soft time windows, *Journal of the Operational Research Society*, **59**, 663–73

Gendreau, M, Guertin, F, Potvin, J-Y and Taillard, É (1999) Parallel tabu search for real-time vehicle routing and dispatching, *Transportation Science*, **33** (4), pp 381–90

Golden, BL and Assad, AA (1988) *Vehicle Routing: Methods and studies*, North-Holland, Amsterdam

Golden, B, Reghavan, S and Wasil, E (2008) *The Vehicle Routing Problem: Latest advances and new challenges*, Springer, New York

Ichoua, S, Gendreau, M and Potvin, J-Y (2006) Exploiting knowledge about future demands for real-time vehicle dispatching, *Transportation Science*, **40** (2), pp 211–25

J Sainsbury [accessed 15 September 2008] Corporate responsibility: our commitments [Online] http://www.j-sainsbury.co.uk/cr/index. asp?pageid=60

Kallehauge, B, Larsen, J and Madsen, OBG (2006) Lagrangian duality applied to the vehicle routing problem with time windows, *Computers and Operations Research*, **33** (5), pp 1464–87

Kara, BY and Verter, V (2004) Designing a road network for hazardous materials transportation, *Transportation Science*, **38** (2), pp 188–96

Karkazis, J and Boffey, TB (1995) Optimal location of routes for vehicles transporting hazardous materials, *European Journal of Operational Research*, **86** (2), pp 201–15

Kolen, AWJ, Kan, AHGR and Trienekens, HWJM (1987) Vehicle routing with time windows, *Operations Research*, **35** (2), pp 266–73

Lau, HC, Sim, M and Teo, KM (2003) Vehicle routing problem with time windows and a limited number of vehicles, *European Journal of Operational Research*, **148** (3), pp 559–69

Letchford, AN, Lysgaard, J and Eglese, RW (2007) A branch-and-cut algorithm for the capacitated open vehicle routing problem, *Journal of the Operational Research Society*, **58**, pp 1642–51

List, GF, Mirchandani, PB, Turnquist, MA and Zografos, KG (1991) Modeling and analysis for hazardous materials transportation: risk analysis, routing/scheduling and facility location, *Transportation Science*, **25** (2), pp 100–14

Maden, W (2006) *Models and Heuristics Algorithms from Complex Routing and Scheduling Problems*, PhD Thesis, Department of Management Science, Lancaster University Management School

McKinnon, AC (2007) *CO_2 Emissions from Freight Transport in the UK*, UK Commission for Integrated Transport, London

McKinnon, AC and Piecyk, M (2008) Measurement of CO_2 emissions from road freight transport: a review of UK experience, *Energy Policy*, **37** pp 3733–42, Logistics Research Centre, School of Management and Languages, Heriot-Watt University, Edinburgh

Min, H (1989) The multiple vehicle routing problem with simultaneous delivery and pick-up points, *Transportation Research A*, **23** (5), pp 377–86

Mingozzi, A, Giorgi, S and Baldacci, R (1999) An exact method for the vehicle routing problem with backhauls, *Transportation Science*, **33** (3), pp 315–29

Montané, FAT and Galvão, RD (2006) A tabu search algorithm for the vehicle routing problem with simultaneous pick-up and delivery service, *Computers and Operations Research*, **33** (3), pp 595–619

Nag, B, Golden, BL and Assad, AA (1988) Vehicle routing with site dependencies, in *Vehicle Routing: Methods and Studies*, ed BL Golden and AA Assad, pp 149–159, North-Holland, New York

OR/MS Today (2008) Vehicle routing software survey, *OR/MS Today*, February [accessed 17 September 2008] [Online] http://www.lion-hrtpub.com/orms/surveys/Vehicle_Routing/vrss.html

Palmer, A (2007) *The Development of an Integrated Routing and Carbon Dioxide Emissions Model for Goods Vehicles*, PhD Thesis, School of Management, Cranfield University

Papastavrou, JD (1996) A stochastic and dynamic routing policy using branching processes with state dependent immigration, *European Journal of Operational Research*, **95** (1), pp 167–77

Secomandi, N (2001) A rollout policy for the vehicle routing problem with stochastic demands, *Operations Research*, **49** (5), pp 796–802

Taniguchi, E and Shimamoto, H (2004) Intelligent transportation system based dynamic vehicle routing and scheduling with variable travel times, *Transportation Research Part C*, **12** (3–4), pp 235–50

Tavakkoli-Moghaddam, R, Saremi, AR and Ziaee, MS (2006) A memetic algorithm for a vehicle routing problem with backhauls, *Applied Mathematics and Computation*, **181** (2), pp 1049–60

Tesco [accessed 15 September 2008] Reducing energy use: what we are doing [Online] http://www.tesco.com/greenerliving/what_we_are_doing/reducing_energy_use/default.page?#L3

Toth, P and Vigo, D (1997) An exact algorithm for the vehicle routing problem with backhauls, *Transportation Science*, **31** (4), pp 372–85

Toth, P and Vigo, D (2001) *The Vehicle Routing Problem*, SIAM Monographs on Discrete Mathematics and Applications, Philadelphia

van Woensel, T, Creten, R and Vandaele, N (2001) Managing the environmental externalities of traffic logistics: the issue of emissions, *Production and Operations Management*, **10** (2), pp 207–23

Walmart [accessed 15 September 2008] Sustainability: climate and energy [Online] http://walmartstores.com/Sustainability/7673.aspx

Wassan, NA, Nagy, G and Ahmadi, S (2008) A heuristic method for the vehicle routing problem with mixed deliveries and pickups, *Journal of Scheduling*, **11** (2), pp 149–61

Wøhlk, S (2008) A decade of capacitated arc routing, in *The Vehicle Routing Problem: Latest advances and new challenges*, ed B Golden, S Raghavan and E Wasil, pp 29–48, Springer, New York

Yang, W-H, Mathur, K and Ballou, RH (2000) Stochastic vehicle routing problem with restocking, *Transportation Science*, **34** (1), pp 99–112

Zarkadoula, M, Zoidis, G and Tritopoulou, E (2007) Training urban bus drivers to promote smart driving: a note on a Greek eco-driving pilot program, *Transportation Research Part D*, **12** (6), pp 449–51

11

Increasing fuel efficiency in the road freight sector

Alan McKinnon

INTRODUCTION

The environmental impact of freight transport is closely related to the amount of energy consumed. This link is particularly close in the case of carbon dioxide emissions, with one litre of diesel fuel emitting 2.63 kg of the gas. It has weakened, however, in the case of other noxious gases as a result of the tightening of vehicle emission standards (relating to pollutants such as nitrous oxide and particulates), the removal of sulphur from fuel and the switch to cleaner, alternative fuels. The desire to cut exhaust emissions, nevertheless, continues to offer a strong incentive to reduce fuel consumption. For most companies, though, the main incentive is economic, as fuel costs represent a large proportion of total vehicle operating costs. For example, they typically account for around 25–30 per cent of the costs of operating a heavy truck in the UK (DFF International, 2008) and this percentage can rise to 35 per cent or more during periods of high oil prices. As oil prices are predicted to increase steeply in future years, improvements in fuel efficiency are likely to yield a healthy financial return as well as climate change and air quality benefits.

It is possible to measure the energy efficiency of a freight transport operation in different ways. The main distinction is between a measure that relates energy consumed to the distance the vehicle travels, known as energy or fuel efficiency (eg kms per litre), and one that expresses it in relation to the amount of freight movement (eg tonne-kms per litre), which is often called energy intensity. Energy intensity is a function both of fuel efficiency and the loading of the vehicle. As the utilization of vehicle capacity is discussed elsewhere in the book (Chapter 9), this chapter will focus on ways of improving fuel efficiency. It should be noted, however, that in formulating an energy conservation strategy for a freight transport operation, it is never enough for a company to maximize fuel efficiency in isolation. Just as much attention should be paid to filling the vehicles on both outbound and return journeys.

Almost all the energy used to move freight comes from the burning of fossil fuels at point of use in the vehicle. The main exceptions are electrified rail freight services and battery-powered delivery vehicles but, globally, these currently account for only a small percentage of freight tonne-kms. In this chapter, therefore, we will concentrate on ways of improving the fuel efficiency of road freight vehicles.

Over the past three decades, a huge amount of research has been done on ways of improving the fuel efficiency of road haulage. Much of the early work focused on the design of the engine and vehicle chassis. There was a tendency to underestimate the contribution that the driver, supervisor and manager could make to improved fuel efficiency. Today, there is much greater recognition of the importance of the human element in fuel conservation. We will begin by examining recent trends in the fuel efficiency of new trucks and then consider what vehicle operators can do to minimize their fuel consumption.

FUEL EFFICIENCY OF NEW TRUCKS

There has been a steady flow of technical refinements to trucks that have raised their fuel efficiency. It has been estimated that over the past 40 years the average fuel efficiency of new heavy goods vehicles (HGVs) has been improving at a rate of around 0.8–1 per cent per annum (IEA, 2007). The rate and sources of improvement have varied between vehicle size and weight classes. For example, for the heaviest category of vehicles, roughly two-thirds of the increase in fuel efficiency has come from advances in engine performance and the remainder from better aerodynamics and tyres (Duleep, 2007).

The main improvements were made in the 1970s and 1980s. The rate of fuel efficiency improvement has been relatively slow since 1990. This is partly because incremental improvements from the refinement of existing vehicle technology have been diminishing, but it is mainly because of the need to meet tightening emission controls, particularly on nitrogen oxide.

It has been estimated that if these controls had not been imposed, average lorry fuel efficiency today could be around 7–10 per cent higher (IEA, 2007). One estimate for the US trucking industry puts this fuel penalty at 15–20 per cent over the period 1988–2010. This illustrates the environmental trade-off that has been made in giving the reduction of noxious emissions priority over fuel economy and carbon dioxide savings.

This trade-off has been further complicated in recent years by the need to introduce new systems to enable lorries to achieve Euro 4 and 5 emission standards. Most truck manufacturers have opted for the Selective Catalytic Reduction (SCR) system, which, it is claimed, yields better fuel efficiency than the alternative Exhaust Gas Recirculation (EGR) system, but which requires the addition of a urea-based chemical called AdBlue to the combustion. Trials have confirmed that SCR does generally improve fuel efficiency, though the percentage fuel savings depend on the nature of the transport operations.

Future opportunities for increasing the fuel efficiency of new trucks are explored in Chapter 7.

VEHICLE DESIGN: AERODYNAMIC PROFILING

The external shape of the vehicle can have a major influence on its fuel efficiency. Streamlining the flow of air over the vehicle body can significantly cut fuel consumption. In 1993 the UK government's Energy Efficiency Office claimed that 'the importance of aerodynamic efficiency and its effect on fuel economy cannot be over-emphasized.' Around the same time, however, the Freight Transport Association issued a word of caution, describing some aerodynamic aids as 'little more than decoration'. Some early adopters of aerodynamic kits complained that they did not achieve the fuel savings claimed by the suppliers and that payback periods were longer than expected. Since then, aerodynamic styling has greatly improved, become more cost-effective and been shown to yield significant fuel savings both in trials and in commercial operation. Trials held in the UK in 1999 found that trucks travelling at speeds of 50mph and 56mph could achieve fuel savings of, respectively, 9.3 per cent and 6.7 per cent following 'aerodynamic intervention' (ETSU and MIRA, 2001). A series of good practice guides (available at www.freightbest-practice.org.uk) and case studies (eg DfT, 2006b) have reported potential fuel savings in the range 6–20 per cent for improved aerodynamic profiling of trucks. Delegates at a workshop organized by the International Energy Agency (2007) indicated that improved aerodynamics could represent 10–20 per cent of all potential fuel efficiency improvements to the HGV fleet, with most of the benefits accruing to larger articulated vehicles making high-speed, long-distance trips. The magnitude of fuel savings from aerodynamic profiling is critically dependent on vehicle speed. A British Transport Advisory Committee (BTAC) trial, for example, found that the fuel saving was only 1.6 per cent for a lorry travelling at 37mph (DfT, 2006a).

Over-cab spoilers have been the most widely used form of profiling, though it is now recognized that around 85 per cent of the potential fuel savings from improved aerodynamics come from the trailer design. This is particularly true in the case of high-cube/double-deck trailers, which are now relatively common on UK roads. An increasing number of double-deck trailers have sloping fronts, permitting up to 10 per cent fuel savings. It has recently been recognized that improved profiling of the rear of trailers can also have a significant impact on fuel efficiency. So-called 'teardrop' trailers that slope downwards at the front and rear have begun to appear on UK roads. Fuel efficiency gains of up to 10 per cent have been reported for these vehicles (*Commercial Motor*, 8 January 2009).

Where aerodynamic profiling involves the use of spoilers, side-skirts and 'spats' over the wheels, additional weight is added to the vehicle, offsetting some of the fuel efficiency benefits. As discussed in the next section, this runs counter to efforts to reduce the tare (or 'empty') weight of the vehicle.

REDUCING THE VEHICLE TARE WEIGHT

Fuel efficiency can also be enhanced by reducing the tare weight of the vehicle. This is also called 'lightweighting'. Greszler (2009: 111) notes that 'the benefits of weight reduction are more significant in weight-limited operations... where less vehicle weight translates directly into increased freight weight, and improved freight movement efficiency. For volume-limited trucks, vehicle weight impacts energy input due to rolling resistance, acceleration and hill climbing.' Use of lighter materials, such as aluminium or carbon fibre, and fittings can substantially cut the tare weight. For example, the US Department of Energy and the American Trucking Association have a programme that aims to reduce the combined tare weight of the tractor and trailer in a Class 8 articulated truck by 2.3 tonnes. This may require a reversal of recent trends towards higher cab specification and the installation of larger fuel tanks, both of which carry a weight penalty. On vehicles meeting higher emissions standards by SCR, the installation of an additional tank for AdBlue further increases vehicle weight. Existing trucks already have widely varying tare weights. One study in Germany found that, across a sample of road haulage operations, the average tare weight of a 40-tonne gross weight vehicle was 14 tonnes while the minimum weight was 11 tonnes (Leonardi and Baumgartner, 2004). One major truck manufacturer has indicated that it is relatively easy to remove just over half a tonne from the tare weight of an articulated truck without adversely affecting its performance or carrying capacity.

Improvements to the fuel performance of new trucks is only one source of fuel savings, however. Companies' vehicle purchasing decisions determine the rate at which new fuel-efficient technologies and designs are applied in practice. The way in which they subsequently operate and maintain the vehicles over a typical 10–15 year lifespan also has a major influence on total fuel consumption.

VEHICLE PURCHASE DECISION

For technical improvements in fuel efficiency to be widely diffused and truck manufacturers to be incentivized to make them, operators will have to attach greater importance to fuel efficiency in their vehicle purchasing decisions. Research in Finland has found variations of 5–15 per cent in the fuel efficiency of different brands of new truck (Nylund and Erkkila, 2007). Comparing the results of the vehicle tests reported in UK trade publications reveals that 10 per cent variations in fuel consumption over a standard trial route are not uncommon for a particular class of vehicle. This suggests that a haulier's choice of vehicle can have a large impact on fuel consumption. Hauliers would be ill-advised, however, to base their purchase decision solely on fuel efficiency. They should analyse the full-life cost of each vehicle and likely residual value before making their choice. Fuel expenditure should be a major component in this calculation. Market conditions can, nevertheless, work against the objectives of improved fuel efficiency where over-specified vehicles (eg with sleeper cabs for day-time operation) are purchased because they retain a higher residual value.

Some companies purchase tractor units that are more powerful than they strictly require for a particular type of distribution operation. This is sometimes attributed to machismo on the part of the transport manager or owner-driver. A more rational explanation is that lorries with more powerful engines tend to retain higher residual values. This longer-term financial benefit, however, must be set against the additional fuel costs incurred in the interim. Because higher-powered vehicles are more highly geared, they tend to suffer greater loss of fuel efficiency at slower speeds. As road networks are getting more congested and average road speeds diminishing, the fuel penalty associated with over-powering is gradually increasing.

VEHICLE MAINTENANCE

There is a huge range of technical imperfections that can prevent a lorry from operating at optimum fuel efficiency (DfT, 2006a). Many of them go unnoticed for weeks, months or years, wasting substantial amounts of fuel quite unnecessarily. Regular maintenance can help to detect and correct these defects. On a day-to-day basis, however, drivers need to be encouraged to look out for obvious signs that a vehicle's fuel efficiency is being impaired. Typical defects include:

- Fuel leaks: a survey reported by the Freight Transport Association (1993) found that leaks in either the fuel supply or injection systems accounted for 44 per cent of fuel-related lorry defects uncovered during maintenance.
- Under-inflated tyres: according to a UK government report (DfT, 2006a), 20 per cent under-inflation of tyres will result in a 10 per cent increase in rolling resistance and cause a 2 per cent reduction in fuel efficiency. Michelin estimate that 58 per cent of tyres in the UK are at least 10 per cent under-inflated and thus incur a fuel penalty of 1.5 per cent or more (Buckley, 2006).
- Mis-alignment of axles: it is estimated that a $1°$ misalignment of a single axle on a multi-axle trailer will raise fuel consumption by roughly 3 per cent, while a $2°$ misalignment will increase it by 8 per cent (Buckley, 2006).
- Poor combustion: the emission of black smoke from the exhaust generally indicates that the fuel is not being properly combusted and energy is being wasted.

The choice of oil for the engine and gear-box can also have a significant impact on fuel efficiency. Impressive claims have been made in recent years for the new generation of synthetic lubricants that 'boast lower viscosity... and create less drag than do conventional mineral oils'. Depending on the state of the vehicle they can yield up to 4 per cent savings in fuel (Anon, 2006).

Major advances have been made in the electronic monitoring of vehicle condition and performance, facilitating the detection of the range of technical shortcomings that depress overall fuel efficiency. Fuel efficiency is being given greater priority in truck maintenance programmes, partly because high fuel prices ensure a healthy payback for such measures, but also because of tightening controls on exhaust emissions.

INCREASING THE FUEL EFFICIENCY OF TRUCKING OPERATIONS

Companies can improve their fuel efficiency in many different ways. Several manuals have been published by government agencies, trade associations, magazines and oil companies providing advice on the broad array of measures that can be applied. At various times in the past, some measures have been hyped as offering a quantum leap in fuel efficiency only to disappoint hauliers that tried to implement them. A good example is the attachment of magnets to diesel engines supposedly to improve combustion efficiency and reduce the amount of unburnt fuel. As a government-sponsored report has pointed out, however, 'There is no evidence that even quite strong magnetic fields can cause ionization in gases or significantly influence combustion. Suppliers have produced little or no evidence that these types of fuel-saving device actually work' (DfT, 2003: 4).

Many of the claims made for fuel economy measures rest on quite flimsy empirical evidence. Some years ago, the US government's Environmental Protection Agency tested 106 fuel-saving devices and found that only five 'indicated a statistically significant improvement in fuel economy without an increase in exhaust emissions' (DfT, 2003: 4). These five related either to changing driver habits or improving the efficiency of air conditioning systems. (This finding on air conditioning cannot be directly extrapolated to other countries, such as the UK, where average summer temperatures are significantly lower than those in most of the United States.)

Another problem with checklists of fuel economy measures is that they often give the impression that all the savings are additive. Claims are often made that individual measures yield fuel savings of 1–3 per cent. In theory, if a haulier implemented 20 of these measures, it might cut its fuel consumption by 20–60 per cent. Research in the United States, for example, has assessed the percentage fuel savings that an average trucker might achieve by applying a range of 10 measures (Ang-Olson and Schroeer, 2002) (Figure 11.1). These savings vary from under 1 per cent for automatic tyre inflation systems to almost 8 per cent for a reduction in maximum speed from 65 mph to 60 mph. If all these savings were cumulative, aggregate savings of 33 per cent might be achieved. In practice, this is unrealistic. Some measures, after all, are counteracting. For example, cutting maximum speed will reduce the effectiveness of 'improved trailer and tractor aerodynamics'.

A fuel economy initiative should not, therefore, comprise a loose collection of measures. It is much more effective to integrate a specific set of measures into a well-structured programme tailored to the needs

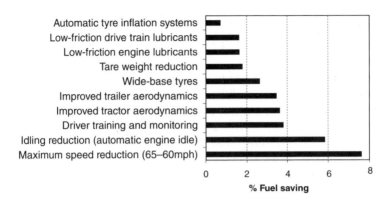

Figure 11.1 Estimated fuel savings from fuel economy measures: US trucking

Source: Ang-Olson and Schroeer (2002).

of particular operators. As part of its Freight Best Practice programme, for example, the UK government has developed a fuel management guide, which not only outlines some of the more promising fuel economy measures, but also sets out a management framework within which these measures can be implemented and their effects evaluated. The oil company Shell has also 'advocated a holistic approach to the whole issue of transport efficiency' and has given this approach the brand name 'Fuel Stretch' (Anon, 2006). Its programme comprises 25 fuel-saving tips, including advice on how to manage the programme.

It is very difficult to assess the overall potential for improving the average fuel efficiency of road haulage operations for several reasons:

- There are many different sources of efficiency improvement.
- There is a complex interaction between different types of improvement measure; in some cases there is mutual reinforcement while in others they are counteracting.
- There are often quite wide variations in the estimates of potential fuel savings from different sources.
- It is often unclear from what baseline potential savings are being calculated, particularly when they are generalized at an international level.

By benchmarking the fuel efficiency of fleets engaged in similar types of distribution operation, one can get a rough indication of potential savings given currently available technology. This is discussed in the next section.

BENCHMARKING THE FUEL EFFICIENCY OF TRUCKS

Several attempts have been made to benchmark the fuel efficiency of truck fleets in countries such as the UK, Germany and Canada. The general message to emerge from these surveys is that even within relatively homogenous sub-sectors there are significant variations in fuel efficiency. Figure 11.2 shows the variability in the average fuel efficiency of lorries of specific types carrying food products (McKinnon and Ge, 2004). The variability was much greater for rigid vehicles than for articulated trucks. The more disaggregated the benchmarking exercise, the less easy it is for managers to dismiss inter-fleet variations in fuel efficiency on the grounds that the transport operations are not directly comparable.

By benchmarking other companies against the most energy-efficient operator in their sector, it is possible to estimate the potential for fuel savings. For example, key performance indicator (KPI) data collected during the course of 'synchronized audits' of transport efficiency in the UK food supply chain were used to estimate by how much energy consumption and fuel costs might be reduced if companies whose energy efficiency was below the average for their sub-sector could bring it up to this mean (McKinnon and Ge, 2004). According to the results of this survey, this would cut the amount of fuel consumed and CO_2 emissions

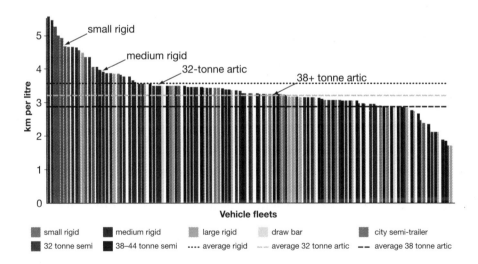

Figure 11.2 Variation in fuel efficiency across vehicle fleets in the food supply chain

Source: McKinnon and Ge (2004).

by 5 per cent, reducing annual fuel costs for the average vehicle by £1,115 (at current prices). Similar analyses have been conducted in other sectors and, in each case, they demonstrate significant potential for cutting fuel consumption while maintaining the same level of freight movement (McKinnon, 2009).

The UK is not alone in benchmarking the fuel efficiency/energy intensity of road haulage. Studies done in other countries have employed different methodologies but arrived at very similar conclusions: for example:

- Germany: a survey of 153 trips made by 50 German hauliers found a wide variation in the ratio of CO_2 emissions to tonne-kms (Leonardi and Baumgartner, 2004). The number of tonne-kms per kg of CO_2 varied from 0.8 to 26. As CO_2 emissions are very closely correlated with fuel consumption, differences in litres of fuel per tonne-km would be similarly wide.
- Canada: a survey of 42 inter-city trucking fleets was conducted across Canada to provide benchmark fuel efficiency data (Transport Canada, 2005). The highest fuel efficiency recorded was 3.01 km per litre for articulated trunking vehicles, with half the fleets surveyed achieving average fuel efficiency values between 2.5 and 3.0 km per litre.

One must always exercise caution in interpreting benchmark data, because some of the variation in fuel efficiency will reflect justifiable differences in the nature of the distribution operation and composition of the vehicle fleet within each sub-sector. The available benchmark data, nevertheless, suggest that there is considerable scope for making further improvements in energy efficiency in freight transport operations given current levels of technology and market conditions. Future advances in technology and strengthening commercial and environmental pressures to economize on fuel will raise the energy-efficiency benchmark even higher.

MORE FUEL-EFFICIENT DRIVING

It is generally accepted that driving style is the single greatest influence on fuel efficiency. Driver training programmes have been shown to improve fuel efficiency by 8–10 per cent. To date over 7,000 drivers have received training under the UK government's Safe and Fuel Efficient Driving (SAFED) programme, with average 'on-the-day' improvements in fuel efficiency of just over 10 per cent recorded (DfT, 2009). If this sample of drivers were representative of the HGV driver population as a whole and if they maintained the improvement in fuel efficient driving observed during the training session, admittedly two large 'ifs', improved driver training could cut total fuel consumption by trucks in the UK by 880 million litres per annum, and CO_2 emissions by 2.3 million tonnes.

Truck simulators are also being used to provide training in safe and fuel-efficient driving techniques. Approximately 550 drivers have undergone training on the English truck simulator, while around 1,000 have been assessed and trained on two truck simulators in Scotland. On average, between the first (pre-training) and second (post-training) run on the Scottish simulators drivers have achieved an average increase in fuel efficiency of 13 per cent.

To derive longer-term benefit from training in so-called 'eco-driving', companies have to maintain awareness of the fuel efficiency issue and incentivize drivers to continue using their skills in fuel-efficient driving. Many companies now offer financial incentives in the form of prizes or bonuses. For such schemes to operate effectively, however, the collection and analysis of fuel data must be seen to be fair and consistent. This can be a complex exercise where drivers regularly switch vehicles and delivery runs (McKinnon, Stirling and Kirkhope, 1993).

It is not only when driving the vehicle that drivers can have a major impact on fuel consumption. By leaving the engine idling unnecessarily, failing to check tyre pressures and not reporting engine problems or oil leaks, drivers waste a lot of fuel. It is necessary therefore to get drivers to adhere to a full set of fuel economy rules.

FLEET MANAGEMENT

Once the right vehicles are purchased and adequately maintained, the fleet manager must ensure that they are deployed in a way that maximizes their operational efficiency. This includes assigning the 'right vehicles to the right jobs'. Available survey evidence suggests that this basic rule of good fleet management is often broken, at the expense of higher fuel consumption by lorries that are bigger or heavier than they need to be for the load they are carrying. Efforts to match the capacity of the vehicle to the size/weight of the load run counter to the common practice of standardizing vehicle weights and dimensions within a fleet. There is scope, however, for improving this match, particularly with the use of fleet management software.

Fleet management can also be reinforced by the appointment of a 'fuel champion' whose job it is to analyse the pattern of fuel consumption, promote fuel saving initiatives and generally instil a fuel-saving culture in the workforce (FTA, 1993). With or without a 'fuel champion', management needs systems in place to monitor fuel consumption and analyse variations in fuel efficiency at a disaggregated level by driver, vehicle, depot and contract. In the absence of such data, it is very difficult to devise an effective fuel management programme. Such a programme will require meaningful and realistic KPIs and targets to give the staff clear goals. Establishing these targets can be difficult given the wide variety of factors that exert an influence on fuel efficiency. Research at the University of Huddersfield (Coyle, 1998), for example, has revealed how the average fuel efficiency of a fleet can be around 10 per cent lower in the winter than in the summer, mainly because more energy is used to heat the vehicle.

CONCLUSIONS

There are numerous ways in which the fuel efficiency of road freight operations can be improved. Those who manufacture, maintain, operate and drive trucks all have a key role to play in minimizing the amount of fuel consumed in moving freight by road. In recent years, a general view has emerged that opportunities for further technical improvements to the energy efficiency of new vehicles are limited and that future gains will come mainly from their operation and maintenance. As discussed in Chapter 7, this view probably underestimates the potential for future technological advances in engine and vehicle design (Baker et al, 2009). Benchmarking surveys also reveal that wider dissemination of current best practice in fuel management by truck operators could substantially reduce the energy intensity of road freight transport. Rising oil prices, environmental taxes, carbon trading, government campaigns and intensifying competition in the road freight market are all likely to promote this dissemination over the next 10–20 years.

REFERENCES

Ang-Olson, J and Schroeer, W (2002) Energy efficiency strategies for freight trucking: potential impact on fuel use and greenhouse gas emissions, paper presented to the 81st Annual Meeting of the Transportation Research Board, Washington, DC

Anon (2006) 25 ways to cut your fuel bill, special supplement, in association with Shell, *Commercial Motor*, March, supplement

Baker, H, Cornwell, R, Koehler, E and Patterson, J (2009) *Review of Low Carbon Technologies for Heavy Goods Vehicles*, Report prepared by Ricardo for the Department for Transport, London

Buckley, H (2006) Stop thirsty tyres, presentation to RHA Scotland and Northern Ireland Annual Conference, Limavady, 4 October 2006

Coyle, M (1998) *Basic Steps to Improving Vehicle Fuel Efficiency*, Transport and Logistics Research Unit, University of Huddersfield

Department for Transport (DfT) (2003) *Fuel Saving Devices*, Good Practice Guide 313, Transport Energy Best Practice Programme, Harwell

DfT (2006a) *Fuel Management Guide*, Freight Best Practice Programme, London

DfT (2006b) *Smoothing the Flow at TNT Express and Somerfield using Truck Aerodynamic Styling*, Freight Best Practice Programme, London

DfT (2009) *SAFED for HGVs*, Freight Best Practice Programme, London

DFF International (2008) *Goods Vehicle Operating Costs 2008*, Road Haulage Association, Weybridge

Duleep, KG (2007) Fuel economy of heavy duty trucks in the USA, Presentation to IEA Workshop, 21–22 June, Paris

ETSU and MIRA (2001) *Truck Aerodynamic Styling*, Good Practice Guide 308, Energy Efficiency Best Practice Programme, Harwell

Freight Transport Association (FTA) (1993) *Fuel Management Guide*, FTA, Tunbridge Wells

Greszler, A (2009) Heavy duty vehicle fleet technologies for reducing carbon dioxide: an industry perspective, in *Reducing Climate Impacts in the Transportation Sector*, ed D Sperling and JS Cannon, pp 101–16, Springer, New York

International Energy Agency (IEA) (2007) *Fuel Efficiency of HDVs Standards and other Policy Instruments: Towards a Plan of Action*, summary and proceedings of workshop on 21–22 June 2007, IEA, Paris

Leonardi, J and Baumgartner, M (2004) CO_2 efficiency in road freight transportation: status quo, measures and potential, *Transportation Research Part D*, **9**, pp 451–64

McKinnon, AC (2009) Benchmarking Road Freight Transport: Review of a Government-sponsored Programme, *Benchmarking: an International Journal* (forthcoming)

McKinnon, AC and Ge, Y (2004) Use of a synchronized vehicle audit to determine opportunities for improving transport efficiency in a supply chain, *International Journal of Logistics: Research and Applications*, **7** (3), pp 219–38

McKinnon, AC, Stirling, I and Kirkhope, J (1993) Improving the fuel efficiency of road freight operations, *International Journal of Physical Distribution & Logistics Management*, **23** (9), pp 3–11

Nylund, N and Erkkila, K (2007) HDV Fuel Efficiency: Methodology, Vehicle Performance and Potential for Fuel Savings, Presentation to IEA Workshop, 21–22 June 2007, Paris

Transport Canada (2005) *FleetSmart: Fuel efficiency benchmarking in Canada's trucking industry*, Office of Energy Efficiency, Ottawa

12

Reverse logistics for the management of waste

Tom Cherrett, Sarah Maynard, Fraser McLeod and Adrian Hickford

INTRODUCTION

Research into sustainable distribution has largely focused on improving the delivery of products through the supply chain from manufacturer to end customer by developing fundamental understanding of the various supply chain operations at work in urban centres. The logistics activities associated with the return of damaged, unsold or returned consumer products back up the supply chain, and the consolidation, handling and disposal of waste products that may result, is becoming of increasing interest in the drive to reduce costs and maximize efficiency within the distribution sector.

With the introduction of the EC Directives on Waste Electrical and Electronic Equipment (WEEE) (2002/96/EC), the Restriction of the Use of Certain Hazardous Substances (RoHS) in Electrical and Electronic Equipment (2002/95/EC) and Packaging and Packaging Waste (94/62/EC), the onus is on retailers and manufacturers to reduce their waste output and better manage their respective logistics operations in this area by participating in specific waste take-back schemes.

The need to effectively manage product returns as part of the supply chain process has become more pronounced since the introduction of the

Directive on Distance Contract (97/7/EC), which stipulates that people who make a purchase via the internet, telephone, fax or mail order can change their minds during a 'cooling-off' period of seven working days after the goods have been received with no explanation for their return being required.

Under this backdrop of increasingly liberal returns policies coupled with a 'throw away' consumer culture, the extent to which product returns contribute to increasing waste and recyclate generation needs to be explored. With a variety of centralized and decentralized supply chain mechanisms being employed to service retailers, there is potential scope for coordinating reverse processes to both reduce collective transport impacts and maximize reuse value from the recyclate generated.

WASTE MANAGEMENT IN THE CONTEXT OF REVERSE LOGISTICS

Reverse logistics has been defined as 'the process of planning, implementing, and controlling the efficient, cost-effective flow of raw materials, in-process inventory, finished goods, and related information from the point of consumption to the point of origin, for the purpose of recapturing value or proper disposal' (Rogers and Tibben-Lembke, 1999). 'Reverse logistics' differs from waste management as the latter is mainly concerned with the efficient and effective collection and processing of waste: that is, products for which there is no longer any reuse potential (De Brito and Dekker, 2003). The definition of 'waste' in this context is important from a legal perspective as the act of 'importing' waste is often forbidden (Fleischmann, 2001). However, there are similarities between some of the processes used by product recovery networks and waste disposal networks, especially in an urban setting (Shakantu, Tookey and Bowen, 2002). These are most evident in the 'supply' side where used products are collected from many, possibly widespread sources and need to be consolidated for further processing and transportation. Major differences do exist between these network types on the 'demand' side however. While a flow of recovered products would be directed towards a reuse market, waste streams eventually end at landfill sites or incineration plants (Figure 12.1) after various treatment processes (Fleischmann et al, 2000).

Depending on the type of reverse process employed, products may not necessarily be returned to their point of origin, but to a different point for recovery (De Brito and Dekker, 2003), and as the level of complexity in reverse logistics operations has increased, there is an increasing need to

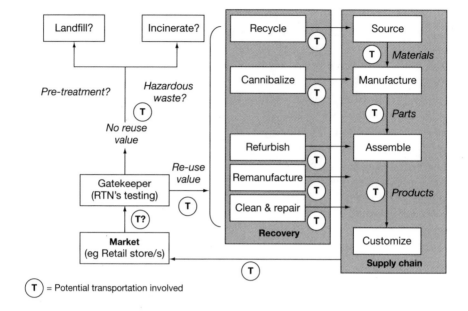

Figure 12.1 Recovery processes incorporated in the supply chain

Source: Adapted from Hillegersberg et al (2001).

address issues of sustainability and integration within the overall supply chain (DfT, 2004). The shipment of materials back to disposal sites and treatment centres is a natural extension of reverse logistics, and better integrating waste management processes within the overall reverse process could help reduce the negative transport impacts.

Within the retail sector, two main mechanisms of returns management have been identified (Halldórsson and Skjøtt-Larsen, 2007). In the centralized reverse supply chain, one organization has responsibility for the collection, inspection, disposition and redistribution of returned items that could be originating from many different retailers. In the decentralized reverse supply chain, multiple organizations could be involved in this process, where individual sales outlets act as their own 'gatekeepers', checking returned product and deciding which reuse/disposition paths items should take. Where the gatekeeping function is taken on at the individual store level, local skills will be needed in product inspection and testing. This is not a trivial undertaking and is a process that could lead to increased waste generation if not tightly managed and coordinated. Four physical network structures for handling retail returns have been identified (DfT, 2004), as outlined below.

Type A: Integrated outbound and returns network

Using a company's own fleet or its logistics providers' vehicles, returns are 'back hauled' from the retail outlets to a regional distribution centre (RDC). The gatekeeper function associated with sorting, checking and deciding the ultimate fate of the returned items (potentially including certain refurbishment processes) is carried out at the RDC. This system works well in a supply chain where the frequency of delivery to stores is high, and the volume of returns is also high.

Type B: Non-integrated outbound and returns network

In this case, a separate network is used for managing returns, typically operated by a third-party logistics provider (3PL) that takes returns (on an 'as and when required' basis) from stores to a separate location where the gatekeeper activities are undertaken by the retail organization. This system works well if the level of returns varies in volume but is generally low.

Type C: Third-party returns management

Where the total management of product returns is outsourced to a third-party contractor, the retailer benefits in that no gatekeeping expertise is required at the individual store level. The 3PL provides this functionality along with a complete returns management process, including supporting technologies, refurbishment and disposition programmes. Centralized gatekeeping processes have the potential to better manage the waste generated during the returns process and maximize reuse potential, as they have greater visibility of the various refurbishment options. This has seen the emergence of 4PLs that undertake 'business process outsourcing' to deliver fully comprehensive forward and reverse supply chain solutions, including refurbishment and disposition management (Mukhopadhyay and Setaputra, 2006).

Type D: Return to suppliers

In this case, goods are returned direct to the suppliers and exchanged for credit. Under these circumstances, retailers may have no gatekeeping responsibilities and little responsibility for returns. Such systems may have additional transport cost implications as the goods have to return to the individual supplier for the gatekeeping function before potential further travel related to refurbishment or disposition.

Waste and recyclate management should be seen as a key component in all reverse logistics processes but should be considered in the context of initial source reduction strategies to minimize waste production (Wu and Dunn, 1994; Marien, 1998). Carter and Ellram (1998) proposed a hierarchy of disposition that suggested that resource reduction (minimizing the amount of materials used in a product, and reducing the waste produced and energy spent through designing more environmentally efficient products) ought to be the ultimate goal of the reverse logistics process. Building on this concept, a simple hierarchy of product disposition 'reduce, reuse, recycle' has been suggested to minimize the impact of product returns (DfT, 2004). Reduction of returns can be attained through better management of the supply chain, particularly where closer collaboration between gatekeeping processes can be realized. Reuse of returns will maximize their asset value through the utilization of effective refurbishment programmes, and where reuse is no longer an option recycling refers to the best route for material recovery of products that cannot be re-sold. Returns that cannot be managed through these three elements will enter the waste stream (Figure 12.1).

To effectively utilize this hierarchy of disposition, businesses need to integrate their current supply chain and process management strategies, and consider collaborating with potential rivals to better utilize existing assets and generate critical mass to make use of specialist service providers. As legislation such as the WEEE directive and the Directive on Distance Contract start to impact on retailers in terms of increasing the volumes and variety of returns, so opportunities for the small to medium-sized enterprise (SME) to cooperate with other organizations in collaborative 'reduce, reuse and recycle' initiatives increase (Shih, 2001).

THE IMPACT OF WASTE TREATMENT LEGISLATION

The Producer Pre-Treatment Requirement of the Landfill Directive was implemented in October 2007, prohibiting businesses from sending non-hazardous waste that had not been pre-treated to landfill (Biffa, 2007). The responsibility for pre-treatment rests with the waste producer and the overall aim of the directive is to reduce the impact of landfill and increase material recovery through recycling. Under the directive, 'pre-treatment' is deemed to have been undertaken when the waste has been through a 'three-point test' in which all three points have been satisfied:

1. It must be a physical, thermal or chemical, or biological process, including sorting.
2. It must change the characteristics of the waste.
3. It must do so in order to:
   - reduce its volume, or
   - reduce its hazardous nature, or
   - facilitate its handling, or
   - enhance its recovery.

In the case of a high-street retailer, pre-treatment can usually be achieved by separating out recyclable material from the general waste stream using different containers, or by sending mixed waste (where separation at-store is not possible) to a sortation facility where recyclate can be recovered. There is no clear guidance as to the proportion of waste that would need to be recovered, only that it is 'significant' and 'consistent'. For waste that is not destined for landfill, the treatment requirements are not applicable.

An online survey of over 600 SMEs and 200 larger corporate businesses (with over 250 employees) looked at the extent of recycling amongst UK businesses and the extent to which SMEs were aware of the pre-treatment requirements (Taylor Intelligence, 2007). The results suggested that there was a general lack of awareness amongst SMEs of the producer pre-treatment requirements and many did not have the facilities or contracts in place to separate out and recover recyclate from the general waste stream. There is clearly a market for both private contractors and local authorities to provide commercial recycling collections to SMEs, the latter highlighted in the government's Waste Strategy 2007, which has introduced a strategic objective to encourage local authorities to assist SMEs to recycle. Given the requirements of the producer pre-treatment legislation, SMEs would do well to coordinate their recycling activities with their neighbours to reduce costs and meet their obligations. The end of 'co-disposal' brought about through the Landfill Regulations 2002 (Landfill Directive 99/31/EC) has seen the number of sites licensed to take hazardous waste drop from around 240 nationally to fewer than 15. The longer-term impact of this is likely to be an increase in average length of haul, given that nearly 42 per cent of hazardous waste is currently transported across regional boundaries (Envirowise, 2005) and there are currently no licensed sites in London or Wales. The Environment Agency estimated that as a result, the cost of collecting and disposing of hazardous waste would increase from £150 million per annum to approximately £500 million.

The EC Directive on Packaging and Packaging Waste (94/62/EC) seeks to reduce the impact of packaging on the environment by introducing specific recovery and recycling targets, and by encouraging more minimization and reuse in this area. The UK was obliged to recover 60 per cent of overall UK packaging waste by the end of December 2008, and more specifically, 60 per cent of all paper and glass. The regulations affect any business that handles more than 50 tonnes of packaging per annum and has an annual turnover of more than £2 million. These businesses include those that put goods or products into packaging as well as those that sell already packaged goods to final users.

Under the regulations, obligated businesses must provide evidence of payment for the recovery and recycling of a specified proportion of their packaging waste (including wood, aluminium, steel, cardboard and plastic). This is done through electronic Packaging Recovery Notes (PRNs) and Packaging Export Recovery Notes (PERNs) issued by the accredited re-processor to indicate how much packaging has been recovered or recycled. As in the 3PL returns management model, businesses have the option to join a packaging compliance scheme that manages the individual company's recovery and recycling obligations (eg purchase of PRNs/PERNs and reporting on compliance to the regulator). The government has acknowledged that the increased recovery of packaging waste is integral to meeting its landfill diversion targets and improving recycling and recovery from waste. The introduction of the regulations has already led to a significant improvement in packaging recycling, increasing from 27 per cent (1997) to 57 per cent (2006).

Using a common type of reusable packaging that complies with an agreed standard (Golding, 1999) and could be exchanged between companies (Kroon and Vrijens, 1995; DfT, 2005) is one way that businesses could reduce such costs. Reusable packaging may not be universally attractive as logistics costs might be adversely affected by additional handling, retrieval and storage requirements. Since manufacturers typically factor the costs of packaging into their prices to customers, the total cost of supply would probably reduce where packaging could be reused, along with end disposal costs (Wu and Dunn, 1994). It is however important to clarify whether the collective processes associated with managing the production, take-back and final disposal of returnable packaging is not more detrimental to the environment than the use of one-way packaging material (Kroon and Vrijens, 1995). While large retail chains often maximize vehicle utilization through backhauling reusable packaging (trays, dollies etc) and other recyclable material, wholesalers have to deliver small loads to many small businesses and for hygiene and cost considerations, it is sometimes impracticable to recover packaging waste (Fernie and Hart, 2001).

The EC directives on Waste Electrical and Electronic Equipment (WEEE) (2002/96/EC) and on the Restriction of the Use of Certain Hazardous

Substances (RoHS) in Electrical and Electronic Equipment (2002/95/EC) aim to reduce the environmental impact of waste from electrical and electronic equipment (EEE) and increase its recovery, recycling and reuse. The directives affect producers, distributors and recyclers of EEE, including household appliances, IT and telecommunications equipment, audiovisual equipment (TV, video, hi-fi), lighting, electrical and electronic tools, toys, leisure and sports equipment. Increased recycling of EEE will reduce the total quantity of waste going to final disposal with producers having the responsibility for taking back and recycling items.

A proposal for a UK National Clearing House (NCH) to coordinate producer responsibility for WEEE was given strong support by industry stakeholders during the third round of consultation carried out by the Department for Trade and Industry (DTI) in October 2004 (DTI, 2004). However, the DTI considered the proposal too complex and issued further consultation, including developing a network of 'designated collection facilities' (DCFs), which could possibly utilize the network of 1,400 existing household waste recycling centres (HWRCs) (Bridgwater and Anderson, 2003). If HWRCs were to play a more significant role in reverse logistics processes, then some of their existing functionality may need to be outsourced to more localized collection systems (eg kerbside/bring-site green waste collections) to free up space for WEEE consolidation (Cherrett and Hickford, 2006).

The WEEE Directive also includes provision for a distributor take-back scheme for retailers, which establishes a network of designated collection facilities (NetRegs, 2006). Retailers who sell or distribute electrical and/or electronic equipment on to the UK market are obliged to ensure customer take-back of these products at the end of their lives, through a range of methods. This can be through the offer of in-store take-back of old products when a direct replacement is sold to a customer, or through joining a retailer take-back compliance scheme, which must offer alternative take-back arrangements. The latter would be expected to accept all WEEE and not just on a like-for-like basis, and would therefore have greater implications in terms of transport. Businesses that collect and transport WEEE (eg at the same time as making a delivery) need to be registered with the Environment Agency as waste carriers. Coordinated compliance schemes could ease the problems associated with handling and tracking the return of goods and the associated packaging back to manufacturers via retail outlets (Bettac et al, 1999).

The gatekeeping function within a reverse supply chain (the point at which returned items are checked to establish whether they can be re-sold, repaired, refurbished, cannibalized, or disposed) can also play an important role in managing the movement of potentially hazardous waste products back up the system. Under the EC 2005 Hazardous Waste

Directive (91/689/EEC), producers of hazardous waste as identified in the List of Waste (formerly the European Waste Catalogue) must register with the Environment Agency before they can move material from their premises. Exemptions from registration apply if less than 200 kg of hazardous waste is produced over a 12-month period, and the premises is a shop or office that is used for the collection of WEEE, and a registered carrier is being used to remove the material. The mixing of hazardous and non-hazardous waste is strictly prohibited and reverse logistics operations where the gatekeeping process leads to significant de-construction and cannibalization need to carefully consider waste separation and segregation. Both of these outcomes can lead to additional transport and handling costs. A waste carrier's licence would be needed and drivers would require special training in order to carry hazardous cargo. The consignee would also be required to keep detailed records of waste disposition and provide quarterly reports to the Environment Agency detailing the quantities and origins of wastes. Such documentation enables the movement of hazardous waste to be tracked and managed responsibly until it reaches authorized disposal or recovery facilities.

REUSE, REFURBISHMENT MARKETS AND TAKE-BACK SCHEMES

Of key importance to reverse logistics networks handling recyclate are the end markets for the retrieved materials. The lack of available markets has long been identified as a barrier that restricts recycling performance, and the Waste and Resources Action Plan (WRAP) was established in 2001 with a view to creating stable markets for recyclables with a specific focus on aggregates, glass, organics, paper, plastics and wood (WRAP, 2006).

Material markets are found on a local, national and global level, and commodity pricing structures can be complex, dependent on a range of factors including the supply of and demand for the recyclate, transportation and handling costs, market competition and overheads (RRF, 2004). China is a key end-market for recyclate emanating from the UK, with exports of recovered paper and plastics standing at 2.7 million and 517,000 tonnes respectively in 2008. This accounted for 55 per cent and 80 per cent respectively of the UK exports of these two materials (WRAP, 2009). Autumn 2008 saw a sharp tail-off in demand for these commodities in China, largely due to the economic downturn, with prices falling between 40 and 60 per cent in one month alone. Exports of recovered paper fell by 40 per cent between October and November 2008 as a direct response.

If a particular recyclate market becomes saturated, with supply exceeding demand, the commodity value decreases, affecting the viability of the collection systems employed. This market behaviour was experienced in Germany when the German Packaging Ordinance referred to as the 'Topfer Decree' was introduced in 1992. This covered all types of packaging waste and obliged manufacturers and distributors to take back packaging for reuse or recycling outside the public waste disposal system. The over-supply of recovered paper resulted in a crash in prices that led to an increase in paper dumped across Europe. The UK recyclate market is influenced by its foreign counterpart (through which exports and imports of materials are exchanged), the virgin commodity market and the PERN market (packaging waste recovery notes as part of the Packaging and Packaging Waste Regulations).

There are many mature markets available for components of WEEE, especially plastic and cathode-ray tubes, ferrous and precious metals. European Metal Recycling (EMR) has an established network of facilities throughout the UK to process WEEE, metal packaging, plastics and rubber (Enviros, 2002). The markets for WEEE are influenced by the age of the material and also the techniques used by the reprocessor to reclaim components with value. Community and charity groups also generate a reuse market for recovered material. Organizations such as the Furniture Reuse Network (FRN, formerly known as Furniture Recycling Network), Community Recycling Network, CREATE UK Ltd, CRISP, ECT Recycling, Realise-It and the SOFA project play an integral role in local and national sustainable waste management. Through local community schemes and social enterprises, materials such as EEE (computers, TVs etc), can be refurbished and reused within the community. There are also established charity markets that export materials to developing countries (eg Recommit that collects and exports computers).

There are a number of businesses that are now targeting the different types of waste/recyclate generated by the retail and business sectors, many providing dedicated services that can be easily integrated into existing reverse networks. Some examples are:

- FareShare (www.fareshare.org.uk)
  FareShare is a national organization that works with over 100 food businesses, wholesalers and retailers to reduce the amount of food waste sent to landfill by redistributing surplus fresh food to day centres and night shelters for homeless people. The scheme has been in operation since 2004 and has 12 centres around the UK. FareShare helps around 25,000 people daily by collecting food from businesses and re-distributing it through their network to disadvantaged people in the community. In 2007, the food collected contributed to over 4.5

million meals, and in the period to 2011 they plan to open another 18 depots nationwide and re-distribute 20,000 tonnes of food annually.

- Auction Assist (www.auctionassist.co.uk/investors.htm)
  Aiming to help people or businesses who may want to sell goods or stock on the internet but do not have the technical abilities, Auction Assist offers an auctioning service on eBay. Items are taken to a local Auction Assist centre, either by the prospective seller or via an arranged collection. From the auction centre, the items are sold to the highest bidder on the internet site and dispatched to the buyer, with any proceeds sent to the original owner. It is unclear how this method of disposal would affect the number of kilometres travelled, since journeys to the auction centres would not normally have been made, and items sold through eBay still need to be sent to the purchaser via traditional methods. Such a system could be beneficial for SMEs that need to find new markets for grade-A customer returns. A similar system (The Auction Assistant) is currently operating in the USA (http://www.theauctionassistant.com).

- RASCAL (http://www.rascal-solutions.com)
  RASCAL provides a comprehensive in-store newspaper and magazine returns-processing system. Retail outlets routinely store product information, including magazine titles, on-and-off sale dates and wholesaler details through their stock management systems. Titles that are due for return are scanned and matched to the details of the relevant receiving wholesaler, which are then transmitted to the RASCAL database. Once a product has been returned, the wholesaler transmits a credit from its system to the consignee. The system, which is used by a range of high street retailers, provides an effective tool to track all returned stock.

- Furniture Reuse Network (FRN) (http://www.frn.org.uk/)
  The Furniture Reuse Network is the national coordinating body for around 400 furniture and appliance reuse and recycling organizations across the UK. The FRN promotes the reuse of unwanted furniture and household effects, with around two million items per year being reused and passed on to low-income families (around 250,000 being domestic appliances). Approximately 90,000 tonnes of waste is diverted from landfill through the FRN network as a result. FRN employs around 3,000 people to collect and deliver furniture and appliances around the UK and has over 160 organizations within its network that refurbish and reuse domestic appliances, with over 300,000 fridges being collected annually alone. The FRN is able to reprocess electrical items and is currently developing a network of

over 35 treatment centres for WEEE and is entering into partnerships with local authorities to collect bulky waste.

- Regenersis (www.regenersisplc.com/)
  It is estimated that over 15 million mobile phones are replaced each year in the UK. The main channels for their disposition are through the retail outlets that sell them, and linked to those are a number of WEEE-compliant schemes offering a specific recycling service. Fonebak is one such scheme, now part of the Regenersis brand, with over 1,000 clients representing every network operator in the UK and many major networks, retailers, manufacturers and charities across Europe. With around 10,000 phone collection points across Europe, it has collected over 3.5 million phones since 2002. It also offers a reverse logistics service, which manages the collection of mobile phones and accessories from over 2,000 outlets throughout the UK.

- Computer Aid International (www.computeraid.org)
  With around 3 million PCs decommissioned in the UK every year, Computer Aid International is a charitable organization that provides high quality, professionally refurbished computers for reuse in education, health and not-for-profit organizations in developing countries. The organization has shipped over 90,000 PCs, mostly distributed to schools and colleges with the active support of host governments of around 100 countries.

MANAGING WASTE AS PART OF A SUSTAINABLE REVERSE PROCESS

Under Section 34 of the 1990 Environmental Protection Act, commercial premises have a 'duty of care' to make satisfactory arrangements for their waste collection (DEFRA, 1990). Generally, businesses will arrange a collection contract with a private waste management company but some authorities also offer rival 'trade waste' services. The Environment Agency has suggested that approximately half of all commercial and industrial waste in England and Wales is produced by SMEs, making up around a third of industrial wastes and two-thirds of commercial wastes (EA, 2005). The difficulties small businesses face in terms of recycling opportunities was highlighted in a waste strategy review (DEFRA, 2006) where it was suggested that only 37 per cent of commercial waste was recycled. The review recognized that smaller businesses often had particular problems obtaining affordable recycling and recovery services, and suggested that coordinating operations across different waste streams was a potential way to improve efficiency and performance.

Schemes to aid SMEs

There are many examples of collection schemes that have been specifically aimed at helping SMEs handle their waste and recyclate and therefore encourage sustainable take-back.

Dove Recycling based in Hampshire (www.doverecycling.co.uk), formed in July 2005, provides a tailored collection system to allow businesses to better manage their recyclable waste. Cardboard, paper, cans, plastic bottles, glass, WEEE, fluorescent tubes and confidential waste can all be sent back through its system. An electric-powered collection vehicle was supplied by Hampshire County Council as part of the EC-funded MIRACLES project and was used to transport the collected cardboard and paper.

Funded through the Landfill Tax Credit Scheme (LTCS), 'BasRap' provides a commercial recycling collection service designed to help businesses in Basildon better manage their recyclate. The scheme, which started as a partnership project between Onyx, Remade Essex and the Basildon Green Business Forum (BGBF), uses dedicated 1,100 ltr euro bins, for the collection of cardboard and plastic wrap materials, which are then sent to an Essex recycling facility for sorting and onward reprocessing at sites within the UK (Remade Essex, 2007). The same partnership approach was adopted by the Norfolk Waste Recycling Assistance Project (NORWRAP), supported by Norfolk County Council. Based on the Basildon scheme, a similar service using accredited waste contractors is available to SMEs in Thetford, Great Yarmouth and Norwich (NORWRAP, 2005)

The 'PaperSave' scheme was a joint initiative between Surrey Chambers of Commerce, Surrey County Council and Business Link Surrey, funded and developed by SITA Environmental Trust along with several local authorities. The scheme provided SMEs with weekly or fortnightly collections of mixed paper and cardboard (Sitatrust, 2005). Funding for the scheme was allocated for nine months in order to establish a high number of participating businesses that would enable contractors to reduce collection costs to a level that would be attractive to SMEs. The first scheme was located on the Holmethorpe Industrial estate in Redhill and was serviced by Reigate and Banstead Borough Council. Feedback from the participants and non-participants demonstrated that service cost was one of the most critical factors in scheme take-up.

Take-back opportunities for SMEs, particularly in the area of small parts returns, could be achieved through utilizing the emerging networks of attended and unattended collection–delivery points (CDPs), Cherrett and McLeod (2005). The use of attended premises, typically convenience stores, petrol stations and post offices (eg Kiala, Royal Mail, Parcel Force, Redpack Network) or unattended locker banks or boxes (eg ByBox,

Bearbox) for returning products back up the supply chain are already well established in the service industry. Such concepts could provide alternative, more effective methods for consolidating small items for take-back.

The potential for joint domestic/commercial collections

Local authorities can set up their own trade waste collections for business customers, and under the Controlled Waste Regulations they can charge businesses for these services. A key driver behind the set-up of such services is the Landfill Allowance Trading Scheme (LATS), which sets challenging targets for the reduction of biodegradable municipal waste sent to landfill (DEFRA, 2005). Trade wastes count against an authority's LATS targets, and there is therefore an incentive for authorities to better address the recycling or composting of biodegradable trade waste and divert it from landfill. This would not only help an authority meet its LATS targets but could also increase its overall recycling rate. Research by Enviros Consulting (2005) showed that nearly 22 per cent of the co-collected waste stream was made up of recyclable paper and card-board, and if such percentages were diverted away from landfill in London this would equate to over 100,000 tonnes as a contribution towards the capital's LATS targets.

Local authorities that offer trade waste collections often do so as a separate entity, using a fleet of dedicated vehicles and hiring out bins to businesses as part of the overall service contract. Within the UK there are a few examples of waste collection authorities facilitating the collection of domestic and commercial waste as part of the same collection round. For recyclate collection, this appears to be a much more efficient use of transport resources, as residential areas encompassing areas of retail/ business can be covered using the same vehicle fleet as part of the same round. All commercial waste collected as part of a joint collection would have to be separated out prior to weighing to meet legal requirements.

New Forest District Council (NFDC) has operated such a joint commercial/domestic waste collection service, allowing SMEs to put out recyclate for collection as part of the domestic round (McLeod and Cherrett, 2006). In their operating model, commercial waste is collected from SMEs that have pre-registered with the council and have acquired a 'duty of care' certificate (defined under the Control of Pollution Act 1974, the Collection and Disposal of Waste Regulations 1984 and the Environmental Protection Act 1990). This waste is collected on the same rounds as the domestic recyclate collection. In research undertaken by McLeod and Cherrett (2006), 13 weekly residual-waste rounds were operated by NFDC, with the proportion of commercial waste collected ranging from 0.1 per cent to 3.2 per cent (97.5 tonnes collected during 2005/06 through the domestic rounds). Such a system is ideally suited to small businesses that may be producing small quantities of waste and do not want to sign up to a large-scale commercial collection service.

The ability of an existing domestic round to collect additional SME waste is dependent on the spare capacity in the refuse collection vehicle (RCV). Spare capacity is needed in terms of both physical space and also in the amount of time available for collecting due to the time constraints associated with crew shift patterns and the operating hours of waste treatment/disposal facilities. A theoretical study, modelling the impacts of incorporating SME commercial waste collections into certain domestic rounds across Rushmoor and Hart in Hampshire, was undertaken (McLeod and Cherrett, 2006). Using data collected from the domestic collection fleets, a total spare capacity of 11.3 per cent (14.4 tonnes) was estimated across the eight modelled rounds, with an additional one hour and 16 minutes of time available for each round. The impacts on round distance, time, revenue generation and cost were investigated, associated with collecting different amounts of commercial waste (3.9 T, 7.4 T, 14.4 T) from random points on the round. The results suggested that additional commercial waste loads of 3.9 T and 7.4 T could be accommodated using the existing domestic collection rounds. For commercial waste volumes of 7.4 T and 14.4 T however, one and two additional trips to the waste disposal sites were needed respectively, which would increase the overall collection costs.

There may be wider environmental benefits to be gained through the introduction of joint domestic/commercial collections. Recycling performance amongst SMEs should improve whilst the volume of waste taken to landfill would reduce. Total vehicle mileage and traffic congestion may be reduced, particularly in shopping areas, if the number of visits by waste collection vehicles could be reduced. The current fragmented situation, where some areas can be serviced by many different collection companies, could be improved if the WCA offered a commercial waste collection service of this type.

CONCLUSIONS

Managing recyclate, in terms of minimizing the costs associated with its separation and transport whilst maximizing any value that can be gained through its recovery, is becoming of increasing interest as part of integrated supply chain management strategies. As a result, many innovative take-back systems have been developed, catering for a wide variety of materials, targeted often at small to medium-sized businesses that often do not generate significant volumes of recyclate to warrant a contract with a major waste contractor, but nevertheless have to comply with their obligations under waste management legislation.

In terms of the options that would have the greatest impact for 'greening' the waste take-back systems, supplying the various treatment/ processing facilities, combined domestic and commercial waste collections, particularly for SME recyclate management, have considerable potential. Coordinated through the local collection authority, these types of combined collection could effectively cater for additional small-volume recyclate consignments on top of the domestic set out, and potentially encourage SMEs to recycle more material.

Utilizing the existing delivery mechanisms serving a retail sector to take back recyclate ('backloading') is the other option for reducing the transport footprint associated with waste management in urban centres. If the combined transport resources across different supply chains could be pooled in some way to create shared take-back schemes, then considerable environmental and financial savings could be gained. There are some fundamental barriers to this, not least the requirement that transport companies seeking to take back waste on behalf of other businesses register their intent with the Environment Agency and obtain a Waste Carrier Licence. Other issues relate to whether retailers would be happy with the image of waste and recyclate from a potential rival business being loaded into their liveried vehicles. This aside, the customer-focused operating characteristics of logistics suppliers mean that many are ill-equipped to handle reverse flows, as the methods of transportation, goods storage and handling are often very different from those used in the forward flow (Halldórsson and Skjøtt-Larsen, 2007).

Some of the key issues that would have to be considered with regard to using existing delivery fleets for take-back are:

- Is there spare capacity on the existing delivery rounds?
  In the case of centralized distribution systems, where single-drop delivery rounds are more prevalent, there may be more potential to take back recyclate as well as returns, depending on any collections that have to be scheduled as part of the return journey. Multi-drop delivery rounds may be problematic as stowage space may be at a premium with multiple delivery calls to make, but there could also be more serious issues relating to the cross-contamination of grade A stock by recyclate or returns. There could also be time conflicts on a multi-drop round with having to collect, consolidate and store recyclate/returns at each delivery point.

- Do the delivery vehicles visit frequently enough to service the waste collection/return goods demands?
  External storage and groupage areas are often at a premium for businesses operating in historic city centres. If a retail store only has a small area set aside for waste and recyclate storage, then it might require a more frequent waste collection service than can be offered through backloading opportunities. The available backloading capacity may vary considerably depending on day-to-day occurrences in the supply chain (eg rejected deliveries, inter-store transfers, promotional stock etc).

- Which materials may be collected?
  In reality, only 'clean' recyclate such as uncontaminated paper, cardboard and plastics would be suitable for take-back using delivery vehicles. Depending on the requirements of the end-processor, there may be limited opportunities further up the reverse supply chain to separate out recyclate, and therefore mixed collections, although desirable, may not be achievable in practice. This could increase handling costs and lead to small, sub-optimal volumes of recyclate passing back up the system.

- What equipment is needed?
  Waste collection typically involves a range of bins, sacks, compacting and baling equipment, lifting mechanisms and specialist waste-collection vehicles. If special equipment is required to consolidate the recyclate or lift it on to the vehicle then this might preclude the use of backloading as a realistic option. The existing equipment used in deliveries (eg roll cages, pallets, dollies) may limit what items can be returned in the vehicle.

- Where does the waste/recyclate have to be delivered to?
  In centralized distribution systems, recyclate and returned products may simply go back to the regional distribution centre. The situation could be more complex if a delivery vehicle being used for backloading has to divert from its schedule to drop recyclate at a specific processing or sortation facility. There may be vehicle-facility compatibility issues where re-processing facilities are not geared up to receive articulated delivery vehicles. Given the fluctuation in recyclate values, end-markets may frequently change as retailers try to maximize the financial return for the material carried. In such instances, the additional mileage travelled to a facility might outweigh the financial returns from the load. In this case, out-of-town groupage facilities might be a viable option to enable delivery vehicles to back load out of the centre to a managed facility from where recyclate is grouped for

onward movement by a waste contractor. This facility in effect would be acting as a traditional 'consolidation centre' in reverse.

- How stable/regular is the demand for waste and return goods collection?
  Ideally, there should be a regular and stable flow of returns and recyclate in a backloading operation to allow effective scheduling of the delivery vehicles. If the demand is highly variable, particularly in cases where seasonal fluctuations are pronounced, then it may be difficult to accommodate effective backloading as part of the delivery structure, as accurately forecasting demand may prove difficult.

REFERENCES

Bettac, E, Maas, K, Beullens, P, Bopp, R (1999) RELOOP: Reverse logistics chain optimization in a multi-user trading environment, in *Proceedings of the 1999 IEEE International Symposium on Electronics and the Environment*, Conference Record of the IEEE International Symposium on Electronics and the Environment, Danvers, Mass, 11–13 May, pp 42–47

Biffa (2007) [accessed 1 April 2009] *The UK Landfill Regulations Pre-treatment Requirements* [Online] http://www.biffa.co.uk/content.php?id=325

Bridgewater, E and Anderson, C (2003) *Capacity in the UK. An assessment of the capacity of civic amenity sites in the United Kingdom to separately collect waste electrical and electronic equipment*, report commissioned by and written on behalf of DEFRA, London [accessed 08 August 2007] [Online] http://www.networkrecycling.co.uk/pdf/weee/ca_site_weee_capacity_in_uk.pdf

Carter, CR and Ellram, LM (1998) Reverse logistics: a review of the literature and framework for future investigation, *Journal of Business Logistics*, **19**(1), pp 85–102

Cherrett, TJ and Hickford, AJ (2006) The potential for local bring-sites to reduce householder recycling mileage, 86th Annual Meeting of the Transportation Research Board paper 07–0719, January, Washington, DC

Cherrett, TJ and McLeod, FN (2005) Missed another home delivery? The potential for local collect points, University Transport Study Group 37th Annual Conference, 5–7 January 2005, Bristol, Volume 2

De Brito, MP and Dekker, R (2003) *A Framework for Reverse Logistics*, Erasmus Research, Institute of Management Report Series Research In Management, Erasmus University, Rotterdam

DEFRA (1990) *Waste Management, The Duty of Care: A code of practice, Environmental Protection Act 1990*, Section 34, DEFRA, London

DEFRA (2005) *Landfill Allowance Trading Scheme (LATS): A practical guide*, DEFRA, London

DEFRA (2006) [accessed 9 October 2007] *The Producer Responsibility Obligations (Packaging Waste) Regulations 2005 Is your business complying?* Summary, January 2006 [Online] http://www.defra.gov.uk/environment/waste/topics/packaging/pdf/packagewaste06.pdf

Department for Trade (DfT) (2004) *The Efficiency of Reverse Logistics*, report prepared for the DfT by Cranfield University School of Management, Sheffield Hallam University, and The Chartered Institute of Logistics and Transport (UK)

DfT (2005) *Make Back-Loading Work for You*, DfT Freight Best Practice Programme

Department for Trade and Industry (DTI) (2004) [accessed 16 January 2007] *Assessment of Responses to the Third Consultation Document: WEEE and RoHS Directives*, UK DTI [Online] http://www.dti.gov.uk/files/file30558.pdf

Environment Agency (EA) (2005) [accessed 15 January 2007] *Commercial and Industrial Waste Survey 2002/3* [Online] http://www.environment-agency.gov.uk/subjects/waste/1031954/315439/923299/1071046/?version=1&lang=_e

Enviros Consulting (2002) [accessed 25 November 2006] Potential markets for electronic and electrical equipment, project funded by the Environment Agency [Online} http://www.londonremade.com/download_files/weee.doc

Enviros Consulting (2005) *Best Practice Guidance: Trade waste recycling report for the Waste Strategy Support Unit*, Greater London Authority, London

Envirowise (2005) [accessed 4 July 2005] *Hazardous Waste Managament: Essential information for businesses* [Online]: http://www.envirowise.co.uk/envirowisev3.nsf/key/hazwaste

Fernie, J and Hart, C (2001) UK packaging waste legislation; implications for food retailers, *British Food Journal*, **108** (3), pp 187–197

Fleischmann, M (2001) *Reverse Logistics Network Structures and Design*, Erasmus Research, Institute of Management Report Series Research In Management ERS-2001–52–LIS, 2001

Fleischmann, M, Krikke, HR, Dekker, R, Flapper, SDP (2000) A characterization of logistics networks for Product Recovery Omega, *International Journal of Management Science*, 28, 653–666

Golding, A (1999) *Reuse of Primary Packaging*, final report prepared for European Commission

Halldórsson, A and Skjøtt-Larsen, T (2007) Design of reverse supply chains: centralized or decentralized structure, in *Managing Supply Chains: Challenges and opportunities*, ed W Delfmann and R de Koster, pp 1–26, Copenhagen Business School Press, Copenhagen

Hillegersberg, J van, Zuidwijk, R, Nunen, J van and Eijk, D van (2001) Supporting return flows in the supply chain, *Communications of the ACM*, **44** (6), pp 74–79

Kroon, L and Vrijens, G (1995) Returnable containers: an example of reverse logistics, *International Journal of Physical Distribution & Logistics Management*, **25** (2), pp 56–68

Marien, EJ (1998) Reverse logistics as a competitive strategy, *The Supply Chain Management Review*, **2** (1), pp 43–52

McLeod, F, and Cherrett, TJ (2006) Optimizing vehicles undertaking waste collection, final report for the DfT September 2006, Unpublished

Mukhopadhyay, SK and Setaputra, R (2006) The role of 4PL as the reverse logistics integrator, *International Journal of Physical Distribution & Logistics Management*, **36** (9), pp 716–29

NetRegs (2006) [accessed 1 August 2009] Equipment distributors and retailers: what you must do [Online] http://www.netregs.gov.uk

Norfolk Waste Recycling Assistance Project (NORWRAP) (2005) [accessed 10 September 2007] *Norfolk's Business Waste Recycling Scheme* [Online] http://www.big-e.org.uk/norwrap/

Remade Essex (2007) [accessed 13 September 2007] About BasRap [Online] http://www.remadeessex.org.uk/page.asp?categoryID=17

Resource Recovery Forum (RRF) (2004) The Impact of Increasing Road Transport Costs on Waste Recovery and Recycling, a report for the Resource Recovery Forum by Ceres Logistics, RRF, Skipton

Rogers, DS and Tibben-Lembke, RS (1999) *Going Backwards: Reverse logistics trends and practices*, Reverse Logistics Executive Council, Pittsburg, PA

Shakantu, W, Tookey, JE and Bowen, PA (2002) Defining the role of reverse logistics in attaining sustainable integration of materials delivery with construction and demolition waste management, in *Proceedings of Creating a Sustainable Construction Industry*, Proceedings of the CIB W107 International Conference on Creating a Sustainable Construction Industry in Developing Countries, Cape Town, 11–13 November, pp 97–103

Shih, L (2001) Reverse logistics system planning for recycling electrical appliances and computers in Taiwan, *Resources, Conservation and Recycling*, **32**, pp 55–72

Sitatrust (2005) *An Investigation of the Opportunities and Barriers to Developing Sustainable Recycling Schemes for Small and Medium Size Enterprises (SMEs), Using a High Density Approach*, Naomi Pitts MSc dissertation [accessed 9 August 2007] [Online] http://www.sitatrust.org.uk/resources/documents/Final_Report_Recycling_for_SMEs_Made_Easy.doc

Taylor Intelligence (2007) [accessed 30 October 2007] *Recycling in UK Plc: A state of the workplace report October 2007 conducted by YouGov* [Online] http://www.taylor-ch.co.uk/eng/About/Taylor-Intelligence

Waste and Resources Action Plan (WRAP) (2006) [accessed 20 November 2006] *The Waste Resources Action Programme* [Online] http://www.wrap.org.uk/

WRAP (2009) [accessed 24 May 2009] The Chinese markets for recovered paper and plastics, *Market Situation Report*, spring [Online]: www.wrap.org.uk/marketreports

Wu, H-J and Dunn, SC (1994) Environmentally responsible logistics systems, *International Journal of Physical Distribution & Logistics Management*, **25** (2), pp 20–38

Part 4

KEY ISSUES

13

The food miles debate

Is shorter better?

Tara Garnett

INTRODUCTION

The concept of 'food miles' first entered public consciousness in the mid-1990s, following the publication of a groundbreaking report by the SAFE Alliance, an environmental organization now known as Sustain. The phrase was originally coined to encapsulate a broad range of environmental, social and economic problems resulting from the globalizing of food supply systems. Since the report's initial publication, however, the phrase's broader, more holistic intent has been superseded by a narrow focus on the environmental (and specifically CO_2) impacts of transporting food over long distances. The basic, simplified message that the food miles label now carries in the public consciousness is that food transport today is excessive and unnecessary, and that, essentially, further is worse and nearer is better.

While this may be the public view, a considerable and growing body of research has sought to take a closer look at this assumption (Foster et al, 2006; Edwards-Jones et al, 2008). Initial research highlighted the need to consider the importance of mode (sea versus air, for example) and of efficiency (of vehicle, of loading, of route) before making conclusions about the merits of one supply chain over the other. Increasingly, however, food researchers have been adopting a life cycle analysis (LCA) approach; this considers transport within the context of food's environmental impacts at all stages in the supply chain, from agricultural production through to storage and cooking in the home and final disposal. Transport is just one element requiring consideration, and with this whole-cycle approach its importance, relative to other stages, can be gauged. Importantly, the LCA approach not only sheds light on the relative importance of different stages in the supply chain, but also allows us to explore what effect a change in one part of the system (say, a shorter transport leg) may have on emissions from other parts.

The purpose of this chapter is to examine what the LCA approach reveals about the importance of food-transport-related CO_2 emissions. We then consider whether the LCA is itself a sufficient analytic tool – whether it is able to capture the broader, more systemic impacts of globalized food provisioning systems and their contribution to climate changing emissions. Finally, since they are at the core of many discussions around food miles, we consider the issue of self-sufficiency and food security; we ask whether a national policy of maximizing the former enhances the likelihood of achieving the latter.

TRANSPORT AND GHGS: IS FURTHER WORSE?

The last few years have seen a number of studies seeking to investigate the correlation between distance and environmental impact. An early example is the *Wise Moves* report (Garnett, 2003) published by the environmental organization Campaign for Better Transport (at that time Transport 2000). This found that food transport accounts for around 3.5 per cent of the UK's GHG emissions. It concluded that there was some correlation between shorter journey distance and lower emissions, but that there were many exceptions, owing to differences in the efficiency of production systems as well as in the mode of travel and logistics. It suggested that the elements of a lower carbon food system included the following:

- Seasonal and indigenous: fresh produce grown during its natural growing season and well adapted to UK growing conditions will be less transport intensive and produce fewer overall CO_2 emissions than non-indigenous foods or those imported out of season.
- Efficient manufacturing: the processing plant needs to be efficiently operated and managed.
- Minimal use of temperature-controlled storage: This should not, in the process, compromise safety standards or generate waste through spoilage.

- Local clustering: the inputs to the product in question must be situated near to the site of production.
- Journey distance: the distance from point of production to point of retail to point of consumption should be minimized.
- Logistical efficiency: the fuel efficiency of a vehicle and the way it is managed and operated are very important. In addition loads must be consolidated and vehicles as full as possible while they are in use.

It also recommended that a life cycle approach to investigating and tackling food related emissions be adopted.

At around this time, DEFRA (2005) commissioned a study to assess whether food miles might be a valid indicator of sustainable development, to be added to its suite of other indicators (DEFRA, 2008). It put greenhouse gas (GHG) emissions associated with food distribution (including from overseas) at approximately 3 per cent of the emissions produced within UK borders (transport's share would be lower, at 2.25 per cent, if the embedded emissions all goods and services imported from overseas were included – Garnett, 2008) and concluded that distance per se was not an adequate gauge of environmental impact. It highlighted too the need to distinguish between different modes of transport, with the hierarchy of emission intensity running from sea, to rail, to road to air – this last being by far and away the most GHG-intensive mode of travel.

Since the publication of these two reports, a host of others have been published. For example, one New Zealand study (Saunders and Barber, 2007) compared the GHG footprint of the British and New Zealand dairy industries and found that per kg of milk solids, the UK's emissions were 34 per cent higher (and 30 per cent more on a per hectare basis) than New Zealand's, even allowing for shipping emissions. Note that there has also been strong criticism of the authors' core assumptions, which have been articulated elsewhere in some detail (Murphy-Bokern, 2007). However, the important point to note here is that the magnitude of emissions from other stages in the life cycle (and hence differences between the same key stages of two comparable products) can outweigh the environmental impacts of the transport element. In the case of livestock products, the main impacts lie at the agricultural stage and the differences in agricultural production are more significant than the differences in transport impacts.

Perhaps most significantly, one observes that a focus on 'food miles' alone can distract from the real issue, the main one in this case being that livestock production is inherently GHG-intensive, wherever it occurs. Our consumption of livestock products in the UK has been estimated to account for around 8 per cent of the UK's total emissions – a figure that takes into account the livestock rearing stage only, and not emissions arising from slaughter, processing, transport and so forth (Garnett, 2008). Globally, livestock production accounts for around 18 per cent of world GHG emissions (FAO, 2006). The key concern, then, is not where the animals are reared but how much meat and how many dairy products we consume in our diets.

The relative importance of transport will not be consistent across food types. For meat and dairy products, the agricultural stage contributes overwhelmingly to GHG emissions associated with these foods, and the impact of transport is less significant. For other kinds of foods, however, such as field-grown fruits and vegetables, transport can be important. Sim et al (2007) look at sourcing options for three kinds of field-grown fresh produce – Gala apples, runner beans and watercress – and assess their global warming and other environmental impacts. They find that the transport stage of the life cycle does indeed make an important contribution to the environmental impact of these products and generally speaking, the further these products travel, the greater their GHG emissions.

For these field-grown fruit and vegetables, Sim et al conclude that when in season it is generally environmentally preferable (from a GHG perspective) for UK consumers to buy British produce rather than produce imported from overseas – although of course we import many foods that cannot be grown here in the UK.

A combination of seasonality and transport distance distinguished by mode may perhaps be a more effective measure of GHG impact than either of these elements alone. It has been argued by many environmental groups that a combination of eating locally and seasonally is a key element (and indicator) of sustainable food consumption (Sim et al, 2007; Soil Association, 2008).

One paper, for example, finds that during the UK apple season, indigenously grown apples are clearly less GHG-intensive than imports. During the summer months however, the localness of the product is not enough, environmentally speaking. Before the UK growing season starts, apples imported from the southern hemisphere have the edge over UK apples from the previous year that have been stored under energy-intensive refrigerated conditions (Milà i Canals et al, 2007).

What is more, when fresh produce is grown outside its natural growing season with the aid of heating and lighting, the 'local is good' assumption receives another blow. One study (Milà i Canals et al, 2007) found that the GHG emissions resulting from the production of Spanish tomatoes, which are grown with little or no heating and lighting, are lower than those of British tomatoes since the latter require considerable inputs of light and heat. Complicating the issue further, a tomato grower might need heat at the beginning and end of the season and not in the middle

– the 'seasonal' tomatoes in the late summer months will have a lower GHG footprint but this is only made possible because of the heating boost that was given at the beginning. One might also add that to justify the investment in the glasshouses, the plants and all the inputs, growers of horticultural products need to extend the season beyond the 'natural' growing season itself.

Resource utilization also affects the balance. The fish-processing company Young's Seafood took the cost-based decision to export its prawn de-shelling operations to Thailand. In anticipation of environmental criticisms it also commissioned a study to assess the GHG emissions arising from transporting the product to Thailand, de-shelling it there and transporting it back again, taking into account all emission sources, and comparing this with emissions from UK operations. The study in fact concluded that no net increase in emissions had occurred, the reason being that the efficiency of the de-shelling operation in Thailand was greater than in the UK (Youngs Seafood Company, 2009).

It is vital to note that the food miles question is about more than GHG emissions; analysis of the merits of production in country x versus country y needs to consider much more than the notion of GHG efficiency, with water use being a case in point. For example, the Almeria region of Spain, where much of its horticultural production is located, suffers from water shortages due in part to unsustainable rates of water extraction by the horticultural sector. According to current climate models, these areas are set to become more arid still as the effects of climate change intensify. One might question the wisdom of continuing to grow horticultural products in highly water-stressed areas, and of making simplistic 'single-issue' decisions. Sim (2006) shows that some Spanish production systems do worse in other non-GHG environmental respects, such as pesticide use. What is more, there can be huge variability between production methods even within the same region, as Milà i Canals has shown for apples. In the case of tomatoes, some growers in Spain now use heating to boost production (López et al, 2006), in which case the GHG benefits of importing them into the UK are contestable (Milà i Canals, 2003).

It is important to note too (Garnett, 2003), that while there may be trade-offs between measures to reduce transport emissions versus those to minimize production-stage impacts, there can also be correlations between transport energy use and other forms of energy use, including for refrigeration. Food transported over long distances also needs to be refrigerated for lengthy periods; many handling stages in the supply chain increase the possibility of waste occurring. What is more, apples from New Zealand may first be stored there before being shipped into the UK, or shipped here and then stored here[1] – a double whammy. There are after all only two main global harvests (northern and southern hemispheres) and so storage will always be needed at some point in the year if we are to maintain year-round supplies.

So far the discussion has focused on transport in general but the air freight issue merits particular attention. Notwithstanding heavy media focus (Blythman, 2007) on air freighted food, the vast majority is actually carried by ship and road. In absolute terms, emissions from air freight as compared with those from shipping and trucks are considerably lower. This said, per unit of food transported, air freight is by far and away the most GHG-intensive mode. Less than 1 per cent of all food is carried by air but it accounts for 11 per cent of all food transport CO_2, including customer car travel to and from the store (AEA, 2005).

Hence, during the UK growing season, air freighted Kenyan green beans are 20–26 times more GHG-intensive than seasonal UK beans (Sim et al, 2007). Of course, people also eat green beans out of season and a non-seasonal analysis would give different results, since heating would be needed to produce the crop in the winter (this is a hypothetical example since beans are not, in fact, grown out of season in this country). For comparison, a relative environmental assessment of rose production in Kenya and Holland found that during the UK winter months, roses imported to the UK from Holland have a GHG burden nearly six times greater than those air freighted in from Kenya (Williams, 2007). This reflects the very high energy requirements of Dutch greenhouses; Kenyan roses, by contrast, are grown using 'free' sunlight.

It is important, however, to emphasize that both have a high footprint. One of the psychological traps of the life cycle approach is that it can prompt dualistic conclusions. The product that has a lower GHG impact becomes 'good' while the other is 'bad', when in fact both have very high impacts – half a dozen Dutch roses contributes around 17.5 kg of CO_2 and even the less GHG-intensive Kenyan ones are responsible for the emission of 2.9 kg CO_2 per half dozen.

For comparison, 2.9kg would 'buy' nearly 6 kg of sugar or 38 packets of crisps or 5 kg of raw broccoli (British Sugar, 2009; Walkers, 2009; Muñoz, Milà i Canals and Clift, 2008). Clearly no self-respecting lover is going to turn up on the doorstep bearing broccoli, but the point is that either–or comparisons can be misleading. There are, moreover, potentially acceptable alternatives: British daffodils for example. This would, of course, involve cultural changes – among other things, in what we define as being 'romantic'.

Evidently, the GHG emissions arising from our food system are not sustainable, and while some of the alternatives suggested (eat local – without regard to season or type of food being consumed) may not necessarily improve on the current situation (or may have unintended consequences in terms of water, diets/health, landscape or biodiversity), this emphatically does not mean that all is for the best in the best of all possible worlds. The findings of LCA need framing within wider perspectives on absolute impacts and on need and consumer behaviour (Milà i Canals et al, 2008).

Of course, the environmental impacts of air freight cannot be considered in isolation from other social and economic concerns. It has been estimated that between 1 and 1.5 million people in Sub-Saharan Africa depend in one way or another upon export horticulture, with 120,000 people directly employed (MacGregor and Vorley, 2006). The contribution overall that flown-in fruit and vegetables make to the UK's GHG emissions is actually very small at around 0.2 per cent; why, one might ask, should poor Africans have to suffer on account of our tender consciences, particularly since we could easily compensate for these emissions by, for example, walking, rather than driving to the supermarket, or opting-out of a few pints down at the pub?

On the other hand, forms of economic development that are environmentally unsustainable are effectively sawing off the branch they are sitting on, particularly since climate models suggest that sub-Saharan Africa will be particularly affected by the negative impacts of climate change (Boko et al, 2007). There is clearly a development-versus-environment dilemma that many organizations are seeking to explore from a diversity of perspectives (Soil Association, 2007; UNCTAD/WHO, 2007; DfI, 2008; Food Ethics Council, 2008), although at this stage there does not appear to be much by way of resolution.

To conclude this sub-section, the evidence seems to be pointing towards the view that while the transport stage is environmentally significant for some products, particularly for field-grown fruit and vegetables, and more particularly still for those that are air freighted, a focus on food miles alone can distract both from the important variables of mode and efficiency and, more importantly still, from the often heftier impacts at other stages in the supply chain. Moreover, some foods, wherever they are grown and however they travel, are inherently more GHG intensive than others.

However while life cycle analysis usefully helps dismantle 'commonsense' assumptions that shorter is better, the approach itself has its limitations. As we discuss in the next section, it is important, with food miles, not to throw the baby out with the bathwater.

TRANSPORT, THE SECOND ORDER IMPACTS AND THE IMPLICATIONS FOR GHGS

There is a view, among some LCA practitioners that the 'concept of food miles is unhelpful and stupid. It doesn't inform about anything except the distance travelled.'[2] This, we argue, is itself a somewhat unhelpful view, for two reasons.

First, transport creates a wide range of social and environmental problems that, albeit not climate related, are nevertheless significant. These include transport's contribution to accidents, noise, air pollution and congestion (Woodcock et al, 2007; AEA, 2005), and the concreting over of natural landscapes. Long-distance food transport also raises major socioeconomic questions concerning globalization, the inequality and concentrated nature of power structures, and the merits or otherwise, for developing-world countries, of developing export-oriented monoculture in preference to building up national self-sufficiency. One needs also to consider the broader role that transport plays in fostering obesogenic environments (Hinde and Dixon, 2005), the homogenization of food culture and the loss of local identity (Lang and Heasman, 2004). These very important issues are the subject of campaigns by a number of non-governmental organizations[3] (Lake, and Townshend, 2006) and consideration by policy makers and researchers alike, and should be included in any thorough analysis of transport's impacts on society and the environment.

Second, the life cycle analysis approach tends to present an a-temporal, 'snapshot' picture of transport and its contribution to GHG emissions. It assesses the impacts now; it has little to say about the way in which transport indirectly contributes to greenhouse gas emissions and does so over time. A different perspective is needed to assess broader trends in transport emissions, or the way in which long-distance transport can contribute to emission-intensive structural 'lock-in', or the way different policy decisions can alter both the emissions picture and transport's relative prominence in it. We discuss these issues in the paragraphs that follow and argue that, using this more dynamic, systemic approach, food miles once more become relevant.

The first systemic issue concerns transport trends and investment decisions. Clearly, as supply chains globalize, there will be more transport. More transport, in the absence of a clean fuels revolution, means that emissions will grow in absolute terms. This is obvious; however – and this is where the second order, indirect impacts start to emerge – these growth patterns have gone hand-in-hand with infrastructural, systemic changes that bring with them their own impacts. As supermarkets and manufacturers commit to securing supplies or locating their manufacturing plants far from home, their decisions give impetus to further investment in new or expanded infrastructure – roads, ports, runways, air freight handling facilities, as is clearly being seen in the emerging economies (India Aviation, 2008). While these construction activities will produce their own direct environmental (including GHG) impacts, more importantly, they foster a situation where supply chains become committed to, and predicated on, long-distance sourcing and distribution. The presence of new infrastructure makes it easier and cheaper to source from further afield, and of course the cost of investment needs to be recouped. This fosters the continuation of, and increase in, long-distance sourcing. By contrast, sources closer to home may be less economically attractive because labour costs are higher. As a result, local enterprises go out of business, leaving no closer-to-home choice available – even where they may be environmentally preferable. This is what we mean by structural 'lock-in'.

It is unclear, in the present economic climate, given the swings in the price of oil and the downturn in the economy, whether these trends are set to continue. One might speculate that in an economically constrained world, long-distance sourcing may start to look less attractive. It is important to bear in mind, however, that all stages in the supply chain are oil dependent and that economic savings are being sought in all areas, including labour. The cost of transport (and hence the argument that local sourcing may be more cost-effective) needs to be balanced against cost elsewhere in the supply chain; it is still entirely possible that for many commodities the more distant source will remain the most economical one.

A further reason why the 'food miles' concern should not be dismissed as unimportant is this: while other industry sectors are beginning, slowly, to clean up their act and even achieve absolute reductions in emissions, green transport fuels are either a long way down the line (hydrogen for example), or environmentally and socially questionable (biofuels) (Searchinger et al, 2008). The growth in transport has so far been the great intractable, unbudgeable problem, with its importance, relative to those of other life cycle stages, growing. This is perhaps an overly pessimistic view, given the scope for making more use of alternative modes of transport such as rail and short sea shipping – and for improving the efficiency of these modes, where there is still considerable scope for improvement. This said, as ever, a combination of political will and economic feasibility is needed.

Finally, for transport and its second order impacts, there is the 'what if?' question to consider. We have already highlighted the fact that products such as tomatoes may be more GHG intensive to produce in a greenhouse here in the UK than their sunnier-climed counterparts. But while this may be the 'correct' life cycle answer today, what if, over the next few years, the UK protected horticulture sector were to invest heavily in cleaner or renewable heating and lighting technologies? There is more immediate technical scope for applying clean fuel sources (biomass, trigeneration, wind and solar) to stationary infrastructure such as commercial greenhouses than there is to moving infrastructure – transport vehicles. Indeed one study found that technically there is potential for UK horticulture to be carbon neutral (Warwick HRI, 2007).

What if, coupled with this, increased desertification in Spain (Chapagain and Orr, 2008) forced its horticulture industry to increase its use of energy-using irrigation (a likely scenario)? In these circumstances the UK tomato may become the less GHG-intensive choice. Alternatively, tomato production in Spain may become totally uneconomic and retailers may turn to regions further afield, where the GHG balance may be less favourable. Of course, what is true of the UK policy could equally be true of Spain. The Spanish horticulture sector could make concerted efforts to apply renewable technologies to its enterprises, and indeed the use of renewable energy is higher in Spain than it is here (PROGRESS, 2008). The point is that the answers given to particular life cycle questions can change, depending on what policy makers actually decide to do and, relative to other life cycle impacts, the prominence of transport may or may not increase.

A final point to note for transport is that in future years, as the impacts of climate change start to hit home in the developing world and agricultural production becomes increasingly vulnerable to climate induced shocks, we may see a growth in imports from rich northern-latitude countries to the developing world. How this affects transport-related emissions remains to be seen but perhaps merits further investigation.

LOCAL VERSUS GLOBAL AND THE SELF-SUFFICIENCY QUESTION

This brings us round to the question of self-sufficiency. Currently we import (in net terms, by value) around 51 per cent of the food we consume (DEFRA, 2007). Our self-sufficiency in terms of calories is probably higher (since we are self-sufficient in grains) but this is of course only one measure of food security. It is worth bearing in mind that the UK has not been self-sufficient in food for hundreds of years. In the 1840s, around 40 per cent of domestic demand was being supplied by imports (Davis, 1979). In the 1890s a third of the meat consumed in

Britain was imported (University of Guelph, 2009), and indeed in London most of the meat consumed came from overseas (Oddy, 2006).

For many environmentalists and development groups there is a link between a more sustainable, equitable and secure food system and one that is more self-sufficient (Oddy, 2006; Sustain, 2008; Fife Diet, 2009). This view is based partly on the view that food miles are a bad thing (with the sophistication of the argument varying), and partly on a sense that one can have more control over the way indigenous goods are produced than those grown on unknown terrain. Growing your own, it is argued, can protect a nation from the vagaries of economic and climatic conditions overseas.

There are several underlying assumptions here, and the security and environmental issues perhaps need to be treated separately. Taking the security question first, is there a specific risk-avoidance argument for shortening the supply chain? This is a difficult question to answer. All supply chains are exposed to risk of one kind or another, and although a shorter supply chain will not be vulnerable to some of the risks threatening a global one, the reverse is also true. The risks may be different but not necessarily of less magnitude. Various recent food safety crises such as BSE, Avian Influenza and Sudan Red are all examples of security risks associated with long-distance sourcing and potentially affecting a large number of people. On the other hand, if we base our food security on the availability of food grown within, say, a 100-mile radius, then we may be at risk of hunger during poor growing seasons, or during a localized outbreak of listeria. Others elsewhere might not be affected, but the health and food security of local people could suffer greatly. Arguably, therefore, a well-prepared business is a flexible one – one that develops as broad a supply and market base as possible in order to spread its risks and respond to events with agility (Garnett, 2003). In short, it can be dangerous to put all one's eggs in one basket.

On the other hand this 'flexible' approach can make life very difficult for suppliers. Without secure long-term contracts and a sense of the volumes they need to produce they cannot plan ahead or indeed invest in some of the cleaner technologies and systems that need to be put in place. Insecure, short-term contracts can undermine food production and thereby reduce food security. More secure, stable arrangements, on the other hand, allow farmers to invest, to plan ahead and indeed to work towards long-term environmental sustainability.

Importantly, we cannot talk about food security without considering our energy security (Food Chain Analysis Group, 2006). As we increase our reliance on energy imports (DTI, 2007), so food grown or manufactured in this country will, relying as it does on energy inputs, be inherently import dependent. It has been argued that we should perhaps be aspiring to achieve food security at the European level, since at this scale energy security is a more achievable goal (DEFRA, 2006). It is also important to point out that measures to reduce the dependence of the food sector on energy inputs will, by this measure, also increase food security.

The environmental arguments are perhaps harder to answer. As highlighted above, the relationship between transport and environmental impact is not always clear, although we have argued that there are additional important, and damaging, second-order consequences of basing economic structures upon globalized provisioning systems. It may also be the case that sourcing more from the UK enables greater control over the quality (and environmental sustainability) of production, although many overseas production systems are in fact highly regulated and controlled by UK retailers.

It is also important to explore self-sufficiency from the perspective of long-term changes in the global climate. While all regions of the world will ultimately suffer from the consequences of a warming climate, agricultural production in northern latitudes (including the UK) may initially benefit. Countries in the southern hemisphere, on the other hand, and particularly those that are already agriculturally vulnerable, are already beginning to suffer the negative consequences of a warmer, more volatile climate. They will not be able to grow as much or as predictably, and so the number of people at even greater risk of hunger will grow (Easterling et al, 2007). There is therefore a strong moral case for the UK and other wealthy northern countries to ensure that their farming sector is robust enough to grow enough food not just for their own populations but for people overseas. There is of course a danger that this point may be used as an argument for maintaining high levels of EU subsidy for EU agriculture – a situation that would be damaging to developing world growers.

Perhaps the key point with respect to food security is that strong local, regional and national supply networks are important, as are global ones, but in all cases they will be strong only if the agricultural base is environmentally sustainable (Barling, Sharpe and Lang, 2008), which in most geographical regions worldwide, is not the case (IAAK, 2008; Food Matters, 2008; Smith et al, 2007). Food security, then, is as much about the 'repeatability' of food production in the long run as the geographical origin of the product, and repeatability requires the maintenance of soil and water quality and of biodiversity, and the reduction of farming-related GHG emissions. The questions of food miles and self-sufficiency are important, but need to be considered as part of the broader challenge of improving the sustainability of the food system as a whole.

NOTES

1. In the latter case the situation is worse since the UK's electricity mix is more carbon intensive than that of New Zealand, which is based largely on hydroelectricity.
2. Dr Adrian Williams quoted in: How the myth of food miles hurts the planet, *The Observer*, Sunday 23 March.
3. For example the Campaign for Better Transport, the Council for the Protection of Rural England, Friends of the Earth, Sustain, Oxfam and others.

REFERENCES

AEA (2005) *Validity of Food Miles as an Indicator of Sustainable Development*, report produced by AEA Technology Environment for DEFRA, July 2005 [accessed 23 August 2009] [Online] https://statistics.defra.gov. uk/esg/reports/foodmiles/execsumm.pdf

Barling, D, Sharpe, R and Lang, T (2008) *Rethinking Britain's Food Security*, A research report for the Soil Association by the Centre for Food Policy, City University, London

Blythman, J (2007) Food miles: the true cost of putting imported food on your plate, *The Independent*, 31 May 2007 [accessed 26 February 2008] [Online] http://www.independent.co.uk/environment/green-living/food-miles-the-true-cost-of-putting-imported-food-on-your-plate-451139.html

Boko, M, Niang, I, Nyong, A Vogel, C, Githeko, A, Medany, M, Osman-Elasha, B, Tabo, R and Yanda, P (2007) Africa climate change 2007: impacts, adaptation and vulnerability, Contribution of Working Group II to the *Fourth Assessment Report of the Intergovernmental Panel on Climate Change*, ed ML Parry, OF Canziani, JP Palutikof, PJ van der Linden and CE Hanson, pp 433–67, Cambridge University Press, Cambridge

British Sugar (2009) [accessed 23 August 2009] British Sugar website [Online] http://www.silverspoon.co.uk/home/about-us/carbon-footprint

Chapagain, A and Orr, S (2008) *UK Water Footprint: The impact of the UK's food and fibre consumption on global water resources*, Volume one, WWF-UK, Godalming, Surrey

Davis R (1979) *The Industrial Revolution and British Overseas Trade*, Leicester UP, Leicester, cited in Food security and the UK: an evidence and analysis paper, Food Chain Analysis Group, DEFRA, December 2006

DEFRA (2005) *Validity of Food Miles as an Indicator of Sustainable Development*, Report produced by AEA Technology Environment for DEFRA, July 2005 [accessed 23 August 2009] [Online] https://statistics.defra.gov. uk/esg/reports/foodmiles/execsumm.pdf.

DEFRA (2006) Food security and the UK: an evidence and analysis paper, Food Chain Analysis Group, DEFRA, December 2006

DEFRA (2007) Origins of food consumed in the UK: 2006, Table 75, Chapter 7, Agriculture in the United Kingdom 2007, DEFRA, London

DEFRA (2008) Sustainable development indicators in your pocket 2008, DEFRA 2008

Department for International Development (DfI) (2008) [accessed 13 February 2008] Buy a Kenyan rose this Valentine's Day, Department for International Development press release, [Online] http://www. dfid.gov.uk/news/files/pressreleases/ethical-valentine.asp

Department of Trade and Industry (DTI) (2007) *Meeting the Energy Challenge: A White Paper on energy*, Department of Trade and Industry, London

Easterling, WE, Aggarwal, PK, Batima, P, Brander, KM, Erda, L, Howden, SM, Kirilenko, A, Morton, J, Soussana, J-F, Schmidhuber, J and Tubiello, FN (2007) Food, fibre and forest products climate change 2007: impacts, adaptation and vulnerability, contribution of Working Group II to the *Fourth Assessment Report of the Intergovernmental Panel on Climate Change*, ed ML Parry, OF Canziani, JP Palutikof, PJ van der Linden and CE Hanson, pp 273–313, Cambridge University Press, Cambridge

Edwards-Jones, G, Milà i Canals, L, Hounsome, N, Truninger, M, Koerber, G, Hounsome, B, Cross, P, York, EH, Hospido, A, Plassmann, K, Harris, IM, Edwards, RT, Day, GAS, Tomos, AD, Cowell, SJ and Jones, DL (2008) Testing the assertion that 'local food is best': the challenges of an evidence-based approach, *Trends in Food Science & Technology*, **19**, pp 265–274

Fife Diet (2009) [accessed 5 March 2008] Think global, eat local [Online] http://fifediet.wordpress.com/

Food and Agriculture Organisation (FAO) (2006) *Livestock's Long Shadow*, Food and Agriculture Organization, Rome

Food Chain Analysis Group (2006) *Food Security and the UK: An evidence and analysis paper*, Food Chain Analysis Group, DEFRA, London http:// statistics.defra.gov.uk/esg/reports/foodsecurity/default.asp

Food Ethics Council (2008) *Flying Food: Responsible retail in the face of uncertainty*, Food Ethics Council, Brighton

Food Matters (2008) *Food Matters: Towards a strategy for the 21st Century*, The Cabinet Office, London,

Foster, C, Green, K, Bleda, M, Dewick, P, Evans, B, Flynn, A and Mylan, J (2006) *Environmental Impacts of Food Production and Consumption*, a report produced for the Department for Environment, Food and Rural Affairs (DEFRA), London

Garnett, T (2003) *Wise Moves: Exploring the relationship between food, transport and CO₂*, Transport 2000, London

Garnett T (2008) *Cooking up a Storm: Food, greenhouse gas emissions and our changing climate*, Food Climate Research Network, Centre for Environmental Strategy, University of Surrey

Hinde, S and Dixon, J (2005) Changing the obesogenic environment: insights from a cultural economy of car reliance, *Transportation Research Part D*, **10**, pp 31–53

India Aviation (2008) Rajiv Gandhi Airport to set up centre for perishable cargo, *India Aviation*, 19 August [accessed 23 August 2009] [Online] http://www.indiaaviation.aero/news/airline/13460/59/Rajiv-Gandhi-Airport-to-set-up-centre-for-perishable-cargo

International Assessment of Agricultural Knowledge (IAAK) (2008) [accessed 23 August 2009] Science and Technology for Development, Global Summary for Decision-Makers [Online] www.agassessment.org

Lake, A and Townshend, T (2006) Obesogenic environments: exploring the built and food environments, *The Journal of the Royal Society for the Promotion of Health*, **126**, p 262

Lang, T and Heasman, M (2004) *Food Wars: The battle for mouths, minds and markets*, Earthscan, London

López, JC, Baille, A, Bonachela, S, González-Real, MM and Pérez-Parra, J (2006) Predicting the energy consumption of heated plastic greenhouses in south-eastern Spain, *Spanish Journal of Agricultural Research*, **4** (4), pp 289–96

MacGregor, J and Vorley, B (2006) *Fair Miles? The concept of 'food miles' through a sustainable development lens*, International Institute for Environment and Development, London

Milà i Canals, L (2003) *Contributions to LCA Methodology for Agricultural Systems: Site-dependency and soil degradation impact assessment*, PhD thesis, University of Barcelona [Online] http://www.tdx.cesca.es/TDX-1222103–154811/

Milà i Canals, L, Cowell, SJ, Sim, S and Basson, L (2007) Comparing domestic versus imported apples: a focus on energy use, *Env Sci Pollut Res*, **14** (5), pp 338–44

Milà i Canals, L, Muñoz, I, Hospido, A, Plassman, K and McLaren, S (2008) *Life Cycle Assessment (LCA) of Domestic vs Imported Vegetables: Case studies on broccoli, salad crops and green beans*, Working paper, Centre for Environmental Strategy, University of Surrey

Muñoz, I, Milà i Canals, L and Clift, R (2008) Consider a spherical man: a simple model to include human excretion in life cycle assessment of food products, *Journal of Industrial Ecology*, **12** (4), pp 521–38

Murphy-Bokern, D (2007) Comments to the Food Climate Change Network on the Comparative Energy and Greenhouse Gas Emissions of New Zealand's and the UK's Dairy Industry (Caroline Saunders and Andrew Barber 2007), commentary circulated and posted on the FCRN mailing list

Oddy, DJ (2006) Food quality in London, 1870–1938, XIV International Economic History Congress, Helsinki, [accessed 5 March 2008] [Online] http://www.helsinki.fi/iehc2006/papers1/Oddy.pdf

PROGRESS (2008) [accessed 5 March 2008] PROGRESS: Promotion and growth of renewable energy sources and systems Final report for the European Commission, Contract no: TREN/D1/42–2005/S0756988, Utrecht [Online] http://ec.europa.eu/energy/res/publications/index_en.htm 20 August 2008

Saunders, C and Barber, A (2007) *Comparative Energy and Greenhouse Gas Emissions of New Zealand's and the UK's Dairy Industry*, Research Report No 297, Lincoln University, New Zealand

Searchinger, T, Heimlich, R, Houghton, RA, Dong, F, Elobeid, A, Fabiosa, J, Tokgoz, S, Hayes, DNS and Yu T-H (2008) Use of US croplands for biofuels increases greenhouse gases through emissions from land-use, *Change Science*, **319**, p 1238

Sim, S, Barry, M, Clift, R and Cowell, SJ (2007) The relative importance of transport in determining an appropriate sustainability strategy for food sourcing, *Int J LCA*, **12** (6), pp 422–31

Smith, P, Martino, D, Cai, Z, Gwary, D, Janzen, H, Kumar, P, McCarl, B, Ogle, S, O'Mara, F, Rice, C, Scholes, B and Sirotenko, O (2007) *Agriculture in Climate Change 2007*: Mitigation contribution of Working Group III to the Fourth Assessment Report of the Intergovernmental Panel on Climate Change, ed B Metz, OR Davidson, PR Bosch, R Dave and LA Meyer, Cambridge University Press, Cambridge and New York

Soil Association (2007) [accessed 14 February 2008] Soil Association to ensure air freighted organic food benefits poor farmers – and challenges UK Government to do same for all air freighted produce, Soil Association Press release, 25 October [Online] http://www.soilassociation.org/web/sa/saweb.nsf/89d058cc4dbeb16d80256a73005a2866/3a1c3d1cc0d10bff8025737f002d919b!

Soil Association (2008) [accessed 9 July 2008] Organic vegetables bicycled in from Berkshire for star-studded charity banquet, Soil Association press release [Online] http://www.soilassociation.org/web/sa/saweb.nsf/d39dda83e1f3c019802570ad005b4516/086031e0e22c8a2380257409002be23d!

Sustain (2008) [accessed 9 July 2008] Sustainable food [Online] http://www.sustainweb.org/sustainablefood/

UNCTAD/WHO (2007) *The Economic Impact of a Ban on Imports of Airfreighted Organic Products to the UK*, International Trade Centre, UNCTAD/WHO, Geneva

University of Guelph (2009) [accessed 23 August 2009] Victorian Agriculture, University of Guelph [Online] http://www.uoguelph.ca/ruralhistory/research/crowley/victorianAgriculture.html

Walkers (2009) [accessed 23 August 2009] Carbon footprint: calculating the carbon footprint of a packet of Walkers Cheese & Onion Crisps [Online] http://www.walkerscarbonfootprint.co.uk/walkers_carbon_footprint.html

Warwick HRI (2007) *Direct Energy Use in Agriculture: Opportunities for Reducing Fossil Fuel Inputs*, Final report to DEFRA by Warwick HRI, DEFRA project AC0401, May

Williams, A (2007) [accessed 14 February 2008] *Comparative Study of Cut Roses for the British Market Produced in Kenya and the Netherlands: Précis report for World Flowers*, Cranfield University, 12 February [Online] http://www.world-flowers.co.uk/12news/news4.html

Woodcock, J, Banister, D, Edwards, P, Prentice, AM and Roberts, I (2007) Energy and transport, *The Lancet*, **370** (9592), pp 1078–88

Youngs Seafood Company (2009) [accessed 9 October 2009] [Online] http://www.youngsseafood.co.uk/company/youngs/corporate_responsibility.asp

14

Sustainability strategies for city logistics

Julian Allen and Michael Browne

INTRODUCTION

Approximately 80 per cent of European citizens live in an urban environment. Due to their large populations and extensive commercial establishments, urban areas require large quantities of goods and services for commercial and domestic use. The growing importance of urban freight transport is related to increases in urban populations and continued economic growth in urban areas. This results in increasing levels of demand for freight transport services (European Commission, 2007).

Urban freight transport and logistics involves the delivery and collection of goods and provision of services in towns and cities. It also includes activities such as goods storage and inventory management, waste handling, office and household removals and home delivery services.

Freight transport in towns and cities responds very effectively to the requirements of modern urban economies. However, it is a major contributor to environmental impacts, particularly to local air pollution and noise and, as a result, has an important impact on the health of the most vulnerable residents of cities. Urban freight activities involve economic, social and environmental issues simultaneously and can result in conflicts. Under current conditions the economic viability of urban areas might actually be benefiting from socially and environmentally damaging freight transport operations. Moving towards a more sustainable urban freight system requires changes and innovations in the public and private sectors.

URBAN FREIGHT RESEARCH AND POLICY MAKING

It would be expected that, because of its importance to the urban economy and urban lifestyles, the topic of urban freight transport would have received much attention from government at the local, regional, national and EU level as well as from researchers. However, surprisingly little attention has been paid to urban freight by researchers and policy makers until relatively recently.

Research into urban freight transport issues took place in the UK during the 1970s. Much of this was related to concerns about the safety of heavy goods vehicles in urban areas, and resulted in studies into transhipment centres and other vehicle restrictions (for example see Battilana and Hawthorne, 1976; GLC London Freight Conference, 1975; Hassell, Foulkes and Robertson, 1978; Nathaniel Lichfield and Partners, 1975). This took place against a backdrop of several national enquiries and reports into freight transport in the UK, such as the work of the Pettit enquiry, the Lorries and the Environment Committee and the Armitage Report (see Pettit, 1973; Lorries and the Environment Committee, 1976; Armitage, 1980). This UK research was not replicated in other European countries, and did not translate into policy making.

The level of urban freight research in the UK diminished, and between the late 1970s and mid-1990s, researchers and policymakers paid relatively little attention to the increasingly severe logistics problems facing urban areas. However, during the late 1980s and early 1990s there was much interest in city logistics and urban transhipment in France and Germany and to a lesser extent the Netherlands, where numerous pieces of research were undertaken. In the case of Germany this frequently led to operational consolidation centre schemes being set up (usually referred to as City Logistik schemes). However, many of these have since closed (Flämig, 2004; Köhler, 2001; Köhler and Groke, 2003).

More recently there has been growing interest in the logistics of collection and delivery services in town and city centres on the part of the UK government, researchers, companies and environmentalists. This renewed interest in urban distribution issues among policy makers was supported by the establishment of a Freight Distribution and Logistics Unit in the Department of Environment, Transport and the Regions

(DETR; now known as the Department for Transport or DfT), and the publication of the 1998 Transport White Paper *A New Deal for Transport: Better for everyone* (DETR, 1998) and the daughter document to the White Paper entitled *Sustainable Distribution* (DETR, 1999). The UK government's determination to recognize and address the problems both faced and caused by urban distribution activities was noted as an important theme within these documents.

The urban freight transport and distribution considerations of local authorities in the UK have traditionally tended to take place as a reaction to problems, usually arising from complaints made by residents and other road users. Most local authorities with an urban remit have not developed coherent freight transport policies to the same extent that they have their public transport policies. However, UK local authorities have been encouraged by central government to focus greater attention on freight transport and to include consideration of urban distribution and its sustainability in their Local Transport Plans over the last decade. The Department for Transport is also encouraging local authorities to include Freight Quality Partnerships (FQPs) in their local transport plans (DETR, 2000).

European and international research into urban freight transport has also increased since the late 1990s (see for example Ambrosini et al, 2001; Meimbresse and Sonntag, 2000; Thompson and Taniguchi, 1999). Several major EC-funded projects have taken place. These have included the following (for further information about these EC-funded urban freight transport projects see Stantchev and Whiteing, 2006; Delle Site and Salucci, 2006):

- researching future urban freight requirements and strategies (such as CITY FREIGHT);
- investigating the feasibility of new logistics concepts for urban distribution and supply (such as CITY BOX);
- focusing on the application of intelligent transport systems (ITS) for urban freight transport (such as GIFTS, MOSCA, eDRUL and SMART FREIGHT);
- concerned with freight terminals serving urban areas (such as FV-2000);
- investigating changing modal split and encouraging rail use (such as UTOPIA, REFORM, IDIOMA and PROMIT);
- urban freight demonstration projects intended to improve freight efficiency and reduce energy use (such as START and projects in the CIVITAS I Initiative including VIVALDI, TELLUS TRENDSETTER and MIRACLES).

The EC-funded BEST Urban Freight Solutions (BESTUFS) thematic network was formed in 2000 and continued until summer 2008. The main objective of BESTUFS was to identify, describe and disseminate information on best practices, success criteria and bottlenecks of urban freight transport solutions. Furthermore, BESTUFS aimed to maintain and expand an open European network between urban freight experts, user groups/associations, ongoing projects, the relevant European Commission Directorates and representatives of national, regional and local transport administrations and transport operators. The project team organized regular workshops and conferences all over Europe and reports about interesting urban commercial transport-related developments, demonstrations and events at European, national, regional and local levels. Topics addressed at BESTUFS workshops included: vehicle access and parking regulations, urban goods vehicle design, e-commerce and last mile solutions, non-road modes for urban distribution, road pricing, urban consolidation centres, public private partnerships in urban goods transport, night delivery, ITS in urban goods transport, and urban waste logistics. The initiative received considerable attention from practitioners as well as from researchers, and all information was made publicly available via the website (BESTUFS, 2008).

In addition, the Institute for City Logistics (ICL) was established in Kyoto, Japan, in 1999. The Institute is a centre of excellence for research and development in city logistics and urban freight transport, bringing together academics and practitioners to exchange knowledge, experience and information through conferences and short courses (Institute for City Logistics, 2008).

The METRANS Transportation Center organized and hosted the first Annual National Urban Freight Conference in North America in 2006. This brought together North American researchers and practitioners to consider urban freight in a specialist conference setting for the first time (METRANS, 2008).

EFFICIENCY PROBLEMS IN URBAN FREIGHT TRANSPORT

Urban freight transport operations are responsible for a range of negative social and environmental impacts. These are relatively well understood and include fossil fuel consumption, greenhouse gas emissions, air pollution, noise, visual intrusion, physical intimidation (of pedestrians and cyclists), road safety and accidents, and road traffic congestion/disruption.

The problems experienced by those performing freight transport and logistics operations in urban areas are far less well understood. These include (Allen et al, 2000):

● traffic flow/congestion issues caused by traffic levels, traffic incidents, inadequate road infrastructure, narrow street layouts and poor driver behaviour;

● transport policy-related problems, including neglect of freight transport issues in town and traffic planning, and other policy issues such as vehicle access restrictions based on time and/or size/weight of vehicle and width of bus lanes;

● parking and loading/unloading problems, including loading/unloading regulations, fines, lack of unloading space and handling problems;

● customer/receiver-related problems, including queuing to make deliveries and collections, difficulty in finding the receiver, and collection and delivery times requested by customers and receivers.

It is important to distinguish between the two different groups who are capable of implementing changes to the urban freight system, namely:

● Public policy makers (especially urban authorities) who make changes to urban freight transport operations through the introduction of policy measures that force or encourage companies to alter their behaviour.

● Freight transport companies that implement initiatives that reduce the impact of their freight operations because they derive some internal benefit from this change in behaviour. These benefits can be internal economic advantages from operating in a more environmentally or socially efficient manner, either through improved economic efficiency or through being able to enhance market share as a result of their environmental stance. Instances of company-led initiatives include increasing the vehicle load factor through the consolidation of urban freight, making deliveries before or after normal freight delivery hours, the implementation of IT for communications or planning purposes, improvements in the fuel efficiency of vehicles, and improvements in collection and delivery systems. Some of these initiatives are technology related, some are concerned with freight transport companies reorganizing their operations, and some involve change in the supply chain organization.

Inefficiencies in urban freight transport can occur as a result of existing road layouts or traffic levels. They can also come about due to non-freight urban transport policies that have unintended consequences on freight transport operations (eg the introduction of bus lanes). Another cause of inefficiency in urban freight transport can result from variations in urban freight transport policy measures in different urban areas or different parts of a single urban area. For example, different access or loading time restrictions or vehicle emissions requirements within different parts of a city can be problematic for companies serving these locations with a single vehicle. It can result in the need for additional goods vehicles and goods vehicle trips. Such inefficiencies can have both financial and environmental impacts and are therefore best avoided from the perspective both of companies and of the wider society. This suggests the need for collaboration between public policy makers with responsibility for freight transport regulations in urban areas, as well as consideration of the benefits of harmonizing such regulations in order to avoid causing operational inefficiency.

The efficient usage of infrastructure in urban areas is of high priority to European cities, as in most cities urban space cannot be further increased for private transport purposes. The management of urban infrastructure usage in terms of time and space is of fundamental importance for city transport planners, resulting in various measures for regulating the use of urban infrastructure. For example, some cities already provide loading zones or bays for commercial traffic in order to improve the working conditions for transport operators in cities and to avoid negative effects due to delivery operations (eg second-lane parking).

Efficient and reliable deliveries are required to support the urban economy, both from local planners' and from the transport operators' sides. In order to reach efficient and sustainable approaches key issues to be taken into account are:

- Vehicles making the deliveries should impose as few social and environmental impacts as possible.
- Planners (from urban, city, municipal or local transport authorities), freight transport companies and other businesses must cooperate to ensure that these objectives are met.
- Urban planners may need to influence or control the movement of goods vehicles.
- Transport companies must optimize operational efficiency to reduce traffic congestion and environmental impact.
- The types of policy measures required depend on factors such as:
  - the economic, social and environmental objectives of the urban authority;
  - the level of freight transport and other road traffic;
  - the size, density and layout of the urban area.

Over the last few years a variety of new experimental schemes have appeared. Information and communication technologies, together with mechanical access gates or variable message signs, have become less expensive and offer a variety of complex new access schemes tailored to the individual infrastructures of delivery areas. Besides the provision of infrastructure, some cities also provide value-added services of loading zones to carry out the deliveries (eg the possibility for short-term storage or support in transhipment).

URBAN FREIGHT TRANSPORT INITIATIVES

Efforts to increase the sustainability of urban freight transport can focus on improving one or more of the economic, social or environmental impacts of these activities, without worsening the impact of the others.

Urban freight transport initiatives to achieve these economic, social and environmental goals can focus on: efforts to improve the efficiency of operations, greater use of environmentally friendly modes, reductions in the demand for freight transport (through reorganization of land-use patterns or supply chain organization), regulations to influence urban transport behaviour and patterns through the implementation of traffic and transport policies, and improvements in technological applications including vehicles, handling equipment and freight facilities.

Companies tend to be most interested in operational and market initiatives, while urban authorities and regional/national governments tend to be most interested in regulations, including those concerned with traffic movement, land use and vehicle technologies.

Various types of urban freight initiatives and experiments have been implemented in European towns and cities over the last decade. The most prominent include:

- Environmental zones: these schemes, which are often aimed at goods vehicles, aim to encourage the use of less polluting engine technologies in urban areas. Schemes have existed for several years in some Swedish cities and have been (or are being) introduced in many other European cities.
- Urban consolidation centres: these schemes can be either voluntary or compulsory and aim to reduce the number of goods vehicles making deliveries to establishments in urban areas by consolidating vehicle loads at centres based in or near the town or city for which they are destined. There are several examples of such centres in the UK (for example the London Construction Consolidation Centre, the Heathrow Retail Consolidation Centre and the Broadmead Retail Consolidation

Centre) as well as in France (in Paris, La Rochelle and Monaco) and in Italy (in Milan and Padua).

- Joint working between public and private sectors: efforts to get policy makers working with other stakeholders in urban freight transport (especially carriers and their customers) can assist in improving understanding between the public and private sectors, aid problem identification and solving, and provide policy makers with an opportunity to receive feedback on their ideas and proposals. Examples of such joint working can be found in the UK (Freight Quality Partnerships) and in the Netherlands (in initiatives developed by Platform Stedelijke Distributie (PSD), the Forum for Physical Distribution in Urban Areas).
- Vehicle access weight/size/time restrictions: these are among the most common types of regulations imposed by policy makers, and include loading and unloading restrictions at the kerbside. Innovations in this field include automated vehicle access control systems (which identify vehicles that are permitted to serve a particular area), the multi-use of road space by time of day in Barcelona, and the Nearby Delivery Area (ELP) scheme in Bordeaux, in which town staff assist with making deliveries.
- Out-of-hours deliveries and reduced noise from operations: the PIEK programme in the Netherlands has researched quiet technologies for urban delivery that could help in reducing the noise associated with night deliveries. A night deliveries scheme operates in Barcelona that makes use of quiet technologies, while in London the Lorry Control Scheme aims to reduce goods vehicle activity and hence noise in residential areas at night.
- Use of home delivery locker banks and collection points: with the growth in home delivery operations in recent years efforts are being made to improve the efficiency of these trips by using lockers banks (such as the Packstation scheme by Deutsche Post in German cities) and shop-based collection points (such as the Kiala scheme that operates in several European countries).
- Use of non-road modes: including the use of tram systems for freight movements (as in the City Cargo scheme in Amsterdam and the Cargotram scheme in Zurich) as well as the use of water-based modes (such as the transport of waste by barge in Liege).
- Lorry-routeing schemes: either voluntary or compulsory schemes to provide suitable road networks and routes for heavy goods vehicles, such as the scheme in Bremen.
- Use/design of environmentally friendly goods vehicles: including the use of environmentally friendly road vehicles such as bicycles and alternatively fuelled goods vehicles. Several urban consolidation

centres make use of such vehicles, including La Petite Reine in Paris, which uses electrically assisted bicycle delivery, and Cityporto in Padua, which uses LPG and electric vehicles. Chronopost in Paris and the Nearby Delivery Area (ELP) scheme in Bordeaux also use electric vehicles.

● Road pricing systems: these initiatives, such as the road pricing schemes in London and Norwegian cities, tend to be aimed at all road users, but do also apply to and affect the road freight industry.

Given the size limitations of this chapter it is not possible to discuss developments with respect to each of the urban freight initiatives listed above. Therefore three of the initiatives that are being commonly used by policy makers and operators in the UK and the rest of Europe will be focused on: i) urban consolidation centres, ii) joint working between public and private sectors, and iii) environmental zones.

URBAN CONSOLIDATION CENTRES

Broadly speaking the key purpose of urban consolidation centres (UCCs) is the avoidance of the need for goods vehicles to deliver part loads into urban areas (be that a city centre, an entire town or a specific site such as a shopping centre). This objective can be achieved by providing facilities in or close to the urban area whereby deliveries (retail, restaurant, office, residential or construction) can be consolidated for subsequent delivery into the target area in an appropriate vehicle with a high level of load utilization. A range of other value-added logistics and retail services can also be provided at the UCC.

Much of the older literature on transhipment centres (and similar public-sector-driven initiatives) can be said to focus on 'the traditional break-bulk form of transhipment being implemented at an urban level on a communal, shared-user basis', with much attention devoted to the use of small vehicles for the urban distribution (McKinnon, 1998).

In contrast, much of the literature since the late 1990s talks of UCCs, which are generally seen to be more flexible and involve break-bulk, transhipment and groupage, often with a focus on maximizing vehicle loads, thereby avoiding the need for vehicles to deliver part loads into urban centres, and with a far greater role for the private sector.

Table 14.1 shows the basic characteristics of five UCC schemes in Europe. These schemes provide a range of operating characteristics, applying to both UK and non-UK schemes, a mix of sectors covered (though predominantly retail and construction, since these are most common), and examples of optional and compulsory scheme partici-

Table 14.1 Key characteristics of selected UCCs

Centre	Location	Sector	Status	Terms of use
Bristol (Broadmead)	UK	Retail	Active	Optional
Sheffield (Meadowhall)	UK	Retail	Active	Optional
London (Construction)	UK	Construction	Closed *	Optional
Monaco	Overseas	All	Active	Compulsory **
Stockholm (Hammarby)	Overseas	Construction	Closed	Compulsory **

Notes: * concept now applied to new site; ** with certain exceptions.

pation. The Stockholm scheme operated for a fixed duration and is now closed; all the others are still operational.

A major literature review identified the main advantages and disadvantages of UCCs (Browne et al, 2005). Table 14.2 shows the main positive and negative issues associated with them. It should be noted that, in many cases, these advantages and disadvantages are not backed up with evidence, but the ones shown here are those that are most frequently referred to in the literature.

There is also some evidence that UCCs can offer the potential to improve the management of the supply chain (Browne et al, 2005). Figure 14.1 illustrates the range of logistics and pre-retail activities that can be carried out by a UCC and the potential benefits of these activities.

In the same review (Browne et al, 2005) 17 schemes were considered in detail and the following results were reported. Reductions in vehicle trips were calculated to range from 30–80 per cent, reductions in vehicle kilometres ranged from 30–45 per cent, improvements in vehicle load factors ranged from 15–100 per cent, and reductions in vehicle emissions ranged from 25–60 per cent. All of these results refer only to the change in transport activity associated with goods handled by the UCC (ie a comparison of the transport activity from the UCC to the receivers when the UCC is used and when it is not for those goods flowing through it) rather than the changes in total freight transport operations and impacts in the area covered by the UCC or the entire town/city.

Table 14.2 Main advantages and disadvantages of UCCs

Main advantages	Main disadvantages
• environmental and social benefits resulting from more efficient and less intrusive transport operations within urban areas • better planning and implementation of logistics operation, with opportunity to introduce new information systems at same time as consolidation centre • better inventory control, product availability and customer service • can facilitate a switch from push to pull logistics through better control and visibility of the supply chain • potential to link in with wider policy and regulatory initiatives • theoretical cost benefits from contracting out 'last mile' • public relations benefits for participants • potential to allow better use of resources at delivery locations • specific transport advantages • opportunity for carrying out value-added activities	• potentially high set-up costs (and sometimes high operating costs) • difficult for a single centre to be able to handle the wide range of goods moving in and out of an urban area, for example due to different handling and storage requirements • can result in an increase in delivery costs due to an additional stage in supply chain which imposes a cost (and often a time) penalty, though this clearly depends on how well the centre is integrated into the supply chain and the extent to which all costs and benefits are considered • a single consolidation centre for an urban area may be unattractive for some suppliers' flows due to the degree of diversion required from normal routes • lack of enforcement of regulations for vehicles not included in the consolidation scheme • loss of the direct interface between suppliers and customers

The potential transport and environmental benefits of UCCs have to be weighed against the potential costs associated with consolidation that can include:

• capital and operating costs of UCCs;
• an additional handling stage in the supply chain;
• security, liability and customer service issues associated with additional companies handling goods.

It is important to note that much urban freight is already consolidated at the intra-company level or by parcels carriers, so the benefits of trying to channel these flows through a consolidation centre may be limited. One of the main issues that remains largely unresolved surrounds the financial viability of UCCs. Those that operate on a voluntary basis and are not controlled by a single landlord all appear to require public funding, despite the promotion of value-added services as part of the UCC offer.

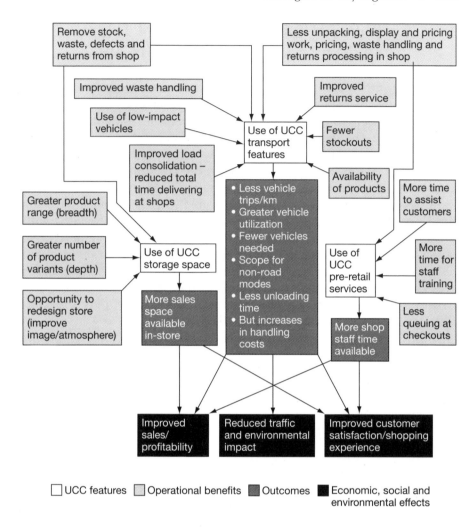

Figure 14.1 Range of potential logistics and pre-retail activities at UCC and possible benefits

UCCs are more likely to break even if participation can be made compulsory through planning or lease agreements, but this is difficult to achieve at present in most cases. Particular attention is required to ensure that private sector contributions are maximized, and that those who benefit from the UCC pay for its operation.

JOINT WORKING BETWEEN THE PUBLIC AND PRIVATE SECTORS

Urban freight transport and logistics involves many different stake-holders with diverse interest (including policy makers, retailers, whole-salers, freight operators, warehousing companies, residents, shoppers and workers). The global movement of people, goods and information has further accelerated the extent of diversification, which makes our lives exciting, for example, by offering the consumer many choices. However, public decision making has required more efforts to coordinate these activities to ensure that they function efficiently, while at the same time minimizing the social and environmental impacts associated with them. In an attempt to reach democratic decisions that will achieve these objectives, policy makers have been working closely with other stake-holders on a range of urban freight issues.

Logistics activities are primarily performed by private companies. However, government (local and national) is expected to play a respon-sible role for many reasons – for example:

- coping with negative externalities such as road congestion and air pollution;
- necessary coordination with other public functions such as city planning, regional economic development and environmental management;
- cross-border administrative issues with relation to international supply chain management.

Ogden (1992) argues that the urban freight system is far more complex and heterogeneous than urban passenger transport. This complexity and heterogeneity are driven by certain key features of urban goods movement, one of which is the range of participants involved in urban freight and the range of perceptions they hold of the 'urban freight problem'. Such complexity can make it difficult to develop successful participation between the public and private sectors.

During the late 1990s in the Netherlands, government became aware that cooperation of the private sector is very important in order to implement public policies. Government therefore sought cooperation with the private sector and began to develop policies in full consultation with the private sector, in order to create win–win situations. This has meant that instead of regulation, local, regional and national governments now sign covenants with organizations representing business or directly with businesses. In these covenants the private sector agrees to behave in a particular way, while the public sector either provides facilities and finance, or reassesses and alters regulations. The policy agenda of PSD in the Netherlands was developed in cooperation with both the public and private sector. The implementation of the policy required the public and private sector to work together in a partnership (Bockel, 2002).

The Japanese national government authorized a set of policies for freight transport entitled 'The New Comprehensive Program of Logistics Policies' in 2001, which was a revised version of an earlier programme, first launched in 1997. Urban freight transport is considered an important area in which to achieve efficient and environmentally friendly logistics systems in Japan. Two quantitative targets were set on 'the load factor of trucks' and 'peak-hour average travel speed' in three major metropolitan areas. In order to realize these targets, the programme highlighted the importance of coordination between public and private sectors, and between national and local governmental agencies, among others. This is why the programme requested the local agencies to establish an independent organization to plan local logistics policies, and new round tables to exchange information on local logistics policies, inviting private representatives from bodies representing carriers and retailers (Browne et al, 2004).

Freight quality partnerships (FQPs) are a UK approach to freight transport partnerships between the public and private sectors that were launched by the Freight Transport Association (FTA) in 1996. The FTA initiative brought together industry, local government and representatives of local and environmental interest groups to pursue the following agenda (FTA, 1997):

- to identify problems perceived by each interest group relating to the movement and delivery of goods in their city;
- to identify measures within the group's competence to resolve or alleviate such problems;
- to identify best practice measures and principles for action by local government and industry to promote environmentally sensitive, economic and efficient delivery of goods in towns and cities.

The FQP initiative was tested in four UK urban areas in 1996: Aberdeen, Birmingham, Chester and Southampton (FTA, 1997).

The UK Government has been promoting FQPs since 1999 (DETR, 1999; DfT, 2003a, 2003b). FQPs can facilitate improved dialogue about urban freight transport issues between local authorities, freight transport companies, retailers, manufacturers and other businesses, local residents and other interested parties. This can lead on to more efficient, less harmful operations. In their guidance document the government state that, 'Freight Quality Partnerships provide local authorities with a means to formalize the consultation and development work undertaken in their sustainable distribution strategy. Authorities have an integral role to play in helping industry, through developing partnerships to progress and develop best practice in sustainable distribution systems, and to find solutions to the issues of greatest concern' (DETR, 2000).

FQPs are a means for local policy makers, businesses, freight operators, environmental groups, the local community and other interested stakeholders to work together to address specific freight transport problems. The FQP provides a forum to achieve good practice in environmentally sensitive, economic, safe and efficient freight transport. The partners can exchange information, experiences and initiate projects regarding urban freight transport.

More than 120 FQPs have been developed in the UK over the last 10 years (FTA, 2008). Their purpose ranges from regional planning through city or town-specific partnerships, to micro-level partnerships (maybe concerned with a few streets) and issue-specific partnerships. FQPs can be formed to address any type of geographical area, but the majority cover urban areas.

FQPs have resulted in a wide range of successful urban freight projects including:

- the production of specialist maps for freight operators and goods vehicle drivers;
- improved road signing;
- information boards and online truck information points (in lay-bys and service stations to provide essential information specific to goods vehicle drivers);
- reviews of parking and loading enforcement regimes and on-street loading/unloading provision.

London is one of the most active UK cities in terms of FQPs. It has four sub-regional FQPs, in central, east (Thames Gateway), south and west London, which act as 'umbrella' groups for all local freight initiatives. Each of these sub-regional FQPs consists of several London boroughs together with private sector participants. In addition there are FQPs in Islington and Brimsdown. The issues addressed by some of these London FQPs are shown in Table 14.3.

ENVIRONMENTAL ZONES

Several terms are often used interchangeably when referring to this topic: these are 'environmental zones' (EZs) 'low emissions zones' (LEZs), 'Umweltzonen', 'Milieuzones', 'Lavutslippssone', 'Miljozone' and 'Miljözon'.

Table 14.3 Issues addressed by selected London FQPs

London sub-regional FQP	Work carried out

Central	<ul><li>Study of out-of-hours deliveries</li><li>Working groups addressing:
	  – urban consolidation centres
	  – loading/unloading provision
	  – out-of-hours deliveries
	  – vans, servicing and utilities</li></ul>

South	<ul><li>Freight industry stakeholder surveys</li><li>Feasibility studies for urban consolidation centres</li><li>Reviewing loading/unloading provision on high streets</li><li>Identifying penalty charge notice hotspots</li><li>Setting up a trial of night-time deliveries</li><li>Organizing seminars</li></ul>
West	<ul><li>Providing an information system for deliveries</li><li>Improved signage for drivers in several locations</li><li>Improved loading provision in Ealing town centre</li><li>Producing delivery and servicing plans</li><li>Reviewing overnight parking provision</li><li>Carrying out delivery and servicing studies in Brent and Harrow</li><li>Review of fly-tipping</li></ul>
East (Thames Gateway)	<ul><li>Urban freight study in Bexleyheath resulting in hotspot identification</li><li>Freight study in Belvedere industrial estates resulting in hotspot identification, lorry map and improved signing</li><li>Mapping expected construction projects</li><li>Mapping existing lorry parking facilities and determining demand for these in the medium to long term</li><li>Developing pilot project for River Thames</li></ul>

An 'environmental zone' (EZ) is a defined geographical area that can only be entered by vehicles meeting certain emissions criteria. The purpose of an EZ is to either restrict or charge the most polluting vehicles if they enter the EZ when their emissions are over the set level. In this way, an EZ can lead to air quality improvements because it capitalizes on recent EU legislation for road vehicles, which has set progressively tighter emission limits on new vehicles manufactured over the past decade. EZs are implemented in locations in which air pollution has reached levels that are dangerous to public health. By introducing the EZ it is hoped that air quality will improve and that this will reduce the health problems and fatalities associated with poor air quality.

As noted by the Low Emission Zone in Europe Network (LEEZEN):

> air pollution is responsible for 310,000 premature deaths in Europe each year... more than caused by road accidents. Air pollution particularly affects the very young and the old and those with heart and lung diseases – both common causes of death in Europe. It also triggers health problems like asthma attacks and increases hospital admissions and days off sick. The human health damage that air pollution causes is estimated to cost the European economy between €427 and €790 billion per year. Because of this danger to health, many countries around the world, as well as the European Union (EU), have set air quality targets to be met. In the EU, it is in order to meet these targets that LEZs are being implemented. (LEEZEN, 2008)

The main air pollution problems today in Europe are particulate matter (PM), nitrogen dioxide (NO_2) and ground-level ozone (O_3). Road traffic is a significant source of both PM and NO_2. The Framework Directive 1996/62/EC describes the legal framework for the assessment and control of air pollution in the European Union. Directive 1999/30/EC set the limit values for PM and NO_2. If the limit values are exceeded, the air quality framework directive requires member states to develop 'plans or programmes' designed to ensure that the limit values are met. An EZ offers one approach by which emissions of these pollutants can be reduced in areas where road traffic makes a significant contribution to air concentrations and thereby (together with other actions) can help authorities to meet the European air quality standards. The EU noise directive will also require development of action plans in some areas, and EZs may be used to address traffic noise problems in affected areas in future (Joint Expert Group on Transport and Environment, 2005).

As mentioned, an environmental zone (EZ) can only be entered by vehicles that meet specified emissions criteria. This can be applied to just goods vehicles, a selection of motor vehicles or all motor vehicles. An EZ therefore differs from the following types of access restrictions that can be placed on goods vehicles in urban areas:

- weight restrictions;
- length restrictions;
- restrictions based on utilization of loading capacity;
- time restrictions;
- permanent street closures and pedestrianization schemes;
- road user charging.

Table 14.4 Key aspects of current environmental zones in Europe

Key aspects of EZs	Practice in current EZs in Europe
Objectives of the EZ	The objective of an EZ is to improve environmental standards in the area in which the EZ is implemented. The main environmental goal is to reduce vehicle pollutant emissions and thereby improve air quality (helping to reduce fatalities and health problems caused by poor air quality). In addition EZs can help to improve other environmental standards by reducing traffic noise and improving road safety.
Geographical area covered by the EZ	Range from small, historic city centres (eg the city centre of Bologna which is 3.2 km^2) to entire cities (eg virtually all of Greater London – which is approximately 1,580 km^2). The vast majority of existing EZs are located in urban areas (as this is where air quality levels tend to be worst), but there are examples of EZs on motorways in Italy and Austria.
Times at which the EZ is in force	Of the EZs already implemented all, with the exception of some of the Italian schemes, operate 24 hours a day, 365 days a year. Some Italian schemes are only in force for certain hours per day during winter months.
Vehicles included in the EZ restrictions	All current EZ schemes cover heavy goods vehicles over 3.5 tonnes. All EZs, with the exception of the Dutch schemes, also include buses and coaches. The London EZ will also include vans over 1.205 tonnes (unladen) and minibuses with over eight seats from 2010. The German EZs cover all vehicles except motorcycles. The Italian schemes include all vehicles.
Emissions standards required by the EZ	Goods vehicle emissions standards required by EZs are based on Euro engine standards. Most current EZs require goods vehicles to meet Euro 2 standards, but some (including London) require Euro 3 standards. Some schemes permit older vehicles to be retrofitted in order to meet the required emissions standards, while others do not. Many Italian schemes require Euro 2 standards for diesel engines and Euro 1 for petrol engines.
Enforcement approaches used in the EZ	Some current EZs use manual enforcement, while others use automated systems. Manual systems typically involve vehicles having to register and then display stickers on windscreens, which are manually checked by police. Automated systems make use of fixed and mobile camera-based ANPR (automatic number plate recognition) and number plate checking with the relevant national vehicle registration body.
Fines imposed on non-compliant vehicles entering the EZ	Range from €40 (and one point in the national traffic penalty register) in Germany to £1,000 in London (approximately €1,250).

However, the above types of access restrictions can be implemented in addition to an EZ. EZ schemes can take many forms based on their objectives, the geographical area they cover, the times at which the EZ is in force, the vehicle emissions standards required for vehicles to enter the zone, the types of vehicles that need to comply with the EZ, and the implementation and enforcement approaches used. EZs are seen as one of the options for helping to improve urban air quality. Table 14.4 summarizes the key features of EZs already implemented in Europe.

Table 14.5 summarizes the EZs that have already been implemented or that are planned to be implemented soon in European countries, based on information currently available.

Table 14.5   Planned and existing environmental zones in European cities and regions (as at May 2009)

Country	Existing and planned EZs
Austria	One scheme on the A12 motorway started in 2007. A scheme in Graz is due to start in 2010.
Denmark	EZs in centre of Copenhagen, in Aalborg and in Frederiksberg have already started. An EZ is being considered in Aarhus, and is part of an environmental policy action plan in Odense (although no decision has been taken yet).
Germany	EZs have already begun operating in 29 cities since 2008. EZs are planned to start in another 10 German cities by 2010.
Hungary	An EZ is planned in Budapest.
Italy	EZs have already been implemented on the A22 motorway, in Bologna and Palermo, and in towns and cities in the following regions (during winter months and specified hours per day): Emilia-Romagna, Lombardy, Piedmont, Venetia and Bolzano-Bozen.
The Netherlands	EZs have already begun operating in nine cities since 2007. Another 10 cities are considering introducing EZs.
Norway	EZs are planned in Bergen, Oslo and Trondheim in 2009 and 2010.
Spain	An EZ is planned in Madrid as part of the Air Quality Strategy.
Sweden	EZs have been implemented in Stockholm, Gothenburg, Lund and Malmo.
UK	An EZ was implemented in London in 2008. It covers virtually the whole of Greater London and is the largest EZ in Europe.

Source: Based on information in LEEZEN; Teuro, 2008; and the authors' own knowledge.

An assessment of the air quality benefits of the Stockholm scheme in 2000 found that emissions of nitrous oxides (NOx) from heavy vehicles within the zone were reduced by 10 per cent and emissions of particulates by 40 per cent. The corresponding reductions in air pollution concentrations were estimated at 1.3 per cent reduction for NOx (with a range of 0.5 –2 per cent) and 3 per cent for particulates (with a range of 0.5–9 per cent), compared with the predicted concentrations without the zone. The air pollution reductions are much lower than vehicle emission reductions because of the relative importance of goods vehicles to total air quality concentrations. The analysis also concluded that the effect of the environmental zone was large when compared with other actions that it was possible for the local city administration to implement (Johansson and Burman, nd).

The Gothenburg EZ has produced the following reductions in vehicle emissions: 3.6 per cent reduction of carbon monoxide (CO), 6.1 per cent reduction of hydrocarbons (HC), 7.8 per cent reduction of NOx and 33.2 per cent reduction of particulate matter (PM) (Roth, 2007; Schoemaker, Dasburg and Allen, 2008).

Evaluation of the EZ schemes in the Lombardy region of Italy has shown daily mean emission reductions of 7 per cent for PM10 and NOx, and 11 per cent for CO (Joint Expert Group on Transport and Environment, 2005).

Monitoring work on the London LEZ has noted some small improvements in air quality since its introduction (Transport for London, 2008). However, it is too early to assess the full impact of this major scheme.

CONCLUSIONS

There are no standard, easily applicable solutions to the problems caused and experienced by freight transport in urban areas. However, the goal ought to be to identify policy measures and initiatives that ensure safe vehicle operation, promote economic vitality and lead to environmental improvement.

Policy makers will probably need to adopt a range of policy approaches to addressing urban freight transport and its relationship with sustainable development. They should make use of both encouragement and compulsion in their efforts. In some cases it will be necessary to impose restrictions on certain aspects of goods vehicle operation and to enforce these restrictions so as to meet safety and environmental objectives (LEZs are an example of this type of approach). In other cases, more progress is likely to be made by working closely with the private sector to improve the efficiency and reduce the negative impacts of urban freight. The FQP approach appears to be achieving some success in raising the level of dialogue between all the parties involved, identifying the key issues and problems, and implementing solutions. Whether the FQP approach can achieve sustained progress in the implementation of economic and environmentally sustainable urban freight solutions across all urban areas in the UK remains to be seen.

Strategies designed by the public and private sector to increase load consolidation and/or less frequent deliveries (through the use of urban consolidation centres, fiscal measures to encourage improved lading factors, or company-led innovations in their supply chains to improve the efficiency of distribution) have the potential to reduce the number of goods vehicle rounds quite considerably. To achieve increased levels of load consolidation can require that policy makers generally try to avoid the unnecessary use of weight and time restrictions on goods vehicle operations, whilst still ensuring that such restrictions are imposed in specific local situations as required.

REFERENCES

Allen, J, Anderson, S, Browne, M and Jones, P (2000) *A Framework for Considering Policies to Encourage Sustainable Urban Freight Traffic and Goods/service Flows: Summary report*, University of Westminster, London

Ambrosini, C, Routhier, J and Patier-Marque, D (2001) Objectives, methods and results of surveys carried out in the field of urban freight transport: an international comparison, paper presented at 9th World Conference on Transport Research (WCTR) in Seoul, Korea, 22–27 July 2001

Armitage A (1980) *Inquiry into Lorries, People and the Environment*, HMSO, London

Battilana, J and Hawthorne, I (1976) *Design and Cost of a Transhipment Depot to Serve Swindon Town Centre*, Laboratory Report 741, TRRL, Crowthorne

BESTUFS (2008) [accessed 24 August 2009] Bestufs.net [Online] http://www.bestufs.net

Bockel, R (2002) PSD: Public private partnerships in the Netherlands for urban freight transport, presentation at BESTUFS workshop on Public Private Partnerships, 12–13 September 2002, Malaga, Spain [accessed 24 August 2009] [Online] http://www.bestufs.net

Browne, M, Nemoto, T, Visser, J and Whiteing, T (2004) Urban freight movements and public-private partnerships in logistics systems for sustainable cities, *Proceedings of the Third International Conference on City Logistics*, ed E Taniguchi and R Thompson, pp 16–35, Elsevier

Browne, M, Sweet, M, Woodburn, A and Allen, J (2005) *Urban Freight Consolidation Centres*, report for the Department for Transport, University of Westminster, London

Delle Site, P and Salucci, M (2006) *Third Annual Thematic Research Summary: Freight transport*, Deliverable D2E-12, EXTR@Web Project, Transport Research Knowledge Centre

Department of the Environment, Transport and the Regions (DETR) (1998) *A New Deal for Transport: Better for everyone*, The Government's White Paper on the Future of Transport, Cmnd3950, The Stationery Office, London

DETR (1999) *Sustainable Distribution: A strategy*, DETR, London

DETR (2000) *Guidance on Full Local Transport Plans London*, 2000, DETR, London

Department for Transport (DfT) (2003a) *A Guide on How to Set Up and Run Freight Quality Partnerships*, Good Practice Guide 335, DfT, London

DfT (2003b) *Freight Quality Partnerships: Case studies*, Good Practice Case Study 410, DfT

European Commission (2007) Background paper for the technical workshop for the Green Paper on urban transport, January 2007, European Commission, Brussels

Flämig, H (2004) The success or failure of city logistics in Germany, presentation at Inter and Intra Urban Freight Distribution Networks, Cityfreight Project Conference, Prague 16–17 December

Freight Transport Association (FTA) (1997) *Delivering the Goods: Best practice in urban distribution*, Freight Transport Association, Tunbridge Wells

FTA (2008) *Freight Quality Partnership Network*, restricted website

GLC London Freight Conference (1975) *The Scope for Transhipment and Consolidation Operations in London: An analysis of available goods vehicle and commodity movement data*, Background paper No 8, April, Greater London Council, London

Hassell, M, Foulkes, M and Robertson, J (1978) Freight planning in London: the total strategy, *Traffic Engineering & Control*, May, pp 231–235

Institute for City Logistics (ICL) (2008) [accessed 25 August 2009] Institute for City Logistics [Online] http://www.citylogistics.org/

Johansson, C and Burman, L (nd) *Swedish Experience with Low Emission Zones*, Environment and Health Protection Administration, Air and Noise Analysis/Stockholm University, Institute of Applied Environmental Research

Joint Expert Group on Transport and Environment (2005) Report from the Working Group on Environmental Zones: Exploring the issue of environmentally related road traffic restrictions, European Commission, Brussels

Köhler, U (2001) City logistics in Germany, in *City Logistics II: 2nd International Conference on City Logistics*, ed E Taniguchi and R Thompson, pp 203–14, Institute for City Logistics

Köhler, U and Groke, O (2003) New ideas for the city-logistics project in Kassel, *Proceedings of 3rd International Conference on City Logistics*, pp 331–43, Madeira

Low Emission Zones in Europe Network (LEEZEN) (2008) [accessed 25 August 2009] Europe-wide information on LEZs [Online] http://www. lowemissionzones.eu

Lorries and the Environment Committee (1976) *Report on Transhipment London, 1976*, PE Consulting Group, London

McKinnon, A (1998) *Urban Transhipment: Review of previous work in the UK*, Report prepared for the Retail and Distribution Panel of the UK Government's Foresight Programme

Meimbresse, B and Sonntag, H (2000) Modelling urban commercial traffic with the model Wiwer, paper presented at Jacques Cartier Conference, Montréal, Canada, 4–6 October 2000

METRANS (2008) [accessed 25 August 2009] 2nd Annual National Urban Freight Conference, 2008 [Online] http://www.metrans.org/ nuf/2007/

Nathaniel Lichfield and Partners (1975) *Chichester Central Area Servicing System: Local interchange depot study*, Nathaniel Lichfield and Partners, London

Ogden, K (1992) *Urban Goods Movement: A guide to policy and planning*, Ashgate, Aldershot

Pettit, D (1973) *Lorries and the World We Live in*, HMSO, London

Roth, A (2007) Greening freight transport in Göteborg – From emissions and efficiency to breakfast cereals, presentation at BESTUFS Workshop on port cities and innovative urban freight solutions, Gothenburg, 22–23 March 2007

Schoemaker, J, Dasburg, N and Allen, J (2008) Quantification of urban freight transport effects II, Deliverable D52, BESTUFS project

Stantchev, D and Whiteing, T (2006) *Urban Freight Transport and Logistics: An overview of the European research and policy*, EXTR@Web Project, DG Energy and Transport, Brussels

Teuro, M (2008) Low emission zone as established in 2006–2010 Madrid Local Air Quality Strategy, presentation at the 8th BESTUFS (Best Urban Freight Solutions) II Workshop on Environmental Zones in European Cities: impacts and opportunities for urban freightport cities and innovative urban freight solutions, Madrid, 13–14 March 2008

Thompson, R and Taniguchi, E (1999) Routing of commercial vehicles using stochastic programming, *First International Conference on City Logistics*, ed E Taniguchi and R Thompson, Institute for City Logistics, pp 73–83

Transport for London (2008) London Low Emission Zone: Impacts Monitoring Baseline Report July, Transport for London, London

Links to relevant EU projects mentioned in the chapter

BESTUFS, http://www.bestufs.net

CITY FREIGHT, http://www.cityfreight.eu/

CIVITAS, http://www.civitas-initiative.org/main.phtml?lan=en

eDRUL (e-Commerce Enabled Demand Responsive Urban Logistics), http://srvweb01.softeco.it/edrul/Default.aspx?lang=en

FV-2000 (Quality of Freight Village Structure and Operations), http://www.freight-village.com/fv2000/

GIFTS (Global Intermodal Freight Transport System), http://gifts.newapplication.it/gifts/

IDIOMA (Innovative distribution with intermodal freight operation in metropolitan areas), http://cordis.europa.eu/transport/src/48343.htm

MIRACLES, http://www.civitas-initiative.org/project_sheet?lan=en&id=8

MOSCA (Decision Support System For Integrated Door-To-Door Delivery: Planning and Control in Logistic Chains), http://www.idsia.ch/mosca/deliverables.phtml

PROMIT, http://www.promit-project.net/

REFORM (Research on freight platforms and freight organization), http://cordis.europa.eu/transport/src/reform.htm

SMART FREIGHT, http://www.smartfreight.info/index.htm

START (Short Term Actions to Reorganize Transport of Goods), http://www.start-project.org/

TELLUS (Transport and Environment Alliance for Urban Sustainability), http://www.tellus-cities.net/

TRENDSETTER, http://www.trendsetter-europe.org

UTOPIA (Urban Transport: Options for Propulsion systems and Instruments for Analysis), http://www.utopia-eu.com

VIVALDI, http://www.civitas-initiative.org/project_sheet?lan=en&id=6

15

Benefits and costs of switching to alternative fuels

Sharon Cullinane and Julia Edwards

INTRODUCTION

As discussed in Chapter 2, freight transport is responsible for a high proportion of the approximately 20 per cent of total global greenhouse gas (GHG) emitted by the transport sector, with emissions from diesel fuel accounting for the majority of this. As a consequence, a great deal of international effort and money is being expended on the development and production of alternative fuels. This chapter analyses the potential of the various alternative fuels (AFs) for use within the freight transport sector and assesses their environmental impacts. It starts with an examination of biofuels and then goes on to consider other alternatives, namely hydrogen and hydrogen fuel cells and gaseous fuels (natural gas, LPG and CNG). The penultimate section considers some of the developments that are currently being implemented in the logistics sector, focusing mainly on electric vehicles, which are being used or trialled in many companies' van and light goods vehicle fleets.

As yet, there seems to be less progress in the use of alternative fuels in heavy goods vehicles, despite distances travelled indicating that the potential benefits derived from the use of new technology would be much greater (Nesbitt and Sperling, 2001). The problem seems to be one of cost. As Deutsche Post (2008) states: 'In contrast to the passenger car sector, almost no "off-the-shelf" alternative fuel commercial vehicles are on offer at a similar cost to comparable conventional vehicles.' Logistics companies are therefore having to trial their own solutions. The final section looks to the future and briefly discusses some possible fuel developments.

THE MAIN TYPES OF ALTERNATIVE FUELS

In this section we will look at the main types of alternative fuels. We start with biofuels as this constitutes probably the most popular AF currently in use.

Biofuels

Much recent attention has been focused on biofuels. This is highlighted economically by the fact that worldwide investment in biofuels rose from US$5bn in 1995 to US$38bn in 2005, owing to substantial investments by companies such as BP, Shell and Ford, and by Richard Branson (Grunwald, 2008).

Biofuels are essentially fuels produced from renewable plant material and oils. The International Energy Agency (IEA, 2004: 26) defines biofuels in the following way: 'Either in liquid form such as fuel ethanol or biodiesel or gaseous form such as biogas or hydrogen, biofuels are simply transportation fuels derived from biological (eg agricultural) sources.'

There are two main types of biofuel:

- biodiesel;
- bioethanol.

Biodiesel (or alkyl esters)

Biodiesel is made from plant and animal oils through a process called transesterification (ie the production of esters from oil or fat). In this process, the fat or oil is reacted with alcohol in the presence of a catalyst to produce biodiesel and glycerine (www.biodiesel.org). The main sources of oil used in the production of biodiesel vary according to country, depending on local growing conditions. In Asia palm oil is the norm, in the United States it is soybean oil and in Europe the norm is rapeseed oil (or canola). Other plant oils that can be used include sunflower oil, cottonseed oil, mustard seed oil, coconut oil and hemp oil. In 2006, the United States produced 250 million gallons of biodiesel, up from 2 million gallons in 2000, but this still only represented less than 1 per cent of total highway diesel fuel used (Union of Concerned Scientists, 2007).

Bioethanol

Bioethanol can be produced from any biological foodstock that contains sugar, or materials such as starch or cellulose that can be made into sugar (IEA, 2004). The main sources of sugars for bioethanol are wheat, corn, sugar beet, straw, maize, reed canary grass, cord grass, Jerusalem artichokes, myscanthus, sorghum, sawdust and willow and poplar trees (ESRU, 2007), although sugar beet and corn account for 80 per cent of all bioethanol produced in the world in 2007 (Sperling, 2008). Bioethanol has been used as a fuel for decades. Brazil has been using bioethanol made from sugar cane since the 1930s, and indeed in the 1980s was selling cars that ran exclusively on such fuel (Sperling, 2008). The United States has also been using bioethanol (produced from corn) for many decades (not so much for environmental reasons as to reduce its dependence on imported conventional oil).

Both biodiesel and bioethanol are usually blended with existing fuel to make them usable. Biodiesel is usually blended with conventional diesel and bioethanol is usually blended with conventional petrol ('gasoline' in the United States), although it can be blended with diesel after some modification (IEA, 2004). Thus, B20 means there is a 20 per cent blend of biodiesel with conventional diesel and similarly E20 means that there is a 20 per cent blend of bioethanol with conventional petrol. As the percentage blend of ethanol increases, so its corrosive impact increases, and over about 10 per cent susceptible conventional vehicle components (particularly the rubber elements) need to be replaced by ethanol-resistant components. However, with biodiesel this problem is reduced. In the United States, the most common blend is B20, but in Germany, Austria and Sweden 100 per cent pure blended biodiesel is used in goods vehicles and buses with only very minor engine modifications (IEA, 2004). Vehicles that can use conventional fuel or any blend of biofuels are known as flexible-fuel vehicles (sometimes called flex-fuel vehicles).

One of the main reasons why biofuels have gained so much attention is that low blends (generally agreed to be up to about 10 per cent) can be used directly in existing cars with no engine modifications, and the refuelling infrastructure is exactly the same as for conventional fuel (ie through fuel pumps). In early 2008, there were 165 biodiesel and 16 bioethanol stations around the UK (Anon, 2008). This makes it very convenient and cheap compared with the development of other renewable fuel alternatives (such as hydrogen, electric power or LNG/CNG), which require major modifications to both vehicles and refuelling distribution systems.

Attention on the environmental impacts of transport is not new. In the 1970s and 1980s the focus was on the use of non-renewable resources (ie oil) following the OPEC oil crisis and an increasing understanding of the effects of transport on the local environment (particularly the health impacts of sulphur and lead). Since the 1990s, however, attention has been focused on the global impacts of pollution, and in particular on the impact of greenhouse gas emissions (particularly CO_2) on climate change. The EU Biofuels Directive was adopted in May 2003.[1] Its aim was to promote the use of transport fuels made from biomass and other renewable sources. The directive sets a reference value of 5.75 per cent (by energy) for the market share of biofuels by 2010. In the case of the UK, a conditional target of 10 per cent for the energy content share of biofuels in petrol and diesel was set for 2020.[2] As part of the UK's 2006 Climate Change Programme, a further target of 5 per cent (by volume) was set for the proportion of road transport fuel to be derived from renewable sources by 2010. To aid in the achievement of this target, a Renewable Transport Fuel Obligation (RTFO) was established for fuel suppliers (which started in April 2008). Under the RTFO, companies are required to measure and report on how much carbon their fuel has saved on a life cycle basis (including land-use changes) (DfT, 2007). In 2008, the government announced that from 2010, the RTFO will reward fuels according to their carbon savings in order to encourage technological advances.

Environmental impacts of biofuels

The emissions issue

Apart from the security of supplies argument, the main reason for the push towards biofuels is their purported environmental benefits. The DfT (2007: 2), for instance, states that 'evidence from lifecycle analysis suggests that sustainable biofuels can offer significant reductions in greenhouse gas emissions compared with fossil fuels and so represent an opportunity to address climate change.' The EPA (2002) calculated that with a 40 per cent biodiesel mix, NOx would increase by around 4 per cent, particulate matter and CO would both decrease by around 22 per cent and hydrocarbons would decrease by about 36 per cent. If the biodiesel mix was increased to 80 per cent, the corresponding figures would be +9 per cent, –40 per cent and –60 per cent. Thus, emissions of most pollutants decrease with the use of biodiesel but emissions of nitrous oxides increase. The big gains are from a near-complete elimination of sulphur emissions, with reductions in hydrocarbons and other local emissions. Results of tests by the International Energy Agency support these findings; they conclude that 'Biofuels (ethanol and FAME biodiesel) generally produce lower tailpipe emissions of carbon monoxide, hydro-carbons, sulphur dioxide and particulate matter than gasoline or conventional diesel fuel.' They state, however, that ethanol-blended gasoline produces more volatile organic compounds (VOCs). They also point out that the hydrocarbons that are produced are different from those in conventional fuels and that the health effects of these hydrocarbons are not yet fully known.

Most research suggests that there will be slight increases in the emissions of nitrous oxides (NOx) as a result of the use of biofuels. However, tests also indicate that once sulphur has been eliminated from fuel (which seems entirely possible in the near term), this will enable the use of powerful NOx-breaking catalysts that cannot be used when sulphur is present. So, in the future, it is possible that the NOx gases can be reduced too, thereby improving the environmental credentials of biofuels.

The change in the level of emissions of carbon dioxide (CO_2) resulting from a switch towards biofuels is much more debatable. The EPA (2002: iii) stated that they were 'not able to identify an unambiguous difference in exhaust CO_2 emissions' between conventional fuel and biodiesel. Other research suggests that there is a 10 per cent increase in the tailpipe emissions of CO_2 when using biodiesel, but that the sequestration effect of growing the plants to start with is calculated to offset this increase (DfT, 2007). Indeed the EPA state that 'it should be noted that the CO_2 benefits commonly attributed to biodiesel are the result of the renewability of the biodiesel itself, not the comparative exhaust CO_2.' This is very interesting given the arguments now looming over the land-use change effects of the push towards biofuels (see section on 'The land-take issue' below). The net effect on life cycle emissions of CO_2 (but see below) is purported to be a reduction of between 10 per cent and 100 per cent, depending on what exactly is included in the calculation (eg the source of the biofuel, the amount and type of fertilizer used in the crop production and the energy used in the production process), the blend of fuel used and the type of conventional diesel to which the biodiesel is added (EPA, 2002). Emissions savings from biofuels can vary widely. The use of wheat-based ethanol produced CO_2 savings from as little as 7 per cent to as much as 77 per cent in the United Kingdom (Defra, 2007).

Turning to energy efficiency, the EU estimates that fuel consumption increases by about 10 per cent with the use of biofuels. The IEA argues that because of the higher cetane number of biodiesel, it has a higher burning efficiency and this, combined with the fact that the lubricity of biodiesel is higher, means that the energy efficiency is just a little below that of traditional diesel.

The land-take issue

Until recently, it was assumed that the benefits of biofuels were mostly positive. However, this notion is now being challenged. In 2007, the DfT (p 3) cautioned that 'major land-use change, particularly deforestation and draining of peat bogs, can completely negate the carbon saving from biofuels as well as causing damage to biodiversity and other ecosystem resources.' However, although local impacts were being recognized, it was not until late 2007, when the OECD (2007) published a report questioning the whole biofuels policy, that the global implications of their widespread use were fully realized. Searchinger (2008: 1) summarized the growing concern:

> Previous studies have found that substituting biofuels for gasoline will reduce greenhouse gases because biofuels sequester carbon through the growth of feedstock. These analyses have failed to count the carbon emissions that occur as farmers worldwide respond to higher prices and convert forest and grassland to new cropland. New analyses are now showing that the loss of greenhouse gases from direct and indirect land-use changes exceeds the other benefits of many biofuels over decades.

The issue is one of demand. For small quantities of biofuels, crops can be grown on marginal land and excess crops or leftover frying fat can be used without causing too much environmental damage. However, as global demand for biofuels increases, this approach is no longer tenable. Inevitably, the prices of the biofuel crops increase, which in turn causes distortions in global agricultural production as a whole, and land previously considered uneconomic is cultivated (including rainforest and wetlands, which contain extensive stores of carbon). In turn, increasing food prices impact particularly hard on the poorest in the world. Grunwald (2008) attributes food riots in Mexico and the destabilization of Pakistan to soaring corn prices, which themselves are a result of increased ethanol production for fuel in the United States. He concludes by stating that 'biofuels aren't part of the solution at all. They're part of the problem,' a view that Sperling (2008: 5) concurs with in relation to the corn ethanol produced in the United States. He states: 'In sum, corn ethanol is expensive and provides no net environmental benefits. The main societal benefit is a small reduction in oil imports, gained at a substantial cost.' According to Anon (2008) the palm oil industry has already used 6.5 million hectares of plantations in Sumatra and Borneo and removed an estimated 10 million hectares of rainforest in order to produce biofuels.

It is in the wake of these arguments raging over the environmental impact of biofuels that the UK government ordered the Gallagher Inquiry to consider the appropriateness of the RTFO target. The resulting report

(Renewable Fuels Agency, 2008) suggested that the 2.5 per cent (by volume) target for 2008/09 be retained but that the 5 per cent target for 2010 should be extended to 2013/14 to allow for more understanding of the life cycle effects (DfT, 2008).

Previous analysis by the EU to assess the impact on prices of the 10 per cent by energy target by 2020 concluded that prices for agricultural raw materials would increase by 3 per cent – 6 per cent for cereals and by 5–18 per cent for oilseeds (DfT, 2007). The IEA (2004) has estimated that displacing 5 per cent of EU petrol and diesel consumption would take 20 per cent of EU cropland. The problem is that biofuels cannot be produced solely from crops grown in the EU and oils would still need to be imported from the United States and Asia (Environmental Audit Committee, 2008). Biofuels targets are now being revised until new research comes up with better solutions.

Hydrogen

Hydrogen is a second key potential alternative energy source for transport. In the early 2000s, hydrogen was being viewed as a panacea for the future and in 2003 the International Partnership for the Hydrogen Economy, established by the US Department of Energy with signatories from around the world, aimed to accelerate the transition to a hydrogen economy (see www.iphe.net). The impetus towards this shift has, however, slowed as problems have emerged.

To date, much of the research into hydrogen as an AF has focused on passenger cars and buses rather than freight vehicles, although there is considerable interest in the potential for hydrogen use in the light goods vehicle (LGV) sector. As the technology improves, and as long as it is viewed as being successful, transferral of this energy source to larger vehicles is likely.

The main form of hydrogen to be used in transport is the hydrogen fuel cell. This is a device that converts hydrogen gas and oxygen into water via a process that generates electricity. Fuel cell vehicles are generally powered by pure hydrogen which comes in the form of compressed hydrogen gas, metal hydrides stored in cylinders or as liquid hydrogen, though any hydrogen-containing feedstock (such as petrol and diesel oil) could be used (DfT, 2000). Proton exchange membrane fuel cells (PEMFC) are being developed for both transport and stationary applications (such as power for warehouses). PEMFCs are not new; they were invented in the 1950s by General Motors and were used by NASA in the Gemini space project. The PEMFC works by harnessing the chemical energy that results from the reaction of hydrogen and oxygen and transforming it into electrical energy. It is very efficient at energy production and is almost totally recyclable.

The main environmental benefit of hydrogen is that its only real tailpipe emission is water vapour. For use in cities this can be very beneficial and it is for this reason that bus companies all over the world are currently trialling them (for instance through the Clean Urban Transport in Europe (CUTE) initiative).

As more research into the use of hydrogen is carried out, however, major doubts have crept in concerning its environmental credentials. The principle issues of contention are fivefold:

- Hydrogen is 'an energy carrier not an energy source' (EurActiv, 2006). This means that it has to be produced from other sources (coal, nuclear etc), so it is only as clean as these source fuels. It can be made from renewable energy sources, such as wind power, but there is concern that if there is a global switch to the use of hydrogen, there will be insufficient supplies of renewables, whose price will increase as a result, encouraging the use of non-renewables again. Even if renewables can be used, in a major study of the benefits of hydrogen fuel for the DfT, Eyre, Fergusson and Mills (2002: 6) concluded: 'until there is a surplus of renewable electricity it is not beneficial in terms of carbon reduction to use renewable electricity to produce hydrogen – for use in vehicles or elsewhere.' They suggest that it is more efficient to use renewables for purposes other than hydrogen formation.
- The pollutant emissions from hydrogen have also been challenged. A report to the DfT (2002: 4) by AEA Technology suggested that 'direct emissions of hydrogen to the atmosphere from human activity may alter the natural chemistry of the atmosphere and exacerbate problems relating to the impacts of photochemical pollution (ozone) and climate change.' Hydrogen is an indirect greenhouse gas with a potential global warming effect, because emissions of hydrogen lead to increased burdens of methane and ozone (Collins, Derwent and Johnson, 2002). It appears that the precise impact of hydrogen on the environment is not yet clear.
- In order to be able to produce hydrogen fuel cells, a small amount of platinum is required (to act as a catalyst). There are substantial negative environmental effects associated with the mining and refining of platinum, including atmospheric emissions of SO_2, ammonia, chlorine and hydrogen chloride (estimated to be around 180 kg of carbon per ounce), but also long-term groundwater and disposal problems (DfT, 2002). If recycled platinum can be used, this reduces the environmental footprint significantly.
- A whole new refuelling infrastructure needs to be developed. Hydrogen filling stations need to be set up globally, requiring a

considerable investment and a great deal of environmental pollution. For vehicles, hydrogen would be purchased in liquid form and the oxygen would be obtained from the air. However, because of its low energy-to-volume ratio, hydrogen is difficult to carry in vehicles as well as to store and distribute (NREL, 2003).

- At present the fuel cells do not allow long-distance travel (ie their range is limited).

In conclusion, hydrogen does not appear to be the 'dream ticket' it was expected to be. Until there is a surplus of renewables from which it can be produced, and until the platinum problem is dealt with, it seems that hydrogen merely transfers the environmental effects from the tailpipe to the electricity generation. In the future, it may be possible to produce hydrogen by 'splitting' water (ie by electrolysis). If this can be done using sunlight, either through photoelectrochemical or photobiological processes, the lifecycle impact of hydrogen production is virtually nothing (NREL, 2003). At present, this technology is not well understood (or some would say that the big oil producers are not in favour of it, so less investment is being made in it). It seems likely that the majority of hydrogen energy will continue to be produced from non-renewables in the foreseeable future.

Gas-fuelled vehicles

Natural Gas (NG)

Natural gas vehicles (NGVs) are methane-powered vehicles. The methane is derived from either fossil sources or biomethane (a raw biogas upgraded for vehicle use). According to the European Natural Gas Vehicle Association (ENGVA, 2007), in 2007 there were 6.7 million NGVs worldwide, including 820,400 in Europe (10.5 per cent of which were trucks). NGVs produce slightly lower emissions of CO_2 than traditional petrol-engined cars and about the same levels of CO_2 as the equivalent diesel-powered trucks. The benefit of NG is that it produces no nitrous oxides or particulate matter. Some manufacturers produce heavy goods vehicles that run purely on NG. Vehicles can be refuelled overnight at depots, which have purchased the required compressors. Dual-fuel NG/diesel or NG/petrol vehicles are also available.

Natural gas is still, however, fossil fuel-dependent, so does not represent a clean fuel. Methane is classed as a greenhouse gas (although the ENGVA argue that it should not be) and has a global warming potential that is 21 times that of CO_2 (for an explanation of this, see Chapter 2). However, NG production from biomass actually reduces emissions of methane as it harnesses the methane normally emitted in the waste disposal process and transforms it into energy. Anaerobic digestion plants extract and process the methane from municipal waste and sewage. At present, although Sweden has plans for 80,000 biogas-powered vehicles by 2010, the UK is still in its infancy stages and has no biogas refuelling stations (Anon, 2008).

Liquid petroleum gas (LPG) and compressed natural gas (CNG)

LPG comes mostly in the form of propane and butane. LPG is a heavy gas derived from the process of petroleum refining and natural gas extraction and is stored in liquid form. In the EU, 66 per cent of LPG comes from gas field extraction and 34 per cent from crude oil refining (AEGPL, 2007). CNG is derived from similar sources but remains a gas when compressed. LPG is now a reasonably common fuel for cars and buses. As an example, 99.8 per cent of Hong Kong's taxis and most new minibuses run on LPG. However, it does require some vehicle modifications, and although there has been an international push towards providing LPG refuelling stations, it is not yet as widely available as conventional fuels, and indeed is not yet available at all in some countries.

Environmentally, the benefits are sizeable reductions in nitrous oxides and particulate matter at the tailpipe. However, both LPG and CNG still originate from fossil fuels, so the well-to-wheel emissions of greenhouse gases are still high. Eyre, Fergusson and Mills (2002: 53) state that LPG does not offer lifecycle carbon benefits compared with diesel and conclude that 'LPG will have a rather marginal impact on either total road fuel energy demand or CO_2 emissions and does not provide a pathway to non-fossil-fuel transport.'

Electric vehicles

Electric vehicles depend on batteries, which are still currently heavy and bulky and only enable a limited distance range to be travelled. Recent improvements in the distance range (now in excess of 250 miles), however, have led to an increase in interest in the use of this technology for van-based home deliveries (MacLeod, 2007) and other van-based operations. Smith Electric Vehicles, for instance, produce a range of smaller trucks (including a 9-t truck), where the batteries are stored on the underside of the truck. These are currently in use by a number of large UK companies. Although electric vehicles are not yet capable of powering larger trucks, there are many hybrid trucks on the road that combine electric and diesel power. Conventional axles can be replaced by electric-driven differential units that produce electricity to help power vehicles up hills and at the same time recharge the batteries when not in use. A growing number of vehicles also use regenerative braking systems that slow the vehicle and simultaneously recharge the battery.

For the freight industry, the attraction of electric vehicles is twofold. They are virtually pollution-free at point of use (emitting almost no tailpipe emissions), and they are much quieter than conventional goods vehicles (producing fewer vibrations). For these reasons they are eminently suitable for use within city environmental zones. On the cost front, they incur no vehicle excise duty (VED) and use no fuel (except electricity). However, the capital cost of the vehicles is considerably above that of conventional vehicles.

Electric vehicles have been in use for deliveries for decades, with the British milk-float being an early and enduring example. The technology is now fairly common in buses and considerable attention has been paid to introducing it into private cars. Academic studies have tended to focus on private transport up-take of this technology (Carlsson and Johansson-Stedmann, 2003; Delucchi and Lipman, 2001; Chan and Chan, 2001). As the pressure increases on logistics companies to become more environmentally friendly, interest in electrically powered goods vehicles looks likely to increase.

Environmentally, the benefit of electric vehicles is an almost total elimination of both tail-pipe emissions and engine noise. The problem remains, however, that batteries must be recharged using electricity and the production of the electricity itself is environmentally unfriendly; the extent of the damage done depends on the ultimate source of the electricity. Until electricity is produced from renewable resources, the burden of environmental damage is merely being transferred from the vehicle upstream to the electricity production process.

CURRENT USE OF AFS IN THE FREIGHT INDUSTRY

As stated earlier, use of AFs in goods vehicles has received less attention than that in passenger cars. Yet, regularly fuelled and maintained in-house, fleet vehicles often run to fixed daily routes, allowing them to be switched to new technology vehicle types before public fuelling infrastructure and networks are widely available. Nevertheless, at present individual companies have to come up with their own solutions to environmental problems. Many logistics companies choose to ignore the problem completely, or rely on EURO vehicle standards to deal with it. The most proactive companies are working with vehicle manufacturers on an individual basis to come up with tailor-made solutions. Some examples of this are given below.

Tesco, Britain's largest supermarket, owns a 25 per cent share of biofuel company, Greenenergy, which buys rapeseed from 1,500 farmers in the UK to make biodiesel. Tesco uses a 50:50 biodiesel mix in its own vehicle fleet (Tesco, 2008). This fact was once prominent on their website. By August 2008, however, there was no mention of this and indeed they are now much more circumspect, stating that 'we recognize that the full impacts of biofuels are complex and any environmental benefit depends on how the biofuels are made,' and 'the full impact of biofuels is not 100 per cent clear.' In April 2007, Tesco launched a fleet of battery-powered home delivery vans with a 100-mile range, claiming that each van saves 21 tonnes of CO_2 per year (Tesco, 2008).

Sainsbury's, another leading UK supermarket, introduced its 'Little Green Van' – an electric delivery van for making its online deliveries. By the end of 2008/09, they hope to be making a fifth of their online deliveries in these vans, carrying the advertising slogan: 'Zero emissions – nothing comes out of this van but great food.' Currently, Sainsbury's (2008: 75) are less committed to the use of biofuels, stating that, although they intend to comply with the RTFO, 'significant questions remain around the overall environmental benefits of biofuels and their impact on the developing world.'

Asda, another supermarket chain and part of the Walmart group, is trialling an electric home delivery van that has a range of 120 miles after charging for 60 minutes.

DHL, now part of Deutsche Post, which describes itself as the biggest logistics company in the world, is trialling various alternative energy vehicles around the world, including biogas, CNG, LPG and electric vehicles. Its policy on biofuels is also currently very cautionary. Its sustainability report (Deutsche Post, 2008), states:

> The use of sustainable biofuels is an important option to consider, and we are developing internal biofuels guidelines to help us make the right choices. Biofuels need to be carefully evaluated because their production might cause adverse social and environmental impacts – of particular concern are the possible consequences for food supplies in poor or developing countries. The public discussion on biofuels is ongoing and we are following it carefully, including through dialogue with relevant stakeholders.

Daf, one of the major truck manufacturers, prides itself on its environmental credentials and frequently wins awards for the environmental attributes of its trucks. It is currently developing a hybrid diesel-electric medium-duty vehicle using a lithium-ion battery. Unfortunately, this example only serves to illustrate how far away the medium–heavy goods vehicle industry is from being able to effectively use alternative fuels, because this prototype vehicle is only capable of travelling 2 km using the battery, despite a battery pack weighing 100 kg (Daf, 2008). As the company's brochure states, this is just enough for driving in and out of the green zones of city centres.

THE FUTURE

It is evident from this chapter that developing new, more environmentally sustainable fuels is complex, partly because in order to make any significant inroads into the consumption of conventional fuels, the scale of production needs to be so vast that unintended and unpredictable secondary issues emerge.

In relation to biofuels, because of the land-take issues and the low efficiency of conventional biofuels, attention is turning to what are termed second-generation biofuels. These are fuels that can be made from waste materials (such as municipal waste) and cullulosic crops (dedicated energy crops) that can be grown on wasteland. According to the EU (EC, 2008: 11), use of cellolosic biomass feedstock allows new methods of biofuel production from 'products, by-products and waste from agriculture, forestry and wood, pulp and paper with more sophisticated chemical reactions'. For instance, according to the IEA (2004), cellulosic feedstocks can be converted into ethanol using lignin (ie the non-cellulose part of the plant), and excess cellulose instead of fossil fuels can be used as the main process fuel, thus producing minimal GHG emissions. As the Royal Society (2008) argues, biofuels may form part of the solution for the future but only a small part, and other solutions will also be required. It appears that hydrogen fuel cells are not going to be the panacea that they were predicted to be. The Intergovernmental Panel on Climate Change (2007) states that by 2030 energy use and carbon emissions from transport are predicted to be 80 per cent higher than current levels. If supply-based solutions cannot be found, it seems that demand management solutions must receive even greater consideration if climate change is to be stemmed.

NOTES

1. Directive 2003/30/EC
2. In terms of biodiesel, a 5 per cent reduction by volume is equivalent to a 4 per cent reduction by energy (DfT, 2008)

REFERENCES

AEGPL (2007) The LPG Industry Roadmap, Brussels

Anon (2008) Reducing fleet carbon emissions with fuel alternatives, *Logistics Business Magazine*, Feb/March, pp 6–10

Carlsson, F and Johansson-Stedmann, O (2003) Costs and benefits of electric vehicles: A 2010 perspective, *Journal of Transport Economics and Policy*, **37** (1), pp 1–28

Chan, CC and Chau, KT (2001) *Modern Electric Vehicle Technology*, Monographs in Electric and Electronic Engineering, Oxford Science Publications, Oxford

Collins, WJ, Derwent, RG and Johnson, CE (2002) The oxidation of organic compounds in the troposphere and their global warming potential, *Climatic Change*, **52**, pp 453–79

Daf (2008) Daf and the environment: "Attention to the environment as a matter of course", Eindhoven

Defra (2006) [accessed 25 August 2009] UK Climate Change Programme [Online] www.defra.gov.uk/environment/climatechange/uk

Defra (2007) [accessed 16 March 2009] *Biofuels: Risks and Opportunities*, Defra, London [Online] http://dft.gov.uk/pgr/roads/environment/rtfo/289579

Delucchi, MA and Lipman, TE (2001) An analysis of the retail and life-cycle cost of battery-powered electric vehicles, *Transportation Research Part D*, **6**, pp 371–404

Department for Transport (Dft) (2000)

DfT (2002) *Platinum and Hydrogen for Fuel Cell Vehicles*, AEA Technology, Harwell

DfT (2007) Biofuels: risks and opportunities

DfT (2008) [accessed 25 August 2009] Carbon pathways analysis: informing development of a carbon reduction strategy for the transport sector [Online] http://www.dft.gov.uk/pgr/sustainable/analysis.pdf

Deutsche Post (2008) 2008_ Sustainability Report [Online] [accessed 17 March 2009] http://www.dp-dhl.com/sustainabilityreport/2008/servicepages/downloads/files/entire_dp_csr08.pdf

Energy Systems Research Unit (ESRU) (2007) [accessed 26 July 2008] What is Bioethanol? [Online] www.esru.strath.ac.uk

ENGVA (2007) [accessed 16 March 2009] European Natural Gas Vehicle Response 15 July 2007 to public consultation on the implementation of the renewed strategy to reduce CO_2 emissions from passenger cars and light-commercial vehicles [Online] http://ec.europa.eu/reducing_co2_emissions_from_cars/doc_contrib/engva_en.pdf

Environmental Audit Committee (2008) *Biofuels: Are they sustainable?* House of Commons, London

EPA (Environmental Protection Agency) (2002) [accessed 25 August 2009] A comprehensive analysis of biodiesel impacts on exhaust emissions, Draft Technical report [Online] www.epa.gov/otaq/models/analysis/biodsl/p02001.pdf

EurActiv (2006) [accessed 26 October 2006] *Hydrogen and Fuel Cells: fake promises?* [Online] www.euractiv.com/en/transport/hydrogen_fuel_cells_fake_promises/article159235

European Commission (2008) *Renewables Make the Difference*, DG for Energy and Transport, Office for Official Publications for the European Communities, Luxembourg

European Natural Gas Vehicles Association (2007) Response to the EU Strategy on CO_2 emissions from the transport sector [Online] www.ec.europa.eu/reducing_ CO2_emissions_from_cars/doc_contrib/engva_en.pdf

Eyre, N, Fergusson, M and Mills, R (2002) *Fuelling Road Transport: Implications for energy policy*, DfT, London

Grunwald, M (2008) The clean energy scam, *Time*, 27 March, pp 28–32 [accessed 20 March 2007] [Online] http://www.time.com/time/magazine/article/0,9171,1725975,00.html

Intergovernmental Panel on Climate Change (2007) Climate Change 2007. Impacts, Adoption and Vulnerability. Contribution of Working Group II to the Fourth Assessment Report of the Intergovernmental Panel on Climate Change, Geneva

International Energy Agency (2004) *Biofuels for Transport: An International Perspective*, OECD, Paris

MacLeod, M (2007) Parcels carriers: what they're doing for the world, *Fulfilment and E-Logistics*, **44**, summer [accessed 25 August 2009] [Online] http://www.elogisticsmagazine.com/magazine/44/parcels-carriers-the-world.shtml

National Renewable Energy Laboratory (NREL) (2003) *New Horizons for Hydrogen: Producing hydrogen from renewable resources*, NREL, Golden, Colorado

Nesbitt, K and Sperling, D (2001) Fleet purchase behavior: decision processes and implications for new vehicle technologies and fuels, *Transportation Research Part C*, **9**, pp 297–318

OECD (2007) Biofuels: Is the cure worse than the disease? SG/SD/RT (2007) 3, OECD, Paris

Renewable Fuels Agency (2008) *Review of the Indirect Effects of Biofuels (the Gallagher Review)* St Leonards-On-Sea, East Sussex

Royal Society (2008) [accessed 25 August 2009] Sustainable biofuels: prospects and challenges [Online] http://royalsociety.org/displaypagedoc.asp?id=28914

Sainsbury's (2008) Corporate Social Responsibility Report, Our Values Make Us Different, J Sainsbury plc, London

Searchinger, T (2008) The impacts of biofuels on greenhouse gases: how land use change alters the equation, The German Marshall Fund Policy Brief [accessed 25 March 2009] [Online] www.gmfus.org/economics/publications/article.cfm?id=385

Searchinger, T, Heimlich, R, Houghton, RA, Fengxia Dong, Elobeid, A, Fabiosa, J, Tokgoz, S, Hayes, D and Tun-Hsiang Yu (2008) Use of US croplands for biofuels increases greenhouse gases through emissions from land-use change, *Science*, **319**, pp 1238–40

Sperling, D (2008) Are biofuels the answer? Paper presented at the International Transport Forum, Leipzig, OECD/ITF

Tesco (2008) Corpoprate Social Responsibility Review, 2008, Tesco plc, Cheshunt, Hertfordshire

Union of Concerned Scientists (2007) [accessed 5 March 2008] Clean Vehicles [Online] www.ucsusa.org/clean_vehicles

Links to relevant EU projects mentioned in the chapter

www.biodieselamerica.org
www.biodiesel.org
www.biodiesel.org.au

16

E-business, e-logistics and the environment

Julia Edwards, Yingli Wang, Andrew Potter and Sharon Cullinane

INTRODUCTION

The fast emergence of information and communication technologies (ICT) in the 1990s dramatically transformed the way companies used their supply chains to achieve competitive advantage. This has led to the emergence of the 'e-business' concept. The term 'e-business' was coined by Lou Gerstner, CEO of IBM. It refers to the transformation of key business processes through the use of internet technologies (IBM, 1997). E-business refers to the use of ITC for the buying and selling of goods and services (also known as e-commerce), collaborating with business partners, and conducting electronic transactions within an organization (Turban et al, 2007). The impact of e-business covers both business-to-business (B2B) and business-to-consumer (B2C) transactions.

The digital revolution has driven the development of e-business. Early applications can be traced back to the 1960s, but e-business only became popular in the 1990s due to the widespread use of the internet. Since 1995, e-business, particularly through online trading activities, has experienced an explosive growth with many companies starting to sell or advertise their products or services on the internet. Many of these developments related to B2C activities. However, by 2000 many of the new dot.com companies collapsed, largely due to their business models being unsustainable. Since then, there has been a period of reassessment, followed by strong double-digit growth (Laudon and Traver, 2008). No longer a niche technology, the internet is a commercial mass medium, with internet penetration rates approaching a quarter of the world's population (Miniwatts Marketing Group, 2009).

The new e-business technologies have led to significant changes within supply chains, with alternative ways of doing business, improved visibility and changes to distribution channels, including new intermediaries. The aim of this chapter is to discuss how these changes have impacted upon green logistics. B2B and B2C logistics are considered separately. In the case of B2B relationships, e-business has particularly focused upon improved efficiency and accuracy. For B2C operations, it has presented new marketing opportunities, affecting the whole nature of distribution channels. However, as companies increase their use of ICT, there is a need to consider the environmental impact of these changes (Crowley, 1998; Hesse, 2002)

BUSINESS-TO-BUSINESS (B2B)

Since the 1960s, there has been an increasing use of inter-organizational systems to improve the efficiency of information flows within businesses. Material requirements planning (MRP) has given way to enterprise resource planning (ERP), enabling whole businesses to operate from a common system. More recently, there has been increasing awareness of the importance of B2B connectivity to achieve better communication and collaboration between an organization and its customers and suppliers (Horvath, 2001; Wilson and Vlosky, 1998). One response to this has been the extended ERP (or ERPII) system. However, with the growth of internet access, electronic marketplaces (EMs) have become more common as they are easier to join for potential participants (Christiaanse, Diepen and Damsgaard, 2004).

Definitions of an EM are diverse. One of the earliest and broadest definitions is offered by Bakos (1991), who referred to an EM as 'an inter-organizational system that allows the participating buyers and sellers to exchange information about price and product offerings'. Daniel et al (2004) narrowed the definition and described EM as 'web-based systems which enable automated transaction, trading or collaboration between business partners'. Using web companies can reduce the complexity and cost of implementation and ease the integration with other systems. EMs are emerging quickly as a viable alternative to large-scale client-server solutions, especially where they are hosted by the technology provider (also known as 'software as service', Cherbakov et al, 2005). In the context of logistics, EMs can be termed electronic logistics marketplaces (ELMs).

Types of electronic logistics marketplace

- Open marketplaces: open ELMs tend to focus on matching the supply and demand of transport with no barriers to entry; examples are online freight exchanges for the spot trading of transport services. Early ELMs were open systems, such as www.teleroute.com, and mainly price driven (Gosain and Palmer, 2004). Hauliers are often reluctant to join an open ELM, as they fear being judged purely on carriage rates and not on total service delivery. A trend was observed that 'early days of freight exchanges must now put less emphasis on open-market exchanges and more on their ability to work with closed communities of users who trade with each other' (Lewis, 2002; Rowlands, 2003). This has resulted in the recent development of closed ELMs, aiming for long-term collaboration between shippers and carriers.
- Private marketplaces: this closed form of marketplace usually connects only one shipper to a range of carriers and works in isolation from any other ELM (Wang, Potter and Naim, 2007). Consequently, this ELM can only help to optimize one company's network. Developing the marketplace normally involves a computer software provider. The leader is responsible for the operation of the marketplace and the information flows through it. Because of its simplicity, there are clear lines of communication with a central point of control. One disadvantage is the set-up costs, particularly in terms of creating an interface between each participating company's system and the marketplace. This also means that companies may be bound to the marketplace. Finally, if a company is involved in a number of these ELMs, it may be exposed to repeated set-up costs.
- Shared marketplaces: these are similar to private marketplaces. However, information can also be communicated between the different ELMs. This happens because all of the marketplaces are hosted by a single organization and share the same platform. Only limited technical modifications are needed to provide connectivity. The integrated nature of the marketplace means it is possible to identify synergies between different distribution networks. However, there is only limited collaboration between companies from different marketplaces, with commercial sensitivity a major concern. The technological requirements of these marketplaces are also lower, with communication using a range of methods.

- Collaborative marketplaces: unlike previous structures, this form of marketplace is led by a consortium of organizations with a common interest in the system. The marketplace provides a community for multiple shippers, carriers and customers, encouraging a reduction in empty running by identifying synergies within product flows and sharing the capacity of carriers. Because multiple supply chains are involved, not only is there a high level of integration between shipper and carrier (vertical integration), but also a greater level of collaboration among shippers, and among carriers (horizontal collaboration). A risk is that most organizations will optimize their own operations, rather than across the whole network. Sharing of information between participants has to be clearly defined, especially for commercially sensitive data.

Figure 16.1 provides a generic overview of ELM operations, although the exact functionality varies between the different types of marketplace.

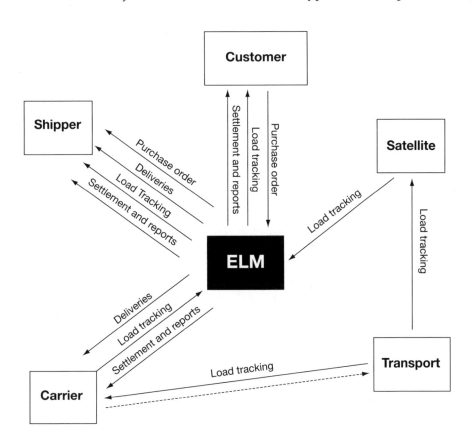

Figure 16.1 Overview of ELM operations

Environmental impact of B2B marketplaces

Many of the environmental benefits from using an ELM can be associated with the economic benefits. A key feature of open and closed ELMs is the ability to make good use of backloads. With open systems, carriers can bid for return loads where the vehicle would otherwise be returning empty. This ad hoc system will not necessarily generate an optimum solution but will reduce the level of empty running by goods vehicles. With a closed system, backloading can be managed more effectively, as the opportunities can be included when the system is planning the whole transport network. Therefore, greater optimization is possible. With a private marketplace, each network will be individually optimized. However, a collaborative ELM provides a global optimum across all networks, enabling outbound and return loads to potentially be provided by different shippers. A constraint to this is the compatibility of vehicles – for example, it would not be possible to backload a chemicals-carrying trailer with food products.

Most of the other environmental benefits arise from the use of closed ELMs due to their limits on who can participate and the greater functionality they offer, particularly in the area of load planning. Because participation is by invitation only, it is possible for shippers to impose constraints on which carriers they use. While traditionally many of these may relate to the vehicles operated, nowadays the opportunity exists to impose environmental criteria too. These could include environmental quality assurance (such as ISO14000) or restricting vehicles to those that meet certain standards (for example, Euro IV engines).

In terms of shipment planning, some closed ELMs allow carriers to input the availability of vehicles on a daily basis. From this, the system can then optimize deliveries so as to make the best use of each vehicle's capacity as well as maximizing the opportunities for backloading. The system will also identify opportunities for consolidation, either within a single network or across different networks depending upon the type of ELM used. If demand exceeds supply, there may also be the chance to delay deliveries to avoid the spot hire of vehicles, which may generate an empty return load.

Finally, many closed ELMs offer the opportunity for tracking and tracing loads. Where this occurs on a real-time basis, it may be possible to identify opportunities to re-route vehicles to avoid areas of congestion, such as those associated with accidents. This may mean that the vehicle needs to travel further. Therefore, from an environmental perspective, the emissions from these extra miles need to be balanced against those arising from the vehicle sitting in congestion.

BUSINESS-TO-CONSUMER (B2C)

Business-to-consumer (B2C) e-commerce is simply electronic retailing using the internet as a medium to place orders for goods, with the consumer interacting directly with the supplier's system. With the advent of internet shopping, the 'store-reach' boundaries of the traditional retailer have been extended literally to the global scale, as retailers are able to offer goods via the internet to the final consumer anywhere in the world, provided each has access to a computer. Such convenience and ease of transaction has resulted in the global retail industry witnessing a phenomenal growth in online shopping. Weltevereden (2007) reported that between 1999 and 2005 online retail sales grew by 720 per cent in the UK, 1,060 per cent in Germany and 1,403 per cent in the Netherlands. Today, over 85 per cent of the world's online population have used the internet to make a purchase (Nielsen, 2008) and B2C e-commerce is regarded as a popular mainstream activity by many consumers. Nevertheless, global headline figures hide a lack of uniformity in the acceptance and take-up of this medium.

Numerous factors (economic, infrastructural, cultural and political) apparently determine both businesses' and consumers' engagement with e-tailing. However, two main reasons for the importance of online shopping among internet users stand out. The first is the readiness of retailers to establish an initial online presence (see Nikolaeva, 2006). For instance, UK food retailers, as early adopters of e-commerce, have developed sophisticated online businesses. The second reason is the willingness of the population to embrace this new shopping experience. In South Korea (a nation known for its acceptance of new technology), 99 per cent of internet users have shopped online (compared with just a third of users in Egypt) (Nielsen, 2008). Consumer mistrust of online companies, the perceived quality of the merchandise they sell and online payment security issues will together partly explain low user transaction levels, although the real engagement with B2C e-commerce in many developing countries may be obscured, as few countries have comprehensive information on online sales and purchases (UN, 2007),

Within Europe, the UK is firmly established as the most developed online market, with online sales amounting to €18.5bn in 2007, considerably ahead of sales amongst its European counterparts: Germany, €13bn; France, €7bn; Italy, €1.1bn and Spain, €1bn (Mintel, 2008). At a global level, with double-digit, year-on-year growth forecasts, the share of online retail sales is set to increase significantly over the coming years, though the online sales growth in the United States is expected to slow to 11 per cent in 2009 (Forrester Research, 2009).

Types of e-retailers

Multi-channel retailers (bricks and clicks)

Most traditional retail companies have set up a multi-channel business model, whereby they have a physical store (bricks) and an online presence (clicks), running both models in parallel (see Agatz, Fleischmann and van Nunen, 2008). Rather than duplicating their efforts, multi-channel retailers usually use existing distribution infrastructure and retail networks (at least initially) to lower their online set-up costs. The presence of physical stores also allows easier product returns options for online customers. Equally, established retailers gain from brand identity and, in some cases, the transferral of their customer base to the online mode (although online shoppers are notoriously fickle when choosing websites to purchase from, often opting for choice, convenience and price over loyalty to any one particular high-street retailer).

From an operations management perspective, multi-channel retailers may benefit from synergies across their respective retail channels (Agatz, Fleischmann and van Nunen, 2008). Many prefer to operate their upstream online businesses from within their general warehouses (integrated fulfilment). As a result, such retailers hold common stock within their pre-existing warehouse set-up. Physical products are shipped from the distribution centres (DCs) to either their physical retail stores or their separate online operations. Under such arrangements, cross-channel visibility is essential to prevent under or over-stocking across the organization.

A highly successful recent venture on the part of multi-channel retailers has been the introduction of a click and collect service, where retailers, notably Argos and Comet in the UK, take advantage of their physical store presence, as goods purchased online can be collected from a store of the customer's choosing in as little as 30-minutes after the original order was placed. This popular option among consumers has added benefits to the retailer, as once in-store customers can be encouraged to make supplementary offline purchases. At peak times, two-thirds of online shoppers may opt for click and collect, potentially making this a lucrative sales opportunity for multi-channel retailers. Retailers who rely solely on a high-street presence (bricks and mortar) are relatively few in number, as multi-channel retailing is now seen as the norm. Multi-channel retailers account for the majority of online sales.

Pure play retailers (e-tailers)

These are dedicated online retailers who use the internet as their only means of trading. Many of these companies are small, and most are relatively young entrants to the retail market. Although not burdened with the costs of running physical stores, their relative inexperience in the retail environment meant that during the late 1990s and into the early 2000s numerous early pure play businesses disappeared. They were either taken over by major retail groups (Vishwanath and Mulvin, 2001) or more frequently, failed owing to losses derived from costly, inefficient order-fulfilment set-ups (Fernie and McKinnon, 2009). For instance, Peapod, the US online grocery, was taken over by Royal Ahold NV. It seemed, at the time, that only large 'niche' pure play retailers would be able to compete with multi-channel retailers. Amazon.com, probably one of the most widely recognized and successful pure play companies, only recorded its first profit in 2001, having launched in 1995. Recent late arrivals to e-tailing, however, have had the opportunity to learn from their predecessors' earlier mistakes (Xing and Grant, 2006), and many are carving sizeable online markets for themselves (Stone, 2008). Indeed some previously conventional retail companies such as Littlewoods and Dixons in the UK have closed their physical stores and become pure online retailers.

At the same time, some pure play e-tailers have developed into multi-channel retailers by opening physical stores in addition to their online business (iParty.com in the United States currently operates out of 50 stores along the East Coast, while UK-based Long Tall Sally has 22 stores nationwide). This transition to a clicks and bricks operation is a much harder conversion for companies, as they have to build in the high fixed costs of managing a store. Thus far, few have been successful in creating a prominent high-street presence.

Mail-order companies

Catalogue and mail-order companies have extended into the online market, seeing the potential of the internet to lure additional younger and wealthier clienteles than those who traditionally bought from catalogues. Online orders in the UK make up half of Findel's mail order sales, with Littlewoods, the UK's market leader, expecting similar revenue sales from its online channel. Boden, originally a catalogue retailer, now receives over 4,000 orders a day on its UK website.

Contrary to initial predictions, companies that retain the printed catalogue as a form of marketing are experiencing growth in this medium; customers favour browsing a printed catalogue before ordering online (flick and click), with many of them then choosing to keep the catalogue for future reference (Royal Mail, 2007).

Wholesalers or producers using the internet to sell directly to customers

Additionally, inventory for online retailers may be held at wholesalers until the orders have been received, then shipped directly to the customer from the wholesaler. The retailer handles only the transaction, not the goods (see Bailey and Rabinovich, 2005). This arrangement is referred to as drop-shipment.

E-auction companies

Some companies sell through e-auction sites such as eBay in addition to other media. Many sell their leftover stock, returns and goods with slight defects on such sites, but increasingly companies are viewing this as just another medium through which to sell their normal goods.

RESTRUCTURING OF THE SUPPLY CHAIN

With the expected growth in online shopping over the next few years, additional DCs, purpose-built e-fulfilment centres and larger vehicle fleets will be required to meet the increased volume of goods that require delivery. This is because, while digitally delivered items (music, holidays and financial services etc) purchased on the internet usually require no physical distribution, the vast majority of goods bought online involve at least one freight trip for delivery to the end customer (Table 16.1). IMRG (2006) estimated that approximately 540 million parcels were delivered to online customers in the UK in 2006. Home Delivery Network Limited, a leading parcel carrier in the UK, alone handles in excess of 116 million items ordered online each year.

This fundamental shift in fulfilment strategies away from high-volume cases and bulk store distribution to smaller customer orders (often of single items) delivered to highly dispersed addresses has environmental implications.

THE ENVIRONMENTAL IMPACT OF E-COMMERCE

Most parcels are delivered in diesel-operated, light goods vehicles (small vans), and total vehicle mileage for this category of vehicle has increased (by 40 per cent over the past 10 years in the UK), highlighting the more frequent movement of smaller quantities of goods. Fuel consumption has

Table 16.1 Items bought online in the past three months

Item	Percentage
Books	41
Clothing/accessories/shoes	36
Videos/DVDs/games	24
Airline tickets/reservations	24
Electronic equipment (TVs/cameras etc)	23
Music	19
Cosmetics/nutrition supplies	19
Computer hardware	16
Tours/hotel reservations	16
Event tickets	15
Computer software	14
Groceries	14
Toys/dolls	9
Sporting goods	8
Automobiles and parts	4
Sports memorabilia	3
Other	20

Source: Nielsen (2008).

also increased, as smaller vehicles consume more fuel per tonne moved than larger vehicles. They also produce more pollution. The average small van (1.5 tonnes) generates around 4.6 times more CO_2 per tonne-km than larger vehicles (DfT, 2003). Yet there appears to be a widely held view among consumers that online purchases and home delivery are beneficial to the environment because they reduce personal travel demand. To reinforce this assumption, some online retailers have been actively promoting the environmental benefits of online shopping (Smithers, 2007).

Several aspects of online shopping appear to offset any initial environmental gains (Sarkis, Meade and Talluir, 2004). These include:

- It involves increased (relatively inefficient) home delivery movements (Kröger, Fergusson and Skinner, 2003).
- Customer orders are smaller (often of single items).
- Customers tend to purchase separate items from several different web-based companies (each requiring separate delivery). Previously, goods would have been bought on one trip to the shops.
- Additional sortation is required to combine multiple customers' orders prior to delivery (de Koster, 2002). Some companies do not deliver the whole of a customer's multi-order in one trip because of the timing of the picking process.
- Additional trips are generated when the time saved by shopping online is converted into travel for other out-of-home activities by either the car owner or other members of the household (Gould and Golob, 1997; Cullinane, Edwards and McKinnon, 2008). As a result, there is an increase in total vehicle miles travelled.
- Internet-browsing encourages people to go shopping for additional and/or supplementary purchases (Skinner et al, 2004). Sourcing information on the internet allows for greater price transparency.
- Goods may be sourced from further afield, requiring more transport.
- There are minimal travel savings for online shopping, when goods, if purchased via the conventional channel, would have been bought as part of an overall multi-activity trip, referred to as a trip chain (Primerano et al, 2008).
- Additional freight movements are created in cases where customers previously walked or cycled to the shops.

Delivery conflicts

Delivery to the home is a key customer service, and can be classified into attended or unattended delivery. For attended delivery, a time slot (delivery window) is agreed between the supplier and the customer, the width and timing (including lead-time) of which are crucial. There is a conflict here between the requirements of supplier and customer. For the supplier, the wider the delivery window, the lower the delivery cost, whereas for the customer, the narrower the delivery window the less time is spent waiting around for the delivery. This conflict is essentially the root cause of why so many companies have trouble entering the online market. Customer satisfaction requires prompt and reliable delivery and this is extremely costly for the supplier as very few customers are willing to pay extra for a timed delivery service. Partly because of the need for wide delivery windows on the part of suppliers, delivery companies have to deal with the problem of failed delivery, when no one is home to receive the delivery;

most shoppers state that they have experienced difficulty in receiving parcel deliveries to the home.

Failed delivery

Estimations of first-time delivery failure rates vary considerably. For instance in the UK, figures range from almost a quarter (McLeod, Cherrett and Song, 2006) to one in every eight attempts (IMRG, 2006). Such delivery failures lead to increased costs on the part of carriers as packages need to be redelivered at a later date. Ultimately, after several failed attempts at delivery, a very small percentage of parcels are returned to sender, or being undeliverable, are disposed of by the carrier.

Handling of customer returns

Online retailers experience far higher product returns than conventional retailers (Park and Regan, 2004), although the return rates depend largely on the type of product in question. Fashion clothing, for instance, has some of the highest return rates at between 20 and 40 per cent. To minimize the impact of returns on their operations, a parcel carrier may choose to collect returned items as part of its usual outbound delivery round. When dedicated pick-up runs are deployed for returns, additional mileage results. Many customers favour returning items via the postal services. In this case, the addition of returned items within the usual postal network will have a negligible environmental impact on the overall postal system.

CASE STUDY: ONLINE BOOKS SUPPLY CHAIN

Owing to their homogeneous nature, books are among the most popular purchases on the internet (PriceWaterhouseCooper, 2007). Yet the apparent ease with which books are purchased online conceals a complicated upstream online supply chain (Figure 16.2). Some 787 million books were produced in the UK in 2006 (Publishers Association, 2007), and there is a plethora of trading relations between the main book industry participants: authors, agents, publishers, printers, distributors, wholesalers, online retailers and consumers. For instance, some 44,000 publishers are thought to be active in the UK alone (KeyNote, 2007). Furthermore, the global book industry is in a constant state of flux, owing to ongoing mergers, acquisitions and supply chain 'swap-arounds'.

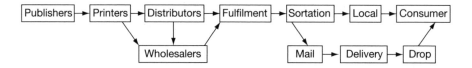

Figure 16.2 The online book supply chain: key players and their trading relationships

Environmental aspects of the online book industry

- Excess new stock: a great deal of uncertainty in the industry surrounds the success of new publications, especially from non-established authors. Inaccurate sales forecasts and poorly planned print-run decisions can leave publishers with excess stock. Online book retailers, acknowledged as experts in the sale of the 'long tail' of slow-moving books, are ideally placed to provide a medium for the disposal of such stock.
- Sale or return: books are usually bought by retailers on a sale-or-return basis (on consignment). Conventional retailers have had no reason to resist new stock because it carries very little supply risk and this practice appears to have transferred to online retailers.
- Reverse logistics: traditionally, return rates in the UK have been as high as 25–27 per cent for paperback books (softbacks), yet there has been little incentive for publishers/distributors to recycle these returns. Assuming on-consignment arrangements will become commonplace amongst online retailers, the reverse flow of returned books will become even more of an issue for book publishers and distributors as online retailers return unwanted stock. This problem is exacerbated, as it appears to be more financially viable to reprint a new book in bulk in the Far East than to attempt to recycle a returned book into the forward supply chain. As a result, a high percentage of returned stock is sent for immediate pulping; even books in near-mint condition, suitable for the secondary (remainders) market, are pulped, and this incidence looks set to increase.
- Packaging: while online retailers receive bulk consignments of books, they deliver small orders, each often containing a single book, to individual homes. One leading online bookseller in the UK has a policy of only shipping orders as individual items, regardless of whether multiple-itemed orders are received.

THE FUTURE

As already mentioned, one of the limitations of the internet is that, in the case of attended delivery, someone has to be available to receive the purchase, and deliveries are often restricted to business hours only. Owing to the impracticalities of this requirement, much work has been undertaken into developing unattended (not at home) delivery solutions that increase delivery flexibility while ensuring delivery security. Issues arise when sensitive product categories, by virtue of either their size or specific handling requirements (for example, those needing refrigeration) are delivered. Alternative delivery solutions include secure home-based reception (or 'drop') boxes and local and community collection-and-delivery points (CDPs). After a first-time delivery failure, instead of making re-attempts, a parcel carrier could use a secure alternative. For the supplier or carrier, time and fuel are saved, while for the customer, delivery is guaranteed. Specialist equipment, however, can be costly, and companies need to be aware of the potential financial outlay. One of the pioneers of the US online grocery market, Streamline, went out of business in late 2000, unable to recoup its investments in providing customers with refrigerated reception boxes (Agatz, Fleischmann and van Nunen, 2008).

At individual residential addresses, for luxury new-builds integral fixed boxes can be installed into property at the time of construction, or alternatively, if the owners wish, an external box can be fitted retrospectively. At an area level, CDPs may be a preferred alternative, where customers retrieve or return items purchased online from a dedicated, secure location (see Weltevereden, 2008). To date CPDs have been used mostly in the B2B market, although their appeal to the B2C market is growing (Fernie and McKinnon, 2009). Little additional consumer travel will result if they are located either near residential areas (eg local stores/ post offices) or at locations often frequented by consumers (eg railway stations).

REFERENCES

Agatz, NAH, Fleischmann, M and van Nunen, JA (2008) E-fulfillment and multi-channel distribution: a review, *European Journal of Operational Research*, **187**, pp 339–56

Bailey, JP and Rabinovich, R (2005) Internet book retailing and supply chain management: an analytical study of inventory location speculation and postponement, *Transportation Research Part E*, **41**, pp 159–77

Bakos, JY (1991) A strategic analysis of electronic marketplaces, *MIS Quarterly*, **15**, pp 295–310

Cherbakov, L, Galambos, G, Harishankar, R, Kalyana, S and Rackham, G (2005) Impact of service orientation at the business level, *IBM Systems Journal*, **44**, pp 653–68

Christiaanse, E, Diepen, TV and Damsgaard, J (2004) Proprietary versus internet technologies and the adoption and impact of electronic market-places, *Journal of Strategic Information Systems*, **13**, pp 151–65

Crowley, J (1998) Virtual logistics: transport in the marketspace, *International Journal of Physical Distribution & Logistics Management*, **28**, pp 547–74

Cullinane, SL, Edwards, JB and McKinnon, AC (2008) Clicks and bricks on campus: the environmental impact of online food shopping, Proceedings of the Logistics Research Network, Annual Conference, September, Liverpool

Daniel, EM, Hoxmeier, J, White, A and Smart, A (2004) A framework for the sustainability of e-marketplaces, *Business Process Management Journal*, **10**, pp 277–90

de Koster, MBM (2002) The logistics behind the enter click, in *Quantitative Approaches to Distribution Logistics and Supply Chain Management*, ed A Klose, MG Speranza and LN Van Wassenhove, pp 131–48, Springer, Berlin

Department for Transport (DfT) (2003) *Key Performance Indicators for the Food Supply Chain*, Benchmarking Guide 78, Department for Transport, London

Fernie, J and McKinnon, A (2009) The development of e-tail logistics, in *Logistics and Retail Management: Insights into current practice and trends from leading experts*, 3rd edn, ed J Fernie and L Sparks, pp 164–86, Kogan Page, London

Forrester Research (2009) *Topic Overview: US online retail*, Forrester Research, New York

Gosain, S and Palmer, JW (2004) Exploring strategic choices in market-place positioning, *Electronic Markets*, **14**, pp 308–21

Gould, J and Golob, TF (1997) *Shopping Without Travel or Travel Without Shopping? An investigation of electronic home shopping*, Institute of Transportation Studies, Center for Activity Systems Analysis, University of California, Irvine Papers UCIITSASWP972

Hesse, M (2002) Shipping news: the implications of electronic commerce for logistics and freight transport, *Resources, Conservation and Recycling*, **36**, pp 211–40

Horvath, L (2001) Collaboration: the key to value creation in supply chain management, *Supply Chain Management: An International Journal*, **6**, pp 205–07

IBM (1997) [accessed 5 June 2007] History of IBM [Online] http://www-03.ibm.com/ibm/history/history/year_1997.html

IMRG (2006) *Valuing Home Delivery: A cost–benefit analysis*, IMRG, London

KeyNote (2007) [accessed 25 August 2009] *Book Retailing on the Internet*, KeyNote Report [Online] http://www.marketresearch.com/product/display.asp?productid=1430685. Accessed 6 April 2008

Kröger, K, Fergusson, M and Skinner, I (2003) Critical issues in decarbonising transport: the role of technologies, Tyndall Centre Working Paper No 36, University of East Anglia, Norwich

Laudon, KC and Traver, CG (2008) *E-Commerce: Business, technology, society*, 4th edn, Pearson, London

Lewis, CN (2002) Freight exchanges, *E-logistics Magazine*, January [accessed 6 May 2008] [Online] http://www.elogmag.com/magazine/16/index.shtml

McLeod, F, Cherrett, T and Song, L (2006) Transport impacts of local collection/delivery points, *International Journal of Logistics: Research and Applications*, **9**, pp 307–17

Miniwatts Marketing Group (2009) [accessed 18 May 2009] Internet world stats: usage and population statistics [Online] http://www.internetworldstats.com/stats.htm,

Mintel (2008) *E-commerce: Europe*, Mintel Report, London

Nielsen (2008) *Trends in Online Shopping: A Global Nielsen consumer report*, February 2008, Haarlem

Nikolaeva, R (2006) E-commerce adoption in the retail sector: empirical insights, *International Journal of Retail & Distribution Management*, **34**, pp 369–87

Park, M and Regan, A (2004) *Issues in Home Delivery Operations*, Research Paper, University of California, Transportation Center, Los Angeles

PriceWaterhouseCooper (2007) *The Internet: This time it's for real*, PriceWaterhouseCoopers Consultants, London

Primerano, F, Taylor, MA, Pitaksringkarn, L and Tisato, P (2008) Defining and understanding trip chaining behaviour, *Transportation*, **35**, pp 55–72

Publishers' Association (2007) *UK Book Industry in Statistics*, 2006, The Publishers' Association, London

Rowlands, P (2003) Freight exchanges, *E-logistics Magazine*, January [accessed 6 May 2008] [Online] http://www.elogmag.com//magazine/25/xchanges.shtml

Royal Mail (2007) *Home Shopping Tracker*, Royal Mail, London

Sarkis, J, Meade, LM and Talluri, S (2004) E-logistics and the natural environment, *Supply Chain Management: An International Journal*, **9**, pp 303–12

Skinner, I, Fergusson, M, Kröger, K, Kelly, C and Bristow, A (2004) *Critical Issues in Decarbonising Transport*, Final Report of the Theme 2 project T222, Tyndall Centre for Climate Change Research, University of East Anglia, Norwich

Smithers, R (2007) Supermarket home delivery service promotes its green credentials, *Guardian*, 12 September 2007, [accessed 6 December 2007] [Online] http://www.guardian.co.uk/environment/2007/sep/12/plasticbags.supermarkets

Stone, A (2008) Small business niche players profit online, *The Sunday Times*, 27 July 2008 [accessed 11 August 2008] [Online] http://business.timesonline.co.uk/tol/business/entrepreneur/article4406065.ece

Turban, E, Leidner, D, McLean, E and Wetherbe, J (2007) *Information Technology for Management: Transforming business in the digital economy*, 6th edn, John Wiley & Sons, New York

United Nations (2007) *Information Economy Report 2007–2008, Science and Technology for Development: The new paradigm of ICT*, United Nations Conference on Trade and Development, UN, New York and Geneva

Vishwanath, V and Mulvin, G (2001), Multi-channels: the real winners in the B2C internet wars, *Business Strategy Review*, **12**, pp 25–33

Wang, Y, Potter, A and Naim, M (2007) Electronic marketplaces for tailored logistics, *Industrial Management & Data Systems*, **107**, pp 1170–87

Weltevereden, J (2007) *Winkelen in het Internettijdperk* [Shopping in the Internet Age] (in Dutch), NAI Ultgevers, Rotterdam

Weltevereden, J (2008) B2C e-commerce logistics: the rise of collection-and-delivery points in the Netherlands, *International Journal of Retail & Distribution Management*, **36**, pp 638–60

Wilson, DT and Vlosky, RP (1998) Interorganizational information system technology and buyer–seller relationships, *Journal of Business & Industrial Marketing*, **13**, pp 215–34

Xing, Y and Grant, DB (2006) Developing a framework for measuring physical distribution channel and 'pure player', *Internet Retailers*, **34**, pp 278–89

Part 5

PUBLIC POLICY PERSPECTIVE

17

The role of government in promoting green logistics

Alan McKinnon

INTRODUCTION

This book contains many examples of companies reducing the environmental impact of their logistics operations. While these corporate initiatives are gathering momentum, it is unlikely that the free market on its own will deliver an environmentally sustainable logistics system, particularly within the required time frame. A key attribute of such a system will be carbon emissions per unit of product delivered that are well below the current level. Logistics will be expected to make a large contribution to the drastic reductions in CO_2 emissions that will be required by 2050 to contain the global temperature increase within 2°C by 2100. Industry cannot be expected to achieve this on its own. It will require concerted action by companies, citizens and government to reach the necessary carbon reduction targets. Governments also have a strong interest in 'greening' other aspects of logistics to improve the general quality of the environment. While great progress has been made over the past 20 years in cleaning exhaust emissions, cutting vehicle noise levels and reducing the involvement of freight vehicles in accidents, the potential exists to attain significantly higher environmental standards.

There has been a long history of government intervention in the freight transport sector. This was traditionally motivated by a desire to correct market anomalies, particularly in the competition between transport modes. In most developed countries, regulatory frameworks were established to control the supply of freight transport capacity, impose obligations on carriers and/or influence the tariffs that they could charge. Over the past 30 years most of these quantitative regulations on freight transport have been removed as part of a general process of market liberalization, to be replaced by qualitative controls designed to maintain operating standards and professionalism in the freight industry (McKinnon, 1998). It is over this period that environmental concerns have begun to play an increasingly important role in the formulation of freight transport policy. It is ironic that while liberalization measures have been facilitating the growth of freight movement, governments have been intensifying their efforts to reduce its impact on the environment.

As explained in Chapter 1, official definitions of sustainability used in the context of freight transport/logistics generally encapsulate the concept of the triple bottom line (Savitz, 2006). This aims to reconcile economic, environmental and social objectives in a fair and balanced manner. Building on the Brundtland Commission's definition of sustainable development, the UK government defined the 'aim of its sustainable distribution strategy' as being 'to ensure that the future development of the distribution industry does not compromise the future needs of our society, economy and environment' (DETR, 1999). As the growth, efficiency and reliability of freight transport are seen as being intimately linked to economic development, governments are naturally reluctant to impose environmental constraints on the movement of goods that would be damaging to the economy. The updated version of the UK government's sustainable logistics strategy, published nine years later, continues to adopt this broad definition of sustainability, aiming to reconcile climate change, competitiveness/productivity, equal opportunities, quality of life, safety, security and health objectives (DfT, 2008a). In this respect they are applying what Whitelegg (1995) calls the 'weak' form of sustainability, in which environmental objectives are traded off against social and economic objectives. The 'strong' form, which involves the imposition of environmental controls regardless of their economic and social consequences, may have to be more widely applied in the future to address the problem of climate change.

Since the 1980s, environmental policies on freight transport have evolved in several respects. First, their emphasis on particular externalities has shifted, partly because of the success of earlier policy initiatives but mainly because of a general re-ordering of environmental priorities at national and international levels. Second, policy objectives have become more wide-ranging and specific, with clearer definition of targets and timescales. Third, the policy 'tool-kit' has been expanded to include a broader range of measures. Some national governments, such as those of the Netherlands, the UK, the United States and France, have been more innovative than others in devising new methods of 'greening' the freight transport system. The more progressive ones have also recognized the need to make freight transport policies sensitive to wider logistical and supply chain trends. As companies now manage transport as an integral part of a logistics strategy, governments must understand the interrelationship between transport and other logistical activities if they are to be able to influence corporate behaviour. For example, a decade ago the UK government acknowledged that 'a sustainable distribution strategy should consider more than just the transport of goods from A to B.' It should also 'encompass supply chain management or "logistics" as well as all modes of transport' (DETR, 1999). Fourth, funding for sustainable distribution/logistics programmes has generally increased to support this broader array of policy measures. Fifth, knowledge has accumulated in government circles of the relative cost-effectiveness of different sustainable logistics strategies. International networking through organizations like the International Transport Forum[1] and the European Union has helped to disseminate this information and identify the most promising measures. There nevertheless remain wide international differences in the nature, scale and resourcing of government programmes designed to improve the environmental performance of logistics.

Although formal policy statements on sustainable freight/distribution/logistics usually emerge from national transport ministries, the environmental impact of freight transport is influenced by a broad spectrum of governmental decisions at central and local levels. The demand for freight movement is affected by government policies on the economy, industry, regional development, energy, land-use planning and recycling, which are the responsibility of several departments. Some of the goals of these various policies are in conflict. For example, efforts to promote industrial development (or 'social cohesion') in peripheral regions typically generate more freight movement per tonne of product produced, while by inflating the real cost of holding inventory, monetary policy can cause companies to tighten just-in-time regimes, often at the expense of poorer vehicle utilization. Differences in the level of tax imposed on different transport modes are often determined more by budgetary requirements than by an assessment of their relative environmental impacts. Although politicians frequently espouse the virtues of 'joined-up' government, in practice there is often little cross-ministry coordination of all the government decisions affecting the freight transport system.

This chapter will focus on the 'green logistics' initiatives of central governments and multinational organizations. Earlier chapters, particularly Chapter 14 on city logistics, have examined the efforts of local government to reduce the environmental impact of logistics.

OBJECTIVES OF PUBLIC POLICY ON SUSTAINABLE LOGISTICS

The UK government declared a fairly comprehensive set of objectives for its 'sustainable distribution strategy' (DETR, 1999). It aimed to:

- improve the efficiency of distribution;
- minimize congestion;
- make better use of transport infrastructure;
- minimize pollution and reduce greenhouse gas emissions;
- manage development pressures on the landscape – both natural and anthropogenic;
- reduce noise and disturbance from freight movements;
- reduce the number of accidents, injuries and cases of ill-health associated with freight movement.

The government addressed all the main externalities associated with logistics, though it excluded visual intrusion (Baugham, 1979), where people object to the appearance of freight vehicles and warehouses in 'sensitive' environments, and community severance, where a transport link carrying large amounts of freight traffic acts as a barrier to social interaction. Several of the objectives were mutually reinforcing. Improving the efficiency of distribution, for example, can reduce freight traffic levels, thus easing congestion and mitigating a range of environmental effects, as well as saving money. Others were potentially in conflict. For example, in the absence of noise-abatement measures, running trucks out-of-hours to make better use of infrastructural capacity can exacerbate the noise problem on busy roads and around distribution centres during the night.

POLICY MEASURES

Governments have a range of policy instruments that they can deploy to reduce the environmental impact of freight transport/logistics. These can be divided into six broad categories:

- Taxation: this comprises mainly fuel taxes, vehicle excise duty (VED) and road-user charges.

- Financial incentives: these can take various forms. For example, they can support capital investment by companies in new equipment or infrastructure, or subsidize the use of greener freight modes or urban consolidation depots.
- Regulation: this can be applied to vehicle design and operation, the status of the freight operators, the tariffs they charge and even the capacity of the freight sector.
- Liberalization: the liberalization, and privatization, of freight markets can also have environmentally beneficial effects by, for example, enabling rail companies to compete more effectively for traffic or giving own-account truck operators permission to backload with other firms' traffic.
- Infrastructure and land-use planning: this includes the construction and management of network infrastructure and terminals, controls on vehicle access to infrastructure and the zoning of land uses for logistics-related activity.
- Advice and exhortation: governments have a role in identifying and promoting best environmental practice in freight transport, often working closely with trade associations.

Under each of these headings, there are many specific measures that can be applied, giving government considerable flexibility in the way it influences the behaviour of organizations involved in logistics. The policy maker must exercise considerable skill however in designing a package of measures that in combination achieve the declared objectives. This can be difficult in the field of sustainable logistics because many of the measures are relatively new and their longer-term impact and relative cost-effectiveness are still uncertain. Nor is there a single optimum policy mix for all countries and regions. The package of measures will always need to be tailored to the particular circumstances of a country's geography, freight market, infrastructure and industrial strategy, as well as the weighting attached by politicians and the public to different environmental effects.

Figure 17.1 shows the interrelationship between some of the more important sustainable logistics measures and the key freight parameters identified in Chapter 1 that link freight-related externalities to economic growth. By modifying these parameters, public policy interventions can reduce the environmental impact of freight transport even within an expanding economy. Figure 17.1 shows that some of the measures are likely to have targeted impact on specific parameters and objectives while others can exert a wider influence on the freight transport system and simultaneously address several policy objectives.

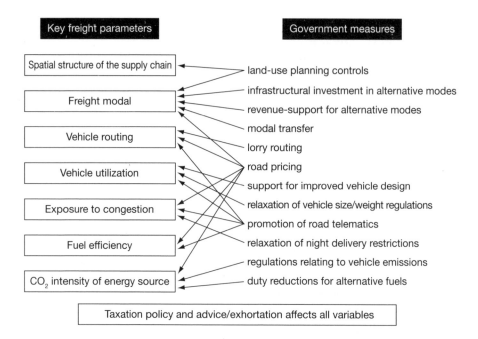

Figure 17.1 Relationship between key freight transport parameters and government transport policy measures

In designing a package of sustainable logistics measures, policy makers must take account of possible 'second-order effects'. There is always a risk that the application of a green measure in one area of logistics will have an offsetting effect elsewhere. The most prevalent second-order effect in this field results from those measures that cut cost in addition to reducing the burden on the environment. These measures are generally lauded for being self-financing and thus commercially attractive to businesses. By reducing the cost of transport per tonne-km, however, they can, perversely, cause a re-adjustment of logistical cost trade-offs and promote developments, such as wider sourcing or greater centralization, that actually generate more freight movement. In some cases it may be necessary to introduce additional taxes and/or regulations to suppress undesirable second-order effects.

The following review of public policy measures will focus on five aspects of sustainable logistics strategy:

- freight transport intensity;
- freight modal split;
- vehicle utilization;

- energy efficiency;
- level of externalities.

REDUCING FREIGHT TRANSPORT INTENSITY

In its White Paper on transport the European Commission (2001: 15) stated that 'We have to consider the option of gradually breaking the link between economic growth and transport growth.' This policy statement did not specifically mention freight, though as Meersman and Van de Voorde (2002: 2) explain: 'the European Commission refers primarily to freight transport when it argues that transport growth should be gradually decoupled from economic growth.' This proposal was not officially adopted as an EU policy objective, however, and it did not appear in the mid-term review of the White Paper. This review document emphasized the need to divorce the growth in mobility from the related externalities rather than to cut mobility relative to GDP (European Commission, 2006). The EU and national governments are committed to promoting economic growth and naturally fear that attempts to constrain increases in the amount of freight movement might adversely affect future growth prospects. Ironically, in recent years, across the EU as a whole the trend in freight tonne-kms has been decoupling from GDP growth though, as far as the environment is concerned, in the wrong direction (European Environment Agency, 2008). The freight transport intensity of the EU economy has been increasing, generating more tonne-kms per billion euros of output. At a national level in the EU, the trend varies widely, with some countries exhibiting pronounced positive decoupling and others significantly reducing freight growth per unit of GDP (McKinnon, Piecyk and Somerville, 2008). In the latter countries, governments can argue that freight transport intensity is already declining, removing the need for explicit transport-reduction strategies. This, for instance, will make it easier for them to meet climate change obligations (McKinnon, 2007). The UK Department for Transport (2008a: 19) argues that 'the decoupling demonstrates that the economic growth in UK GDP is not currently reliant on freight tonne-km growth and therefore economic growth is not directly linked to increased greenhouse gas emissions due to freight activity.' At least some of this freight–GDP decoupling, however, is likely to be the result of manufacturing operations being offshored to low-labour-cost countries, taking with them all the externalities associated with the inbound logistics operation. While national environmental footprints are then reduced, freight transport intensity and total freight-related externalities are increased at a planetary level. Statistical evidence of decoupling in one country should not, therefore, be taken as grounds for complacency on the part of freight transport policy makers.

As the magnitude of the global warming challenge becomes more apparent, it may ultimately be necessary for government to introduce explicit policies to curb the growth of tonne-kms. How then might this be achieved? It might have to be done as part of a deliberate down-sizing of national economies to bring the level of material consumption down to a more sustainable level. Alternatively, ways might have to be found of reducing freight tonne-kms within an expanding economy. This would require changes to the structure of supply chains, arresting and then reversing the geographical changes in production and distribution systems that have been key drivers of freight traffic growth for several decades. Promoting a return to more localized sourcing, greater vertical integration of production and more decentralized warehousing could all reduce freight transport intensity, but would require a reversal of well-established business trends. A series of fairly draconian measures might have to be imposed to achieve this, including steep increases in taxation, the re-introduction of quantitative controls on capacity in the freight sector and a moratorium on infrastructural development to allow traffic congestion to worsen and act as a constraint on future traffic growth. Because freight transport tends to have a relatively low price elasticity, tax levels would have to rise steeply, especially in those countries where they are currently low, to achieve a significant traffic reduction. If oil prices rise sharply in the medium to long term, market forces may relieve governments of the need to raise transport taxes (Fiorella et al, 2008). It is worth noting, for example, that the increase in the world price of oil over nine months, between September 2007 and June 2008, inflated diesel fuel prices in the UK by a greater margin than five years of the government's radical 'fuel-duty escalator' policy, which increased fuel taxes by 5–6 per cent per annum in real terms between 1994 and 1999.

Much less controversial and more cost-effective are government initiatives that encourage companies to reduce the amount of freight movement within their existing logistical systems and pattern of trading links. This can be achieved by, for example, routing vehicles more directly, probably with the support of computerized vehicle routing and scheduling (CVRS) as discussed in Chapter 10, or establishing swap arrangements between producers, as currently happens in the petroleum sector. As part of the UK government's Freight Best Practice programme, for example, companies are given advice on the use of CVRS (DfT, 2007), while in the Netherlands the government operated a 'transport prevention' programme for several years that gave companies guidance on ways of reducing their demand for freight movement by rationalizing their logistics operations.

SHIFTING FREIGHT TO GREENER TRANSPORT MODES

Getting freight off the road network and on to trains, barges and ships has traditionally been seen by policy makers and politicians as the most promising way of easing the environmental and congestion problems associated with goods movement. In most countries this would involve reversing a long-term modal shift to road. In Eastern Europe the shift from rail to road has been a much more recent and dramatic phenomenon that will be difficult to stop let alone reverse in the foreseeable future. Despite the efforts of governments around the world to stem the erosion of freight traffic from rail to road, in most countries this trend has continued. One of the few exceptions has been the UK where, partly as a result of the privatization of the state-owned rail freight company and the emergence of new operators, rail increased its share of the domestic surface freight market (ie road + rail) from 8.0 per cent in 1995 to 11.6 per cent in 2006 (DfT, 2008b).

All six categories of policy measure listed earlier can be used to rebalance the modal split. As observed in Chapter 6, some measures can be used to make rail and water-borne transport more attractive, while others can deter companies from using more environmentally damaging modes. This combination can exert pull and push pressures on companies' modal split decisions. Some of the major measures are discussed below.

Taxation

Differential levels of duty can be imposed on fuel consumed by different modes. Currently in the UK, diesel fuel used in trucks is taxed at 54 pence per litre, while that burned in diesel locomotives hauling freight trains attracts a tax of only 7 pence per litre. Not all fuel taxation is environmentally progressive, however. The most glaring anomaly is the exemption of aircraft kerosene from taxation, despite the fact that most of its pollutants and CO_2 are emitted high in the atmosphere where their damaging effect (or 'radiative forcing') is much greater than exhaust emissions from surface transport. Most air freight moves internationally and is bound by international treaties, mainly the Chicago Convention of 1944 and around 3,000 bilateral agreements between countries, which prohibit governments from taxing aviation fuel. It is likely to be only a matter of time before this historical legacy is corrected.

The introduction of road-user charging for trucks can also favour a switch to rail and water. The German government, for example, estimated that the

Maut would encourage a 6 per cent shift in long-distance freight tonne-kms to these alternative modes (McKinnon, 2006).

As discussed in Chapter 4, in an ideal world taxes on the various transport modes would be set at levels that internalized their marginal social/environmental costs. Within most countries, governments are still a long way from full application of the 'polluter-pays principle' to the freight sector. The internalization of the environmental costs of freight transport is currently high on the transport policy agenda in the EU and is likely to be implemented over the next 5–10 years.

Financial incentives

These can take various forms. The nature of government financial support for greener transport operations varies widely, reflecting differences in the ownership of the service and infrastructure providers, the nature of the freight market, competition policy and rules governing the award of state aid. Support typically comprises capital grants for rolling stock/vessels and terminal development, discounted infrastructure access payments or operating subsidies/revenue support grants. Such financial aid is usually conditional on the freight operator and/or client demonstrating that adequate environmental benefit accrues from the use of the alternative mode. For example, the Freight Facilities Grant Scheme, which has been in operation in the UK since 1974, provides capital support for rail freight investment where it can be demonstrated that environmental benefit will result from the use of rail rather than road. This benefit is calculated financially by estimating the number of 'sensitive lorry miles' that will be removed from different classes of road and multiplying them by appropriate monetary values for the environmental impact per mile. The grants awarded on the basis of this calculation effectively 'buy the removal of lorries from the road system' (DfT, 2009: 55). For example, between 1997 and 2008, a total of 38 freight facilities grants (FFGs) were awarded in Scotland with a total value of £58 million, predicted to remove 32.4 million lorry-miles per annum from Scottish roads (Scottish Government, 2009). A similar set of Waterborne Freight Grants is now available to incentivize a shift of freight from road to inland waterways and coastal shipping. At the EU level, the Marco Polo programme has been set up to promote, mainly by means of financial incentives, the use of intermodal transport services incorporating trunk haulage by rail, inland waterway or sea. The second phase of this programme, extending from 2007 to 2012, has the ambitious objective of diverting the equivalent of the forecast growth in international road tonne-kms in the EU to intermodal services.

Regulation

For much of the 20th century the governments of developed countries tried to use quantitative controls on the capacity and pricing of the road freight sector to protect rail freight operations against intermodal competition. This strategy proved largely ineffective, however, and was abandoned with the deregulation of the trucking industry in most developed countries between 1970 and 2000 (McKinnon, 1998). The governments of these countries appear to have little interest in the re-imposition of quantitative licensing or tariff restrictions on road transport to engineer a modal shift by regulation. Instead priority is being given to the liberalization of rail freight operations and the creation of commercial conditions in which rail can compete more effectively with road. Within Europe the EU and individual member states are also trying to improve the 'interoperability' of rail freight services among national rail networks to allow rail to exploit more effectively its comparative advantage in long-distance freight transport.

Infrastructural measures

In some countries the growth of rail freight is constrained by inadequate track capacity, particularly at peak times in and around conurbations, a lack of network access points, and physical constraints on the size and weight of rolling stock. In European countries governments have been actively investing in the installation of rail sidings, lengthening of refuges / loops, strengthening of track to support heavier rolling stock, expansion of the loading gauge, construction of freight-only lines and the development of intermodal terminals.

IMPROVING VEHICLE UTILIZATION

Despite the heavy emphasis that has been given to modal shift in government transport policies, in most countries road transport is going to remain by far the dominant mode of freight transport for the foreseeable future. Sustainable logistics policies must also therefore exploit the potential for improving the utilization of road freight capacity. For a given amount of freight movement, raising vehicle load factors reduces vehicle-kms, cutting transport costs, congestion levels, energy consumption and emissions. Chapter 9 examined the various methods that companies can use to improve vehicle fill. Here we will consider how much leverage government can exert on this critical parameter. Again, all six categories of policy measure can be used, to a greater or lesser extent, to influence vehicle utilization.

Taxation

In theory higher taxes on the ownership and/or operation of trucks will give companies an incentive to use them more efficiently. It has long been argued that the influence of taxes on vehicle load factors will be stronger and more targeted if they are related to the carrying capacity of the vehicle and the distance it travels. Over its first three years, for example, the Swiss Heavy Vehicle Fee (HFV) is reckoned to have significantly improved truck loading, particularly on backhauls. It is claimed that, 'the main reason for the more powerful effect of the HVF was its incentive for fully exploiting the logistic potential to optimize utilization of the vehicle fleet and especially avoiding empty runs' (Swiss Federal Office for Spatial Development, 2004: 22).

Financial incentives

As the vehicle operator gains a commercial benefit from improved loading, it should not be necessary for the government to provide an additional financial incentive. Governments at both central and national levels, however, have subsidized the development of urban consolidation schemes in an effort to rationalize the movement of freight in towns and cities. Browne et al (2005) review a range of urban consolidation initiatives around the world that have benefited from public support and created systems within which companies delivering and collecting goods in urban areas can combine loads and thereby improve vehicle fill. Their work suggests that such schemes generally require a continuing public subsidy to survive.

Regulation

The loading of vehicles is partly a function of the size and weight limits imposed by government. As mentioned in Chapter 9, vehicle utilization can be measured in terms of weight or volume. Many loads either weigh-out before they cube-out or vice versa, leaving some weight- or volume-carrying capacity unused. By relaxing maximum size and/or weight limits companies can consolidate loads, thus using some of this excess capacity. Both economic and environmental benefits can flow from such a measure, even after allowance has been made for any second-order modal shift or traffic-generating effects (McKinnon, 2005). In recent years, several studies have been conducted in the United States (Transportation Research Board, 2002), the Netherlands (ARCADIS, 2006), Germany (Umwelt Bundes Amt, 2007), UK (Knight et al, 2008) and the EU (Transport and Mobility Leuven et al, 2008) to assess the relative costs and benefits of permitting longer and heavier vehicles, and have arrived at differing conclusions. Government decision making on the issue of vehicle sizes and weights has been influenced mainly by concerns about safety, public opinion and the competitiveness of rail freight services. In some countries, it has been conditioned more by lobbying and emotion than hard facts.

Liberalization

Deregulation of the trucking sector has generally been accompanied by improvements in vehicle utilization (Cooper, 1991; McKinnon, 1998). When freed of operational constraints on backloading, vehicle movements and tariff levels, carriers can generally use their vehicle assets more intensively to yield economic and environmental benefits.

Advice, exhortation and accreditation

Several governments run advisory, benchmarking and promotional programmes to encourage companies, among other things, to improve the utilization of their vehicles. It may seem strange that governments feel the need to provide such support, given that efficient utilization of vehicle capacity is a core business skill and a key determinant of profitability. The advice is targeted as much at shippers, as at carriers however, and often publicizes new operational practices and technology in an effort to accelerate their uptake. A later section of this chapter gives examples of government advisory/accreditation schemes.

INCREASING ENERGY EFFICIENCY

Governments' efforts to raise the fuel efficiency of freight transport operations are often subsumed within general energy efficiency programmes spanning all sectors of the economy. These programmes usually comprise a combination of 'carrots and sticks', the 'carrots' taking the form of advisory/auditing services and financial support for the implementation of energy-saving technology and the main 'stick' being high fuel duty. They are motivated as much by a desire to cut total energy costs and reduce dependence on imported fossil fuels, as by environmental objectives. Again, a variety of policy measures can be deployed.

Raising fuel duty

The level of fuel consumption in the road freight sector is relatively sensitive to changes in fuel price. During the period of the UK government's 'fuel duty escalator' policy (1994–1999), the fuel duty rose around 30 per cent in real terms and the average fuel efficiency of road haulage operations increased by approximately 9 per cent. It is not known how much of this efficiency gain was due to the tax policy.

Subsidizing driver-training schemes

Such schemes offer a relatively cost-effective means of improving the fuel efficiency of trucks and vans and usually yield supplementary benefits in reduced accident involvement and lower insurance costs. The government-sponsored Safe and Fuel Efficient Driving (SAFED) programme in the UK, for example, has so far provided on-the-road training for over 7,000 drivers. Case studies of companies using this programme indicate average fuel savings ranging from 2.6 to 12 per cent (DfT, 2006). Regular training updates and incentive schemes can help to ensure that improvements in driving behaviour are maintained. Truck simulators have also been used for this purpose and offered comparable fuel savings, though their relatively high capital and operating costs generally make them less cost-effective.

Enforcing/reducing speed limits

As a rough average for heavy goods vehicles, every one mph reduction in speed saves approximately 0.8 per cent of fuel (Southwest Research Institute, 2008). Simply enforcing existing speed limits can thus significantly cut fuel consumption and emissions. Anable and Bristow (2007), for example, argue that effective enforcement of the 70 mph speed limit in the UK (for all road vehicles) would save roughly 1 million tonnes of road transport-related carbon emissions annually by 2010. Governments can go further and lower speed limits on particular classes of road for particular types of vehicles. They can also insist upon mandatory installation of speed governors to ensure that trucks adhere to speed limits, as is currently the case in the EU though not in the United States.

Imposing fuel economy standards for new vehicles

As noted in Chapter 11, the Japanese government is pioneering the development fuel economy standards for trucks with its 'Top runner' programme. Despite the formidable practical problems, both the US government and European Commission are considering a similar initiative.

Incentivizing scrappage of older vehicles

Evidence from Canada suggests that the average fuel efficiency of heavy trucks more than 10 years old is around 24 per cent lower than that of the average heavy truck (Transport Canada, 2005). Retiring elderly vehicles and replacing them with newer models can, therefore, effect substantial fuel savings. Some governments, most notably that of Spain, have used public funds to accelerate this process.

Advice, exhortation and accreditation

These 'soft' initiatives, which were discussed above, are more widely and intensively applied to improve fuel efficiency than to raise load factors. The adoption of energy intensity, expressed as the ratio of freight movement to fuel consumed (eg tonne-kms per litre), as a sustainable logistics metric encourages companies to optimize fuel efficiency and vehicle loading simultaneously.

CUTTING EMISSIONS RELATIVE TO ENERGY USE

The externalities of freight transport can vary independently of vehicle utilization and energy efficiency. Those associated with air pollution have been separately controlled by the imposition of emission standards for vehicles and fuel (see Chapter 2). The reduction in pollutants such as nitrogen oxide (NOx) and particulate matter (PM10) has been achieved by making technical modifications to vehicles, while sulphur has had to be removed from the fuel during the refining process. In the case of trucks, separate though similar sets of emission standards have been devised by the EU, the United States and Japan and tightened at 4–6 year intervals. This has induced a dramatic decline in emissions from new trucks over the past 20 years. Countries in other parts of the world have tended to adopt the EU or US emission standards. As developing countries acquire many of their trucks on a second-hand basis from Western countries they inherit vehicles meeting the emission standards, typically with a delay of five or six years.

Legislation and directives relating to emissions from diesel-powered non-road vehicles (eg locomotives, barges and domestic shipping) have lagged behind those of road vehicles by an average of five to seven years. This has partly eroded these modes' environmental advantage relative to road transport, particularly as they have tended to use cheaper and dirtier bunker fuel that contains more impurities. Regulatory authorities in the EU, United States and Japan are currently trying to harmonize worldwide emission standards for non-road diesel vehicles, partly to make it easier for manufacturers of these vehicles to standardize their production.

While good progress has been made in cleaning exhaust fumes from land-based freight transport modes, relatively little has been done until recently to cut pollution from international shipping. Talley (2003: 287) described ship engines as 'the dirtiest combustion sources per ton of fuel consumed'. Although, globally, they consume only around 2 per cent of fossil fuels they are responsible for 14 per cent of NOx emissions and 16 per cent of sulphur emissions. They can account for much higher proportions of sulphur dioxide emissions along shipping lanes and in the vicinity of major ports. The failure of the shipping industry to upgrade its environmental standards in line with those of land-based freight modes can be attributed to the lack of inter-governmental action and failure of the international organization responsible for shipping, the International Maritime Organization (IMO) to prioritize emission reductions. It illustrates how, in the absence of public intervention, environmental standards in a major industry can remain woefully inadequate. Much of the initiative in the greening of shipping operations has been taken by port authorities, because emissions from ships can represent a large proportion of air-borne pollutants in the surrounding area. The Port of Los Angeles, the largest port in the United States, has set particularly ambitious targets for cutting ship-related emissions, forcing vessels to use low-sulphur fuels, reduce speeds in the vicinity of the harbour and to use shore-side electricity as the power source when docked.

GOVERNMENT-SPONSORED ADVISORY AND ACCREDITATION PROGRAMMES

Governments in several countries have established programmes that promote the adoption of good environmental practice in the logistics sector. Good examples of such programmes can be found in the UK and United States.

UK Freight Best Practice (FBP) programme

This programme provides advice to companies about a broad range of measures that improve the efficiency and reduce the environmental impact of freight transport operations (www.freightbestpractice.org.uk). It has produced numerous reports and brochures, runs workshops and has established online tools for monitoring and benchmarking energy efficiency. Until recently the programme was concerned solely with the movement of freight by lorries. It is now being extended to cover van traffic and promote the use of alternative, more environmentally friendly transport modes. Recent market research has established that companies obtaining advice from the FBP showed a significantly greater propensity to implement a range of fuel savings measures (Lawson, Michaelis and Waldron, 2007). It also suggested that the FBP was a very cost-effective means of promoting the decarbonization of freight transport operations (at approximately £8 of public funds per tonne of CO_2 saved).

US SmartWay programme

This programme was set up by the US Environmental Protection Agency (EPA) in 2004 to help shippers to 'reduce their transportation footprint' (www.epa.gov/oms/smartway). It provides advice and management tools to companies, approves emission-reducing products and services that transport companies can use, offers financial support for green technologies such as anti-idling devices for trucks, and helps companies obtain loans from private sources for other 'green' investments. Around 1,000 shippers and carriers have joined the SmartWay Transport Partnership, membership of which 'helps companies to build supply chain management strategies that integrate energy efficiency, air quality and climate change directly into the transportation decision-making process'. Carriers meeting specified environmental criteria can gain differing levels of accreditation. An increasing number of US shippers, such as Wal-Mart, are insisting that their carriers are SmartWay-accredited. The EPA also advertises the SmartWay brand, thus helping participating companies to derive a marketing advantage from greening their freight transport operations.

CONCLUSION

Government policy towards freight transport has greatly evolved in recent decades, recognizing the need to see transport as part of a larger logistical system, to manage its environmental as well as economic impacts, and to deploy a wider range of measures to achieve long-term sustainability. There are, nevertheless, wide international variations in the nature, extent and resourcing of government initiatives in the field of green logistics. Those countries that are still at an early stage in the development of sustainable logistics strategies can learn from those, such as the UK, United States, Netherlands and France, that have longer experience. Given the magnitude of the environmental challenges now facing us, particularly from climate change, even the governments of these more progressive countries will have to give much greater priority to the greening of logistics in the years ahead.

NOTE

1. Formerly the European Conference of Ministers of Transport

REFERENCES

Anable, J and Bristow, AL (2007) *Transport and Climate Change: Supporting document to the CfIT Report*, Commission for Integrated Transport, London [accessed 25 August 2009] [Online] http://www.cfit.gov.uk/docs/2007/climatechange/

ARCADIS (2006) *Monitoringsonderzoek Vervolgproef LZV: Resultaten van de Vervolgproef met Langere of Langere en Zwaardere Voertuigcombinaties op de Nederlandse Wegen*, ARCADIS, Arnhem

Baugham, CJ (1979) *Public Attitudes to Alternative Sizes of Lorry*, Supplementary Report no 509, Transport and Road Research Laboratory, Crowthorne

Browne, M, Sweet, M, Woodburn, A and Allen, J (2005) *Urban Freight Consolidation Centres*, report for the Department for Transport, London

Cooper, JC (1991) Lessons for Europe from freight deregulation in Australia, the United Kingdom and the United States of America, *Transport Reviews*, **11** (1), pp 85–104

Department of the Environment, Transport and the Regions (DETR) (1999) *Sustainable Distribution: A strategy*, HMSO, London

Department for Transport (DfT) (2006) *Companies and Drivers Benefit from SAFED for HGVs: A Selection of Case Studies*, Freight Best Practice Programme, London

DfT (2007) *Computerized Vehicle Routing and Scheduling (CVRS) for Efficient Logistics*, Freight Best Practice Programme, London

DfT (2008a) *Delivering a Sustainable Transport System: The logistics perspective*, DfT, London

DfT (2008b) *Transport Statistics Great Britain*, The Stationery Office, London

DfT (2009) *Mode Shift Benefit Values: Technical report*, DfT, London

European Commission (2001) *Transport Policy for 2010: Time to decide*, European Commission, Brussels

European Commission (2006) *Keep Europe Moving: Sustainable mobility for our continent*: Mid-term review of the European Commission's 2001 Transport White Paper', Brussels

European Environment Agency (2008) *Climate for a Transport Change: TERM 2007 – indicators tracking transport and environment in the European Union*, European Environment Agency, Copenhagen

Fiorella, D, Schade, W, Beckmann, R, Fermi, F, Köhler, J, Martino, A, Schade, B, Walz, R and Wiesenthal, T (2008) *High Oil Prices: Quantification of direct and indirect impacts for the EU*, HOP research project, European Commission, Brussels

Knight, I, Newton, W, McKinnon, A, Palmer, A, Barlow, T, McCrae, I, Dodd, M, Couper, G, Davies, H, Daly, A, McMahon, W, Cook, E, Ramdas, V and Taylor, N (2008), *Longer and/or Longer and Heavier Goods Vehicles (LHVs): A study of the likely effects if permitted in the UK: Final report*, TRL Published Project Report 285, TRL, Berkshire

Lawson, K, Michaelis, C and Waldron, D (2007) *Freight Best Practice Programme Impact Assessment: Final report*, Databuild, London

McKinnon, AC (1998) The abolition of quantitative controls on road freight transport: the end of an era? *Transport Logistics*, **1** (3), pp 211–24

McKinnon, AC (2005) The economic and environmental benefits of increasing maximum truck weight: the British experience, *Transportation Research Part D*, **10** (1), pp 77–95

McKinnon, AC (2006) A review of truck tolling schemes and assessment of their possible impact on logistics systems, *International Journal of Logistics: Research and Applications*, **9** (3), pp 191–205

McKinnon, AC (2007) CO_2 emission from freight transport in the UK, Commission for Integrated Transport, London [accessed 25 August 2009] [Online] http://www.cfit.gov.uk/docs/2007/climatechange/

McKinnon, AC, Piecyk, MI and Somerville, A (2008) Decoupling, recoupling and the future growth of road freight, *Logistics and Transport Focus*, **10** (12), pp 40–46

Meersman, H and Van de Voorde, E (2002) Utopia and goods transport observations at decoupling economic growth and demand for transport, paper presented at the European Conference on Mobility Management, Ghent, 15–17 May

Savitz, AW (2006) *The Triple Bottom Line*, Jossey-Bass, San Francisco

Scottish Government (2009) [accessed 25 August 2009] *Freight Grants* [Online] http://www.scotland.gov.uk/Topics/Transport/FT/freightgrants1

Southwest Research Institute (2008) Heavy duty vehicle fuel consumption and GHG emissions improvement: preliminary simulation results, presentation to National Academy of Sciences hearing on Fuel Economy Standards, Washington, DC, 4–5 Dec

Swiss Federal Office for Spatial Development (2004) *Fair and Efficient: The distance-related Heavy Vehicle Fee (HVF) in Switzerland*, ARE, Berne

Talley, WK (2003) Environmental impacts of shipping, in *Handbook of Transport and the Environment*, ed DA Hensher and JK Button, pp 279–91, Elsevier, Oxford

Transport and Mobility Leuven et al (2008), *Effects of Adapting the Rules on Weights and Dimensions of Heavy Commercial Vehicles as Established within Directive 96/53/EC*, Report for the European Commission, Brussels

Transport Canada (2005) *Canadian Vehicle Survey: Summary report*, Transport Canada, Ottawa

Transportation Research Board (2002) *Regulations of Weights, Lengths and Widths of Commercial Motor Vehicles*, Special Report 267, Committee for the Study of the Regulation of Weights, Lengths and Widths of Commercial Road Vehicles, Washington, DC

Umwelt Bundes Amt (2007) *Longer and Heavier on German Roads: Do megatrucks contribute towards sustainable transport*, Umwelt Bundes Amt, Dessau

Whitelegg, J (1995) *Freight Transport, Logistics and Sustainable Development*, World Wide Fund for Nature, London

Index

NB: page numbers in *italic* indicate figures or tables

Abukhader, S 6
accidents 38–39, *39*
  and rate in EU 39, 40
Adamowicz, W 73
Adams, J G U 9, 75
Ad-Blue 145, 231
Aeronautics Research in Europe, Advisory
    Council for (ACARE) 154, 156–57
Affenzeller, J 38
Agatz, N A H 328, 335
Ahmadi, S 218
air freight (and) 153–57
  air cargo trends 153–54
  capacity increases 154–55
  fuel efficiency improvements 155–56
  reduction in externalities 156–57
Air Quality Damage Cost Guidance (DEFRA) 81
Airbus 153, 154, 155, 157
Allen, J 146, 286, 301
Alligier, L 94
alternative fuels 306–21 *see also* biofuels;
    electric vehicles; gas/gas-fuelled
    vehicles *and* hydrogen
  and current use in freight industry 316–18
Altes, T 187
Ambrosini, C 284
Anable, J 354
analytical framework/key parameters 19–22,
    20
Anderson, C 249
Ando, N 220
Ang-Olson, J 235
Armitage, A 9, 283
Aronsson, H 5, 14, 22, 113, 114, 118
Aryee, G 107

Asda 137, 206
  and alternative fuels 317
Assad, A A 216, 219
atmospheric emissions/pollution 32–37, *33*
  global effects of 34–6
    and Kyoto Protocol categories 34–5, *35*
  local effects of 36–37
    carbon monoxide (CO) 37
    hydrocarbons (HCs) 36
    nitrogen oxides (NOx) 36
    ozone (O_3) 37
    particulates 37
    sulphur dioxide (SO_2) 37
  regional effects of 36
    acid rain 36
    photochemical smog 36

Bailey, J P 330
Baker, P 168, 171, 172, 179
Bakos, J Y 323
Baldacci, R 218
Ballou, R H 220
Banner, S 150
Barber, A 267
Barling, D 276
Bask, A H 110
Battilana, J 283
Baublys, A 72
Baugham, C J 344
Baumgaertner, M 225, 233
Beamon, B 102, 111–12
Bennathan, E 9
Berbeglia, G 218
Bettac, E 249
Beulens, A 107, 108

Beuthe, M 72, 78
Biehl, M 107
biofuels 136, 307–12, 318 *see also* definition(s)
  biodiesel/alkyl esters 307–08
  bioethanol 308–09
  environmental impacts of 309–12
    emissions 309–10
    land-take 311–12
  and Royal Society (2008) 318
Black, I 10, 24
Bletjenberg, A 15
Bloemhof, J M 115
Blythman, J 270
Bockel, R 295
Bode, S 157
Boffey, T B 221
Böge, S 9
Boko, M 271
Bowen, F E 16
Bowen, P A 243
Boyes, G 149
Brandão, J 218, 219
Bräysy, O 218
Bridgwater, E 249
Bristow, A L 354
British Standards Institution 56, 58
Brodin, M H 5, 14, 22, 113, 114, 118
Browne, M 12, 17, 24, 146, 291, 295, 352
Browning, B 201
Brundtland Commission 4, 342
Buckley, H 234
Burbidge, J L 103
Burman, L 301
Burns, R 86
business-to-business (B2B) 323–26
  environmental impact of 326
business-to-consumer (B2C) (and) 327–30
  e-auction companies 330
  mail order companies 329
  multi-channel retailers (bricks and clicks)
    328
  pure lay retailers (e-tailers) 328–29
  wholesalers/producers 330

Canessa, M 168
capacitated vehicle routing problem (CVRP)
  216
carbon auditing 49–67 *see also* carbon
  footprinting *and* case studies
carbon calculators/software tools 17
Carbon Check 58
Carbon Disclosure Project 65
carbon footprinting 49–60, *50, 52, 54, 66*
  guidelines for 50–51
  success factors in 59–60
Carbon Trust 17, 51, 56, 175, 176, 177, 189
  Good Practice Guide 319 177
CarbonView 58
Carlsson, F 316
Carson, R T 73
Carter, C R 13, 246

Case for Rail, The 151
case studies (of/on)
  carbon auditing of road freight transport
    operations in UK 60–65, 62, 64, 65
  container train load factors 130–31, 131
  e-business/e-logistics: online books supply
    chain 333–34, 334
  taxes on road freight (UK) 93
CE Delft 69, 72, 75, 79
Chan, C C 316
Chan, K T 316
Chao, I-M 219
Chapagain, A 274
Chartered Surveyors, Royal Institute of
  (RICS) 175
  and Green Value Report (2005) 175, 187
Chen, I J 111
Cherbakov, L 324
Cherrett, T J 24, 249, 254, 255, 256, 333
Christianse, E 323
Christopher, M 203
Civic Trust 12
Clean Transportation, International Council
  on 160, 161
Clean Urban Transport in Europe (CUTE) 313
Clements, A 204
Clift, R 270
Climate Change, Committee on 4, 154, 155 *see
  also* research
Climate Change, Intergovernmental Panel on
  140
Coase, R H 70
Collaborative Transportation Management
  (CTM) 201
Collins, W J 313
Commercial Motor 143, 232
Community Recycling Network 251
computerized vehicle routing and scheduling
  (CVRS) 348
Contingency Valuation Method 73–74
Cooper, J C 10, 353
Corbett, J J 158
Cordeau, J-F 218
corporate social responsibility (CSR) 45
Coyle, M 240
CREATE UK Ltd 251
Creten, R 222
Crowley, J 323
Cruijssen, F C A M 204
Cullinane, S L 24, 332

Daf diesel/electric vehicles 317–18
Damage Function approach 72–73
Damsgaard, J 323
Daniel, E M 323
Danzig, G B 216
Dasburg, N 301
Davies, J 181
Davis, R 274
Davis, T 107
De Brito, M P 243

de Koster, M B M 332
definition(s) of
    biofuels 307
    carbon footprint 49–50
    electronic marketplace (EM) 323–24
    environmental management standards
        (EMS) 41
    GHG sink 58
    green supply chain management (GCSM)
        16–17
    reverse logistics 243
    sustainability 342
Dekker, R 13, 243
Delle Site, P 284
Delucchi, M A 316
den Boer, L C 37
Derwent, R G 313
Dessouky, M 222
Deutsche Post/DHL 306–07, 317
development of greener vehicles, aircraft and
        ships see individual subject entries
    air freight 153–57
    rail freight operations 150–53
    road freight 141–50
    shipping 157–62
dial-a-ride (DARP) 218
Diepen, T V 323
Disney, S M 104, 105, 205
Dixon, J 272
Dror, M 221
Duhamel, C 218
Duleep, K G 230
Dunn, S C 14, 246, 248

Easterling, W E 276
e-business, e-logistics and the environment
        (and) 202, 322–38 see also case studies
    business-to-business (B2B) 323–26 see also
        main entry
    business-to-consumer (B2C) 327–30 see also
        main entry
    electronic logistics marketplaces (ELMs)
        324–25, 325
    environmental impact of e-commerce
        330–34, 331, 334 see also online
        shopping
    future for 335
    restructuring of supply chain 330
ECMT (Paris) 68, 71, 72
Eco-Indicator 99 method for impact
        assessment 115
Economic Co-operation and Development,
        Organization for (OECD) 9, 311
ECT Recycling 251
Eddie Stobart Ltd 138
Edwards, J B 332
Edwards-Jones, G 265
Eglese, R W 218, 219, 222, 224
Ejsmont, J A
electric vehicles 315–16
electronic logistics marketplaces (ELMs)
        324–25, 325

electronic marketplaces (EMs) 323–24
Ellram, L M 13, 246
Energy Information Association (EIA) 148,
        149
energy security 275–76
Energy Systems Research Unit (ESRU) 308
enterprise resource planning (ERP/ERPII
        system) 323
Environment, Food and Rural Affairs,
        Department for (DEFRA) 35, 52, 58, 75,
        80, 81, 253,
267, 274, 276
Environment, Transport and the Regions,
        Department of the 15
Environment Agency 128, 247, 253
Environmental Audit Committee (2008) 312
environmental costs of logistics (and) 68–97
    arguments for and against internalization
        of 69–72
    external costs allocated to road freight
        vehicles 80–81, 82, 83
    foreign-registered HGVs 85–87, 87
    heavy goods vehicles 83–85, 84, 85
    internalization of external costs 79–93
    internalization of external HGV costs across
        Europe 87–89, 88
    light goods vehicles 89–91, 89, 90
    monetary valuation of 72–79, 74, 76, 77 see
        also environmental damage
    overview of internalization – UK road
        freight sector 91–93, 92
    taxes/charges borne by road freight
        operators 79–80, 81
    traffic congestion 77–78, 78
    use of marginal or average/aggregated
        costs for externalities 78–89
environmental damage 72–77
    cost of 73–75, 74
    cost of avoiding 75
    and monetary values 73–74, 77
    summary of costs of 75, 77, 76, 77
environmental impacts of freight transport see
        freight transport
environmental indices 115
environmental KPIs 119
Environmental Management and
        Assessment, Institute of (IMEA) 41, 42
Environmental Pollution, Royal Commission
        on (RCEP) 34
Environmental Protection Agency (EPA) 45,
        309, 310
environmental rating system GREENSTAR
        (Australia) 186
environmental standards 41–42 see also
        international standards
    BS7750 42
    Eco-Management and Audit Scheme
        (EMAS) 42
    environmental management (EMS) 41
    ISO 14000/14001 42
environmental sustainability 3–30 see also
        research into green logistics

rhetoric and reality 17–19, 18
environmentally responsible logistics (ERL)
    14–15
Erkut, E 221
Esper, T L 201
Euro emission standards 145, 149
EURO vehicle standards 316
EUROCONTROL 156
European Aluminium Association 142
European Commission (and) 12, 72, 73, 88,
    131, 150, 158, 282
    BESTUPS 285
    ExternE study 73
    fair and efficient pricing policy 69
    fuel economy standards 355
        for trucks 144
    limits on CO2 149
    REDEFINE and SULOGTRA projects 11
    White Paper on Transport (1992) 131–32
European COST 321 programme 12
European Emissions Trading Scheme 94
European Environmental Agency (EEA) 69,
    87, 347
European Federation of Transport and
    Environment 79
European Logistics Association (ELA) 171
European Metal Recycling (EMR) 251
European Natural Gas Vehicle Association
    (ENGVA) 314
European Parliament/Council of Ministers 69
European Union (EU) (and) 70, 75, 114, 343 see
    also legislation, EU
    accident rate in 39
    air pollution 298
    Best Urban Freight Solutions (Bestufs)
        programme 12
    biofuels 310, 312, 318
    economy 11
    emission standards 355
    Freight Action Plan (EC, 2007) 133
    Greening Transport initiative 133
    Integrated Maritime Policy 132
    Marco Polo programme 350
    Trans-European Network programme
        (TEN-T) 134
    TREMOVE project 43
exhaust gas recirculation (EGR) 145, 231
Eyefortransport 14
Eyre, N 313, 315
Eyring, V 161

Fairholme, N 44
Faruk, A C 17
FEHRL European National Highway
    Research Laboratories 38
Fergusson, M 313, 315, 332
Fernie, J 248, 329, 335
figures
    analytical framework for green logistics 20
    average speed on a primary road in the UK
        223

bad practices from four sources of supply
    chain uncertainty: examples 109
carbon footprint, different types of 50
carbon footprint, horizontal and vertical
    dimensions of 66
carbon footprint, steps to calculating 52
changes in UK floor space by usage (1998 to
    2004) 170
Chatterley Park Distribution Centre 188
CO2 emissions from road freight transport,
    factors affecting 65
costs: distance-related charges and external
    costs of road freight transport 2002) 88
costs: internalization of external costs by
    HGV category 85
costs: internalization of external costs by
    LGVs in UK 91
costs: total external costs imposed by
    foreign-registered trucks in UK 87
costs: total external costs of HGV activity in
    UK 85
costs: total external costs of LGV activity in
    UK 90
daily demand fluctuation in food sector:
    per cent by volume 200
different load factors for container train
    services (examples) 131
domestic freight transport moved by mode
    (Great Britain, 1976–2006) 125
domestic freight transport moved (Great
    Britain): mode share for selected
    commodities (2006) 127
ELM operations, overview of 325
estimated average CO2 intensity values for
    freight transport modes 129
estimated fuel savings from fuel economy
    measures: US trucking 236
evolving perspectives and themes in green
    logistics 7
extended supply chain 112
five-fold classification of constraints on
    vehicle utilization 199
framework of assessment for developing
    sustainability in warehousing 174
impact pathway approach to valuing
    environmental effects 74
improvement in truck productivity in UK
    197
Logistics Triad Uncertainty Model 110
online book supply chain: key players and
    trading relationships 334
percentage of lorry-kms travelled with
    weight and volume-constrained loads
    207
process map for yoghurt 54
recovery processes incorporated in supply
    chain 244
relationship between speed and fuel
    consumption for light duty diesel
    vehicle 224
three supply chain scenarios 104

traditional supply chain *102*
uncertainty circle model *108*
variation in fuel efficiency across vehicle
fleets in food supply chain *237*
vehicle speed and CO2 emissions:
articulated vehicle over 40 tonns gvw
78
Flight International 155
Fiorella, D 348
Flämig, H 283
Fleichmann, M 328, 335
Fleischmann, M 243
Food Chain Analysis Group 275
Food Ethics Council 271
Food Matters 276
food miles debate 265–81
and food security 275–76
life cycle analysis (LCA) approach to 265–71
local vs global and the self-sufficiency
question 274–76
transport and GHGs – is further worse?
266–71
transport, second order impacts and
implications for GHGs 272–74
food safety crises/BSE 275
Forrester, J W 103, 104
Forrester Research 327
Foster, C 265
Foulkes, M 283
Fraser, J 9
Freight Facilities and Waterborne Freight
Grants (UK) 79
freight quality partnerships (FQPs) 295,
301–02
Freight Route Utilization Strategy for British
Rail network 151
freight transport 4, 5, 31–48 *see also* urban
freight
environmental impacts of see accidents;
atmospheric emissions/pollution and
noise pollution
environmental standards for 39–42
mandatory 40–41, *41*
voluntary/management 41–42
measuring environmental impact of 42–45
by macro-level assessment 42–44, *44*
by micro-level assessment 44–45
Freight Transport Association (FTA) 80, 207,
231, 234, 239, 295
Freightliner 135, 150
Friedrich, R 77, 79
Fu, I 220
Fu, Z 218
fuel duty escalator policy 71
fuel efficiency *see* increasing fuel efficiency in
road freight sector
Fulton, L 32

Galle, W P 16
Galvão, R D 218
Gardner, B 205

Garnett, T 15, 24, 266, 267, 268, 269, 275
Garreau, A 15
gas/gas-fuelled vehicles 314–15
compressed natural gas (CNG) 315
liquid petroleum gas (LPG) 315
natural gas (NG) 314–15
Gavaghan, K 16
Gazeley 170, 183, 184, 186
and Chatterley Park Distribution Centre
188–89, *188*
eco-templates 187
and John Lewis Partnership 187–88
Ge, Y 198, 203, 237
Geary, S 107, 108
Gendreau, M 219
Germany (and)
City Logistik schemes 283
fuel taxation 349–50
Packaging Ordinance 251
Gilmore, D 17
Giorgi, S 218
global warming potential (GWP) 34–35, 57
Golden, B L 216, 219
Golding, A 248
Goldsby, T J 15, 106, 107
Golob, T F 332
Going Green (PE International study, 1993) 18
Gosain, S 324
Gosier, R 196
Gould, J 332
government role in promoting green logistics
(by/and) 340–60
cutting emissions relative to energy use
355–56
government-sponsored advisory and
accreditation programmes 356–57
improving vehicle utilization 351–53
increasing energy efficiency 353–55
objectives of public policy on sustainable
logistics 344
policy measures 344–47
reducing freight intensity 347–48
shifting freight to greener transport modes
349–51
Grant, D B 329
Green Book (HM Treasury, 2003) 81
Green Logistics project (EPSRC) 130
green supply chain management (GCSM)
16–17
green supply chains 111–16, *112*
green performance measures for 113–16
GreenBuildings.com 169
Greenhouse Gas Protocol 56
greenhouse gases (GHG) 31, 49, 266–74
listed by UN IPCC (1996) 34
Grenoble, W 15
Greszler, A 142, 232
Groke, O 283
Grunwald, M 307, 311
Guide, V D R 13
Guiliano, G 154

Gunter, H 111, 117

Halldórsson, A 244, 257
Hampson, J 16
Handfield, R B 16
Hanson, S 154
Hart, C 248
Hassell, M 283
Hawthorne, I 283
Heasman, M 272
Helms, M M 113, 115–16, 118
Henrickson, C T 15
Hervani, A A 113, 115–16, 118
Hesse, M 171, 172, 187, 323
Heymann, E 158
Hickford, A J 24, 249
Hinde, S 272
Holmen, B A 32
Holmstrom, J 205
Holt, D 15
Home Delivery Network Limited 330
Horvath, L 323
Hosoda, T 105
Hout, T M 103
Huge-Brodin, M 15
Hugo, A 114, 115
hydrogen 312–14
  environmental credentials of 313
  and proton exchange membrane fuel cells
    (PEMFC) 312–13

Ichoua, S 219
Impact Pathway Approach 73
increasing fuel efficiency in the road freight
    sector (by) 229–41
  benchmarking fuel efficiency of trucks
    237–38, 237
  fleet management 239–40
  fuel efficiency of new trucks 230–31
  increasing fuel efficiency of trucking
    operations 235–36, 236
  more fuel-efficient driving 238–39
  reducing vehicle tare weight 232–33
  vehicle design: aerodynamic profiling
    231–32
  vehicle maintenance 234
  vehicle purchase decision 233
INFRAS 43, 72
Insight 17 see also surveys
Intergovernmental Panel on Climate Change
    (2007) 318
International Assessment of Agricultural
    Knowledge (IAAK) 276
International Energy Agency (IEA) 230, 231,
    307, 308, 309–10, 312, 318
International Maritime Organization (IMO)
    158, 356
International Road Transport Union (IRU) 32,
    70
international standards
  guidelines 53

ISO 14000/series certification 14, 53
ISO 14064:1 (2006) 55
International Transport Forum 343
Isoraite, M 72

Jackson, G C 11
Jahre, M 13
Janić, M 38
Japan (and)
  Comprehensive Assessment System for
    Building Environmental Efficiency
    (CASBEE) 186
  emission standards 355
  Energy Conservation Law 144
  freight transport policies 295
  fuel economy standards – Toprunner
    programme 355
  Institute for City Logistics (ICL) 285
Jayaraman, V 13
Jennings, A 12
Johansson, C 301
Johansson-Stenman, D 316
Johnson, C E 313
Johnson, E 175, 180
Johnson, F 16
Johnsson, G 6
Jones, D T 103

Kahn Ribeiro, S 140
Kallehauge, B 217
Kan, A H G R 217
Kanter, J 160
Kara, B Y 221
Karkazis, J 221
Kassel, R 158
Khoo, H H 114
KingSturge 171, 175, 186, 187
Kirkhope, J 239
Klassen, R D 16
Knight, I 195, 208
Köhler, U 283
Kohn, C 15, 114
Kolen, A W J 217
Kröger, K 332
Kroon, L 248
Krusch, O 225
Kyoto Protocol 34
  and gas emissions 56
  system of GHG accounting 158

Lake, A 272
Lalwani, C 106
Lamming, R 16
Landfill Tax Credit Scheme (LTCS) 254
Lang, T 272, 276
Laporte, G 218
Larsen, J 217
Lau, H C 218
Laudon, K C 323
Lawson, K 357
Le Blanc, H M 113

Lee, H L 103
legislation (EU)
  Biofuels Directive (2003) 309
  Directive 70/157/EEC (vehicle noise
    standards) 38
  Directive 1999/30/EC 298
  Directive 2001/43/EC (vehicle tyre noise
    regulations) 38
  Directive on Distance Contract (97/7/EC)
    243, 246
  Directive on Packaging and Packaging
    Waste 94/62/EC 247
  Directives on Waste Electrical and
    Electronic Equipment (WEEE) 242, 246,
    249
  EU Council Directive 93/53/EC on vehicle
    length 208
  Energy Performance Buildings Directive
    185
  EURO emission standards 40–41, 41
  Framework Directive 1996/62/EC 298
  Fuel Quality Directive 152
  Hazardous Waste Directive (91/689/EEC)
    249–50
  Landfill Directive 99/31/EC 247
  noise directive 298
  Non-Road Mobile Machinery (NRMM)
    legislation 152
  Packaging and Packaging Waste (94/62/
    EC) 242, 251
  Restriction of the Use of Certain Hazardous
    Substances (RoHS) in Electrical and
    Electronic Equipment (2002/95/EC) 242
  White Paper on transport (2001) 347
legislation (UK)
  Climate Change Act 49
  Collection and Disposal of Waste
    Regulations (1984) 255
  Control of Pollution Act (1974) 255
  Environmental Protection Act (1990) 253,
    255
  Landfill Directive, Producer Pre-Treatment
    Requirement of 246–47
  Landfill Regulations (2002) 247
  Sustainable Distribution (White Paper,DETR,
    1999) 284
  Working Time Directive 209
Léonardi, J 225
Letchford, A N 219
Lewis, C N 324
Lewis, I 202
Li, L Y O 218
Li, S 105
Lieb, R 15
life cycle analysis (LCA) 17, 45, 167, 265–66
Lipman, T E 316
List, G F 221
Logistics, UK Institute of 13
logistics see environmental costs of logistics
logistics companies and rail freight 138
Logistics Management, Council of 13

López, J C 269
Lorries and the Environment Committee
    (1976) 8–9, 283
Low Emission Zone in Europe Network
    (LEEZEN) 298
low emission zones (LEZs) 296, 301
Lysgaard, J 219

MacGregor, J 271
MacIntosh, A 153
McKinnon, A C 10, 11, 22, 23, 24, 35, 43, 60, 61,
    87, 129, 171, 196, 198, 199, 201, 203,
    205, 210, 222, 223, 237, 238, 239, 290, 329, 332,
    335, 342, 347, 350, 351, 353
McLean, E 322
McLeod, F N 24, 254, 255, 256, 333
MacLeod, M 315
MacLeod, P 180
Maddison, D 70, 74, 75
Maden, W 222, 224
Madsen, O B G 217
Mansell, G 202
Marchant 23
Marien, E J 246
Mason-Jones, R 107, 108, 110
material requirements planning (MRP) 323
Mathur, K 220
Matthews, H S 15
Meade, L M 202
Meersman, H 347
Meimbresse, B 284
Melnyk, S A 16
METRANS Transportation Center 285
  and National Urban Freight Conference
    (USA, 2006) 285
Michaelis, C 357
Milà i Canals, L 268, 269, 270, 271
Millen, R 15
Mills, R 313, 315
Min, H 16, 218
Mingozzi, A 218
Mitchell, R C 73
Mode Shift Benefit Values (DfT, 2009) 81
Montané, F A T 218
Montreal Protocol 56
Mukhopadhyay, S K 245
Mulvin, G 329
Muñoz, I 270
Murphy, P R 5, 8, 13, 14
Murphy-Bokern, D 267

Nag, B 219
Nagy, G 218
Naim, M M 23, 103, 104, 105, 324
National Atmospheric Emissions Inventory
    (NAEI) 81
Nesbitt, K 306
Netherlands 348, 358
  public and private sectors 294–95
Network for Transport and the Environment
    158

Network Rail (UK) 128, 135
New Deal for Transport: Better for Everyone, A (DETR, 1998) 284
Newing, R 204
Niemeier, D A 32
Nikolaeva, R 327
noise pollution 37–38
  European standards for 38
Nominated Day Delivery System (NDDS) 201
Nordhaus, W 77
Norfolk Waste Recycling Assistance Project (NORWRAP) 254

Oddy, D J 275
O'Donnell, T 103
Ogden, K W 11, 12, 294
online shopping 330–35, *331, 334 see also* case studies
  and customer returns 333
  delivery conflicts of 332–33
  failed delivery of 333
  and offsets to environmental gains 331–32
onward delivery 204–05
optimizing routing of vehicles (and) 215–28
  environmental impact 221–24
    congestion 222–24, *224*
    emissions auditing 222, *223*
  types of problem 217–21
    arc routing 220–21
    backhauls 218
    dial-a-ride (DARP) 218
    dynamic VRSP 219–20
    non-homogeneous vehicles 218–19
    open VRSP 219
    pick-up and delivery 218
    stochastic 220
    time windows 217–18
    transportation of hazardous materials 221
  vehicle routing problems 216–17
  vehicle routing/scheduling problems (VRSPs) 215
OR/MS Today 217
Orr, S 274
Ortiz, J 175

Padgett, J 168, 173, 175
Padmanabhan, P 103
Palmer, A 222
Palmer, J W 324
Pantelides, C C 102
Papastavrou, J D
Pappis, C 168, 173
Park, M 333
particulate matter (PM10) 32, 355
Paulraj, A 111
Paxton, A 9
Peck, H 107, 108
Perez-Lombard, L 175
Perotti, S 171, 172
Peters, M 10

Pettit, D 8
Piecyk, M 23, 43, 61, 210, 223, 347
Pigou, A C 68
Pistikopoulos, E 114, 115
Poist, R F 5, 8, 13, 14
polluter-pays principle 71
Pope, C A 33
Potter, A 104, 105, 106, 107, 113, 205, 324
Potvin, J-Y 218, 219
Pout, C 175
Prater, E 107, 109
Primerano, F 332
PROGRESS 274
Prologis 186
  low carbon warehouse 187
Punakivi, M

Quariguasi Frota Neto, J 114, 115

Rabinovich, R 330
Rahimi, M 222
rail and water industries (and) 135–38
  freight grants 137
  greener transport modes for freight users 136–37
  modal transfer 137–38
rail freight 150–53
  carrying capacity of 150–51
  energy efficiency of 151–52
  and reducing externalities 152–53
Rail Safety and Standards Board (RSSB) 130, 151
Ramser, J M 216
Rao, K 15
Rao, P 15
Raux, C 94
recycling/recycling organisations 13, 251–53
reducing environmental impact of warehousing *see* warehousing, environmental impact of
Reed, R 172
references 25–30, 45–48. 66–67, 95–97, 120–23, 139, 163–66, 190–92, 210–14, 225–28, 240–41, 259–62, 277–81, 302–05, 319–21, 335–38, 358–60
Regan, A 333
regenerative braking 151
Reghaven, S 216
regional distribution centre (RDC) 172
renewable green energy sources 182
research into green logistics (and) 5–17, 7
  aircraft efficiency (Committee on Climate Change) 155
  city logistics 11–12
  corporate environmental strategies 13–15
  green supply chain management (GSCM) 16–17
  model for 19–22, 19, 20
  reducing freight transport externalities 8–11, 10
  reverse logistics 13

research (into/on)
  airframe technology (for Committee on
    Climate Change, 2008) 155
  biofuels 310
  fuel economy (Volvo) 143
  fuel efficiency (Finland) 233
  fuel efficiency (National Academies of
    Science, USA, 2007) 144
  fuel efficiency (University of Huddersfield)
    240
  fuel savings from reducing tare weight
    (USA) 142
  hydrogen use 313
  transport efficiency (Helsinki) 205
  urban freight 12, 283–85
  zero carbon warehousing (GBC) 189
restructuring of logistics systems/supply
    chains 101–23 *see also* supply chains
  and consequences/conclusions 119–20
  gaps in our understanding of and priorities
    for research into 116–18
  green supply chains 111–16 *see also main
    entry*
reverse logistics for waste management *see*
    waste management
rhetoric and reality 17–19
Ricci, A 77, 79
risks and food security 275–76
Rizet, C 17
road freight 141–50 *see also* increasing fuel
    efficiency in road freight sector
  trucks 141–46, 142
    carrying capacity of 141–43
    energy efficiency of 142–45
    and reducing externalities 145–46
  vans 146–50, *147*
    carrying capacity of 146–48
    energy efficiency of 148–9
    and externalities 149–50
road pricing systems 290
Robertson, J 283
Rogers, D S 243
Rogers, P 37
Roth, A 301
Rousseau, J-M 218
Rowlands, P 324
Rushton, A 12
Rust, A 38

Sainsbury 216
  and Little Green Van 317
Salucci, M 284
Samuelsson, A 198
Sanchez Rodriguez, V 23, 110
Sandberg, U 38
Sansom, T 78
Saremia, A R 218
Sarkis, J 16–17, 113, 115–16, 118, 202
Saunders, C 267
Saunders, T 169
Savitz, A W 342

Schipper, L J 32
Schmidtchen, D 70
Schoemaker, J 301
Schroeer, W 235
Schroten, A 37
SCOR model 108, 111
Scrase, I 169, 172
Sea and Water organization 136
Searchinger, T 273, 311
Secomandi, N 220
security risks and long-distance sourcing 275
selective catalytic reduction (SCR) 145, 160,
    231
Setaputra, R 245
Shah, N 102
Shakantu, W 243
Sharp, C 12
Sharpe, R 276
Shell 107
  and Fuel Stretch 236
Shepherd, C 111, 117
Shih, I 246
Shimamoto, H 219
shipping 138, 157–62
  carrying capacity of 159
  energy efficiency of 159–60
  and externalities 160–61
  and pollution 356
Sim, M 218
Sim, S 268, 269
Simons, D 103
Singh, R K 118
Single European Market 131
Single European Sky legislation 156
Skinner, I 332
Skjøtt-Larsen, T 244, 257
Slater, A 15, 222, 224
small to medium-sized enterprises (SMEs)
    246, 247, 253
  and waste management 254–55
Smith, M A 107
Smith, P 276
Smithers, R 331
Soil Association 268, 271
Somerville, A 347
Somerville, H 157
Song, I 333
Sonneveld, K 206
Sonntag, H 284
Southwest Research Institute 354
Spain, horticulture industry in 274
Sperling, D 306, 308, 311
Srivastava, R 13
Srivastava, S K 16–17
Stalk, G Jr 103
Stank, T P 15, 106, 107
Stantchev, D 284
Stehly, M 151
Stern, N 77, 84
Stern Review 84–85
Stevens, G 102

Stirling, I 239
Stock, J 13
Stone, A 329
Storey, R 149
study/ies (on)
 costs and benefits of longer/heavier
   vehicles (EU, Germany, Netherlands,
   UK) 353
 environmental and economic impact of
   LHVs in Germany (UBA) 208
 food miles and sustainable development
   (DEFRA, 2005) 267
 GHG and food miles (New Zealand) 267
   (New Zealand)
 road transport and environmental impact
   (Germany) 9
Supply Chain Council 108
supply chain(s) 102–20
 and bullwhip effect 103–06, 119
 dynamics 102–05
 end-to-end 17
 green 111–16 see also green supply chains
 management and transport logistics 106
 performance measures for traditional 111
 research 116–18
 restructuring of 330
 scenarios 104–05, 104
 traditional 102–03, 111, 102
 and transport, managing uncertainty in
   106–10, 108, 109, 110
Survey of Foreign Vehicle Activity in Great
   Britain (FVA survey, DfT 2003) 86
Survey of Privately-Owned Vans (DfT, 2004) 89
surveys (by/of) 14–15, 17–18
 company environmental strategies
   (Murphy and Poist, 1995) 14
 company environmental strategies (PE
   International, 1993) 14
 Company Van Survey (UK, 2003–2005) 147
 company vans (DfT 2004) 89
 Continuing Survey of Roads Goods
   Transport 43
 green supply chain (Gavaghan et al) 16
 recycling amongst UK businesses and
   SMEs (Taylor Intelligence, 2007) 247
 supply chain professionals (Insight, 2008)
   14
 supply chains (Insight) 14
 Transport KPI (UK government) 198
 UK National Road Traffic Survey (NRTS,
   DfT 2007) 83, 89
 UK road goods transport (CSRGT, DfT
   2006) 83
 US firms on corporate environmental
   policy 13–14
Sustain 265, 268, 275
Sustainable Distribution Strategy (DETR) 196
Sustainable Rail Programme (RSSB, 2007) 153
sustainability strategies 167–68
sustainability strategies for city logistics (and)
   282–305
 efficiency problems in urban freight 285–88

environmental zones (EZs) 296–301, 299,
   300
 joint working between public and private
   sectors 294–96
 urban consolidation centres 290–93 see also
   main entry
 urban freight research and policy-making
   283–85
 urban freight transport initiatives 288–90
   see also urban freight transport
Sweet, M 12
Swiss Federal Office for Spatial Development
   352
Swiss Heavy Vehicle Fee (HFV) 352

Talley, W K 356
Talluri, S 202
Taniguchi, E 12, 219, 220, 284
Tapio, P 11
Tavokkoli-Moghaddam, R 218
Teo, K M 218
Tesco 137, 138, 205, 216
 and Greenenergy biofuel company 317
third-party logistics provider (3PL) 245
Thompson, L S 9
Thompson, R 284
Thornhill, N F 103
Tibben-Kembke, R S 243
Tilanus, B 198
Tookey, J E 243
Toth, P 215, 216, 218
Towill, D R 103, 105, 106, 107, 108, 110
Townshend, T 272
Toyota Material Handling 181
Tozer, D 159
Tracey, M 15
traffic congestion, cost of 77–78, 78
transferring freight to greener transport
   modes (and) 124–39, 125, 126 see also
   case studies
 characteristics of main freight transport
   modes 126–28, 127, 128
 environmental impacts of main freight
   transport modes 129–30, 129
 European Union measures for 133–34
 European Union policy 131–32
 rail and water industries 135–38 see also
   main entry
 UK government measures for 134–35
 UK government policy/key policy
   documents 132–33
Trade and Industry, Department for (DTI)
   249
Transport, Department for (DfT) 61, 63, 79, 83,
   126, 130, 137, 148, 149, 150, 196, 197,
   204, 208, 235, 246, 271, 295, 309, 310,
   311–12, 313, 331, 347, 349, 350
 Choosing and Developing and Multi-modal
   Solution (DfT, 2008) 135
 as DETR 4, 11, 196, 203, 205, 284, 295–96,
   342, 343, 344
 Freight Facilities Grant (FFG) 134

Freight Quality Partnerships 284
Rail Environmental Benefit Procurement
    Scheme (REPS) 135
Transport Dept for Sustainable Distribution
    Fund 134
Transport and Environment, Joint Expert
    Group on (2005) 298
Transport and Mobility Leuven 208
Transport Canada 355
Transport Innovation Fund (TIF, UK) 134
Traver, C G 323
Trebilock, B 180, 181
Treloar, G 168
Trienekens, H W J M 217
Tritopoulou, E 221
Tsiakis, P 102
Tsoulfas, G 168, 173
Turban, E D 322

uncertainty circle model 107–08, 110, *108, 110*
    see also supply chain(s)
UNCTAD/WHO 271
Union of Concerned Scientists 308
United Kingdom (and) 11, 208, 284, 358 *see*
    also legislation (UK)
Air Quality Archive (2008) 60
BREEAM (Building Research Establishment
    Environmental Assessment Method)
    186, 187, 190
British Rail monopoly 128
British Transport Advisory Committee
    (BTAC) 232
British Waterways 128
Business Enterprise and Regulatory
    Reform, Department for (DEBRR) 152
Climate Change Programme (2006) 309
Energy Efficiency Best Practice Programme
    175
Energy Efficiency Office 231
Freight Best Practice programme 134–35,
    195, 236, 348
Freight Facilities Grant Scheme (UK) 350
freight facilities grants (Scotland) 350
freight quality partnershps (FQPs) 295–96
freight transport policy 132–33
Freight Transport Association (FTA) 295,
    296
Gallagher Inquiry re RTFO target 311–12
government fuel duty escalator policy 354
government key policy documents of last
    decade 132
government objectives for sustainable
    distribution strategy 344
Green Building Council (GBC) 169, 183,
    184, 189
Infrastructure Planning Commission (IPC)
    134
London and Low Emission Zone 44
London Freight Conference (1975) 283
Non-Domestic Energy Performance
    Certificates 185
Rail Regulation, Office of 135

renewable energy policy 184
Renewable Fuels Agency report (2008) 312
Renewable Obligation Certificates (ROCs)
    184
Renewable Transport Fuel Obligation
    (RTFO) 309, 311–12
Safe and Fuel Efficient Driving (SAFED)
    programme 221, 238, 354
Transport for London (2008) 301
and vehicle height 208
Waste Strategy (2007) 247
United Nations (UN) 34, 327
Inter-governmental Panel on Climate
    Change (UN IPCC) 34, 35
greenhouses gases listed by (1996) 34
United States of America (USA) (and) 11, 13,
    158, 201, 358
American Petroleum Institute 160
American Trucking Association 232
Chicago Convention (1944) 349
Department for Energy 142, 232
    and International Partnership for the
        Hydrogen Economy 312
Environmental Protection Agency 235
    Smartway programme 357
emission standards 355
fuel economy standards 355
fuel economy standards for trucks 144
LEED (Leadership in Energy and
    Environment Design) 186, 190
Transportation Research Board 353
urban consolidation centres (UCCs) 288–89,
    290–93, *291, 292, 293*
urban freight transport 283–90
    efficiency problems in 285–88
    initiatives 288–90
    and Pettit enquiry 283
    research and policy making 283–85

Vachon, S 16
Van de Voorde, E 347
Van der Vorst, J 107, 108
Van Hoek, R 16
van Nunen, J A 328, 335
van Woensel, T 222
Vandaele, N 222
vehicle licensing statistics (DfT 2008) 89
vehicle routing and scheduling problem
    (VRSP)/software 215–16, 217
vehicle utilization, measuring 196–98
    empty running 198
    space-utilization/vehicle fill 198
    tonne-kilometres per vehicle per annum
        96–97, *197*
    weight-based lading factor 197–98
vehicle utilization, opportunities for
    improving 195–214
vehicle utilization and truck capacity, factors
    affecting 199–209, *199*
    capacity restraints at company premises
        209
    demand fluctuations 200–201, *200*

design of packaging and handling equipment 206
geographical imbalances in traffic flow 202
health and safety regulations 209
incompatability of vehicles and products 206–07
just-in-time (JIT) delivery 202–03
lack of cooperation across supply chain 203–04
  and horizontal/vertical collaboration 204–05
lack of inter-functional coordination 203
lack of knowledge of loading opportunities 201–02
priority given to outbound deliveries 203
unreliability in logistics schedules 205–06
vehicle size and weight restrictions 207–08, 207
working time restrictions 209
vendor-managed inventory (VMI)/strategy 104–05, 205
Verter, V 221
Vigo, D 215, 216, 218
Vishwanath, V 329
Vlosky, R P 323
volatile organic compounds (VOCs) 310
Vorley, B 271
Vrijens, G 248

Waldron, D 357
Wallace, L 153
Walley, N 41
Wal-Mart 216, 357
Walter, F 93
Walton, S V 16
Wang, Y 24, 324
Ward, D 152
warehouse
  lighting 177–78, 177, 178
  mechanical handling equipment 179–82
  temperature 175–76
warehousing, environmental impact of 167–92
  framework for assessing 173
  and increasing resource intensity 171–72
  scale of 168–70, 170
  ways of reducing (by) 173–89 see also warehouse
    designing sustainability into buildings 185–89, 184, 187, 188
    harnessing green energy 182–85, 183
    improving energy efficiency 173, 175–82, 174
Wasil, E 216, 219
Wassan, N A 218
waste management 242–62
  in context of reverse logistics (and) 243–46, 244
    integrated outbound and returns network (Type A) 245
    non-integrated outbound and returns network (Type B) 245

return to suppliers (Type D) 245
third-party returns management (Type C) 245
and hazardous waste 249–50
and household waste recycling centres (HWRCs) 249
impact of legislation for 246–50, 253, 255 see also legislation (EU) and legislation (UK)
as part of sustainable reverse process 253–56
and potential for joint domestic/commercial collections 255–56
reuse, refurbishment markets and take-back schemes 249, 250–53
  Auction Assist 252
  Computer Aid International 253
  FareShare 251–52
  Furniture Reuse Network (FRN) 251, 252
  RASCAL 252
  Regenersis 253
  Waste and Resources Action Plan (WRAP) 250
schemes to aid SMEs 254–55
systems 13
Waterborne Freight Grants (WFG) 135, 350
Watts, G R 37
Weeks, J 13
Weidner, M 222
Weltevreden, J 327, 335
Wetherbe, J 322
Whang, S 103
White, A 201
Whitehead, B 41
Whiteing, T 284
Whitelegg, J 9, 15, 342
Wikner, J 105
Wilkinson, S 172
Williams, A 270, 277
Williams, L R 201
Wilson, D T 323
Wise Moves report (2003) 266
Wøhlk, S 221
Woodburn, A 10, 22, 23, 130
Woodcock, J 272
World Business Council for Sustainable Development 4
  and World Resources Institute 55, 56, 59, 60, 61, 169
Wu, H-J 14, 246, 248
Wyatt, K 177

Xing, Y 329

Yang, W-H 220
Young, R 15
Yrjola, H 205

Zarkadoula, M 221
Ziaee, M S 218
Zoidis, G 221